EUROPE'S BALKAN MUSLIMS

NATHALIE CLAYER
XAVIER BOUGAREL

Europe's Balkan Muslims
A New History

Translated by
Andrew Kirby

HURST & COMPANY, LONDON

First published as *Les musulmans de l'Europe du Sud-Est (XIXe-XXe siècles)*,
© Editions Karthala, Paris, 2013
This English translation first published in the United Kingdom in 2017 by
C. Hurst & Co. (Publishers) Ltd.,
41 Great Russell Street, London, WC1B 3PL
© Nathalie Clayer and Xavier Bougarel, 2017
Translation © Andrew Kirby, 2017
All rights reserved.
Printed in India

Distributed in the United States, Canada and Latin America by
Oxford University Press, 198 Madison Avenue, New York, NY 10016,
United States of America.

The right of Nathalie Clayer and Xavier Bougarel to be identified
as the authors of this publication is asserted by them in accordance
with the Copyright, Designs and Patents Act, 1988.

A Cataloguing-in-Publication data record for this book
is available from the British Library.

ISBN: 9781849046596

This book is printed using paper from registered sustainable
and managed sources.

www.hurstpublishers.com

CONTENTS

List of Maps	vii
Acknowledgements	ix
Terminology	xi
Glossary	xiii

Introduction   1

1. From the Ottoman Provincial Autonomies to the Eastern
   Crisis (1800–1876)   11
   When the Ottoman Empire in Europe started to disintegrate   11
   *Reforms, the establishment of bureaucracies and the formation of new
   elites*   20
   New relationships between Muslims and Christians   26
   The multiple networks of Balkan Islam   31
   From the first scholarly discourses to the first identity constructions   36

2. From the Eastern Crisis to the End of the Empires (1876–1923)   45
   The strengthening and weakening of the Balkan states   45
   Migrations and population exchanges   52
   *Muslims caught between non-Muslim national states and the
   Ottoman Empire*   57
   Politicisation of identities and the slow development of nationalism   64
   The central importance of the question of reforms   70
   Balkan Muslims between representations and practices   74

3. From the End of the Empires to the Advent of Communism
   (1920–1944)   79
   *From one World War to the other: territorial reconfigurations and the rise
   of authoritarianism*   79

CONTENTS

Nationalisation of societies and ideological radicalisation	86
Muslims between emigration, the agrarian question and the construction of minorities	90
Partial nationalisation, strengthening and control of the Islamic institutions	95
The specific forms of mobilisation of the Muslim populations	100
Beyond the "reformers"/"conservatives" opposition	107
A Balkan Islam within new networks	111
"European Islam", "modern Islam" and local practices	117

4. **From the Advent of Communism to its Fall (1944–1989)** — 123
   Between Cold War and nationalist fervour — 123
   Authoritarian modernisation and anti-religious policies — 128
   Different ways in which national identities crystallised — 131
   Scientific socialism and national mythologies — 145
   The contrasting development of the Islamic institutions — 150
   The Bosnian exception: a pan-Islamist current under communism — 158
   The transformations of Islam through the prism of anthropology — 162

5. **From the Fall of Communism to European Integration (1989–2001)** — 167
   Between Yugoslav disintegration and Euro-Atlantic integration — 167
   "Transition" and the "return of religion" — 174
   The Balkan Muslims' politicisation — 177
   Closer links between Islam and national identity — 192
   The renewal and fragility of Islamic institutions — 197
   Neo-Salafism: what transformations of Balkan Islam does it reveal? — 201

Conclusion — 209

Notes — 227
Bibliography — 239
Index — 269

LIST OF MAPS

Map 1: Spatial distribution of Muslim populations in Southeast Europe (early 21st century)   3
Map 2: Linguistic distribution of Muslim populations in Southeast Europe (early 21st century)   5
Map 3: Southeast Europe in the first half of the nineteenth century   14
Map 4: Southeast Europe after the Treaty of Berlin   47
Map 5: Southeast Europe and the Balkan Wars   48
Map 6: Southeast Europe in the Interwar Period   81
Map 7: Southeast Europe during the Second World War   85
Map 8: Southeast Europe during the Cold War   125
Map 9: Southeast Europe at the beginning of the 21st century   171

ACKNOWLEDGEMENTS

We would like to thank the Institut d'études de l'Islam et des sociétés du monde musulman (IISMM) and its directors, Hamit Bozarslan and Bernard Heyberger, for encouraging us to write this book. We would also like to thank the late Alexandre Popovic, Nadège Ragaru, Galia Valtchinova, Fabio Giomi and Jeanne Hersant for giving us the benefit of their knowledge of Balkan Islam. Responsibility for the content of this book, and for any errors that may have crept in, is, of course, ours alone. Finally, we would like to thank Andrew Kirby for providing the translation from French to English.

TERMINOLOGY

Writing a book about the Muslims of Southeast Europe necessarily involves using specific concepts from different languages, including Arabic, Ottoman, Turkish, Albanian, Bosnian/Croatian/Serbian, Bulgarian, Greek and so on. We have decided to use the Arabic word without italics for discussion of major concepts in Islam (for example: fatwa, waqf, madrasa, ulama, etc.). For concepts which are less dominant, though still relating to Islam in general, we have opted for the Arabic word in italics (for example: *umma*, *ijtihad*, *zakat*, etc.). And finally, for local religious practices and institutions we have primarily used the word in Turkish (for example: *cemaat*, *tekke*, *mevlud*, etc.), or in some other Balkan language in certain specific cases.

GLOSSARY

Alevis	Name taken by the Kizilbash in the twentieth century.
armatoles	Greek militias charged by the Ottoman authorities with maintaining order in some peripheral regions of the Empire.
Ashkalis	National identification adopted by some Gypsies of Macedonia and Kosovo from the 1990s onwards.
ayan	Great provincial notable.
baba	literally "father"; title given to the spiritual leaders of some Muslim mystical brotherhoods, in particular the Bektashis.
başmüftü	Grand mufti at the head of the Islamic institutions in Bulgaria, Romania and, in theory, Greece.
başmüftülük	Post of grand mufti.
Bektashis	Members of a Muslim mystical brotherhood whose doctrine combines different elements (Sunni, Shiite, Hurufi, etc.) and which spread above all in Anatolia and Southeast Europe from the sixteenth century onwards, when it was used by the Ottoman authorities to absorb heterodox elements, while being itself often regarded as heterodox by the ulamas.

GLOSSARY

In 1826, the brotherhood was banned by Sultan Mahmud II, but managed to survive unofficially and to resurface. In Albania, it was recognised unofficially in the inter-war period, and then recognised officially in 1945 as a fully-fledged religious community.

bey (or *beg* in Bosnia-Herzegovina)	Major landowner.
Bosniaks (Bosnian: *Bošnjaci*)	Members of the Bosniak nation, called the Muslim nation until 1993, present above all in Bosnia-Herzegovina and in Sanjak.
Bosnians (Bosnian: *Bosanci*)	Inhabitants of Bosnia-Herzegovina, independently of national and denominational affiliation.
boyar	Member of the landowning nobility of Moldavia and Wallachia.
cadi	Judge at a sharia court.
Caliphate/Caliph	Successor to the Prophet at the head of the *umma* (the community of believers); from the late eighteenth century the Ottoman sovereign was considered to be Sultan of the Ottoman Empire and Caliph, i.e. the spiritual leader of all Muslims; the Ottoman Caliphate was abolished in 1924, one year after the sultanate.
Çams	Albanian-speaking Muslims from North-West Greece and South-West Albania.
cemaat	Assembly of the faithful; from the late nineteenth century, this term has also been used to designate the local Islamic institutions.
cem evi	Place where the Alevis-Kizilbash perform their ritual, called *cem*.
darülharb	Literally "territory of war"; i.e. "territory of the infidels"; countries under non-Islamic sovereignty.

GLOSSARY

darülislam	Literally "territory of Islam"; territories under Islamic sovereignty.
dede-baba	Literally "grandfather-father", spiritual leader of the Bektashi brotherhood.
dergah	Dervish establishment.
ders	Lesson; term used in the twentieth century to mean the lessons given by an expert in religious sciences to disciples gathered around him, most often in a mosque.
dervish	Member of a Muslim mystical brotherhood.
devşirme	practice of collecting non-Muslim boys, converting them to Islam and bringing them up in the Sultan's palace; this practice, which existed from the second half of the fourteenth century, became rare in the second half of the sixteenth century, and ceased completely in the first half of the seventeenth century.
Diyanet (*Diyanet İşleri Başkanlığı*)	Literally "Presidency of Religious Affairs"; official Islamic religious institution, reporting to the prime minister, put in place in republican Turkey (initially under the name of Directorate of Religious Affairs) in order to manage Islam in Turkey following the abolition of the caliphate and of the post of *şeyhülislam*.
dönme	Crypto-Jewish Muslims, inspired by Sabbataï Tsevi (seventeenth century), living mainly in Salonica.
džemat	See *cemaat*.
Egyptians	Identification adopted by some Gypsies of Macedonia and Kosovo from the late 1980s onwards.
fatwa	Legal opinion delivered by a mufti.
fethullahcıs	Members of the neo-Sufi movement founded

GLOSSARY

	in Turkey by Fethullah Gülen, particularly active in the fields of education, the economy and the press.
fikh	Islamic jurisprudence.
Goranis	Slavic-speaking Muslims living in the south of Kosovo and in the north-east of Albania.
hadiths	Traditions relating to the deeds and sayings of the Prophet.
Halvetis	Members of the most widespread Muslim mystical brotherhood in Southeast Europe, the Halvetiyye, which developed through its different branches from the late fifteenth century, often with the support of the Ottoman political and religious authorities. It faced strong competition in the eighteenth and nineteenth centuries from the Naqshbandis. In the post-Ottoman period, its networks remained fairly dense in Albania, Kosovo and Macedonia.
Hanafism (adj: Hanafi)	Official *madhhab* (legal school) of the Ottoman Empire, to which Balkan Muslims historically belong.
hankah/hanikah	Dervish establishment.
hatt-i şerif	Literally "noble rescript" or "noble written edict", term used to mean the Gülhane edict, which launched the *Tanzimat* in 1839.
hijab	Veil, headscarf
hoca	Teacher of religion; sometimes a synonym for imam.
hospodar	Name given to the sovereigns of Moldavia and Wallachia.
Hurufism	Cabalistic-type doctrine that assigns numerical values to the letters of the Arabic alphabet.
hutbe	Sermon pronounced at Friday prayers.

GLOSSARY

ijtihad
: reasoned interpretation supported by the Islamic reformists.

ilmiyye
: Hierarchy of high-ranking religious specialists put in place in the Ottoman Empire, and then in some successor states, bringing together all the ulamas.

Islamism
: In the late nineteenth century, a political-religious current seeking to revive Ottoman Islamic society, sometimes in a pan-Islamist version. From the second half of the twentieth century, a political movement aspiring to put Islam and the sharia back at the centre of the political system of Muslim countries.

jadidism
: Reformist movement led in the Russian Empire by the Tatar Ismail Gasprinski (1851–1914).

janissary
: member of the elite Ottoman troops created in the fourteenth century and abolished in 1826, formed of recruits taken from the *devşirme* and, from the late sixteenth century, by volunteers.

jihad
: Holy war.

Kadiris
: Members of the Kadiriyye brotherhood, from the name of its eponymous saint Abdulkadir Geylani (Baghdad, twelfth century). In Southeast Europe, several branches of the brotherhood established their networks at different times. Some centres are still active today in Albania, Kosovo, Macedonia and Bosnia-Herzegovina.

Kadizadelis
: Members of a movement, named after the preacher Kadızade Mehmed (1582–1635), native of Balikesir, in western Anatolia. This movement appeared in the early seventeenth century, preaching a fundamentalist Islam, in the sense of a return to the Islam of the

GLOSSARY

	times of the Prophet and his companions, and of the fight against the *bid'at* (bad innovations), including some Sufi practices (such as dancing and listening to music), visiting tombs, or consuming tobacco and coffee. The Kadizadelis are said to have still been active in Sarajevo in the eighteenth century.
kalâm	Islamic theology.
kanun	Secular law.
kaza	Local administrative unit, below a sanjak.
Kemalism	current of thought favouring the reforms led by Mustafa Kemal in Turkey, between 1923 and 1938: adoption of the Latin alphabet, reform of education, reform of dress (abolition of the veil for women, wearing of hats for men), abolition of the sharia courts and adoption of the civil code, etc.
kiraathane	Reading room.
Kizilbash	literally "red-heads"; population having beliefs and practices influenced by Safavid Islam of the sixteenth century and far removed from the dominant Sunni doctrine: cult of Ali (the Prophet's son-in-law) and the first imams; esoteric interpretation of the Quran; cult of certain personalities such as Bedreddin Simavi, Otman Baba, Sarı Saltık, Haji Bektash; Hurufism; specific rituals.
kleft	Bandit.
kmet	Sharecropper.
knez	Christian notable in the Serbo-Montenegrin space.
komitaji	Member of a secret committee or of a revolutionary committee.
kryegjysh	Literally "principal grandfather"; name given to the head of the Bektashi brotherhood in Albania from 1929.

GLOSSARY

madhhab	Legal school in Sunni Islam; the *madhhab*s, which appeared in the eighth and ninth centuries, are four in number: Maliki, Shafi'i, Hanbali and Hanafi. The latter is the official *madhhab* of the Ottoman Empire and the one to which Balkan Muslims historically belong.
madrasa	A place of education primarily involved in teaching Islamic religious learning, though other subjects are also taught there.
meclis	Assembly, council.
mekteb	School, more specifically a school of the traditional type, a religious school.
Melamis	Mystics following the Melami "way of the blame" (in its extreme version, committing bad acts in order to be blamed; in its non-extreme version, dissimulation of the mystical states, integration in society); in the late nineteenth century, a brotherhood founded by Muhammed Nur Al-Arabi in Macedonia, which played a role in the development of the Young Turk movement and which, in Southeast Europe, spread mainly in Macedonia, Kosovo and Albania.
menšura	Accreditation of a religious leader by the *şeyhülislam* of Istanbul.
mescid	A place of prayer without a minaret.
Mevlevis	Sometimes called whirling dervishes, because of the form of their ritual (a kind of dance in which they whirl around); the Mevlevis are members of the Mevleviyye, taking their name from their eponymous saint Mevlana Celadeddin Rumi (Konya, thirteenth century). Music and poetry were particularly cultivated in this rather urban and elitist brotherhood, which had a limited, but significant, number of *tekke*s in Southeast Europe, as in Sarajevo and Salonica.

GLOSSARY

mevlud	Poem in honour of the birth of the Prophet; by extension, ceremony during which this poem is recited, held to mark different occasions.
millet	Term designating the religious communities in the Ottoman Empire; towards the end of the Ottoman period, the concept evolved to mean the Muslim community, as well as a group of non-Muslim religious communities that were officially recognised and had institutional links with the Ottoman state structures. However, the term has had multiple meanings, evolving with political and social transformations, and could refer to "the people" and, increasingly, the "nation".
müceddid	Renewer of the Islamic religion.
müderris	Teacher of religious sciences.
mufti	Legal consultant issuing fatwas (legal opinions).
müftülük	Post of mufti.
muhacir	refugee; literally, one who has undertaken an emigration comparable to the *hijrah* of the Prophet and his companions from Mecca to Medina, i.e. from the territory of the infidels to the territory of the believers.
mujahedeen	A warrior taking part in *jihad*.
mütevelli	Administrator of a pious foundation.
nahiye	District.
Naqshbandis	Members of the Naqshbandiyye brotherhood which spread from Central Asia to Anatolia and then to Southeast Europe in the fifteenth century. However, it was in the nineteenth century in particular that new brotherhood networks developed, spreading an Islam that was closely linked to the sharia,

GLOSSARY

	including in Southeast Europe, particularly in Bulgaria and Bosnia-Herzegovina where it supplanted the Halveti brotherhood. Features of the Naqshbandis that distinguish them from the other groups of dervishes were their application of the principle of "solitude in the crowd", their ritual that was often performed in silence, and their pronounced "orthodoxy".
neo-Salafism	Religious current deriving from the *salafiyya* of the late nineteenth century, offering a strict and anti-Western interpretation of Islam and seeking to imitate in all things the Prophet and his companions, the "pious ancestors" (*al-salaf al-sâlih*).
neo-traditionalism	Religious current preaching a revival of Islamic tradition.
nizam-i cedid	Literally "the new order"; refers to the series of reforms implemented by Sultan Selim III (1789–1807); the term ended up meaning the new army that was produced by the reforms.
Ottomanism (Turkish: *osmanlılık*)	The Ottomanism supported by the promoters of the *Tanzimat* developed in Ottoman society more as the idea of a common citizenship than that of a nation. The Ottomanism of the Young Ottomans was synonymous with patriotism, constitutionalism and the extolling of Islamic values.
paşalik	Ottoman region governed by a pasha.
pan-Islamism	A word which appeared in the late nineteenth century to refer to the policies, real or imagined, promoting an Islamic union, i.e. a political union of Muslims under the authority of a caliph or another leader.
Pomaks	Bulgarian-speaking Muslims from Bulgaria or Greece.

GLOSSARY

poturica	Literally, "one who has made himself Turk"; generally used pejoratively to refer to local converts or their descendants.
reformism	Religious current influenced by Islamic tradition and European thought, seeking to reform the institutions of Islam by affirming the compatibility of Islam with Western modernity while rejecting materialism.
reis-ul-ulema	Literally, "chief of the ulamas"; title given to the head of the Islamic religious hierarchy in Bosnia-Herzegovina from 1880, in Yugoslavia from 1930, and in Macedonia, Montenegro and Serbia from the 1990s.
rescript	Administrative act written by an authority such as the Sultan.
"revival process"	Campaign launched by the Bulgarian authorities in 1984 with the aim of completely assimilating the Turkish minority.
revivalism	See neo-traditionalism.
Rifais	Members of a relatively popular brotherhood whose ritual was characterised, on some occasions, by mortification (piercing parts of the body with spikes, chewing pieces of broken glass, licking red-hot iron or hot coals, etc.). Its eponymous saint, Ahmad al-Rifa'i, lived in the twelfth century. While the brotherhood spread in several regions of Southeast Europe during the Ottoman period, today it is active mainly in Macedonia, Kosovo, Albania and, although only on the margins, in Bosnia-Herzegovina (among Albanians).
Roma	Main national identification of the Gypsies from the 1990s onwards.
Rumelia	Literally, "land of the Rum" or "land of the Romans"; during the Ottoman period, this

	term was used to mean in particular that part of the Balkan Peninsula under Ottoman domination.
rüşdiye	Lower secondary schools opened in the Ottoman Empire from the late 1830s onwards which, unlike the madrasas, did not teach only religious subjects but emphasised "profane" subjects.
Sadis	Members of the Sadiyye, a brotherhood that was quite close to the brotherhood of the Rifais (ritual including piercings, power over snakes); its eponymous saint lived in Syria in the fourteenth century. The brotherhood spread in Southeast Europe from the late seventeenth century onwards, particularly in Kosovo, Macedonia and Albania. Ali Pasha of Ioannina seems to have contributed to the spreading of the brotherhood in the late eighteenth to early nineteenth centuries.
salafiyya	Religious reform movement of the late nineteenth century, which envisaged both a return to the Islam of the "pious ancestors" (*al-salaf al-sâlih*) and the use of reason and science, in order to lead the Muslim world towards the progress associated with Western modernity.
şalvar	Baggy trousers worn by women.
sanjak	regional administrative unit in the Ottoman Empire, below a vilayet in the administrative hierarchy, but above a *kaza*; more specifically, name given to the region covered by the sanjak of Novi Pazar because of its particular status after 1878.
sharia	Islamic law, or more correctly, doctrinal, social, cultural and moral norms, laid down by the Quran and the hadiths.
Shazilis	Members of an Arab mystical brotherhood,

GLOSSARY

	present particularly in North Africa and Egypt, with only a small presence in Southeast Europe, mainly in Bulgaria and Kosovo, at the time of Abdülhamid, who favoured it.
shaykh	Spiritual leader of a Muslim mystical brotherhood.
şeyhülislam	Mufti of Istanbul, at the head of the Islamic religious hierarchy of the Ottoman Empire.
Sufi	A Muslim mystic.
Tanzimat	Literally "reorganisations"; term used to refer to the reform policy conducted by the Ottoman authorities between 1839 and 1876, and, by extension, that period.
tafsir	Exegesis of the Quran.
tarikat	Literally "path", which one follows in order to approach the Divinity; Muslim mystical brotherhood.
tekke	Dervish establishment, led by a spiritual master, a shaykh.
Tijanis	Members of a brotherhood founded in the Maghreb in the eighteenth century by Ahmad al-Tijani (1737–1815), present above all in West Africa, and which spread in Albania from the early twentieth century through the pilgrimage to Mecca. Its doctrine is reformist, in the sense that the brotherhood does not have *tekke*s, does not have a spectacular *zikr*, and its adepts emphasise a direct link with the Prophet and strict adherence to the sharia.
timar	Prebend, generally non-hereditary, granted by the Sultan to a soldier or a civil servant, bringing its holder an income in exchange for services to be rendered (providing men for the army, etc.).

GLOSSARY

Torbesh	Slavic-speaking Muslims of Macedonia.
türbe	Tomb; more particularly, a tomb of a saint.
"Turko-Islamic synthesis"	Current of thought promoting a synthesis of Islam and the past of the Turkish nation as a point of reference for religion, identity and ethics. While it originates in Ottoman authors of the late nineteenth century, it was openly promoted in Turkey only from the 1980s onwards.
ulema-medžlis	Literally "council of the ulamas"; council at the head of the Islamic institutions of Bosnia-Herzegovina from the Austro-Hungarian period to the end of the Second World War and of South Serbia in the inter-war period.
ulama	A religious specialist, trained in the religious sciences (*ilm*).
umma	Community of believers.
vilayet	Ottoman province governed by a vali, divided into sanjaks, *kaza*s and *nahiye*s.
vladika	Bishop.
Wahhabism (adj.: Wahhabi)	Salafist-type religious current, founded by Muhammad Ibn Abd-Al Wahhab (1703–92), preaching a return to Islam in its original form. Wahhabism therefore rejects any non-literalist interpretation of the Quran and tradition. It also rejects the *madhhab*s, and prohibits invocation of the saints or the Prophet Muhammad for the purpose of intercession, which is why it is hostile to Sufism and the veneration of the tombs of saints.
waqf	mortmain property or pious foundation, including both institutions with a socio-religious purpose (mosques, *tekke*s, madrasas, libraries, *imaret*s ("soup kitchens"), hospitals, etc.) and assets and properties (land, houses,

GLOSSARY

	shops, mills, etc.) providing income to enable the former to function.
Yücelciler	members of an organisation founded in Skopje in 1937, of Turkish inspiration, called "Yücel" ("accomplish yourself").
zakat	ritual alms-giving.
zaviye	dervish establishment; in the Balkans, a small establishment or one situated in a private house.
zikr	literally "remembrance"; repetition of formulas and names of God during a Sufi ritual; by extension, Sufi ritual.

INTRODUCTION

One of the principal features of Southeast Europe is its great religious diversity; for several centuries an Orthodox Christian majority has coexisted with less numerous groups of Muslims, Catholics, Protestants and Jews[1] in an area measuring 765,000 sq km, about one and a half times the size of France. This book deals only with the Muslim communities, which emerged during the expansion of the Ottoman Empire over the period running from the fourteenth through to the seventeenth century and, to a lesser degree, that of its territorial shrinkage between the eighteenth and twentieth centuries. As we shall see, there has been fierce longstanding debate about how these communities originated, and we do not seek to provide any precise or definitive answer here. It should however be pointed out that the Muslim presence in the Balkan Peninsula may be attributed primarily to the conversion of local Christian populations and, in the eastern part of the Peninsula, to the settlement of Islamicised Turkish-speaking populations from Anatolia, followed in the nineteenth and twentieth centuries by *muhacirs*[2] (refugees) from Crimea and the Caucasus. The Islamicisation of local populations, which occurred to a far greater degree in some regions than in others, mainly took place between the fifteenth and eighteenth centuries, although continuing through to the early twentieth century. This was due to a combination of factors that were political (such as local elites being absorbed into the Ottoman elites), socio-economic (such as their joining certain corporations) and specifically religious (such as the weakness of Christian Churches in certain areas). Whilst these factors combined in different ways depending upon the region and the period, they do allow us to refute arguments presenting a caricatured vision of the Islamicisation of

Southeast Europe as the result of forced conversion, sheer material opportunism or sudden religious revelation. In this case, as in others, historical processes are more complex than nationalist and religious propagandas would have us believe.[3]

This work presents both a political and a religious history of Muslims in Southeast Europe in the nineteenth and twentieth centuries. The analysis of political change over the course of the past two centuries includes all Muslims in the sociological sense of the term (people of Muslim family tradition and culture, independently of how religious they might be). However, in our discussion of religious change we focus solely on believers in Islam. This distinction between "sociological" Muslims and Muslim believers is of particular significance for studying the twentieth century, given the rapid secularisation of Balkan societies.

At this time of writing, the beginning of the twenty-first century, there are in Southeast Europe around 8 million "sociological" Muslims, that is, 12.5 per cent of the total population of this region of the world. This number is of necessity an approximation, as the last two decades have seen large and often dramatic population movements. Also, in population censuses, some people who are Muslims in the sociological sense of the term declare themselves to be non-religious or make no declaration of their religious convictions. The geographical distribution of the Balkan Muslims is very uneven: while they form an absolute or relative majority in three of the region's states (Kosovo, Albania and Bosnia-Herzegovina), they form a substantial minority in three other states (Macedonia, Montenegro and Bulgaria), and a small minority in the other five states (see Table 1 and Map 1). However, even in the states where they are only a small minority, the Muslims may form a compact population at regional level, as in Serbian Sanjak or in Western Thrace, in Greece.[4]

Language is another, equally important, criterion in understanding the diversity of the Balkan Muslim populations. Four major linguistic and national groups can be distinguished (see Table 2 and Map 2):

– the Muslim Albanians (around 4,300,000 people, and around 80 per cent of the Albanians of Southeast Europe), who speak Albanian and live principally in Albania, Kosovo, Western Macedonia, South Serbia and Montenegro.[5] Many Muslim Albanians from Albania have also settled in Greece since the early 1990s, and smaller groups of Muslim Albanians from Kosovo and Macedonia have lived in Croatia and Slovenia since the 1960s;

INTRODUCTION

Map 1: Spatial distribution of Muslim populations in Southeast Europe (early 21st century)

- the Bosniaks (around 2,150,000 people), who speak Bosnian (formerly Serbo-Croatian) and live predominantly in Bosnia-Herzegovina, Serbia and Montenegro (Sanjak), Kosovo and Macedonia.[6] Many Bosniaks also settled in Croatia and Slovenia from the 1960s;
- the Turks (around 880,000 people), who speak Turkish and live primarily in Bulgaria, Greece (Western Thrace region), Macedonia, Romania (Dobruja) and Kosovo. There are also many Turks originating from Bulgaria and other parts of Southeast Europe who have settled in Turkey;
- the Muslim Roma (around 330,000 people), who speak Roma and other vernacular languages and who are present across the region except in Romania—there are many Roma living in Romania, but they are Christians.

In addition to the four major groups, there are small groups whose national identity is often poorly defined, such as the Bulgarian-speaking Pomaks in Bulgaria and Greece, the Macedonian-speaking Torbesh in Macedonia and Albania, the Serbian-speaking Goranis in the south of Kosovo, or the Tatar-speaking Tatars in Romania, in the Dobruja region. Since the 1990s, migrants of African or Asian descent have accounted for a significant proportion of the total Muslim population in Greece and Romania. At the same time, several hundred thousand Albanians and Bosniaks fleeing war or economic crisis have migrated to Western Europe, North America and Australia, where there are now large, politically and religiously active diasporas.

While this distribution by linguistic and national groups provides an initial idea of the diversity of the Balkan Muslim populations, it must be treated with a degree of caution. In regions where different Muslim populations coexist, such as Western Macedonia, the south of Kosovo, Romanian and Bulgarian Dobruja or Western Thrace, many individuals are bilingual or multilingual and some move from one national group to another. More generally, the linguistic diversity of the Balkan Muslim populations can be traced back to the Ottoman era, though national identities only crystallised later in Southeast Europe, as we shall see in this book. Today, changes in identification still occur, from the Pomak and Roma groups to the Turkish group in Bulgaria and Greece, from the Torbesh group to the Albanian or Turkish groups in Macedonia, and from the Gorani, Roma or Turkish groups to the Albanian group in Kosovo. While the statistics give us an approximate snapshot of the

INTRODUCTION

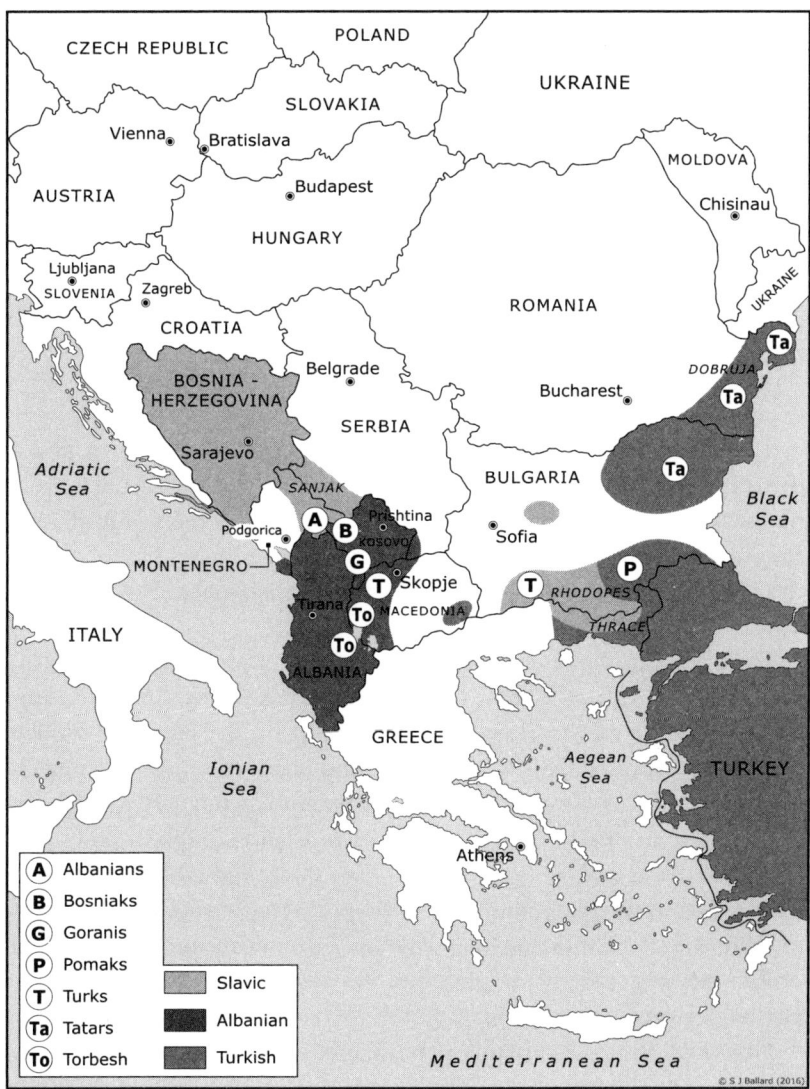

Map 2: Linguistic distribution of Muslim populations in Southeast Europe (early 21st century)

Balkan Muslim populations today, we must not forget the history that brought us to this point, that is to say the demographic, cultural and political processes that shaped the ways in which Balkan Muslims identified themselves during the nineteenth and twentieth centuries.

Separated from the rest of the world by the Iron Curtain, Balkan Muslims were rarely discussed during the Cold War, and their very existence was ignored by Western and Muslim public opinion. However, following the collapse of the communist regimes, these Balkan Muslims were thrown dramatically into the spotlight. The break-up of Yugoslavia, the war in Bosnia-Herzegovina in 1992–5 and that in Kosovo in 1998–9, the massacres and the accompanying waves of refugees, brought these Muslim communities of Southeast Europe to the attention of Western and Muslim public opinion. The majority of that public opinion sympathised with their suffering and even manifested active solidarity. Thus, during the 1990s, the Balkan Muslims were perceived above all as being one of the groups of victims of the former communist regimes, and as the principal victims of the "ethnic cleansing" carried out by the Serbian nationalists in Bosnia-Herzegovina and Kosovo. The most important of the works that have helped to create this victim image is without doubt the book *Witness to Genocide* by the American journalist Roy Gutman, awarded the Pulitzer Prize in 1993.[7]

From 2001, following the end of the Yugoslav wars and the 9/11 attacks in the United States, the image of Balkan Muslims as victims faded, and was partly replaced in the West by the image of Balkan Muslims radicalised by fundamentalist and terrorist networks, threatening the stability of Southeast Europe, or even the whole of Europe. The titles of certain works that have appeared in English in recent years, such as *Islamic Terror and the Balkans*[8] and *The Coming Balkan Caliphate*,[9] bear witness to this turning point. These two opposing images relate to indisputable realities: the Bosniaks of Bosnia-Herzegovina and the Albanians of Kosovo were indeed the principal victims of the Yugoslav wars, and Islamic terrorist networks did establish themselves in Southeast Europe.

However, these two realities mask other essential transformations affecting the Balkan Muslim populations. Victims of the Serbian "ethnic cleansing", the Bosniaks and Albanians were also active players in the break-up of the Yugoslav Federation, as indicated by their political and military mobilisation in favour of independence in Bosnia-Herzegovina and in Kosovo. More generally, as we shall show in this book, the 1990s were characterised by the establishment of political parties representing the different Muslim populations of Southeast Europe; those parties put forward national agendas that differed greatly from one country to another. Likewise, the image of Islamic terrorists or fundamentalists infiltrating and "distorting" Balkan Islam conceals the fact that the Jihadist networks present in Southeast Europe have only a marginal influence among the local Muslims and that the internal diversity of Balkan Islam is organised around other actors and other issues, as we shall show.

While the Iron Curtain disappeared to the East, Islam became a recurrent theme in media and electoral discourse in Western Europe, following the establishment of large permanent Muslim communities there and the rise of xenophobic parties of the extreme right. In this context, some researchers such as Olivier Roy or Jørgen Nielsen,[10] and some Muslim intellectuals such as Tariq Ramadan,[11] predicted or hoped for the coming of a "European Islam". Generally, these discussions were limited to the countries of Western Europe, at a time when political unification of the European continent had not yet been established. At the same time, another discourse was developing that presented Balkan Islam as a model of tolerant, European Islam, ready for use by Western European Muslims but threatened by the fundamentalism coming from the Arab world. The best example of such a discourse is that of Stephen Schwartz, an indefatigable champion of the fight against Saudi influence in Southeast Europe.[12] It goes without saying that such a caricature ignores the diversity of Balkan Islam and the complexity of the links which, yesterday just as today, bind it to the Muslim world. The question of the European identity of Balkan Islam is crucial, above all for the Balkan Muslims themselves; it is a question we shall seek to answer at least in part in this book. At the same time, the fact that specialists of Islam in Europe are increasingly including Southeast Europe in their comparative analyses and studies is to be welcomed, bearing in mind the enlargement of the European Union to include the Balkan countries.[13]

Finally, the two decades since the fall of the communist regimes have seen increased academic output on Southeast Europe and its Muslim communities. With regard to their history, a new edition of Alexandre Popovic's seminal work *L'islam balkanique. Les musulmans du sud-est européen dans la période post-ottomane*, which first appeared in 1986, was republished in 2009.[14] In addition to this work, which covers all the Balkan countries and the whole of the post-Ottoman period up until the 1980s, mention should be made of work by Nathalie Clayer and George Gawrych into the origins of Albanian nationalism,[15] Mary Neuburger and Ali Eminov on the Muslims of Bulgaria,[16] Konstantinos Tsitselikis and Samim Akgönül on the Muslims of Western Thrace,[17] Stefanos Katsikas on Islamic reformism in Southeast Europe,[18] Nathalie Clayer and Éric Germain on Islam in inter-war Europe,[19] together with Armina Omerika on the Young Muslims organisation in Bosnia-Herzegovina.[20] In Southeast Europe itself, the fall of the communist regimes allowed the publication of many works on the history of the Muslims and of Islam in the region; for reasons of space we can mention here only the works of Ali Basha and Shyqyri Hysi in Albania,[21] Fikret Karčić and Enes Karić in Bosnia-Herzegovina,[22] and Valeri Stojanov, Mihail Gruev and Aleksej Kalionski in Bulgaria.[23] At the same time, several anthropologists published the results of their field research: Tone Bringa on Muslim identity in a village in central Bosnia,[24] Ger Duijzings on religion and the politics of identity in Kosovo,[25] Kristen Ghodsee on transformations of Islam in Bulgaria,[26] Burcu Akan Ellis on the identity and memories of urban Muslims in Macedonia.[27] Finally, some books and special issues of journals on the current situation of the Balkan Muslims have appeared, such as the book edited by Hugh Poulton and Suha Taji-Farouki[28] or the collections edited by Xavier Bougarel or Kerem Öktem.[29]

In 2001, the authors of this book edited a collection entitled *Le nouvel islam balkanique. Les musulmans, acteurs du post-communisme 1990–2000*,[30] focusing on the one hand on the development of relationships between Islam and politics in the first decade of post-communism, and on the other on the resumption of exchanges between Balkan Islam and global Islam. What was missing, however, was a work that placed these recent developments in a longer historical perspective. In order to fill that gap, twelve years later, we have written this book on the Muslims of Southeast Europe in the nineteenth and twentieth centuries. In each chapter we look first at the geopolitical, political and socio-cultural context, before exploring in more detail the political and socio-cultural changes specific to the Balkan Muslims (in the sociological sense of the term), the different debates about Islam and about the relationships between religious identity and national identity, together with the changes in the religious institutions and in the beliefs and practices of the believers themselves. In this way, we hope to further knowledge about the history of Southeast

INTRODUCTION

Europe and its Muslim populations, leading to better understanding of the political and religious transformations under way in this part of Europe. In parallel to this, we aim to show that whilst the experience of Muslims in Southeast Europe is in many ways specific, it cannot be understood without taking into account the ties linking them to the rest of the Muslim world.

Table 1: The Muslims of Southeast Europe at the beginning of the twenty-first century (estimates)

	Number of Muslims	*Percentage of the total population*
Albania	1,950,000	70.00%
Bosnia-Herzegovina	1,800,000	45.0%
Bulgaria	900,000	12.0%
Croatia	60,000	1.5%
Greece	450,000	4.0%
Kosovo	1,600,000	90.0%
Macedonia	700,000	33.0%
Montenegro	100,000	16.0%
Romania	70,000	0.3%
Serbia	250,000	4.0%
Slovenia	50,000	2.5%
Total	8,000,000	12.5%

Estimates based on the following population censuses: Albania 2001 and 1941; Bosnia-Herzegovina 1991 and UNHCR estimates 1996; Bulgaria 2001 and 2011; Croatia 2001; Greece 2001; Kosovo 1991; Macedonia 2002; Montenegro 2003 and 2011; Romania 2002; Serbia 2002; Slovenia 2002.

Table 2: National distribution of the Muslims of Southeast Europe at the beginning of the twenty-first century (estimates)

	Albanians	*Bosniaks*	*Turks*	*Romas*	*Others*
Albania	1,900,000	–	–	40,000	10,000 Slavic-speakers
Bosnia-Herz.	5,000	1,790,000	–	5,000	
Bulgaria			650,000	120,000	130,000 Pomaks
Croatia	20,000	40,000	–	–	–
Greece	250,000 immigrants from Albania	–	90,000	30,000	30,000 Pomaks 50,000 others*
Kosovo	1,500,000	25,000	10,000	40,000	25,000 Goranis
Macedonia	500,000	20,000	80,000	50,000	50,000 Torbesh
Montenegro	25,000	70,000	–	5,000	–
Romania	–	–	35,000	–	25,000 Tatars 10,000 others*
Serbia	60,000	150,000	–	30,000	10,000 Goranis
Slovenia	5,000	40,000	–	5,000	–
Total	4,300,000	2,150,000	880,000	330,000	not calculated

* Muslims originating from Africa or Asia

Estimates based on the following population censuses: Albania 2001 and 1941; Bosnia-Herzegovina 1991 and UNHCR estimates 1996; Bulgaria 2001 and 2011; Croatia 2001; Greece 2001; Kosovo 1991; Macedonia 2002; Montenegro 2003 and 2011; Romania 2002; Serbia 2002; Slovenia 2002.

1

FROM THE OTTOMAN PROVINCIAL AUTONOMIES TO THE EASTERN CRISIS

(1800–1876)

When the Ottoman Empire in Europe started to disintegrate

At its greatest extent, the Ottoman Empire stretched over three continents: Europe, Asia and Africa. It included highly varied lands and populations that the sultans integrated within the empire and governed in very different manners depending upon the period and region in question.

The Ottoman conquest of European lands started in the middle of the fourteenth century and lasted for a very long period, by the end of which they had asserted their control over a large part of Southeast Europe, extending as far as Hungary. However, this power was exercised only indirectly in the provinces furthest from the capital and in the least accessible regions. Gilles Veinstein has defined three circles for the classical period (sixteenth–seventeenth centuries).[1] The furthest from the centre was that of the Ottoman possessions north of the Danube (Moldavia, Wallachia, Transylvania, Hungary); for these areas, integration—consisting of relationships of protection, tribute or administration of defensive military zones—was limited, and the Muslim presence was non-existent or very small. The second circle comprised the territories that bordered on Venice or Austria (Bosnia, Montenegro, Serbia, Albania, Greece); these areas were integrated into the Ottoman Empire to a greater degree through implementation of the *timar* land system (prebends), although often under specific local regimes (particularly with regard to taxes). The presence of Islam in this second circle was generally greater than in the outermost circle, as a result of the conversion of local populations to Islam. Finally, the innermost circle was made up of the regions closest to the Ottoman capital (Bulgaria, Thrace, Macedonia, Thessaly, Dobruja), where central power had been established the longest and most directly—although these regions also included areas enjoying a certain degree of autonomy. In these regions the Muslim population, and in particular the Turkish-speaking population, was more numerous.

After suffering several minor, and indeed temporary, territorial setbacks, the Ottoman Empire experienced its first significant territorial losses in Europe after the failure of the second siege of Vienna in 1683. These losses were far from definitive and inevitable. Hungary was certainly lost, but Morea (that is to say, the Peloponnese), in the south of the Balkan Peninsula, was regained in 1715. Likewise, the Austrian presence in Bosnia and Serbia did not last. The turn of the eighteenth and nineteenth centuries marked the beginning of a critical period for the Ottoman Empire in Europe. It was symbolised by the emergence of a new name to designate the region—"the Balkans"—which went on to replace the "Turkey-in-Europe" of the Europeans and the "Rumelia" of the Ottomans. It was the German geographer Johann-August Zeune who proposed that this peninsula in the south of Europe be given the name of the Bulgarian mountain chain, which at that time was still believed to cut the peninsula in two.[2] However, the name "Balkan Peninsula" came to prevail only towards the end of the nineteenth century, when the Ottoman territorial loss had become apparent to all to see.

Several interdependent factors contributed to the weakening of the Ottoman possessions in Europe in the early nineteenth century and the growing autonomy or even separation of some of its territories. The imperialist appetites of the Great Powers, the military and fiscal reorganisations undertaken by the sultans since the late eighteenth century, the autonomy of leading provincial notables and, more generally, changes in the balance of power within the provincial and central Ottoman elites played an important role. Local rebellions, some of which were inspired by the first stirrings of nascent nationalisms, were not the only factors here. Indeed, recent studies[3] show that the formation of Greece, Serbia and Romania was a far from linear process and that it was not the result simply of nationalist struggles to emancipate nations oppressed by a declining empire and build modern states in their stead, as the nationalist narrative would have us believe (see Map 3).

In the early nineteenth century, in addition to Russia, with which the Ottoman Empire was regularly at war, Napoleonic France and Britain came to disturb the geopolitical equilibria in the Eastern Mediterranean and Southeast Europe. Thus, the Ionian Islands, along with the island of Corfu, which were under Venetian control, were incorporated into the French Empire in 1797, before being placed under Russian protectorate and Ottoman suzerainty three years later. From 1807 to 1814, they formed an autonomous republic under French protectorate and then became a British protectorate from 1815 to 1864, when they were incorporated into the Kingdom of Greece. In 1805, following the defeat of the Austrians by Napoleon, the Treaty of Pressburg also gave the French Empire Istria, which, with Dalmatia, Croatia and part of Slovenia, formed the Illyrian Provinces. In 1815, following the fall of Napoleon, the Congress of Vienna restored Austrian domination over these regions. Further east, from 1802, the Romanian principalities saw Russia's position as protective power confirmed, although they remained under the suzerainty of the Ottoman Empire. Ten years later, Russia annexed Bessarabia.

The Serbian border area was controlled by the Ottoman army, and enjoyed a special status. The Christian population there did not rise up against the Sultan but against the exactions of the janissaries, the elite Ottoman troops. This and the pressure exerted by Russia led at first to a degree of autonomy. However, for several decades this fluctuated as a function of internal and external circumstances. The first Serbian insurrection took place in 1804, under the leadership of a notable, Karađorđe (Black George) Petrović, who was supported by the Tsar. However, Napoleon's Russian campaign, launched in 1812, allowed the Sultan to regain control of the *paşalik* of Belgrade. Nevertheless, in order to avoid this border area becoming depopulated, the Sultan was obliged to grant it autonomy once again, and another notable, Miloš Obrenović, was formally recognised as the representative of the region's *knez*s (Christian notables). Miloš took advantage of a second revolt that broke out in 1815 and Russian support at the Congress of Vienna to obtain official autonomy for the *paşalik*, which became a principality. Two years later, he had Karađorđe killed and decapitated when the latter returned to Serbia, and offered his head to the Sultan as a proof of his own loyalty. In the

Map 3: Southeast Europe in the first half of the nineteenth century

early 1830s, by means of several imperial decrees, the Sultan recognised Serbia as a hereditary vassal principality. However, the emergence of an intense political struggle between the prince and the "constitutionalists", the latter seeking a more liberal administration, favoured a degree of re-Ottomanisation of the principality. Indeed, the Sultan intervened in 1838 to impose a Constitution called the "Ottoman Constitution". This constitution limited the prince's power by setting up a council comprising seventeen members who were accountable to the Sultan. Moreover, the Porte regarded the prince only as a bey, that is to say as a governor, appointed and invested by the Sultan, and the council as a sort of *meclis*[4] (council), equivalent to the assemblies of local notables established in the rest of the Empire. While this new political order favoured reform, it also introduced political instability and led, in 1842, to Karađorđe's son Alexander being imposed as the new prince, but now without the right of hereditary succession. In 1844, the Sultan also appointed Toma Vučić-Perišić, one of the leaders of the "constitutionalist" party, to the position of commander-in-chief of the army.

Montenegro—which occupied a much smaller area than the state we know today—seems to have followed a more linear path to autonomy, although that path was just as long and was partly bound up with external factors, particularly political and financial support from Russia. In the late eighteenth century, the victory of the Montenegrin troops over the governor of Shkodër consolidated the power of the *vladika* (bishop) Petar I Petrović Njegoš (1784–1830). Beginning in 1798, Petar I began to draw up a first book of laws and to create specific institutions for this small territory. His successor, Petar II Njegoš (1830–51), was the first to bear the title "sovereign of the Montenegrins". During his rule, the first border agreements were signed with the Ottoman Empire and the Habsburg Empire, confirming the autonomy of a small territory in which the bishop continued his efforts to achieve centralisation, although not without resistance on the part of the local chiefs.

The situation of the Romanian provinces, placed under the double aegis of the Ottoman Empire and of Russia, shifted between 1820 and 1856, first towards a reassertion of Ottoman power, and then to greater protection from Russia, whose imperialist ambitions far outweighed any support for incipient national awareness. In 1821, a revolt against the "Ottoman yoke" was launched by Ypsilantis, a member of the *Philiki Hetairia* ("Society of Friends"), founded in Odessa by "enlightened"

Greek merchants. The absence of the hoped-for support from Russia, and the profound disagreements between the *Philiki Hetairia* and the local insurgents led by Tudor Vladimirescu, resulted in the revolt being suppressed with ease by the Ottoman army. Paradoxically, this reassertion of Ottoman control was accompanied by a degree of Romanianisation of local power. A revolt had also broken out at the same time in the Peloponnese, and so the Ottoman authorities feared a Greco-Romanian alliance. They therefore had the Phanariot princes, descended from the great Greek families settled in the Phanar district of Constantinople/Istanbul, replaced by Romanian princes in their stead. However, new Russo-Turkish conflicts in 1825–7 and in 1828, which were settled by the Treaty of Adrianople (1829), restored Russia's status as protector of the Principalities, while leaving Ottoman suzerainty in place. Indeed, Moldavia and Wallachia were even reorganised by the Russians and new Constitutions (called "Organic Regulations") were introduced. In 1848, a national, liberal movement developed in the two Principalities, linked to the revolutionary unrest that was breaking out elsewhere in Europe. It was quelled by joint action on the part of the Russians and Ottomans and, by the Convention of Balta-Liman (May 1849), the two empires reaffirmed their joint rule.

Finally, in the second decade of the nineteenth century, a very complex combination of factors led to the independence of the southernmost part of the Balkan Peninsula, Greece. The autonomy of the local Ottoman notables, and in particular that of Ali Pasha, governor of Ioannina (who died in 1822), the military reorganisations and the tensions within Istanbul's elites, seem to have played a significant role in the formation of the Kingdom of Greece. However, other factors can also be identified, such as the action of the *Philiki Hetairia* guided by a Greek imperial ideology, the growth of Philhellenism in Western Europe and, above all, the conflicting interests of the Great Powers. Partly fomented by the *Philiki Hetairia* from Odessa and Constantinople, a revolt was launched in the Peloponnese and on some islands by local notables, who had their own interests, and by the leaders of Christian militias (*klefts* and *armatoles*), who had been hard hit by the military reorganisations which had sought to eliminate them over the course of the previous twenty years. Philhellenes from Western and Southeast Europe came to fight at their side, and an Assembly held at Epidaurus proclaimed a Constitution. The Ottoman troops, caught up in the Romanian provinces and

Ioannina, had difficulty containing these rebellions, which were, however, weakened by internal disagreements. The Porte was able to regain control in the Peloponnese thanks to the intervention of Ibrahim Pasha of Egypt in 1825–6, while his father Muhammad Ali put down the rebellions in Crete. Soon after, Russia issued an ultimatum to the Ottoman Empire, forcing it to recognise Russia's increased role as protector of the Romanian Principalities and Serbia. However, Ottoman troops took back Athens the following year. In 1827, Russia, France and Britain decided to intervene in order to push the Sultan to accept mediation between himself and the insurgents. The destruction of the combined Ottoman and Egyptian fleet at Navarino did not cause the Sultan to yield. Russia then decided to attack the Ottoman Empire in the Balkans and in Eastern Anatolia. At the London Conference of 1830, Britain and France, seeking to avoid the Empire collapsing in Europe to Russia's advantage, succeeded in obtaining recognition of Greek independence with the guarantee of the Great Powers. Two years later, a kingdom of Greece was established; Prince Otto of Bavaria was placed at the head of the new kingdom and would reign until 1862.

This geopolitical context in Southeast Europe, characterised by the growing influence of Russia, which had been regarded as the protector of Orthodox Christians since the Treaty of Küçük Kaynarca (1774), was dramatically shaken in the middle of the nineteenth century by the Crimean War (1853–6). Sparked by an incident in the Holy Places in Jerusalem, this war between Russia on the one side and the Ottoman Empire allied with France and Britain on the other was a major turning point in the balance of power in Europe, as well as for the Ottoman Empire and the Balkan Peninsula. Under the new order there was greater intervention on the part of France, Britain, Austria, Prussia and Piedmont-Sardinia (Italy from the 1860s), and Russia's influence was limited. In this context, Serbia, Montenegro and the Romanian Principalities were able to achieve increasing autonomy.

Serbia was placed under the protection of the Great Powers and the Porte intervened in Serbian internal affairs for one last time in 1858; the last Ottoman garrisons were driven out nine years later. Although the political scene in Serbia was shaken by internal struggles between different actors supported by one great power or another, the Serbian state was strengthened under Miloš (1858–60), his son Mihailo (1860–68) and then his great-nephew Milan (1868–89). The defeat of Russia had even more significant consequences for the Romanian Principalities. Russia was forced to withdraw from those principalities and to return southern Bessarabia to Moldavia and the Danube Delta to the Ottoman Empire. Moreover, the fact that Wallachia and Moldavia, still under Ottoman suzerainty, were also placed under the guarantee of the Great Powers resulted in the following years in what the French historian Catherine Durandin calls a "national shift" (*"un basculement national"*).[5] The complex balance of power between the Great Powers allowed the internal debate about the union of the two Principalities to move in favour of such a project. In 1859, Alexandru Ioan Cuza was elected *hospodar*, sovereign of Wallachia and Moldavia. Late in 1861, the Ottoman authorities finally gave way and recognised him on a temporary basis. Overthrown in February 1866, he was replaced by Prince Charles of Hohenzollern, who ruled under the name Carol I as a vassal of the Sultan, but this time with hereditary title. The "post-Crimean" context also tended to strengthen Montenegro. Shortly before the end of the war, Petar II's place was taken by his nephew Danilo (1852–60). Danilo was not a bishop, and was the first to bear the title of prince, recognised by the Habsburgs and Russia. The new prince succeeded in consolidating his power externally. Under pressure from Russia and the Habsburg Empire, in 1859 the Ottoman Empire was compelled in the wake of fighting on the border of the sanjak of Herzegovina to recognise the de facto Ottoman–Montenegrin border, confirming a significant enlargement of Montenegrin territory. Under Nikola (1860–1918), who continued to benefit from Russian support, there were recurrent clashes on the borders with the Ottoman Empire.

In this new period, the geopolitical equilibria in the region were gradually called into question, not only by Russia's desire to regain its influence or by the conflicting interests of the Great Powers, which often used the principle of nationalities for their own ends, but also by the appearance of Balkan irredentist movements. These movements sought the "liberation" of their "co-nationals" or their co-religionists, or, at least, the enlargement of their own states' territory at the expense of the Ottoman Empire. From the 1860s, the consolidation of the new political entities meant that they could begin to implement irredentist plans that had appeared twenty years earlier and were connected to nascent national ideologies. On the Serbian side, the *Načertanije* ("Plan") of the Serbian Prime Minister Ilija Garašanin (who held office from 1843 to 1852 and from 1861 to 1867), drawn up in 1844, aimed to achieve the liberation and unification of the Serbian people. It envisaged a kind of reconstitution of the medieval Serbian Empire, which would also extend to Bosnia-Herzegovina, Montenegro and the north of Albania. This plan, the first concrete manifestation of which was a propaganda drive using a network of agents in the Ottoman Empire and the Habsburg Empire, was sometimes also conceived as a programme guaranteeing freedom of worship for the non-Orthodox. In Greece, the *Megali Idea* ("Great Idea") emerged in 1844, during discussions on the Constitution between the Prime Minister, Ioannis Kolettis, and King Otto. Adopting a similar approach to the *Načertanije*, the idea was to resuscitate the Byzantine Empire in order to bring all the Greeks together in one state, with Constantinople as the capital. It should also be mentioned that a work of a somewhat different nature, the celebrated epic poem of the Montenegrin Petar II Njegoš entitled *The Mountain Wreath*, was published in 1847, and thus at roughly the same time. That poem told of the fight against the Turks and the forced conversion to Christianity of the local Muslims.

Only after the Crimean War did these plans lead to concrete actions in support of the insurrections breaking out in the Ottoman Empire—Serbia, for example, supported uprisings in Herzegovina and Bulgaria—and to alliances. Thus Serbia, stimulated by the dynamic of Italian unification, renewed contact with Greece in 1860–61. The alliances, however, were established later, with Montenegro (1866), Greece (1867) and the Romanian Principalities (1868). Agreements were also entered into with Bulgarian revolutionaries in 1867, while an attempt was made to form an alliance with the Yugoslav movement that was developing in the Habsburg Empire. The arrival of Prince Milan, who developed closer relations with the Habsburg Empire (Austria-Hungary from 1867), rendered these alliances ineffective for a time. However, in this context, the revolts of the Christian populations of Rumelia were able to spark the powder keg. The first revolts that broke out in Herzegovina and Montenegro were quickly suppressed by the Ottoman authorities. However, the revolt that broke out in Crete in 1866 triggered a serious crisis for the Ottoman Empire, which was forced to grant autonomous status to the island in 1868, set out in an "Organic Regulation". Finally, revolts in Herzegovina and Bulgaria triggered the Eastern Crisis in 1875. The following year, Montenegro and Serbia declared war on the Ottoman Empire, while administrative, social and ideological changes accelerated in both the new territorial entities and the Empire itself.

Reforms, the establishment of bureaucracies and the formation of new elites

Alongside these geopolitical changes, the first three quarters of the nineteenth century saw numerous reforms or "reorganisations"—to capture the meaning of the word "*Tanzimat*"—which characterised the policy of the Ottoman authorities between 1839 and 1876. These reorganisations brought about certain changes to the societies of Southeast Europe. National historiographies have generally presented a picture of new states modernising and Westernising themselves as soon as they were freed from the "Ottoman yoke", while the Ottoman Empire gradually became the "sick man" of Europe. This view distorts the reality in two ways. Firstly, reforms were introduced in both the new entities that wholly or partially freed themselves from Ottoman rule and in the Ottoman Empire itself. And secondly, in this Ottoman, or already post-Ottoman, Southeast Europe, where the great majority of the population was rural and illiterate, the most significant changes occurred only in the aftermath of the Crimean War, and indeed not before the years 1860–70.

Thus, Kostas Kostis has shown that the Greece of Otto (1834–63) remained largely a pre-modern state: the central government concerned itself only with settling conflicts between notables and did not seek to establish direct control over the whole territory.[6] In Greece, as in Serbia and in the Romanian Principalities, the political system, highly dependent on the Great Powers, remained autocratic. The constitutionalism that certain groups desired became a reality in those areas only in the 1860s: 1864 in Greece, 1866 in Romania and 1869 in Serbia. A constitution would be proclaimed in Istanbul some ten years later, in 1876, by the Sultan, who was concerned to avoid the intervention of the Great Powers. Michael Palairet has shown that, even from an economic point of view, freedom from Ottoman rule did not automatically mean economic progress.[7] Autonomous Serbia, for example, was significantly less prosperous at that time than the Ottoman Bulgarian and, to a lesser degree, Bosnian regions, which were open to European markets.

The Greek, Serbian and Moldo-Wallachian societies experienced change through agrarian transformations (industrialisation had as yet scarcely taken off). These societies changed further with the strengthening of the administrative apparatus and the appearance of new administrative and intellectual elites, who arrived from outside (the Habsburg Empire, Russia, Istanbul), or were educated in local or foreign (Western European, Russian) schools. This resulted in the dissemination of new ideas and a first attempt at political organisation. In Serbia, where the prince prevented the formation of a class of large landowners, a section of these new elites formed the "constitutionalist" movement, which led a first series of administrative and educational reforms in the years 1840–50. A liberal movement then asserted itself in the late 1850s, opposing the conservatives. However, there was a significant divide between the liberal bureaucratic elites and the peasants, who supported the sovereign. In Romania, the land reform of 1864 changed the economic and social relationships between boyars (landowners) and peasants, which had already been affected by the Constitution imposed by Russia in 1848. This reform put an end to serfdom and allowed peasants to own land, but did not eliminate the large properties or the economic domination of the boyars. However, the king introduced political alternation between conservatives and liberals, the latter being recruited from among the new elites that emerged from the merchant bourgeoisie and the intelligentsia, educated in France, in particular. In Greece, the state itself inherited 70 per cent of the arable lands which had formerly belonged to the Sultan and to the large Ottoman landowners. It would hold them until the land reform of 1864. The new "middle class" that was being formed—often civil servants—would only assert itself politically in the following years. While religion held an important place in these new political entities, the Orthodox Church, recognised as the dominant Church, was not above politics and was nationalised following the granting of autonomy (Serbia in 1832) or independence from the Patriarchate of Constantinople (Greece in 1833, Romania in 1866).

On the Ottoman side too, which was (as we shall see later) where virtually all the Muslims of the Peninsula lived after the 1840s, society was transformed over the first decades of the nineteenth century, though to varying degrees. As Maurus Reinkowski has explained, for the Ottoman authorities it was a case of putting in place infrastructures to meet the Empire's financial needs.[8] That required control of all the regions, including the remote regions that were relatively autonomous but were under threat, mainly from European imperialism. Nevertheless, the changes were the result of a process that was less rational and linear and more ambiguous and heterogeneous than has previously been thought.

The first Ottoman military reforms date back to the eighteenth century. They were reinforced by the introduction of a professional army, the *Nizam-i Cedid* army, by Sultan Selim III (1789–1807), then by the decision taken by Sultan Mahmud II (1808–39) in 1826 to abolish the janissaries, and the introduction of conscription in the mid-1840s (although this conscription never applied to the whole population, as Christians, among others, were de facto exempted). In the early 1830s, Mahmud II reined in the leading *ayans* (local notables) who had carved out significant autonomy for themselves, such as Ali Pasha of Ioannina, Mustafa Pasha Bushatli in the Shkodër region, or Osman Pazvanoğlu in Vidin. In 1839, after the Empire had suffered a defeat at the hands of the troops of Muhammad Ali of Egypt, Mahmud II's successor, Abdülmecid (1839–61), proclaimed the famous *hatt-i şerif* (rescript or written act) of Gülhane, which launched the *Tanzimat* reforms. Senior officials were sent from the capital to replace the local governors, and a new bureaucracy was put in place. Although they were supposed to collect taxes directly, the tax farming system would soon be reintroduced. In this way, changes were wrought to a large part of the administrative and military system, and also the economic and tax system, except in certain border areas like Bosnia and Albania. In these two provinces there was strong resistance from certain sections of the local elites—too often interpreted in national or proto-national terms. Most of the notables sought to avoid the loss of their military and tax prerogatives which, with land, constituted the basis of their power. In Bosnia, this resistance would be eliminated by force in 1850–51; in Albania, the main revolts were put down in the 1840s, although certain areas, in particular those close to the borders, retained a special status.

In Ottoman Rumelia as a whole, the most important changes took place after the Crimean War. With the new imperial rescript of 1856, which recognised the Sultan's subjects as equal citizens, a new land law (1858) authorised private property. In particular, the provincial administration was reformed following an initial experiment in the province of Niš, bordering the principality of Serbia, between 1861 and 1864. The new system was introduced in 1867 in the Danube vilayet, under the aegis of Midhat Pasha, and the Prizren vilayet was created. The new administrative structures involving the creation of *meclis* (councils), which brought the administrators together with Muslim and non-Muslim notables, were extended to all vilayets from 1871. However, this administration was put in place with a great deal of pragmatism and therefore differed greatly from place to place. Changes were more easily made where the means of communication had been improved—for example, between 1857 and 1860 a first railway line was built in Dobruja by a British company; a line between Ruse and Varna was opened in 1867; and from 1869 onwards several sections of a Balkan railway, which was to connect Istanbul to Vienna, were built thanks to Baron Hirsch.

The reforms also required new bureaucrats to be trained. To this end, following the founding of military schools from the late eighteenth century (Engineering School in 1795, Medical School in 1827, Military Academy in 1834), civilian higher education schools were established in Istanbul (the School for Cadis in 1855 and the School of Civil Administration in 1859), while some *rüşdiye*s[9] (lower secondary schools) were opened in the capital from 1838–9 onwards and then in the European provinces from the end of the 1840s. These *rüşdiye*s had nothing to do with the madrasas, the religious schools, since they taught non-religious subjects to a greater degree and the curriculum was no longer organised around learning books but around progression through school years. Some young people were also sent to study in Western Europe, particularly France. A new impetus was given by the setting up of a Ministry of Education in 1857, and even more so by the Regulations of Education in 1869 for the introduction of public instruction, designed to secularise education and disseminate Ottomanism (*Osmanlılık*). The intention was also to counter the influence of other school networks (Greek, missionary, etc.) which were attracting increasing numbers of the Christians of the Balkans both inside and outside the Empire. Thus, the foundation of new Ottoman schools went hand in hand with the administrative reforms in the sanjak of Niš, and then in the Danube vilayet, where Midhat Pasha also sought to attract Bulgarian children, although without much success.

The years 1830–76 were therefore characterised by the end of the hegemony of the local Muslim notables. They had to cope with the power of the new governors who came from other regions of the Empire, and with that of foreign consuls and agents who appeared on the local scene after the Crimean War, marking the physical presence on Ottoman lands of the Great Powers, Greece and Serbia. New economic and intellectual elites, which appeared as a result of the administrative and economic changes, also gradually became involved in politics: merchants, often Christian, benefiting from the economic growth, and new Christian and Muslim elites (bureaucrats, teachers), educated within the different educational networks which were gradually spreading.

For these new elites, the press and the printed word which expanded from the years 1830–40 onwards, and even more from the 1860s, became highly important instruments of communication and expression. They led to a new relationship being built up between the authorities, emergent public opinion, and a budding liberal current inspired by the young Italian liberals. The Ottoman authorities very soon began to use the press. In Rumelia, official newspapers were published in a number of vilayets (Danube 1865, Bosnia 1866, Ioannina 1868, Salonica 1869), in Turkish and in the local language. However, in addition to the press published by Christians, newspapers with a greater or lesser degree of independence, published by Muslims, also appeared during the 1860s, such as *Gülşen-i Saray* ("The Palace Rose Garden") in Sarajevo or *Mecra-i Efkâr* ("The Course of Ideas") in Ruse. Others appeared in Salonica in the 1870s. These periodicals were part of the impetus generated by young civil servants in the capital, who over the early 1860s launched press titles that took part in political debate. The Young Ottomans (who appeared at the same time as other "youth movements" in the region— the Unified Serbian Youth in Serbia and the "Junimists" of Romania) criticised the actions of the Ottoman authorities. Under the aegis of Namik Kemal, they criticised the authoritarianism, submission to the Great Powers and neglect of the Islamic heritage. They opted for constitutionalism and parliamentarianism and therefore sought to connect liberalism with Islamic tradition.

The new Muslim bureaucratic elites had a profile, an openness to the Western world (through their knowledge of foreign languages) and a place in society that was no longer that of the scribes and the ulamas, the holders of Islamic religious knowledge. They did compete with those scribes and ulamas, but still in a very limited way. Before the Crimean War, education remained very largely under the control of the ulamas, some of whom supported the reforms while others opposed them. However, these new elites, who did not want the Empire to reject its Islamic tradition and heritage, also ended up criticising the reforms.

The reforms were supposed to introduce new relationships between the state and religion in the Empire. The rescript of 1856 guaranteed non-Muslims respect for their traditional immunities, freedom of worship and property rights. All the Ottoman subjects were declared equal with regard to taxation, justice and education. All had the same access to employment and could go to the same schools, but all were required to submit to conscription or to pay the *bedel* (the tax payable in place of conscription). In reality, non-Muslims were not integrated into the Ottoman army and paid the tax instead. Non-Muslims also developed their own school networks, while relatively few of them held positions in the administration. Despite the principles of the rescript, certain political and social differences between Christians and Muslims continued to exist. The policy of equality, which went hand in hand with an Ottomanist policy that sought to develop an Ottoman patriotism, quickly reached its limits.

For example, the institutionalisation of the non-Muslim religious communities, initiated as part of the policy of equality, ended up reinforcing the differences, particularly in terms of education. In fact, in the 1860s, ten years after the recognition of a protestant Armenian community, the principal *millets* (non-Muslim communities) adopted new regulations and new bodies (1860–62 for the Orthodox Christian or "Rum" community, 1863 for the Gregorian Armenian community, 1865 for the Jewish community). The Roman Catholics were not recognised as a *millet* because they were subject to a spiritual authority outside the Empire; their fate was governed above all by the treaties negotiated between the Ottoman Empire and the protective powers (France, Habsburg Empire). In each case, the consequences of this institutionalisation differed with regard to the centralisation of the community or the increased role of the laity, as religious and political changes were influenced by other factors (the role of other states, missionary activities, socio-economic composition of the communities).

In the Balkan Peninsula, the largest non-Muslim community, the Rums (Orthodox Christians), would split. From the 1850s, a movement appeared among the Slavic-speaking populations against Hellenism and the Patriarchate of Constantinople. From 1860 onwards, some Bulgarians, on the basis of economic and social changes that were sometimes only of very local significance, claimed their ecclesiastical autonomy from the Patriarchate. The Porte, which had an interest in slowing the growth of Hellenism and perhaps also the growth of a Bulgarian revolutionary movement that had been on the rise with the support of the diaspora since 1867, allowed a Bulgarian Exarchate to be created in 1870. The following year, in a similar way it granted authorisation to the Serbs to establish an Orthodox seminary in Prizren.

In fact, the political, economic and socio-cultural changes that occurred between 1800 and 1876 gave rise to new balances of power in

Southeast Europe—between Christians themselves, but above all between Muslims and Christians.

New relationships between Muslims and Christians

The reshaping of Southeast Europe during the first three quarters of the nineteenth century had important consequences for relationships between Muslims, who had always been a minority in that area in numerical terms, and Christians, who, although in the numerical majority, had an officially inferior political status until the *Tanzimat* reforms.

For many Muslims, the conflicts, the revolts and the emancipation of the Balkan territories from Ottoman rule, brought death or exile or placed them in circumstances in which survival was difficult. National or international agreements that were intended to guarantee their civil, economic and religious rights were rare, and rarely observed, or were introduced only once the Muslim population had shrunk to small groups.

Thus, the few Muslims living in the territory of the embryonic Montenegrin state were unable to maintain their presence because of massacres, forced conversions or departures. And so, after the disappearance of the *poturica* (Muslim descendants from local converts) of Old Montenegro in the eighteenth century, it was the turn of the Muslims living in the region inhabited by the Vasojević tribe to disappear in the years 1852–8, either due to forced conversions or else because they left to avoid conversion.

In "Old Greece", their co-religionists, who accounted for around 10 per cent of the population, did not manage to survive despite the guarantees provided by certain national and international agreements. The period of conflicts in the 1820s provoked a number of massacres and departures, as well as some forced conversions to Christianity. According to the first constitutions, the remaining Muslims enjoyed freedom of worship, but could not benefit from the citizenship that was reserved for those who believed in Jesus Christ. The first international agreements signed in 1826–8 concerning the region in revolt contained provisions relating to the compensation that the Muslim owners of expropriated lands should receive (or the Ottoman State, in the case of religious foundations). In particular, through the agreements that followed between 1829 and 1832 and which led to the creation of an independent Greek state, Britain, France and Russia sought to guarantee not only freedom of worship but also the equality of all subjects in the new state, regardless of their religion. They also wanted Muslim property to be protected and Muslims to have the right to "reciprocal optional migration" (in the same way as the Empire's Orthodox Christians). It is interesting to note here the seeds of the idea of population exchange between Greece and the Ottoman Empire. However, under the reign of King Otto (1833–62) and at the beginning of the reign of his successor George I, until the Eastern Crisis, the Muslims of "Old Greece" numbered no more than a few hundred, primarily on the island of Euboea, but also in central Greece and the Peloponnese. In the absence of laws specifically applicable to them, their status was determined only by the successive constitutions (1844 and 1864) that established Orthodox Christianity as the dominant religion (while tolerating the other religions), and stipulated that all inhabitants were equal before the law. However, they frequently encountered harassment and difficulties in their daily lives.

North of the Ottoman possessions, in the *paşalik* of Belgrade the situation of the Muslims had already been insecure in the eighteenth century, on account of frequent Christian revolts. This led to many leaving for the urban centres or for regions further from the borders. The revolts in the early nineteenth century, which also led to massacres, increased these departures and led to the gradual disappearance of Muslims from a territory to which many Christians came from different regions of Rumelia and the Habsburg Empire. The rescript of 1830, which granted autonomy to that territory, enlarged by an additional six districts (*nahiye*), stipulated that the only Muslims who could stay were those living in towns and cities with an Ottoman fortress, and obliged the others to sell their lands and leave. Nevertheless, thanks to the intervention of the Ottoman governor of Belgrade, the departures were delayed for some years. The Muslims of the Morava valley did, however, leave shortly after the promulgation of the 1833 rescript, even though it granted them a period of five years. The Muslims of the Drina valley were persuaded to leave or were driven out in 1834, with the exception of two villages (Mali Zvornik and Sakar), which were protected and managed to remain under the jurisdiction of the Ottoman fortress of Zvornik, on the Bosnian bank of the Drina. In 1862, in the reign of Prince Mihailo Obrenović, friction between Muslims and Christians in Belgrade worsened. A convention was then agreed between Serbia and the Ottoman Empire that obliged the entire civil Muslim population to leave the principality. Only the soldiers of four garrisons (Belgrade, Šabac, Smederevo and Kladovo) remained, along with Gypsy Muslims, or those who declared themselves to be such. However, in 1867 these garrisons also had to leave. The few remaining Muslims—Gypsies or Muslims who passed themselves off as such—now came under Serbian administration, which resulted in the first regulations concerning the official recognition of Islam, promulgated in May 1868.

So, from the early nineteenth century, many Muslims living in Montenegro, Greece or Serbia were forced to move and settle elsewhere in Ottoman lands. Some, from Greece in particular, emigrated to Anatolia; others took refuge in what was still Rumelia, swelling the flows of *muhacirs*, those Muslims who were fleeing the *darülharb* ("territory of war" or "territory of the infidels") to join the *darülislam* ("territory of Islam"). For Russia's advances in Crimea and the Caucasus also provoked several large waves of migration to the Empire. In the last decade of the eighteenth century, tens of thousands of Tatars had already left the Crimea (annexed by Russia in 1783) and settled in Dobruja, a region situated between the Danube and the Black Sea and forming a buffer zone between the two empires. In the late 1820s, a wave of Nogay Tatars took refuge there after Russia had annexed Bessarabia. Moreover, the Ottoman authorities adopted a policy of repopulating the Dobruja by settling these refugees and other Muslims arriving from various provinces of the Empire. The Ottoman authorities created an ad hoc commission to manage the flow of tens of thousands of Crimean Tatars and Caucasian Circassians following the Crimean War. This commission became an office of the Ministry of the Interior in 1870. The new town of Mecidiye/Medgidia was even founded in Dobruja, named after Sultan Abdülmecid. However, Tatars and Cherkesses were also settled elsewhere in Anatolia, and in the Balkan Peninsula: in South Serbia, Kosovo, Bulgaria, Macedonia, and even in Thessaly. Thus, the Ottoman authorities were able to strengthen the Muslim presence in certain areas. Nevertheless, the social integration of these *muhacir*s was not always easy, as living together with the surrounding Christian populations generally proved difficult. Moreover, these Muslims were often among the first to leave for Istanbul and Anatolia at the time of the 1877–8 conflicts. Conversely, the departure of Christian populations also changed the balance between the religions in certain regions of the Balkan Peninsula. This was the case in the eastern regions. For example, during the Russo-

Ottoman war of 1828-9, Bulgarians and Gagauz (Turkish-speaking Christians) were encouraged by Russian propaganda to move further north. Others followed their example, although some would subsequently return to Ottoman lands.

At a more local level, a number of factors contributed to changes in the demographic balance between Christians and Muslims. The relative decline of the Muslim population in certain regions (for example, Bulgaria) was caused by a higher birth rate among the Christians, but also by the military service obligation introduced by the reforms. Only Muslims were required to perform military service, and so Muslims suffered a higher death toll in the Empire's recurrent wars. Christians settled in very large numbers in the urban centres, where the share of the Muslim element decreased accordingly. In the western part of the Balkan Peninsula, on the other hand, there were areas in which Christians converted to Islam under varying degrees of duress. In the northern regions of Epirus, Ali Pasha of Ioannina was responsible for the Islamicisation of several regions over which he imposed his authority. In current Kosovo and the current north of Albania, Albanian-speaking or Slavic-speaking Christians converted in order to integrate into the dominant element.

Relations between Muslims and Christians changed not only in terms of demographic balance, but also politically, economically and socially. In the new entities that were Greece, Montenegro and the *paşalik* of Belgrade (that is to say, Serbia), Muslims not only lost their dominant status, but those who remained were totally marginalised. In the Ottoman Empire, general changes gradually occurred that improved the status of Christians—or rather of certain Christians—although the Muslims' dominant political status was not truly challenged. While the *Tanzimat* rescripts (1839 and 1856) proclaimed the equality of all the Sultan's subjects regardless of their religion, that equality remained no more than a principle, particularly in the provinces. Conscription ended up applying only to Muslims, with Christians being required to pay a tax instead, as we have seen. Positions in the civil service and government continued to be occupied almost exclusively by Muslims. Above all, land remained largely in Muslim hands. In Bosnia-Herzegovina, for example, 91 per cent of landowners were Muslim, while 95 per cent of the *kmets* (sharecroppers) were Christian. The agrarian question and the peasants' economic and social claims thus remained of central importance in provincial life, even leading to insurrections (Crete in 1841, 1858 and 1866–9, Herzegovina in 1875, Bulgaria in 1876).

Nevertheless, the political and tax reforms, as well as the new political and economic relations with the Great Powers, did favour positive changes for certain non-Muslims, who enjoyed a greater share of local power whether in the villages or in the mixed *meclis* (councils) put in place at different levels by the Ottoman authorities. Non-Muslims, particularly Orthodox Christians, grew wealthy through the trade they were able to develop with foreign countries. In terms of religion, there were still constraints on public worship and it remained impossible for Muslims to convert to other religions. In 1846, crypto-Christians in the Black Mountain region north of Skopje (Skopska Crna Gora) were severely punished for seeking to declare themselves Christians in order to avoid military service. However, Christian religious activities increased and became more visible, in particular from the 1860s onwards: the Catholic and Protestant missionary networks grew and churches were built in urban centres such as Bitola, Mostar and Shkodër. Under the 1856 rescript, non-Muslims also became free to establish their own schools. The number of such schools, which provided an education in Greek, Bulgarian, Serbian or Romanian, increased more rapidly than the number of new Ottoman schools. A Hellenic literary society (*Syllogos*) and an Epirote Society were created in Constantinople, in 1861 and 1871 respectively, to spread Greek culture. This religious and cultural dynamism was bound up with the economic growth experienced by Christian merchants and with the support of the Great Powers or the new Balkan political entities, which were now represented locally by consuls or agents.

Faced with these changes, the Balkan Muslim elites, or a part of them, began to feel a relative loss of status, even though they (at least partially) retained their political and economic supremacy. Some of them saw their local power not only reduced by the central authorities, but also competed for by new Christian or Jewish economic and intellectual elites. This feeling manifested itself in more overt reactions; where measures to implement the equality of Christians and Muslims were enforced locally and disrupted the economic and social equilibria, they sometimes caused unrest. While complex relationships based on rivalry, imitation or adaptation became established between the Muslim elites and the non-Muslim elites of the Balkans (and the West), Islamic institutions and practices also underwent changes associated with this context.

FROM OTTOMAN PROVINCIAL AUTONOMIES TO EASTERN CRISIS

The multiple networks of Balkan Islam

In the early nineteenth century, there was no major difference between Islam as practised and lived in the European part of the Empire, and the Islam of the Anatolian provinces. It was conveyed through the same institutions, which often had Istanbul at their heart, even though Balkan Muslims had more frequent contacts with non-Muslims, Christians in particular. However, in both the European part of the Empire and Anatolia, the form and practice of Islam was far from homogeneous, on account of the multiplicity of networks and actors through which the religion of the Prophet Muhammad was interpreted and disseminated. What were these networks and who were these actors?

Islamic practice was organised around the mosques (or *mescid*s[10] in the case of places of prayer that did not have a minaret) where Muslims offered up their ritual prayers and where *hutbe*s (sermons) were given on Friday or on other occasions (when they were referred to as *vaz*s). The *cemaat*[11] (local community) met there around the imam, who often also gave lessons to the young children (boys, and to a lesser extent girls), teaching them the Quran and sometimes the rudiments of arithmetic and writing. In some towns, the mosque formed part of a complex, including also a madrasa, that is to say a school in which religious specialists, the ulamas, were trained in religious knowledge (Arabic language, the Quran, Quranic exegesis, knowledge of the hadiths or deeds and sayings of the Prophet, Islamic jurisprudence, logic, rhetoric) and some profane sciences. They then became cadis (judges) or *müderris* (teachers) who in turn taught young Muslims. The famous madrasas founded in Rumelia included the Gazi Husrev-beg madrasa in Sarajevo (1537). However, the most important remained those in Istanbul: the madrasas of Fatih and Süleymaniyye. A particular feature of the Ottoman Empire compared to the rest of the Muslim world was that a hierarchy of religious specialists, the *ilmiyye*, was gradually established; that hierarchy could almost be regarded as a high clergy that was accountable to the authorities, with the *şeyhülislam* ("Head of islam") at its head, who was also the mufti of Istanbul. This hierarchy included the cadis and the *müderris*, the importance of whose posts (and whose remuneration) varied according to the town where they were employed. The madrasas were also organised in a hierarchy, those of Fatih and Süleymaniyye being the best and having the best, and best remunerated, teachers.

The positions of the cadis and the *müderris* in provincial society were quite different. The cadis presided over the sharia courts and made judgments according to a body of law that included, in addition to sharia (Islamic law), the *kanun* (secular legislation) and the imperial orders. They also had notarial, administrative and even municipal powers and duties. The cadis were also consulted by non-Muslims. The role of the *müderris* had more to do with transmitting religious knowledge, and sometimes profane knowledge (medicine, mathematics, etc.). It was often the *müderris* who became muftis, that is to say the legal experts consulted in order to obtain a fatwa (a legal opinion on any subject). However, the mufti was also considered to be the highest religious authority in the town or region, and as such could have the ability to mobilise people socially and politically either in favour of or against the political authorities. Only a small minority of the Muslims in the Balkan regions studied in the Balkan madrasas, most of them in the area in which they were born. The best students left to study in the best madrasas of the Peninsula, in the Empire's capital, and, less often, in the Arab provinces.

Religious knowledge could be acquired simply from a teacher in a mosque. It could also be acquired in a *tekke*, that is, in a dervish establishment, led by a spiritual teacher, a shaykh. These establishments, which were sometimes called *zaviye*, *dergah* or *hankah/hanikah*, could be part of complexes including mosques and madrasas, or else separate. In the Balkan Peninsula, as in the rest of the Muslim world, Ottoman expansion led to the setting up of Muslim mystical brotherhoods, called *tarikat*s (literally, "paths"), at all levels of the population. Balkan dervishes are often associated with the Bektashi brotherhood. In fact, numerous different brotherhood networks were established in the Peninsula, beginning with the Halveti networks, often close to the Ottoman authorities in the classical period (sixteenth–seventeenth centuries), but also the Naqshbandi, Bektashi, Kadiri, Rifai (whom Western travellers sometimes called the howling dervishes), Mevlevi (the famous whirling dervishes), Melami, etc. Their followers sought to achieve knowledge of the divine by following a mystical approach, guided by a spiritual master through different practices and rituals that varied between the different brotherhoods (spiritual retreat, tireless recitation of formulae, dance and breathing techniques, chanting, mortification, etc.). Beyond the individual mystical searching, the spiritual connections between disciple and teacher and between the disciples themselves, as well as the material resources that these religious groups had, allowed them to play a social and political role.

In fact, the *tekke*s, founded or endowed by leading figures of the Empire and local notables, possessed property in mortmain (land, shops, mills, etc.) from which they obtained income that enabled them to pay the officiants and feed the dervishes and passing guests. This system of waqfs (pious foundations) was not restricted to the dervish establishments, as most of the mosques and madrasas functioned in the same way. The provincial notables had an interest in this, as it enabled them to circumvent the impossibility of passing property on to their descendants, by appointing the latter as, for example, *mütevelli* (administrators) of the waqfs, with the income that came with that appointment.

Finally, we must mention the *türbe*s, or tombs. These tombs, which were often, but not always, associated with the brotherhoods, were the object of individual or collective devotion, in the form of individual visits or collective pilgrimages. In the Balkans, many of these tombs, frequented by Muslim—and non-Muslim—believers seeking the fulfilment of a wish, healing of an illness, etc., were the tombs of saints associated with the conquest of those regions or the local history of Islam. The local people believed that repeated visits to certain particularly venerated tombs, such as the *türbe*s of Ajvaz Dede in Prusac (Bosnia), Sari Saltik in Kruja (Albania) or Demir Baba in Deli Orman (Bulgaria), could replace the pilgrimage to Mecca, which required financial resources that not all the Muslim faithful had.

Through these various institutions, different Islamic currents and religious practices spread among the Muslims of Rumelia, who assimilated and adapted them according to their knowledge, expectations and inclinations, and the context of the period. In the nineteenth century, all the Muslims in the Peninsula were Sunni Muslims of the Hanafite school, or at least were officially regarded as such by the authorities. In fact, there were Kizilbash (in Turkish: *kızılbaş*; literally "red heads") groups, particularly in some eastern regions of the Peninsula (Dobruja, Deli Orman, eastern Rhodope, Thrace), who still retained the beliefs and practices inherited from the first period of colonisation of those regions, influenced subsequently by the Safavid Islam of the sixteenth century. Those beliefs and practices were far removed from the dominant Sunni doctrine: worship of Ali (the Prophet's son-in-law) and the first imams; esoteric interpretation of the Quran; worship of certain personalities such as Bedreddin Simavi, Otman Baba, Sari Saltik, Haji Bektash; hurufism (a cabalistic-type doctrine that assigned numerical values to the letters of the Arabic alphabet); and specific rituals. However, it is wrong to regard them as Shiites (as is frequently the case in the literature), even if some of their descendants describe themselves as such today, often because of recent Shiite proselytising. The Kizilbash (today also called Alevis), who were sometimes integrated in Bektashi networks from the end of the sixteenth century, were not alone in Southeast Europe in professing an esoteric Islam. The members of the various mystical brotherhoods also combined an exoteric approach with a mystical approach. However, the latter was not necessarily synonymous with heterodoxy. As in Anatolia, many brotherhood networks (Naqshbandi and Halveti in particular) insisted on the importance of the sharia. Moreover, many ulamas were also shaykhs, and many ulamas not only practised an esoteric Islam, but also performed magical acts (divination, astrology, making of talismans, etc.), such as the Bosnian cadi Muhibbi, who was active in the first half of the nineteenth century.[12] Nevertheless, at certain times in Rumelia there were anti-brotherhood orthodox currents, such as the Kadizadelis who came to prominence in Bosnia in the eighteenth century. These currents denounced certain practices they judged to be heterodox (visiting tombs, listening to music and dancing during rituals, etc.).

How did these Islamic networks in Southeast Europe evolve in the first three quarters of the nineteenth century? Geopolitical changes meant that the Islamic institutions were scarcely able to survive in the embryonic Montenegro. In Greece, some isolated institutions, such as the mosque in Chalcis (Euboea), continued to function with some difficulty. In autonomous Serbia, the presence of the garrisons probably enabled some sharia courts, mosques and *tekke*s (such as the Sadi *tekke* in Belgrade) to continue as, until 1868, the Muslims there remained subject to Ottoman legislation.

In the Balkan territories that remained under full Ottoman rule, these institutions were gradually affected by the reforms, especially after the Crimean War. And they would be more so in the time of Sultan Abdülhamid. The reform that had the greatest impact on the functioning of the Islamic institutions was that concerning the waqfs. In 1826, Sultan Mahmud II created a Ministry of the Waqfs, in order to improve and centralise their management, but also to divert some of their income to the state, which needed to finance its reforms. It is generally considered that this management—which in practice was centralised to varying degrees—hindered the functioning of some mosques, and especially the madrasas and the *tekke*s. In any event, it obliged the ulamas and shaykhs to find other means of existence and therefore altered their position in society. It also led to the creation of offices of the waqfs, in which local Muslim notables were involved and where economic and political issues began to come into play. This reform also took supervision of the religious foundations away from the cadis. The cadis, accused of corruption, were the subject of other reforms. In 1855, a School for Cadis (*muallim-hane-i nüvvab*) was founded in Istanbul to train them in a "modern" way. In 1864, the reform of provincial administration brought new *nizamiye* courts (reorganised courts) that were set up alongside the sharia courts. As far as the *müderris* were concerned, their quasi-monopoly over education was, as we have seen, only very slightly weakened.

Nevertheless, it cannot be said that the ulamas were marginalised by these reforms aimed at secularising the Ottoman institutions. Indeed, David Kushner and others have shown that many ulamas played an active part in these reforms which, either because of their limited scope in certain provinces in particular, or because there were no other qualified officials, left the ulamas an important place in society and in the workings of the administration.[13]

The Islamic networks in Rumelia, which were affected by these reforms of general application, also evolved for other reasons. In some regions, conversions to Islam occurred. This was the case in Epirus where Ali Pasha of Ioannina implemented a highly coercive policy. It was also the case in the mountains of northern Albania and in Kosovo, where being Christian was a stigma. On the other side of the Balkan Peninsula, the Islamic networks were strengthened by the settlement of Muslim populations there and by the massive presence of Ottoman troops fighting against Russia. Thus, Šumen became an important centre of Islamic culture from the end of the eighteenth century/beginning of the nineteenth century, through the spreading of mystical currents and the production of manuscripts of the Quran. The period seems, moreover, to be one in which Islamic orthodoxy was strengthened in the Balkans. The Ottoman authorities banned the Bektashi brotherhood in 1826, shortly after abolishing the janissaries. In Rumelia, as in Anatolia, their *tekke*s were destroyed or given to other brotherhoods and their property seized.

Even though the Bektashi brotherhood ultimately survived this blow, particularly in the Albanian regions, where it even expanded in the last quarter of the nineteenth century, other mystical networks which were far more attached to the sharia grew in strength in the early part of the century: Halveti networks (from Ohrid and Prizren to Tirana and Sarajevo) and Naqshbandi networks (in particular in Bosnia and in the Bulgarian territories), which upheld the sharia against infidels and heretics. Other brotherhoods, sometimes less "orthodox", such as those of the Rifais, the Sadis, the Kadiris and the Shazilis, also expanded and helped to strengthen the links within the Muslim element, increasingly establishing themselves in the countryside and playing a part in the diversification of Islam in the Balkan Peninsula.

Despite this internal diversity, and despite the similarities with the Islam practised in Anatolia, from this time onward some Westerners and Balkan Christians formed essentialist images of the Islam and the Muslims of Southeast Europe.

From the first scholarly discourse to the first identity constructions

From the first half of the nineteenth century, the political interests of the Great Powers and the development of nationalisms led to a scholarly production about the presence of Muslims in Southeast Europe, and in particular on the presence of non-Turkish-speaking Muslims who spoke Slavic languages or Albanian. If these Muslims did not speak Turkish, who were they? What was their relationship with the Christians of the Balkan Peninsula? What should be their fate in the context of the regional geopolitical changes? At the time, one answer to the first question prevailed: they were descendants of groups of Balkan populations that had converted to Islam. However, differing interpretations of the process of Islamicisation reflected different views of Ottoman domination. They also illustrated different ways of conceiving the relationship of these Muslims to Europe and to "national bodies" that were in the process of asserting themselves, or different views of the power relationships at play between ethno-religious groups at the time this discourse was being built up. But all in all, these non-Turkish-speaking Muslims were regarded as specifically Balkan because of their language, and were thus viewed as different from the Turkish Muslims. This discourse strongly influenced subsequent scholarship.

FROM OTTOMAN PROVINCIAL AUTONOMIES TO EASTERN CRISIS

In 1829, the German historian Leopold von Ranke wrote that it was a mistake to regard the "Turks" (i.e. the Muslims, according to the terminology of the time) of Bosnia and Albania as intruders, and that to wish to return them to Asia would be an historical absurdity.[14] Reading between the lines, this discourse could be understood to mean that it would therefore be legitimate to drive the Turkish-speaking Muslims out of the Peninsula, as "non-natives". At no time was consideration given to the fact that they had lived there for several centuries, or that it was difficult to determine their ethno-linguistic origin because of multilingualism and the fact that Turkification, or, on the contrary, Slavisation, Albanianisation, etc., might have taken place. Some considered that the natural fate of the non-Turkish-speaking Muslims would be to convert back to Christianity, as the French geologist and traveller Ami Boué wrote in 1840, and that their conversion would be facilitated by the idea that their ancestors had been Christians, and that they had an interest in converting to Christianity.[15] In 1876, the Austrian ethnographer Felix Kanitz made a similar remark about the Bulgarian-speaking Muslims of the Loveč region, north of Mount Balkan.[16] And the princess of Romanian origin, Elena Ghika, went even further when, in her articles published in French and Italian periodicals (under the pseudonym Dora d'Istria), she separated Muslim identity from Turko-Ottoman identity for Albanian Muslims: no community of believers, no "fanaticism", no demeaning of women, no political submission; for the Albanian Muslims were conditioned by their "Aryan race", which distinguished them from the Turkish Muslims. For her, this indifference towards the Sultan and the Islamic religion could even propel these Albanian Muslims to turn towards Christianity if they saw that to do so would be in their interest, in the same way as they had once seen an interest in converting to Islam. All the more so as, in her view—despite their religion—these Muslims, like the Slavic-speaking Muslims of Bosnia-Herzegovina, had retained "the character, not only the national energy, but also a large part of the customs, and often even the names of their ancestors".[17] Other authors, such as the Greek Panayiotis Aravantinos in his *Chronicle of Epirus* published in 1856,[18] cited the case of the Muslims who took advantage of the *Tanzimat* reforms to declare themselves Christians, for example the Shpatiotes in the district of Elbasan in 1846.

Moreover, the idea that conversion to Islam was only partial and that the conversion of these various Muslim groups was only superficial started to become a feature of the discourse about the non-Turkish-speaking Muslims of the Balkans. The authors cited above and others speaking more specifically about the Albanian-speaking Muslims—such as Victor Adolphe Malte-Brun, John Hobhouse (Lord Broughton), William Martin Leake, Demetrio Camarda, and above all Johann Georg von Hahn—cited a number of elements which, in their view, demonstrated this superficiality: their crypto-Christian character, that is to say the fact that they had, according to these authors, secretly remained Christians; the mixed marriages they had contracted with Christians; the fact that, in certain cases, women and children remained Christians while the men converted; or the existence of Christian elements in their practices, and in particular their custom of celebrating Christian feasts and visiting Christian places of worship.[19]

As regards the Albanian Muslims more specifically, the idea also arose that they were different from the Turkish Muslims because they had adopted a different Islam, supposedly less orthodox and more "free thinking": that of the Bektashi brotherhood or more generally that of the "Alevi" currents, who revered the Prophet's son-in-law Ali. This would become an even more central theme after 1877–8, as the process of building an Albanian national identity intensified. For Dora d'Istria in particular, what she regarded as the "choice" of an Islam she called Shiite was associated above all with a European identity. In her view, the Albanian Muslims of the south, like the Persians, had chosen this form of Islam because it was compatible with the Aryan race, unlike Sunni Islam, which she thought better suited to the Asiatic race of the Turks.[20]

Taking just as essentialist a view, several Western observers of the time considered Islamicisation to have affected different ethno-linguistic groups to differing degrees according to their psycho-social characters. According to this view, the Albanians and the Slavs, who were warrior peoples, had converted because they valued their freedom more highly than their beliefs, unlike the Greeks or the Wallachians, who had therefore been less likely to convert to Islam.

Other, less essentialist and more nuanced discourse on Islamicisation, formulated by outside observers and by local Christian actors, reflected to a greater degree the relationship to the Ottoman past and present, as well as the different power relationships between ethno-religious groups in the Empire and abroad. This discourse depicted conversion to Islam most often as having taken place under duress, or even as having been violently imposed. The practice of *devşirme*, the systematic collection and enslavement of Christian children who were converted to Islam and educated in the Sultan's palace, was the example most often raised. It illustrated the "oriental barbarism" and the "Turkish yoke" from which freedom had just been, or had to be, achieved. Other conversions were also considered forced conversions. Several Croatian, Serbian and Western authors repeated the figure of 30,000 young Bosnians who were forced to convert to Islam and join the janissaries following the conquest of the region by Mehmed II in 1463. According to Bulgarian authors, the Pomaks (Bulgarian-speaking Muslims) of Loveč were also converted to Islam by force at various times. One Bulgarian intellectual had no hesitation in forging a document on this subject which would subsequently be used many times as proof of forced conversion to Islam. The chronicle of Pope Metodi Draginov, which was supposed to go back to the seventeenth century but which was, in reality, "retranscribed" in the 1860s by Stefan Zakhariev from a nineteenth-century chronicle, spoke of the forced conversion of the Bulgarians of the Čepino region in the Rhodopes, and above all, as Maria Todorova has emphasised, betrayal on the part of a member of the Greek high clergy.[21] The purpose was to justify the demands for emancipation from the Patriarchate of Constantinople.

In contemporary analyses, while conversion to Islam also appeared as a means of avoiding pressure or violence, it was often presented as reflecting a certain degree of pragmatism, not to say opportunism, in order to secure the advantages that were reserved for Muslims. In particular, it was argued that nobles converted so that they could continue to enjoy their lands. For some regions, such as Bosnia-Herzegovina, this argument is not unconnected to the agrarian question and the social relations between the beys, who were Muslim landowners, and the *kmet*s (sharecroppers), who were almost exclusively Christian.

Religious or politico-religious factors were also called on to explain Islamicisation, in particular heresies that had supposedly facilitated conversion to Islam. Indeed, some authors believed that the Muslims of Bosnia-Herzegovina were descendants of local Christians who had belonged to a separate church (neither Catholic nor Orthodox) influenced by Catharism, Paterenism or Bogomilism, the latter having arrived from Bulgaria. This argument, which first appeared in the literature in a work by the secretary of the French consulate in Travnik in 1822, later spread among Serbs and Croats seeking to prove that the Muslims were

Slavs capable of being rallied to their cause. In 1865, this question was the theme of a meeting of the Serbian Scholarly Society. In particular, Božidar Petranović published a work in 1867 in which he sought to portray the Bogomils as former Orthodox Christians.[22] In Croatian circles, the response came from Franjo Rački, author of the work *The Bogomils and the Patarenes*, published in Zagreb in 1870;[23] Rački, with Bishop Josip Strossmayer, argued in favour of a Yugoslavism that sought to bring together the Orthodox and Catholic Churches. The theory spread rapidly among non-Balkan authors, who set themselves to explaining the conversion of the Pomaks in a similar way by the disappearance of the Paulicians, descendants of the Bomogils. Thus, Konstantin Jireček thought that some Bogomils had become Muslims even before the Ottoman conquest of Bulgaria, in particular in the Loveč region, where the Pomaks lived.[24]

It is true that the Greek, Romanian and Serbian nationalisms were at that time developing an anti-Ottoman, or even anti-Turkish, element bound up with the legitimisation of the new political order and irredentism. The myth forged around the battle of Kosovo against the Ottoman army in 1389 fed Serbian irredentism, which was directed above all towards Bosnia-Herzegovina. In the 1860s, Bulgarian nationalists in the diaspora in Romania and Serbia exchanged the "Greek enemy", at the heart of the quarrel with the Patriarchate, for the "Turkish enemy". And the Hungarian nationalists used anti-Ottoman arguments to arouse support for the struggle against the Habsburg Empire. However, at the same time, those who were crafting these national constructions sought to include in the nation those Muslims who spoke the same language. Vuk Karadžić (1787–1864) conceived of a Serbian nation defined by language (the Štovakian dialect) and not by religion. In the Habsburg Empire, Illyrism also developed from 1830–40 as a linguistic nationalism that did not take religion into account, and thus prepared the way for the appearance of Yugoslavism in the 1860s. Finally, Bulgarian patriots sought to prove that the Pomaks were Bulgarians.

And what of the Balkan Muslims in these first three quarters of the nineteenth century? Did they build specific collective identities for themselves? The Ottomanism supported by the promoters of the *Tanzimat* reforms developed in society more as the idea of a common citizenship than of a nation. The Ottomanism of the Young Ottomans was a synonym for patriotism, constitutionalism and the extolling of Islamic values.

It was favourably received by the new Balkan Muslim elites, who followed what was happening in the Ottoman capital.

This was the case, for example, in Bosnia, where the introduction of the reforms in the late 1860s was accompanied by the creation of the first—official and unofficial—press organs, which promoted an Ottoman patriotism that was synonymous with reformism. That patriotism was also tinged with a local patriotism. Mehmed Šakir Kurtćehajić (1844–70), who launched a newspaper at that time, disseminated this Ottomanism associated with the notions of reform, progress, education and science, but equally replete with a local Bosnian patriotism rooted in the history and specific characteristics of the province, whilst also echoing Serbian and Illyrian nationalisms. For some notables, such as Ibrahim-beg Bašagić, this was also combined with drawing on Islamic tradition.

A small section of the Balkan Muslim elites began to be receptive to a certain Turkism or pan-Turkism, inspired by the vision of the Turkish peoples in a continuum from Central Asia to Central Europe, which Western Turkology was in the process of forging. Students from the Ottoman Empire who travelled to Western Europe from the middle of the nineteenth century played a role in spreading these new ideas, alongside Hungarian and Polish exiles, who had sought refuge in the Ottoman Empire after the failure of the 1848 revolutions. In 1869, Mustafa Celaleddin Pasha, a Pole who converted to Islam, published in Istanbul a work in French, entitled *Les Turcs anciens et modernes*,[25] in which he emphasised the closeness in ethnic terms of Europeans and Turks, who he argued belonged to the "Touro-Aryan" branch of the Aryan race.

Above all, in Istanbul and the western fringe of Rumelia, some members of the Muslim elite were receptive to Albanianism, that is, the idea of the existence of an Albanian nation. Some Westerners, Arbëresh (Albanian-speaking Greek-rite Catholics from Calabria and Sicily) and Orthodox Christians of the Ottoman Empire who had been influenced by Hellenism, had been developing this idea since the early nineteenth century. The first Muslim Albanianists appeared after the Crimean War. They were part of the new Ottoman elites who had been educated in the brand new Ottoman schools or who had spent time abroad, and the first constructions of Albanianism developed at the same time as the liberal Young Ottomans movement emerged. More specifically, after the Crimean War, in the second half of the 1860s, reforms to the administration, the rise of the provincial press, the projects to develop primary education, the distribution of books in Albanian by the British and Foreign Bible Society and the threat of Hellenism, led the Ottoman authorities and some intellectuals to turn their attention to the question of the use of a vernacular language such as Albanian. Discussions ensued in the Ottoman capital concerning the choice of an alphabet. Those discussions failed both because the Ottoman government seemed to abandon the idea of introducing teaching in another language in the new schools, and because the Albanianists could not agree among themselves. Orthodox Christians supported the Greek alphabet, while the Catholics argued for the Latin alphabet. As for the Muslims, they were divided between supporters of the Arabic alphabet, a totally invented, new alphabet and the Latin alphabet.

The Albanian-speaking Muslim elites could not fully support the identity constructions that arose in Orthodox Christian circles and were closely linked to Hellenism. Their way of modelling an Albanianism closely linked with Ottomanism was necessarily different. Shemseddin Sami Frashëri (1850–1904), an Ottoman intellectual who was a native of Epirus (in the south of current-day Albania), and who was influenced by his Oriental education received from private tutors and especially by the time he spent at the Greek Zosimea secondary school in Ioannina, was one of the leading figures of this nascent Muslim Albanianism. In his play *Besa or the Given Word of Trust*, performed for the first time in 1874 and published in 1875 in Istanbul,[26] he put Albanians on the stage in front of the Ottoman public, as he wanted to highlight "national virtues" and not the "foreign virtues" presented by the Ottoman theatre. In that play he defended the notion of dual loyalty: a loyalty to the Ottoman Empire, the general homeland (*vatan-i umumi*), and a loyalty to Albania, the special homeland (*vatan-i hususi*). However, there is an ambiguity in this Albanianist discourse of Shemseddin Sami Frashëri; in the foreword, he explained that he had decided to present the life and customs of the Albanian people because the latter were "an integral part of the great Islamic nation and members of the Ottoman State".[27] He therefore emphasised not only the Ottoman identity of the Albanian people, but also their Muslim identity, leaving the Christian part of the nation to one side. Once again, the weight of religious identifications made itself felt. For the competing definitions of Albanianism were the result of a dual process of stimulation by and reaction to the West on the one hand, and Hellenism and Ottomanism on the other. These changes were motivated firstly by the question of the destiny of the European territories of the Empire, and secondly by the question of education (in the broad meaning of the term), the press, and written language too. The Eastern Crisis, which erupted from 1875–6 onwards, triggered a fundamental shift in both these issues.

2

FROM THE EASTERN CRISIS TO THE END OF THE EMPIRES

(1876–1923)

The strengthening and weakening of the Balkan states

The Ottoman Empire, hit by political and economic crisis, responded to the Christian revolts in Herzegovina (1875) and Bulgaria (1876) with bloody repression. Serbia and Montenegro then decided to declare war on the Empire (1876), but were quickly defeated. In April 1877 and despite Sultan Abdülhamid's ascension to the throne, the attempts of the Conference of Ambassadors to have the Empire launch a number of reforms, and the proclamation of the Ottoman Constitution on 23 December 1876, Russia once again went to war against the Ottoman Empire. After the final victory of the Russian troops, the Treaty of San Stefano (signed just outside Istanbul in March 1878) recognised the independence of Serbia, Montenegro and Romania, all of whose territories were enlarged. It drew the contours of a Greater Bulgaria extending to Macedonia and the Aegean Sea. This partition considerably lessened Ottoman sovereignty in the Balkan Peninsula, even severing the Ottoman capital to the east from Albania and Epirus to the west. A few months later, however, in July 1878, the Treaty of Berlin restored to the Sultan part of the lands he had lost (see Map 4).

This treaty was less detrimental to the Ottomans than the Treaty of San Stefano had been, and recognised the official independence of

Serbia, Montenegro and Romania. It also created a small autonomous Bulgarian principality, as well as an Ottoman province called "Eastern Rumelia", south of the Balkan mountain chain. Eastern Rumelia was placed under the sovereignty of the Sultan but enjoyed administrative autonomy. This province's direct dependence on the Empire would prove very short-lived, as it was annexed by the Bulgarian principality in 1885. The Treaty of Berlin also confirmed the extension of the territories of Serbia (Niš, Pirot, Vranje regions), Montenegro (Nikšić, Kolašin, Podgorica regions, followed by Bar and Ulcinj in 1880) and Greece (with the annexation of Thessaly and the Arta region in Epirus). Finally, Bosnia-Herzegovina came under military occupation by the Habsburg Empire, that is, Austria-Hungary. The Balkan Ottoman territories were thus reduced to Thrace, Macedonia, today's Kosovo, the sanjak of Novi Pazar (where Austro-Hungary was entitled to establish garrisons), Albania and Epirus.

Ottoman sovereignty in the Balkan Peninsula was not challenged again by physical violence until after the Balkan Wars (1912–13), when Ottoman possessions were reduced to the small territory of Eastern Thrace (see Map 5). A few years later, a new territorial division of the region would emerge at the end of the First World War and the resulting collapse of the Russian (1917), Austro-Hungarian (1918) and Ottoman (1923) empires.

However, this period cannot be regarded simply as one of inevitable loss of Ottoman sovereignty. Between the two periods of crisis—1875–8 and the decade 1912–22—it is possible to speak of a strengthening of the states in the region, including the Ottoman state, at the same time as processes of weakening were also at work.

After 1878, in the context of the new status quo established by the Great Powers, the new Sultan, who had rapidly ended parliamentarianism, became increasingly authoritarian in his leadership. In the 1890s, in particular, the Sultan introduced a series of reforms that strengthened the role of the state and transformed relations between the state and its subjects–citizens. The development of communication networks (telegraph, roads, railways), public administrations and schools, the use of the press, improved tax collection, and conscription helped to assert the presence of the Ottoman state in its Balkan territories. Following the losses of territory of the years 1878–81, Sultan Abdülhamid nevertheless partly refocused his attention on the Arab provinces, as François Georgeon has shown.[1]

FROM THE EASTERN CRISIS TO THE END OF THE EMPIRES

Map 4: Southeast Europe after the Treaty of Berlin

Map 5: Southeast Europe and the Balkan Wars

FROM THE EASTERN CRISIS TO THE END OF THE EMPIRES

During this period, the state apparatus in the other Balkan states seeking to play a full part in the international system also underwent consolidation. For example, Kostas Kostis argues that in Greece the apparatus of state started to assert itself from the years 1870–80 onwards, following the fall of King Otto: it distributed the sizeable landholdings it held, opened up the territory by building roads and railways, reorganised the army to fight against foreign enemies, limited the power of the local elites and neutralised the restive peasantry.[2] The development of infrastructures, bureaucratisation and militarisation were characteristics widely shared by the other Balkan countries at this time. In addition to this, patriotism and nationalism thrived, instilled by schools, youth organisations, the Church and the army (although not always from the same perspective). This included a strong irredentist component, a desire to liberate the "brothers" still under the "Ottoman yoke". In Serbia, the myth of Kosovo became central (the 500th anniversary of the battle of Kosovo was celebrated in 1889). In Greece the *Megali Idea* ("Great Idea") turned minds and energy towards Macedonia in particular, even though this was not always official policy. In Bulgaria, there were calls for a Greater Bulgaria, as briefly envisaged by the San Stefano Treaty. The Romanian irredentists claimed Southern Dobruja. As in the Ottoman Empire, these changes were facilitated by the development of the education system and the press.

However, the emerging educated "middle class" provided fertile ground for opposition and radical movements, which combined national and social claims. Secret societies flourished everywhere. Revolutionary groups multiplied. With the exception of two inter-state conflicts (the Serbo-Bulgarian war in 1885–6 and the Greco-Turkish War that broke out in 1897 following the Cretan crisis in 1896), the violence emanated above all from these groups and organisations, which recruited many young people and were sometimes supported by governments. The bands formed by such organisations fought each other in Macedonia, in a bloody guerrilla war. The assassination of the Austrian archduke Franz Ferdinand by Gavrilo Princip in Sarajevo on 28 June 1914 is another example of this type of violence.

The strengthening of state structures, in the wake of adaptation by Balkan states to the international political and economic system established after the Crimean War, had other limits. The states of the Balkan Peninsula were unable to conduct reform alone and ended up being placed under international economic control. They were also weakened by rivalries between opposing political groups, often seeking support from one or another of the Great Powers (Russophiles against Austrophiles in Serbia, for example). In some countries, such as Serbia and Romania, antagonism between elites and the general population deepened; in 1907 there was even a peasant revolt in Romania.

The Ottoman Empire, for its part, suffered a string of crises at the end of the nineteenth century. From 1894, troops called Hamidiye, recruited among the Kurds, committed a series of massacres of Armenians in Anatolia. The Armenian crisis even reached the Ottoman capital in 1895–6 when a group of Armenians linked to a revolutionary political organisation took over the head office of the Ottoman Bank and made an attempt on the Sultan's life. Further massacres were then committed against the Armenians. These events had significant repercussions in the European part of the Empire—particularly as the "Macedonian crisis" had taken on a new dimension. The struggle taking place since the 1870s between the supporters of the Bulgarian Exarchate and the supporters of the Patriarchate of Constantinople intensified as of 1893. The same was true of the "Macedonian question", created by the revision of the Treaty of San Stefano and linked to that struggle. In 1893, the Internal Macedonian Revolutionary Organisation (*Vătrešna Makedonska Revoljucionna Organizacija*—VMRO) was formed, which favoured autonomy for Macedonia. The following year, the Greeks founded a competing organisation, the *Ethniki Hetairia* (the "National Society"). In 1895 appeared a second Macedonian revolutionary organisation, the Supreme Organisation (*Vărhovna Organizacija*), operated from Bulgaria. It fought in favour of Bulgaria's incorporation of Macedonia. Secret committees recruited komitajis and created *çetes*[3] (in Turkish: guerrilla bands), which exerted pressure on the population and confronted each other on the ground, especially after the violent suppression of the failed Ilinden revolt in 1903. Serbs and Greeks then also established guerrilla bands. According to İpek Yosmaoğlu, 8,000 people were killed in Macedonia between 1903 and 1908, and more than half of them were civilians.[4] This situation led, from 1902, to the intervention of the Great Powers in order to preserve the status quo. However, their reform plans, interventions and setting up of a new police force largely failed to convince, not least because of their differing interests.

The formation of the Young Turk movement in the mid-1890s and the revolution that broke out in the Ottoman Empire in 1908 were not unconnected to these developments. The movement opposing the Hamidian regime—modelled on the other Balkan secret organisations—was also a reaction to the difficulties caused by the situation in the Balkans, and Macedonia in particular. Moreover, as Erik-Jan Zürcher has shown, the Young Turks—including the future founder of the Turkish Republic, Mustafa Kemal, who was born in Salonica and first trained in Salonica and Bitola—were "children of the borderlands".[5] The main centres of the Young Turk revolution were precisely Salonica and Manastir/Bitola, where the officers of the Second and Third Armies (Thrace and Macedonia) decided to act after the Reval meeting of June 1908, which saw Russia and Great Britain propose a more restrictive reform plan for Macedonia. However, the re-establishment of the Constitution of 1878, to which the Sultan agreed, weakened the Ottoman Empire's position in the Balkan Peninsula, even though the Young Turk insurgents succeeded in winning over the Macedonian and Albanian revolutionary organisations. In fact, Bulgaria proclaimed its official independence, Austria-Hungary annexed the province of Bosnia-Herzegovina, which it had occupied since the Berlin Congress, and the Cretan Assembly proclaimed a union with Greece (that was not recognised until 1913).

Events then accelerated. A counter-revolution and the removal of the Sultan in 1909 was followed by an intense power struggle between the Committee of Union and Progress, set up by the Young Turks, and various other political groups. Italy launched war to take possession of Tripolitania (1911). Revolts in Albanian border regions (1911–12) were politicised, and the activity of the guerrilla bands in Macedonia resurfaced, along with mutinies in the Army of Rumelia (1912). Montenegro, Serbia, Bulgaria and Greece, encouraged by Russia, took advantage of the weakening of the Empire to launch a joint attack on it in October 1912. This marked the start of a decade of conflict which saw the two Balkan Wars (1912–13), the First World War (1914–18) and the Greco-Turkish War (1919–22).

This decade of violence had a profound impact on the region's geopolitical situation: the Ottoman Empire lost most of its territory in the Balkan Peninsula, succeeding in retaining only Eastern Thrace. An Albanian state was created, against the wishes of the Balkan allies but in line with the interests of Austria-Hungary and Italy. It was occupied by different armies during the First World War (Greek, Serbian, Italian,

French and Austro-Hungarian) and then escaped from the Italian mandate and became truly independent in 1920. Bulgaria, a loser in the second Balkan War and the First World War, was unable to retain the conquests it had made in the first Balkan War. Romania, on the contrary, was awarded Southern Dobruja, in addition to Habsburg Transylvania. The Austro-Hungarian Empire, which took advantage of its victories at the beginning of the First World War to occupy Montenegro and a large part of Albania and Kosovo, disappeared at the end of the war. Its Balkan territories were included in the Kingdom of Serbs, Croats and Slovenes created on 1 December 1918. Montenegro also disappeared, included in the new state, alongside Slovenia, Croatia, Bosnia-Herzegovina and Serbia (together with Kosovo and Macedonia, conquered by Serbia in 1912). Greece extended its territory in Epirus, Macedonia and Thrace. However, after the Turkish reconquest of 1922, it lost the lands it had conquered in Asia Minor since 1919. The Ottoman Empire, which retained only Eastern Thrace in the Balkan Peninsula and lost its Arab provinces, was replaced by the Republic of Turkey on 29 October 1923.

This decade had profound consequences both for the populations of Southeast Europe and for those of Anatolia. The methods employed by the various regular and irregular armies (which went as far as genocide in the case of Armenians) and the population exchanges that were carried out, on a voluntary or compulsory basis, were to have profound consequences and lead to even greater upheavals than those of the preceding decades, which had already affected relations between Christians and Muslims and between the emerging Balkan nations.

Migrations and population exchanges

Between 1877 and 1912, already one of the main consequences of the territorial enlargement and strengthening of the Balkan states was the dramatic drop in the number of Balkan Muslims in the territories that had passed into non-Ottoman domination, and the increase in their number in the European Ottoman provinces. During the wars, tens of thousands died or left for the Ottoman Empire, and the migratory flows continued afterwards. After the Eastern Crisis, the number of Muslims in Romanian Dobruja fell from 50,000 in 1880 to 35,000 in 1911. In the new Bulgarian principality, the Russo-Turkish war led to the loss of a third of the Muslim population (from 900,000 to 600,000). Then, in the same territory enlarged by the addition of Eastern Rumelia, the number of Muslims fell from 770,000 in 1880 to 600,000 in 1910. Between 1878 and 1914, over 60,000 also left Bosnia-Herzegovina for the Ottoman Empire. In 1910 there were still around 612,000, that is, 32 per cent of the Bosnian population (compared to 39 per cent in 1878). In Thessaly, which had become Greek, only 3,500 Muslims remained in 1907, and 2,900 in 1911, compared to 40,000 in 1880. In Crete, of the 73,000 Muslims (26 per cent of the total population of the island) only 28,000 (8 per cent) remained in 1911.

Even though the demographic decline was not as radical as in the preceding period, since significant groups stayed despite everything, particularly in Bosnia-Herzegovina, Bulgaria and Romania, it was still a major phenomenon. This decline has been the subject of many analyses which have discussed its numbers, causes and nature. For some, it was a case of "ethnic cleansing", seeking the systematic elimination of the Muslims, which continued until the Yugoslav Wars of the 1990s. Others, without using the term "ethnic cleansing", have considered the forced migration and expulsion of the Muslim populations as being mainly connected to the construction of the Balkan states and the ensuing "de-Ottomanisation", to use Bernard Lory's phrase.[6] However, recent historiography has produced some more nuanced analyses, in particular when examining the local level, giving a more complex view of the variety and degree of constraints (and sometimes opportunities) that engendered these huge, but very heterogeneous, migratory flows.

In Bulgaria, as Milena Methodieva has shown,[7] the change in the balance between Muslims and non-Muslims occurred above all in the western and central parts of the new territories, while the proportion of Muslims remained significant in the east, including in the towns (Ruse, Šumen, Plovdiv, Varna, Vidin). While the overall reduction in the percentage of Muslims was mainly due to emigration, it was also, to a lesser extent, the consequence of a lower birth rate. The Russian, and then the Bulgarian, authorities slowed the return of refugees after the Turco-Russian conflict of 1877–8. They subsequently adopted an ambiguous policy based on nationalism and de-Ottomanisation, and above all a loose approach that allowed local actors great latitude, particularly concerning land. (Many Muslims were driven to sell up and leave, or even to leave without selling their land; Muslim religious institutions suffered as well.) Thus local socio-economic relations played a significant role in creating the migratory flows. The Bulgarian authorities ended up taking measures (particularly with regard to military service, from which Muslims could be exempted by paying a tax) to reduce emigration in order to burnish the country's image abroad, and also for economic reasons. Milena Methodieva also provides a nuanced view of the departure of the elites. While many left, some ulamas and landowners remained, and new elites—comprising teachers and journalists—took over from those who had departed.

Thessaly, the region awarded to Greece in 1881, saw continual departures of Muslims—essentially from the urban centres. However, according to Nicole Immig,[8] these were not forced migrations. The factors that drove them were more economic and social than related to ethnic violence or discrimination. There was no military conflict and no centrally-decided policy of expulsion. Here again, it was more the fact that Muslims' rights were only partially respected at the local level, allied with a degree of ostracism, that drove them to leave either individually or as families. The situation was different in Crete, where violence played a large part, particularly after the uprisings of 1896–7 and 1905. Many of the island's Muslims fled to the Dodecanese Islands (Rhodes and Kos), Cyrenaica, Anatolia and the Near East.

In Romania, where the Constitution had been amended in compliance with the clauses of the Berlin Treaty, so that it no longer linked citizenship to Christianity, the Muslims living in Dobruja, along with the other inhabitants of the region, were subjected to internal colonialism. Here, the factors driving migration were not local and did not affect only the Muslims. Until 1909, Dobruja had an exceptional status, under which its inhabitants (Muslims and Christians) lacked political rights and some civil rights. They were granted only a "local citizenship", to use the expression of Constantin Iordachi.[9] They only gained full citizenship through a number of laws passed between 1909 and 1913. The Muslims, like the other inhabitants of Dobruja, were represented in the Assembly from 1909, and the exceptional administrative regime was abolished in 1913. Moreover, the special administration went hand in hand with the state monopoly over the redistribution of land, the majority of which had until then been held by Muslims. The state inherited lands from the Ottoman state, migrants, and those who were unable to pay their taxes. The redistribution of properties to Romanians or Aromanians acted as a catalyst for the colonisation of the region. The population increased considerably, tripling between 1878 and 1912, with the Romanians becoming the majority, including in the towns and cities, at the expense of the Muslims and Bulgarians.

In Bosnia-Herzegovina, the arrival of Austro-Hungarian troops in July 1878 provoked armed resistance. That resistance was short-lived. Nevertheless, some Muslims chose to leave, for reasons similar to those mentioned for Bulgaria. While the numbers of emigrants were higher following certain crises (introduction of military service in 1881–2, repression of the movement for religious autonomy in 1901–3, annexation of the province by the Austro-Hungarian Empire in 1908), departures occurred throughout the period. However, the real number is lower than that suggested by some authors. Local ulamas went as far as issuing fatwas affirming that the province was still part of the *darülislam* ("territory of Islam") and that there was therefore no reason for Muslims to emigrate to the Ottoman Empire (a theme that would be taken up by the Egypt-based reformer Rashid Rida in 1909, who assured the Muslims of Bosnia-Herzegovina that they were not obliged to emigrate since they were able to perform their religious duties without hindrance). As Alexandre Toumarkine has shown,[10] the Austro-Hungarian authorities did not encourage emigration. At times they even took action to slow it. One of the reasons for this was to demonstrate the Dual Monarchy's role in protecting and "civilising" the Bosnian Muslims. The occupying authorities sought above all to sever the links with the Ottoman Empire.

For the Ottoman Empire, this influx of refugees, who were called *muhacir*s (as if they had undertaken an emigration comparable to the *hijra* of the Prophet and his companions from Mecca to Medina, that is, from the land of the infidels to the land of the believers), was double-edged. In 1878, the Ottoman capital received around 200,000 refugees from Southeast Europe and the Caucasus. That population proved a fertile mobilising ground when unrest occurred. In May 1878, the ulama Ali Suavi attempted to overthrow the Sultan, with the assistance of a group of *muhacir*s. On the other hand, this partially-controlled influx of refugees was also used to boost the population—and particularly the Muslim element—in certain regions. Many refugees were settled in the border regions of Rumelia (current Macedonia, Kosovo and northern Albania), as well as in Thrace. Specific districts were built in the towns to receive them, as in Vuçitrn/Vushtrri, Shkodër or Manastir/Bitola. Several commissions, including the General Commission for the Administration of Muhacirs (1878–94) presided over by the Sultan, were created to manage the problems associated with their arrival. However, as Alexandre Toumarkine and Malte Fuhrmann have shown, there were limits to the changing and somewhat hesitant policy of acceptance and resettlement.[11] The refugees sometimes preferred to resettle in a place of their choice, or even to return to their region of origin. Having initially encouraged emigration, the Ottoman authorities then sought to dissuade those wishing to leave, so as to maintain a Muslim presence in the lands that had passed into non-Muslim sovereignty. Ottoman diplomats and administrators also took different views on the subject. It was only after the annexation of Bosnia-Herzegovina by Austria-Hungary in 1908 that a leader of the Committee of Union and Progress envisioned a wide-ranging plan for the large-scale resettlement of the Muslims of Bosnia-Herzegovina in Macedonia. Attempts were also made in Epirus, but all these plans remained unsuccessful.

Muslims were not the only ones to migrate. Many Christians emigrated—sometimes temporarily—from the Ottoman European territories, and particularly from Epirus and Macedonia, to the new Balkan countries, where they provided a labour force in various sectors, went into commerce or studied. Many others emigrated to the Ottoman capital for the same reasons. Migrants also headed to Egypt and, at the turn of the century, to America, or even Australia. The growth in violence in Macedonia further accentuated this emigration, which also helped to increase the proportion of Muslims in the Ottoman Balkan territories. While, overall, those territories had always had a Christian majority, Ottoman statistics claimed they had a slight Muslim majority (51 per cent) in 1911, on the eve of the First Balkan War.[12] That figure is part of the statistical war of the time and seems doubtful. Nevertheless, there was a real change during these thirty years in the demographic balance, in favour of Christians in the new Balkan states and in favour of Muslims in the Ottoman Empire.

The decade of wars that began in 1912 brought a new dimension to migrations in Southeast Europe: population exchanges. According to Erik-Jan Zürcher,[13] the Balkan Wars, during which the violence was particularly intense (massacres, forced conversions, expulsions), caused the displacement of around 800,000 people. Half of these displaced persons were Muslims. Following the rapid defeat of the Ottoman troops, they followed the retreating army and emigrated to Istanbul with a view to potential resettlement in Anatolia. The first population exchange then took place between Bulgaria and the Ottoman Empire. A protocol signed on 29 September 1913 provided for a voluntary exchange involving the Bulgarians of Eastern Thrace and the Muslims living on the other side of the new Bulgarian–Ottoman border. A joint commission was set up to settle the question of the refugees' property. Early in 1914, the Committee of Union and Progress and the militia of the Special Organisation (*Teşkilat-ı mahsusa*) drove 200,000 Orthodox Christians living in coastal areas to leave for the Greek Aegean islands. The Ottoman authorities then wished to sign a similar protocol with the Greek authorities, but that did not happen. In August 1920, after the First World War, a clause in the Treaty of Neuilly authorised a voluntary exchange between Greece and Bulgaria.

In the eyes of some politicians, the events unfolding in Anatolia (including the Armenian genocide) made population exchange an essential part of the resolution of the conflicts. Following the defeat of the Greek army in Asia Minor in 1922, the Orthodox Christian populations (between 400,000 and 500,000 people) followed the retreating troops to Greece. In addition, 250,000 Orthodox Christians and 50,000 Armenians left Eastern Thrace for Greece. Fridtjof Nansen, High Commissioner for Refugees at the League of Nations, proposed an exchange, which this time would be compulsory. The Greek authorities saw in this a solution to the arrival of refugees en masse. Turkey agreed on condition that the Muslims of Western Thrace be exempted, while Greece demanded that the Orthodox Christians of Constantinople also be excluded from the exchange. The Treaty of Lausanne was signed in July 1923 under the auspices of the League of Nations. That treaty ratified the displacements that had already taken place and rendered compulsory the population exchange between Greece and Turkey, based on religious criteria: the Orthodox Christians of central Anatolia (most of whom spoke Turkish) and the Black Sea had to leave for Greece, while the Muslims of Greece (except those of Thrace), some of whom were Greek-speaking, were compelled to emigrate to Turkey.

Muslims caught between non-Muslim states and the Ottoman Empire

Despite the massive and continuous departures of Muslims for the Ottoman Empire, large groups of Muslims remained in the new entities that had been carved out of the Ottoman territory. The Austro-Hungarian province of Bosnia-Herzegovina, Bulgaria and, to a lesser extent, Romania, Montenegro, Serbia and Greece had sizeable Muslim populations. The international situation had changed and in 1878 the Treaty of Berlin granted some rights to Muslims in those countries and to non-Muslims in the Ottoman Empire, in a spirit of reciprocity. More specifically, for each of the new countries (Bulgaria, Montenegro, Serbia and Romania), different articles of the treaty stipulated that no one could be penalised in terms of their civil or political rights, or access to public sector jobs and other sectors of activity, on the basis of their religious affiliation. The treaty also stated that "freedom and outward exercise of all forms of worship shall be assured to all persons belonging to [the country], as well as to foreigners",[14] and that "no hindrance shall be offered either to the hierarchical organization of the different communions, or to their relations with their spiritual chiefs". The treaty also contained clauses relating to property rights. Muslim or other property owners who established their personal residence outside these countries "may continue to hold there their real property, by farming it out, or having it administered by third parties". Joint commissions were entrusted with settling "all questions relative to the mode of alienation, working, or use on the account of the Sublime Porte of property belonging to the State and religious foundations (vakoufs), as well as of the questions regarding the interests of private persons engaged therein". For its part, the Ottoman Empire also had to pledge to respect the rights of all, without distinction as to religion (including before the courts), and to assure the freedom and exercise of worship. It also had to guarantee the rights of the priests, pilgrims and monks, to recognise the right of protection for diplomats and consuls, to preserve the status quo in the Holy Places and to guarantee the rights of the monks of Mount Athos. However, nothing was imposed upon Austria-Hungary, which was mandated by the treaty to occupy Bosnia-Herzegovina. In April 1879, the Convention of Constantinople (or of Novi Pazar) signed by the two empires required the Dual Monarchy to recognise the Sultan's *de jure* sovereignty over the province (Muslims could pronounce the Sultan's name at the beginning of Friday prayers) and guaranteed the religious freedom of Muslims as well as their links with their spiritual leader in Istanbul. As for Greece, by the Convention of Constantinople of July 1881, it agreed to respect "the lives, property, honour, religion and customs of those of the inhabitants of the districts"[15] which were ceded to it in Thessaly. Those inhabitants must enjoy "exactly the same civil and political rights as Hellenic subjects of origin". And in the same way as the other Balkan countries, Greece also pledged to respect the rights of property, freedom and exercise of worship, as well as the ties between the Muslims and their spiritual leader. It was also stipulated that the sharia courts could continue to deal with "purely religious" matters, and that Muslims would be exempted from military service for three years.

This desire of the Great Powers to guarantee the rights of groups that were not yet referred to as "minorities" was important for the maintenance of Muslim populations in the new Balkan states. Throughout the whole of the period, laws were also passed, decisions taken and measures adopted at the national level concerning political and civil rights, property, religious institutions, schools and the sharia courts, creating specific conditions in each state. Often guided by "nationalising" and "civilising" projects, these laws could nevertheless contravene international agreements. Above all, their enforcement depended on the will of and the constraints upon different types of actors at different levels (national, regional, local). Hence the clear departures from the legal order with regard both to politics and economics and to religion; hence the difficulties that Muslims encountered on a daily basis; hence the departure of many of them, as we have seen.

Particularly with regard to religion, there was a trend for state authorities to seek to control the Islamic religious hierarchies to a greater or lesser extent (just as they did with the Christian hierarchies) and to weaken their links with the Ottoman Empire. This was generally accompanied by moves to appropriate the waqfs (or to control their income), as well as to appoint the highest religious officials, previously paid by the Ottoman state, and make them a part of the civil service. In the case of Bulgaria and, above all, Bosnia-Herzegovina, where the new authorities went as far as trying to create institutions that were de facto independent from Istanbul, high levels of tension would result.

In Greece, Crete and Romania, the political and administrative authorities did not really seek to shape the Islamic institutions within their territory. Instead, they contented themselves with controlling them. In Thessaly, the four (and then five) recognised muftis were appointed and removed from office by royal decree and became civil servants paid by the state, in the same way as school teachers. There is no mention of cadis or sharia courts. It was the muftis who, with the elected commissions, managed the waqfs at the local level. In Crete, which became autonomous in 1898 under the aegis of a Christian High Commissioner, the new constitution of 1899 granted the Muslims rights and freedoms, but no new centralised religious hierarchy was created. Likewise, the integration of the "new territories" into the Greek kingdom in 1913 (Epirus, Macedonia, Crete and the Aegean Islands) did not lead to the establishment of hierarchical institutions. In any event, the war scarcely lent itself to that.

Romania also saw the establishment of mechanisms of control, nationalisation and even restriction, without a true structure being set up at the national level. The waqfs, including the highly important waqf of Gazi Ali Pasha in Babadag, were seized by the state, which redistributed land to the mosques and paid some salaries itself. From 1880, two muftis on the public payroll were able to practise in Tulcea and Constanța. The imams at the largest mosques also had their salaries paid by the state, as would all their colleagues from 1904. Sharia courts only operated from 1886, in Tulcea and Constanța. There would be four more in 1914, when Romania gained Southern Dobruja. The famous madrasa in Babadag was able to reopen only in 1889. In 1901 it was transferred to Mecidiye/Medgidia, where it would operate partly on the model of the Romanian schools. Meanwhile, the small "traditional" madrasas would gradually be closed (not necessarily to the displeasure of the Muslim reformists).

In Serbia and Montenegro, where Muslims were less numerous, the Islamic institutions were now represented and directed by a mufti, appointed by the highest authorities of the state but accredited by the *şeyhülislam* of Istanbul. The Serbian mufti was a civil servant and resided in Niš. He was responsible for the waqfs (which had largely been confiscated by the state), the enforcement of family law and the religious hierarchy. After the conquest of today's Sanjak, Kosovo and Macedonia in 1912, he became the "grand mufti", with muftis being appointed in each of the conquered regions. In Montenegro, cadis were also appointed in Podgorica, Bar and Ulcinj, with the status of civil servants. They were appointed by the Montenegrin sovereign, upon a proposal from the mufti. Lower religious officials continued to be paid locally out of the income of the waqfs or donations from the population. In 1908–9, tensions arose between the Montenegrin authorities and the mufti (a Pomak from Tikveš in Macedonia), resulting in the latter leaving the country for the Ottoman Empire. The fact that he was replaced only in 1912 by a mufti of local origin, appointed by the king, is a sign of the complexity of the challenges facing the holder of the position at the time.

In Bulgaria and Bosnia-Herzegovina, where the largest Muslim populations were to be found, much more significant steps were taken to establish Islamic institutions independent of the Ottoman hierarchy. In Bulgaria, where religious organisations were closely overseen by the Ministry of Foreign Affairs and Religion, these steps were timid at first and concrete results were achieved only with difficulty after official independence in 1908. While the intention of the authorities was to limit and oversee the links with Istanbul by creating an independent hierarchy, any such purpose was kept in check by reciprocity vis-à-vis the Bulgarian Exarchate, which had its seat in Istanbul but also had close links with Bulgaria. In 1895, a first attempt was made to establish the mufti of Sofia as head of a religious hierarchy, producing sharp reactions in Bulgaria and in the Ottoman Empire. Under the temporary orders of 1880 and 1895, which regulated the functioning of the local Islamic institutions, the cadis were removed and their prerogatives were handed to the muftis, a typical development in post-Ottoman Southeast Europe. These muftis were chosen by the local Muslim population, appointed and paid by the Bulgarian government, but also confirmed by the *şeyhülislam*. Documents concerning Bulgaria clearly show that this situation could cause significant tensions when the local political and administrative authorities interfered in the appointment and removal of the muftis, or when Istanbul decided not to accredit them. Interference and tensions were just as palpable in the administration of the waqfs, which was entrusted to local councils. In a way, the setting up of a national hierarchy in the wake of the country's independence still resulted from a dual oversight. It was a protocol signed between Bulgaria and the Ottoman Empire that established the status of the muftis, waqfs and religious schools. In particular, an office of grand mufti was created. The holder of this office was chosen from among the local muftis for a term of five years and had to be accredited by the *şeyhülislam*. The grand mufti was head of all Bulgarian Muslims and was responsible for the waqfs and schools. In 1913, a new agreement between the two states provided for a school for cadis (*medrese-i nüvvab*) to be opened to train religious officials locally. However, implementing these agreements was complicated. In 1910, the muftis and the grand mufti were elected but it was impossible to obtain accreditation of the latter because of the deterioration in relations between Bulgaria and the Empire. Five years later, the grand mufti even left the country because of the war and the position remained vacant until 1920, soon after the passing of new "Regulations on the Organisation and Administration of the Muslim Religious Institutions in Bulgaria". The training school for religious officials did not open until 1922.

In Bosnia-Herzegovina, the Austro-Hungarian authorities took action much more quickly to forge institutions independent of Istanbul. In 1880, the *şeyhülislam* sought in vain to impose a mufti from the Ottoman Empire. As soon as the following year, an official from the Austro-Hungarian administration was of the opinion that local institutions needed to be gradually built up. In 1882, the fact that the *şeyhülislam* named the mufti of Sarajevo "mufti of Bosnia" spurred the Austro-Hungarians to action. They gave the mufti, Mustafa Hilmi Omerović, the new position of *reis-ul-ulema* (literally, chief of the ulamas) and set up an *ulema-medžlis* (council of ulamas) comprising four members, modelled on the way the Christian Churches worked. The following year, a Commission of the Waqfs was created (this would be strengthened in 1894) and the sharia courts were reformed and brought into the Austro-Hungarian judicial system. A school to train cadis was opened in 1887. When the *reis-ul-ulema* retired in 1894, he was replaced by Mehmed Tevfik Azapagić (author of a fatwa that called on Muslims not to emigrate) without *menšura* (accreditation) from the *şeyhülislam*, thus confirming the independence of the local hierarchy put in place by the Dual Monarchy. However, some Bosnian Muslims did react to this situation. In fact, from the 1890s, and in a similar vein to the claims by the Serbian notables of Bosnia-Herzegovina, some ulamas and Muslim notables claimed autonomy for their religious institutions in order to avoid the ruin of the Muslim religion, which they believed to be in peril. They also demanded that the requirement for the *reis-ul-ulema* to be accredited by the *şeyhülislam* be respected. The Austro-Hungarian authorities fought for a long time against this movement for religious autonomy which, for some more radical elements, was linked to a demand for autonomy of the province under the sovereignty of the Sultan. It was not until after the annexation of the province in 1908 that the authorities acceded to these demands for autonomous administration of religious affairs, waqfs and schools. Thenceforth, the *reis-ul-ulema* was chosen by the emperor from among three candidates named by a curia and then accredited by the *şeyhülislam* resident in a state—the Ottoman Empire—that could no longer claim sovereignty over Bosnia-Herzegovina.

FROM THE EASTERN CRISIS TO THE END OF THE EMPIRES

During the First World War, the Austro-Hungarian authorities, who from 1916 occupied two-thirds of the Albanian state as defined in 1913, also put in place religious institutions that were independent of Istanbul. At the head of those institutions was a mufti general (*Myftiu i Përgjithshëm*), who was also called the Cadi of cadis, and a Higher Sharia Council comprising the mufti general and two other ulamas. The regulations made no reference to the *şeyhülislam*. The functions of cadi and mufti were also merged.

Thus before the First World War the Muslims of Southeast Europe who had passed into non-Muslim sovereignty continued to be linked to the Ottoman Empire, even in Bosnia-Herzegovina, and the efforts of the Balkan states to cut them off from Istanbul met with only partial success. In Bulgaria, Muslims observed the official Ottoman celebrations and contributed to support campaigns launched in the Empire. In all the Balkan countries, Muslims regarded the Sultan-Caliph and the Empire as their protectors and looked to the Ottoman authorities to defend their rights. In Sofia, they could address their concerns through the Ottoman High Commissioner installed in the Bulgarian capital. Messages or delegations were sent directly to Istanbul from Bosnia-Herzegovina. In 1902, the main leader of the movement for religious autonomy, Ali Fehmi Džabić, went to the Ottoman capital, from where he was unable to return because of the opposition of the Austro-Hungarian authorities, who saw him as the agent of the Sultan's "pan-Islamist" policy.

In fact, while Abdülhamid's "pan-Islamism" was largely a construct of the Great Powers' imagination, the Sultan did inaugurate a policy concerning Muslims abroad, and particularly the Muslims of the lost Ottoman territories. For François Georgeon,[16] the Caliphate, which Abdülhamid made into a key institution, was also an ideological response to the decline of the Empire. It was, as well, a case of mirroring the policies of the Great Powers and the Balkan states towards the Christians in the Ottoman Empire. The Sultan-Caliph could not accede to all the demands, as is evidenced by his policy of cautious support for the Bosnian movement for religious autonomy. The Ottoman authorities did, nevertheless, take a number of actions to link the Muslims of the Balkan states to the ideological and cultural developments taking place in the Empire. As Milena Methodieva and Akşin Somel have shown for Bulgaria, for example,[17] the Ottoman Empire intervened in various ways in local Muslim educational networks: through diplomatic interventions, financial support for the maintenance or opening of schools, appointing teachers, paying their salaries, providing books and maps and awarding grants to enable Muslims to continue their studies in the Empire. This policy of awarding grants, or at least accepting these Muslims in schools in the Empire, extended to the Muslims of Bosnia-Herzegovina and those of Montenegro and other countries which did not have secondary schools or higher education institutions for Muslims.

In addition to the spiritual and political links which still bound them to the *şeyhülislam* and the Sultan-Caliph, other unofficial channels enabled the Muslims of the Balkan countries to maintain relations with the Ottoman Empire. The flows of migrants created new networks: members of acquaintanceship networks emigrated but maintained links with those who had remained; some emigrants returned and property owners, while residing abroad, had their properties managed by intermediaries. Mobility and correspondence through these networks were common. In addition, the press that was developing both inside and outside the Empire helped to create a public space beyond the Ottoman borders and to disseminate information. As a result, for example, the Muslims of Bosnia-Herzegovina could easily, when pressing their claims, make reference to the situation in Eastern Rumelia, Egypt and Romania, where the religious leaders were accredited by the *şeyhülislam*. From the 1890s in particular, new transnational networks emerged which increased these links between Balkan countries, and between those countries and the Ottoman Empire, namely networks of opponents to the Hamidian regime in exile. Some of them were in Romania, such as Ibrahim Temo, and in Bulgaria, whereas some of their companions left for Egypt or Western Europe. Their journalistic and political activism provided another way in which links were maintained with the Empire. They also favoured a politicisation of ethnic and/or religious identities, different from that promoted by the Sultan, and which was nourished—both inside and outside the Ottoman Empire—by the assertion of Balkan nationalisms.

Politicisation of identities and the slow development of nationalism

Whether they lived in the new Balkan states or in the Ottoman Empire, the Muslims of Southeast Europe, like their Christian neighbours, were now faced with the growth of Balkan nationalisms (Serbian, Croatian, Romanian, Bulgarian, Macedonian, Greek and Montenegrin). These nationalisms were reflected in state policies driven by a desire to join the "concert of civilised nations" and were synonyms for "de-Ottomanisation". They were also reflected in the—violent or non-violent—activity of nationalist and irredentist individuals or organisations. The Balkan Muslims were also faced with the Sultan's policy of reinforcing an Ottomanism that had a strong Islamic strand. They were still directly or indirectly experiencing the consequences of the policies of the Great Powers, whether that be Austria-Hungary's semi-colonial policy in Bosnia-Herzegovina or their imperialist policies with regard to the Ottoman Empire. This context favoured a gradual politicisation of the identities of the Muslim populations (and of the Christian populations), the great majority of whose members were still rural and illiterate. This was, however, a somewhat hesitant process, and one that was neither linear nor homogeneous; it frequently peaked during periods of violence, which favoured the polarisation of identities. Moreover, this politicisation had two main dimensions—the one national and the other religious—which were not always separate. The Muslims of Southeast Europe made relatively little use of national categories which, paradoxically, seem to have been of greater significance in the Ottoman Empire.

Several intellectual and political currents developed there at the same time among Ottoman Muslims, and combined Ottomanism, Islamism (with the aim of reviving Ottoman Islamic society, sometimes in a pan-Islamist version) and Turkism (also in a pan-Turkist version). However, in the European part of the Empire, including in the capital Istanbul, Albanianism developed too, closely linked to the fate of the Balkan Ottoman territories. Having appeared, as we have seen, before 1875, Albanianism was given fresh impetus with the Eastern Crisis. In 1877–8, the threat of the disappearance of the Empire in Europe caused Albanian nationalism to burst onto the international scene, with the formation of the "League of Prizren" (1878–81), an episode that was exploited by certain notables of the vilayet of Ioannina and of the Ottoman capital and which subsequently gained widespread mythic status as a national gathering. The aim was to create an Albanian–Greek entity if the Empire disappeared, or if it did not, to form an autonomous Albanian vilayet and prevent certain Ottoman lands from passing under non-Muslim sovereignty. This first shock led some Albanian intellectuals to start to mobilise wider circles—above all, Christians—through language and schools. While Abdülhamid regarded the Albanian

Muslims as the pillars of the Empire in Europe by virtue of their being Muslim (and disregarding their Albanianism), at times the Ottoman authorities also used Albanianism to counter Greek, Bulgarian and Serbian irredentism. Thus, certain Ottoman territories were presented as having been inhabited since antiquity by Albanians who were descendants of the Pelasgians and who still formed a majority of the population (and the majority of whom were, moreover, Muslim). However, the most important turning point for the development of Albanianism and for its large-scale politicisation did not arrive until twenty years after the League of Prizren, with the crisis of 1896-7. At that time, the future of the European provinces was even more uncertain, because of the Macedonian and Cretan questions, and a generation of Muslims emerged who had been educated in the new Ottoman schools and disputed the Sultan's policy. For their part, Austria-Hungary and Italy, who were competing for control of the Adriatic, began to stimulate an "Albanian consciousness", and locally, Albanianism began to play a part in the balance of power. These developments occurred at the same time as, and were connected to, the emergence of the Young Turk movement, which affected many Muslims, in Macedonia in particular, including Albanians. Following the Young Turk revolution in 1908, Albanianism was used within the Empire by the defendants of decentralisation and, more generally, by the opponents of the Committee of Union and Progress, although the latter did seek to bend Albanianism to its own purposes by Islamising it and, for example, by promoting the Arabic alphabet as the alphabet of the Albanian language. In 1912, the defeat of the Ottoman army in the first Balkan War finally led a group of Albanians, formed around Ismail Kemal bey Vlora, to separate Albanianism from Ottomanism and declare Albanian independence on 28 November 1912, in order to save those territories from occupation by the neighbouring Balkan countries. Under pressure from Austria-Hungary and Italy, the Great Powers recognised that independence in 1913.

However, a particular feature of Albanianism was that it developed among both Christians (Orthodox and Catholic) and Muslims. How was the idea of the Albanian nation forged in this context, particularly with regard to religion? A non-denominational discourse began to take shape from the period of the Eastern Crisis. This discourse was directed in particular at foreigners ("the Albanians are Albanians before they are

Christians or Muslims", "religion is not important for Albanians"). The aim was to legitimise the non-emigration of Albanian Muslims to Anatolia should the Ottoman Empire disappear in Europe, and to allow the creation of an Albanian state in Europe, despite its Muslim majority. To achieve that, two other themes were developed alongside this concept of national unity above religious affiliation. The first of these was the Pelasgian or Illyrian origin—depending on the version—that allegedly made the Albanian nation "one of the most ancient nations of Europe". The second, and more important, was the supposed superficiality and non-Sunni (hence "non-fanatical", as it was supposed to be) nature of Albanian Islam, since Islam, unlike Christianity, posed a problem of compatibility with Europe according to the commonly accepted Eurocentric view. However, within each religious group different ways appeared of defining oneself as "Albanian", through a religious (Orthodox, Catholic or Muslim) identity. In reality, by 1912 Albanian national identification was still not widely established; it had taken hold to very differing degrees in the different regions and social groups. Among Muslims, it spread mainly among the educated young, most of whom were from the southern regions. It was also supported by the beys (large landowners) when it was in their interest to do so. It also appeared among some reformist ulamas. Locally, it was able to affect factions mobilised by Albanianists, but could then take on a very different meaning.

Alongside Albanianism, Turkism also developed in the European part of the Empire, particularly from the mid-1890s, and to an even greater extent after the Young Turk revolution. Young Turkism, which attracted the young graduates from the civil and military colleges, was partly tinged with Turkism. Following the Young Turk revolution, the policy of the Committee of Union and Progress (which had its Central Committee in Salonica), although also based on Ottomanism and Islamism, leaned towards a certain Turkification of the non-Turkish elements of the Empire. A Turkism that rejected Ottomanism and was fed by the pan-Turkist ideas brought to the Empire by some Azeris and Tatars (such as Yusuf Akçura), developed only from 1911–12 onwards, and especially after the Balkan Wars and the loss of almost all the European territories. Clubs were then created by the *Türk Ocaklan* ("Turkish Hearths") organisation.

These ideologies found an echo among the Muslims of Bulgaria and Romania, who, as we have seen, maintained close relations with the Empire, particularly as Ottoman political exiles settled there. The politicisation of identities was also very gradual and heterogeneous in these two countries, where it was also stimulated by the nation-building processes and by the resentment generated by mistreatment of Muslims and infringement of their rights. It owed much to the press, the theatre (the works of Namik Kemal enjoyed particular success) and literature. In the case of Bulgaria, studied by Milena Methodieva,[18] we can see how the terms *millet* (nation) and *vatan* (homeland) evolved, retaining multiple meanings. The *"vatan"* could be the place of one's birth, Bulgaria, or the Ottoman Empire. Ottomanism could be understood in a supra-denominational sense, although most of the time it was regarded as concerning only Muslims. Turkism, spread from 1906 onwards by exiles, seduced educated young people with its strong anti-imperialist and anti-Hamidian components and its opposition to Greek and Armenian separatisms. The Young Turk movement also had significant success in Bulgaria as a result of revolutionary impulses among the young.

In Bulgaria as in Romania, a Tatar identity also became established. This identity was separate from the Turkish identity, but was often linked with it by pan-Turkism. Its establishment was facilitated by the fact that Tatar emigrants from Russian lands, or their descendants, sometimes lived together in separate urban districts, had their own schools, and came into conflict with their Muslim co-religionists for economic and social reasons. They could also be more receptive to reformism and in particular the Jadidism of the famous Tatar reformer Ismail Gasprinski (1851–1914). Gasprinski even visited Bulgaria in the early twentieth century, but declared that Turks and Tatars shared a common origin and must therefore unite around the question of reforms. The arguments put forward therefore had less to do with religion than with origins, history and language.

For their part, after 1878, the Bulgarian authorities promoted another intra-Muslim identification. They presented the Pomaks (Bulgarian-speaking Muslims) as Muslim Bulgarians. This category was introduced in the 1905 census. The policy of conversions promoted by the Bulgarian Orthodox Church was not implemented, except during the Balkan Wars, when the military authorities assisted in forcing Pomaks to undergo mass conversions. However, the project to assimilate the Pomaks—regarded as martyrs forcibly converted to Islam—led to the establishment of some schools specifically intended to educate them and integrate them into the Bulgarian nation. These measures had little effect and the Pomaks continued to see themselves as Muslims, with a number of them emigrating to the Ottoman Empire. In the first months of independence in 1878, some twenty Pomak villages in the Rhodopes even revolted against their possible annexation to Eastern Rumelia and succeeded in officially returning to Ottoman sovereignty in 1886.

The case of Bosnia-Herzegovina was more complex. The Muslims there—who were Slavic-speaking like their Christian neighbours—were caught between the developing Serbian and Croatian nationalisms and the policy of the Austro-Hungarian authorities. Benjamin Kállay, who administered the province, was the mastermind behind that policy, which consisted primarily of promoting a supra-denominational "Bosnianism" (*bošnjaštvo*). In fact, this Bosnianism succeeded in mobilising only a small circle of Muslim notables. However, by doing so, and as Xavier Bougarel has shown,[19] it moved towards a first expression of a Bosnian Muslim national identity. Thanks to the Bogomil theory, according to which the Muslims of Bosnia-Herzegovina converted immediately after the Ottoman conquest in order to preserve their customs and retain their lands, the local Muslims acquired an origin myth and a historical narrative that distanced them from Ottomanism, while at the same time justifying their conversion to Islam. However, some members of the newly-emerging intelligentsia educated in the new Austro-Hungarian schools, such as Safvet-beg Bašagić, hesitated between identifying themselves as Croats, identifying themselves as Serbs, and with Bosnianism. In his study of this young Bosnian Muslim, who was the son of an Ottoman reformer accepting the new administration, and who received both a European and an Oriental education, Philippe Gelez has shown that identity choices were made according to the possibilities opened up by education and social strategies, and, above all, that those choices were neither definitive nor clear-cut.[20] Safvet-beg Bašagić hesitated between a Bosnian Muslim identity and a Croatian national identity, before moving away from the latter. He moved between provincial patriotism and Muslim universalism, between Ottoman heritage and the desire for Europeanisation. Moreover, the movement for religious autonomy led by conservative ulamas and landowners ended up pushing the majority of Bosnian Muslims towards a primarily religious identification. This politicisation of the Muslim identity was reinforced by the institutionalisation of communitarianism (through the recognition of cultural and religious autonomy for the Serbs and Muslims) following the death of Benjamin

Kállay in 1903. Associations were created, such as the Muslim cultural association *Gajret* ("Zeal") in 1903, and community-based political parties appeared, the first of which was the Muslim People's Organisation (*Muslimanska Narodna Organizacija*—MNO), created in 1906. This politicisation, a synonym for mobilisation in the name of the Muslim community, was nonetheless associated, for the intelligentsia, with national identifications that were Croatian or Serbian depending on the inclinations, hopes and plans associated with political developments within the Austro-Hungarian Empire or outside (Serbia, Ottoman Empire). However, if we are to gain a better understanding of the Bosnian case, we must also consider the issue of reforms that set the conservative milieus against the young intellectuals.

The central importance of the question of reforms

In the years 1860–70, the Young Ottomans, formed around Namik Kemal, opposed the policy of the Sultan and the reformist ministers, and argued for a liberal form of Ottomanism synonymous with patriotism, constitutionalism and the extolling of Islamic values. The Young Ottomans rejected what they saw as an autocratic Westernisation. With the Eastern Crisis, they also took up the idea of a "Unity of Islam" (*ittihad-i islâm*) which was being promoted at that time by Jamal ad-Din al-Afghani (1838–97), a Muslim of Iranian origin who would make two lengthy stays in the Ottoman capital (1870–71 and 1892–7) and would travel throughout the Muslim world and Europe. He was one of the promoters of a reform movement called *salafiyya*, which envisaged both a return to the Islam of the "pious ancestors" (*al-salaf al-sâlih*) and the use of reason and science, in order to lead the Muslim world towards progress (he refuted the famous conference of Ernest Renan on the incompatibility of Islam and science). This movement, which was not always in phase with Abdülhamid's policy, spread rapidly at the very end of the nineteenth century, thanks in particular to Muhammad Abduh (1849–1905) and Rashid Rida (1865–1935), who in 1898 launched the famous journal *al-Manâr* ("The Lighthouse") in Cairo. This Islamic reformism affirmed the compatibility of Islam and "modernisation" and was influenced as much by Islamic tradition as by European thought, although strongly opposed to materialism. It also affected the central provinces of the Empire, where Muslims from Russia and the Caucasus were also advocating reform, in particular the reform of education, a field in which Ismail Gasprinski, a Tatar from Crimea educated in Moscow, was a leading figure.

After the Young Turk revolution and thanks to the freedom of the press, forms of Islamism and reformism other than the Arab *salafiyya* surfaced in Istanbul, more strongly tinged with Turkism or Ottomanism. Journals supporting these ideas were launched, such as *Sırat-i müstakim/ Sebilürreşad* ("The Straight Path/The Font of Orthodoxy") or *Beyanülhak* ("The Presentation of the Truth"). These journals were widely circulated, including among the Muslims of Southeast Europe. This was also a time when, in this spirit, reforms of the religious education delivered in the madrasas were undertaken in the Ottoman Empire. In 1908, a new programme was prepared for the theology faculty, placing greater emphasis on the history of the disciplines, while a madrasa specialising in training madrasa teachers was opened along the lines of a lay teacher training school, offering new subjects (history of religion and philosophy). In 1910, a "Regulation of the Reforms of the Madrasas" was published. In the following years, several specialised, reformed madrasas opened in the Ottoman capital. More generally, the reformers—whether religious or lay—wanted to introduce new methods into *tafsir* (Quranic exegesis), *fıkh* (Islamic jurisprudence) and *kalâm* (theology), although in different ways according to whether their convictions were more or less modernising, conservative or nationalist. Nevertheless, all shared the desire to renew Islamic thought. They identified with a tradition of Islamic revivalism, and rejected materialist ideas.

The development of these reformist currents also affected the Balkan Muslims living outside the Empire's borders. It was, above all, a generation of young lay people emerging in the 1890s that took up these currents in order to argue for reforms in different sectors and to question the authority of the incumbent elites (particularly the religious elites). This phenomenon was clearly visible in Bulgaria and Bosnia-Herzegovina—where the largest Muslim populations were to be found—and in Romania.

In the new Bulgarian state, this new generation, educated in the *rüşdiye*s or the local madrasas (or potentially both) and sometimes in the Ottoman Empire, consisted mainly of teachers and journalists. The end of the Stambolov regime allowed them to launch newspapers, open *kıraathane*s (reading rooms), set up theatre groups and organise teachers' associations. Through these new institutions they opened up a debate, (which was also stimulated by the journalistic activity of the Young Turk exiles), and sought to introduce reforms, opposing the traditional elites in a very critical way. As elsewhere in the Muslim world, they were driven by a feeling of economic backwardness, political dependence and moral decline, affecting both the Muslims of Bulgaria and those of the Ottoman Empire to whom they remained linked, and indeed all their co-religionists belonging to the *umma* (community of believers). In Bulgaria they faced problems in education, as well as the interference of the Bulgarian authorities in religious matters, in the management of the waqfs and in the election of muftis. As regards schools, the Muslims of Bulgaria had some *rüşdiye*s, *mekteb*s and madrasas which were specific to them and were regarded as private schools. While they could benefit from public subsidies, in reality they received little and a significant gap opened up between Muslim schools and Bulgarian schools. In particular, many of the teachers were not sufficiently qualified, which was a source of great dissatisfaction for the reformers. In the Empire, the reformers also witnessed the penetration by the Great Powers and repeated political crises. As in the rest of the Muslim world at that time, debate initially focused on the issue of ignorance and the need for educational reforms. For the reformers, Islam did not stand in the way of progress in education and science, as demonstrated by the brilliant past of Islamic educational institutions. The problems stemmed from the corruption of the religious elites. The arguments also concerned the administration of the waqfs, the role of women (who now had to be educated) and morality. Politically, the reformers wanted Muslims to participate in Bulgarian political life in a community-based and not an individual way, as did the notables—religious and lay—whose authority they were challenging. In addition to these debates, at the turn of the nineteenth and twentieth centuries, the young Bulgarian Muslim reformers specifically focused on the reform of schools. They did this by introducing new programmes and new teaching methods (which they called *usul-i cedid*, literally "new method") and by improving teaching standards. To do that, they created a teachers' association and organised conferences, the first of which was held in 1906. They also opened *kıraathane*s, where their newspapers were read. They raised money to fund schools, for example at theatre performances which sought to instil the new ideas. They fought against the established elites by attacking them in their newspapers, but their desire to change the status of women does not seem to have produced any concrete results. Nor did women participate in public debate.

FROM THE EASTERN CRISIS TO THE END OF THE EMPIRES

The situation in Romania was similar, save in terms of intensity. But things were different in Bosnia-Herzegovina. The position of Muslims vis-à-vis the authorities was different in the Austro-Hungarian province, as some notables—lay and religious—had been co-opted into the local administrative structures. Here too, reformism was supported by a young lay generation that appeared in the 1890s. In this context, faced with the conservative elites among whom the movement for religious autonomy was developing, reformism was reinforced by the Austro-Hungarian reforming policies (for example, in the area of education). The issue of education and school enrolment was just as central for Bosnian reformers as it was in Bulgaria in their fight against the traditional elites. In particular, they disputed the ulamas' monopoly over the interpretation of Islam by promoting *ijtihad* (reasoned interpretation), and spread among their local Muslim readership the ideas of the leading reformist authors—Jamal ad-Din al-Afghani, Muhammad Abduh, Ismail Gasprinki, etc. As in Bulgaria, they had no hesitation in using their newspapers to launch debates on the waqfs, the teaching of Islam, the issue of women, and even reform of the law. They ended up establishing "Muslim" (*musliman*) as the term to be used to refer to Bosnian Muslims, instead of "Turk", which had been used until then in everyday language, and "Mohammedan", which had been introduced by the Austro-Hungarian administration. However, there were differences between Bosnia-Herzegovina and Bulgaria. In Bosnia-Herzegovina, the reformers argued for the use of the vernacular language with the Latin or Cyrillic alphabet, deeming that the Arabic alphabet should be abandoned. Also, the issue of women was not merely debated; real progress was made in enrolling girls in schools, especially in Sarajevo. In the 1910s, Bosnian Muslim women began to find a public voice by publishing literary texts, and participated in groups and associations after the First World War, as Fabio Giomi has shown.[21] Finally, in Bosnia-Herzegovina, in the early twentieth century, an important figure appeared on the Bosnian Muslim scene who occupied a place halfway between the ulamas and the intelligentsia. This was the reformist ulama Džemaludin Čaušević (1870–1938). Born in the north-west of the province, he gained his higher education in Istanbul (at the new School for Cadis and the School of Law) and in Cairo, where he attended lectures given by Muhammad Abduh. Following his return to Bosnia-Herzegovina, he became a teacher of Arabic and then a teacher at the local School for Cadis (*Šerijatska Sudačka Škola*). Very soon, he was appointed to the *ulema-medžlis* (1903) and found himself responsible for matters concerning religious education. He too disseminated the thinking of the reformist authors in the newspapers he published in Serbo-Croatian, using the Arabic alphabet. In 1913, he was elected to the head of the religious hierarchy and became *reis-ul-ulema*, a position he would hold until 1930.

These reformist currents, which remained in the minority among the Muslims of Southeast Europe, fed into different ways of thinking about Islam in a society undergoing very significant changes. But what was the situation with regard to religious practices and the representation of those practices in studies of the subject?

Balkan Muslims between representations and practices

There are relatively few accurate sources and accounts concerning the day-to-day practice of Islam among the Muslims of Southeast Europe during this period. The studies produced by the academic institutions founded in the Balkan Peninsula at the time, if not politically biased, at least involved a significant degree of reification and must be used with caution. The same is true of the studies produced by Westerners, who also had a tendency to give greater weight to certain themes such as syncretism or heterodoxy.

In Bosnia-Herzegovina, the Austro-Hungarian authorities created the Provincial Museum (*Landesmuseum/Zemaljski Muzej*) in 1888 in order to forge a specific Bosnian identity and distance the province from Serbian and Croatian nationalisms. Contemporary ethnographic work, which often concerned the material culture and customs of the Muslims, followed these lines. The journal published by the museum and other studies carried out at the time also contain interesting information on the very common magical and healing practices, as well as on the *türbe*s and the *tekke*s, but have less about "orthodox" Islam. Antun Hangi's book on the *Life and Customs of the Muslims of Bosnia-Herzegovina* published in Sarajevo in 1906 took a normative approach to the practices of the local Muslims: "Bosnian Muslim men and women perform the majority of their religious duties correctly. Our Muslim goes five times a day to the house of prayer, the mosque, in order to pray to God."[22] Moreover, more attention was paid to history and origins than to practices. Here, the theory that the Bosnian Muslims were descended from Bogomil ancestors was central, particularly as it was strongly bound up with the agrarian question. The purpose of this thesis, which proposed that the Bogomil nobility had converted voluntarily in order to retain their lands, was to legitimise the agrarian status quo, thus benefiting Muslim landowners regarded as indigenous people who had owned the land since the Middle Ages.

The Bogomil theory, which was taken up by local Muslims such as Safvet-beg Bašagić, was partly refuted at the time by Serbian authors from Bosnia-Herzegovina and Serbia. They regarded the Muslims as "Islamicised Serbs". Yet their feelings about their Muslim "co-nationals" could be ambiguous. Jovan Cvijić, who established himself at the time of the First World War as the leading figure of Serbian geography and ethnography, was of the opinion that all the positive attributes of the "Islamicised Serbs" were to be attributed to their local "Dinaric" origin, while all that was negative came from their religion. He attributed their supposed indolence, ignorance and naivety to the influence of the Quran and Islam. In his famous book, *La Péninsule balkanique*,[23] Cvijić concluded that these individuals, caught between their national character and their Muslim character, could not but be disturbed. He recommended not a return to Christianity but education of these populations so that they might free themselves from their religion and develop a national consciousness. As we have seen, this was a similar approach to that adopted by the Bulgarians towards the Pomaks. The position of Serbian authors towards the Albanian Muslims was, on the other hand, clear-cut. Most contemporary studies presented the Albanians as having converted to Islam immediately, and they were said to have supported the Turkish oppression and become the most fearsome oppressors, driving out some Serbs and Albanianising others. In 1913, Jovan Tomić[24] explained, on the subject of the Albanians of Old Serbia (i.e. Kosovo) and Sanjak, that it was necessary to dam "the devastating river" of Albanians leaving the "true Albania" to invade the Sanjak of Novi Pazar, Old Serbia and Macedonia. The purpose of his book was to shed light on the role of the Albanian Muslims in the "violent spreading" of Islam among the Serbian people. For Tomić, ever since the Christian peoples had begun their attempts to liberate themselves, the Turks had used the Muslim Albanians to stifle these stirrings of independence and to propagate Islam. Thus, like others of his compatriots, he championed the argument that there existed in certain regions "*Arnautaši*" (literally "Albanianised people"), in other words Slavic populations who had been Islamicised and then Albanianised. The political impact of this argument was significant, as it made it possible to claim lands, such as today's Kosovo, that were largely inhabited by Muslim populations that they regarded as having originally been Slavs/Serbs. Similar ideas can be found in some Greek authors, particularly where they argued that the Bektashi Muslims were Greeks who were Islamicised and then Albanianised (see for example Dimitris Hassiotis in 1878).[25] The problem with these theories is that they sought to deduce the "true" ethnic–national nature of these Muslims without taking any account of their feelings.

In the case of Albania, Bektashism was used by the Albanians themselves to further Albanianism. As we have seen, Bektashism was a Muslim mystical brotherhood that was banned by the Sultan in 1826. However, it continued to exist semi-clandestinely, particularly among members of the Ottoman elites and in the south of the Albanian provinces. The particular feature of Bektashism was that it granted a central place to Ali, the Prophet's son-in-law, and his family, who were persecuted by the Ummayad caliphs, and emphasised esotericism and an initiatory path towards the level of the "perfect man", requiring divine knowledge. Bektashi beliefs in the nineteenth century also included the idea of the presence of the divine nature in every being and everything. The brotherhood networks, which created a very strong bond between adepts and their spiritual leader, together with various other characteristics of the brotherhood, would be used by both the Young Turks and the Albanianists in support of their political ends. Thus, the brotherhood's doctrine was presented as a liberal doctrine and the Bektashis as free thinkers, "freemasons" of Islam. More specifically, the doctrine was linked to Albanian nationalism by Naim Frashëri who, in 1896, published *The Little Book of the Bektashis*.[26] In this work, he sought to instil a national sentiment in the Albanian Bektashis by transforming the concepts of love and knowledge, linking them to the homeland and the nation rather than to the divine. Two years later, he published a long poem on the martyrdom of Hüseyin (the son of Ali) in Karbala, through which he promoted the unity of the nation against its enemies.

Many Western authors also showed an interest in Bektashism and the "reinvention" of Bektashi doctrine. They emphasised its opposition (and that of Alevism and the Kizilbash) to Sunni Islam, as well as its supposed closeness to Christianity. Frederick W. Hasluck,[27] who travelled in the Balkans and Anatolia in the early twentieth century, provided an accurate picture of the establishment of Bektashi *tekke*s and constructed a theory on the basis of that description. Yet he also participated in the reinvention. He constructed an audacious parallel between how, in his view, the Seljuk sovereign Alaeddin used the Mevlevi brotherhood in the thirteenth century to attract Anatolian Christians and how he considered Ali Pasha of Ioannina had used the Bektashi brotherhood in the early nineteenth century to convert Albanian Christians. According to his thesis, both cases had involved the use of mystical doctrines that were "conciliatory" towards Christianity to merge the two religions for political ends. He argued that one of the principal means used by the dervishes was to make sanctuaries accessible to both parties, by associating them with both Muslim saints and Christian saints (Sari Saltik/Saint Nicholas, for example). According to Hasluck, in this way the Muslim sanctuaries were rendered "ambiguous" in order to spread the brotherhood and convert the Christian populations. Hasluck also argued that there was a national element since, in that period of development of Albanianism, Ali Pasha sought to use the Bektashi/Sunni, heterodoxy/orthodoxy opposition to create an Albanian state that was independent of the Sultan.

In fact, that opposition too was reinvented in the time of Abdülhamid through his policy of "correcting" deviant beliefs. In the Balkans, this policy affected the Bektashis, the Kizilbash, Muslims who did not regularly practise their faith and crypto-Christians (in Kosovo and central Albania), in whom Christian missionaries also showed an interest. From the years 1880–90, the Ottoman authorities established Quranic schools and sent *hocas*[28] (religious teachers) and preachers to some regions, such as the vilayet of Kosovo, especially as the Albanian Muslims there were considered to be pillars of the Empire. More generally, the teaching of Islamic morals was strengthened in the modern-type schools in order to consolidate the loyalty of Muslim subjects. The Sultan even offered hairs from the Prophet's beard to some of those subjects, such as the inhabitants of Durrës and Vlorë early in 1908. While conversions to Islam did take place, especially in northern Albania and in the north of the vilayet of Kosovo, they were only an indirect consequence of this imperial policy. Social pressure and the higher status enjoyed by Muslims in regions where Christians had few alternative strategies played a more direct role. The expansion of some brotherhood networks within the Balkan borders was also only indirectly attributable to the Sultan's policy. The Sultan had surrounded himself with shaykhs, among whom were members of the Naqshbandi, Halveti and Kadiri networks, which extended into rural areas. The Naqshbandi network also strengthened its presence in Bosnia-Herzegovina, where a new *tekke* was founded in Visoko shortly before the First World War by the shaykh Hadži Hafiz Husni Efendi Numanagić, who became mufti of Travnik in 1914. Born in Fojnica, he was a scholar and mystic educated in Sarajevo and then in Istanbul, Medina and Cairo—another example of how individuals moved between the Arab provinces, the Ottoman capital and Southeast Europe.

Nevertheless, this reinforcement of orthopraxy did not prevent currents that were deemed "heterodox" from developing in some regions. This was the case with Bektashism in the south of today's Albania (which did, however, at times move closer to the "orthodox" currents). Also, in the western part of the Ottoman lands, "Alevisation" (development of the cult of Ali and his family) occurred in some brotherhoods and some ritual practices spread that were normally rejected, such as body piercing. Generally, the practice of magic remained very widespread: dervishes and *hoca*s made amulets and talismans to provide protection against the evil eye for people (including Christians who asked for them), and to protect animals, fields and homes. A particular mystical current spread from Macedonia, driven by Muhammad Nur al-Arabi (who was born in Egypt and died in Strumica in Macedonia in 1888). His mystical path—heir to the Melami ("way of the blame") movement and consequently called Melamiyye-Nuriyye—was the product of a reformed Sufism, rejecting all outward signs of affiliation (including adhesion to the sharia and openly expressing mystical states), the miracles and the hereditary succession of shaykhs. This movement spread in Macedonia and in Kosovo (where there were also some women's *tekke*s), Albania and the Ottoman capital. It spread in particular among religious and non-religious men of letters, including the military. Like the *dönme*s (crypto-Jewish Muslims living in Salonica), these circles provided favourable ground for the Young Turk revolution. Melamis also played a leading role in the pro-Ottoman insurrection that broke out in central Albania in 1914–15, after the country had gained its independence. Finally, and particularly in the Ottoman Empire, young Muslims of Southeast Europe belonging to the non-religious elites began to be attracted by materialism and positivism, or at least were supporters of a laicisation—or even a secularisation—of society, which they would advocate or put in place following the collapse of the Ottoman Empire.

3

FROM THE END OF THE EMPIRES TO THE ADVENT OF COMMUNISM

(1920–1944)

From one World War to the other: territorial reconfigurations and the rise of authoritarianism

The collapse of the Russian Empire and the Austro-Hungarian Empire at the end of the First World War (1914–18), and then the fall of the Ottoman Empire at the end of the Greco-Turkish War (1919–22) represented a major turning point in world history. The consequences were also highly significant in Southeast Europe. Quite apart from the trauma suffered by the populations affected by the wars and the forced displacements that accompanied them, a new political order emerged in the aftermath of the Great War. During the Paris Peace Conference a new political map was drawn by the various treaties signed in 1919 and 1920. The Kingdom of Serbs, Croats and Slovenes, whose existence had been proclaimed on 1 December 1918, was recognised by the Treaty of Saint-Germain in September 1919. This young Yugoslav state included very heterogeneous territories which, before the decade of war, had belonged to Serbia, Montenegro, the Ottoman Empire and Austria-Hungary. The borders of the Albanian state, which had been established in 1913, were also confirmed, while Greece and Romania saw their territories significantly extended at the expense of the Ottoman Empire and Bulgaria. At the end of the Greco-Turkish War, the Treaty of Lausanne, signed in 1923, ratified the loss of the lands that Greece had conquered in Asia Minor and, in Europe, left Turkey Istanbul and Eastern Thrace (see Map 6).

The new equilibrium was fragile in several ways. These territorial reconfigurations fed certain irredentisms. Firstly, Bulgarian irredentism looked to the lands occupied in Thrace and Macedonia during the war and to Southern Dobruja, which had passed into the hands of the Romanians. There was also an Albanian irredentism, which looked to the regions inhabited by Albanian-speakers in "South Serbia" (i.e. current Sanjak, Kosovo and Macedonia), and a Greek irredentism directed towards northern Epirus. Finally, Turkish irredentism, as set out in the National Pact adopted in 1920, looked to the territories lost under the Treaty of Sèvres (particularly Western Thrace). While these irredentisms were often backed by refugee groups or opposition politicians, the states also made use of them when it suited their interests.

The competing policies of Italy, France and Germany also played a significant role in weakening the regional equilibria. Italy, whose influence over Albania increased considerably from 1926, tended to support Albanian irredentism, Macedonian nationalism and Croatian nationalism, against the new Yugoslav state. France supported the Little Entente formed by Czechoslovakia, Romania and Yugoslavia, and then the Balkan Pact signed in 1934 by Yugoslavia, Romania, Greece and Turkey. However, from 1933 onwards, Germany became an increasingly significant economic pole for the Balkan countries. On the eve of the Second World War, more than 70 per cent of Bulgarian exports, just under 50 per cent of Yugoslav exports and more than 40 per cent of Romanian exports went to the Third Reich.

Internal equilibria were also fragile. Significant political changes occurred in the inter-war period, often linked to internal crises. In the aftermath of the Great War, liberal regimes were established in some Balkan countries, but struggled to survive. In Bulgaria, the agrarian leader Aleksandar Stamboliski was appointed prime minister in October 1919. He denounced Bulgarian irredentism and looked to the peasants for support, but was assassinated in 1923. Following an authoritarian government that violently suppressed a communist revolt, a Democratic Entente led the country from 1926 to 1931. Romania, which was regarded as a regional power with its 18 million inhabitants, rebuilt itself around a new liberal constitution adopted in 1923. Despite the various opposition

FROM THE END OF THE EMPIRES TO COMMUNISM

Map 6: Southeast Europe in the Interwar Period

groups, the liberals, with the support of the king, dominated the political scene until 1928 against foreign interests and the centrifugal tendencies from the provinces. However, in 1928, the national peasant movement won the elections and opened the economy to foreign capital.

The political scene was even more troubled in the neighbouring countries. The Kingdom of Serbs, Croats and Slovenes, where politics was characterised by a strong opposition between centralising tendencies (mainly, but not solely, Serbs) and decentralising, even confederalist ones (mainly, but not solely, Croats), was shaken by repeated government crises. The kingdom's first constitution was adopted only in June 1921. Subsequently, the power struggles between parties and political factions, fed to a greater or lesser degree by opposing nationalisms, led to tensions that culminated in 1928 with the assassination in parliament of Stjepan Radić, leader of the Croatian Peasant Party (*Hrvatska Seljačka Stranka*—HSS). In Albania, under the rule of a regency council, the political landscape fell into two opposing camps from 1920 onwards, before coming into conflict in 1924. Ahmet Zogu, who had dominated the political scene until then, was forced to flee to Yugoslavia. However, the "revolutionary" government lasted only six months. As for Greece, following the failure to realise the *Megali Idea* ("Great Idea") in Asia Minor, the monarchy was abolished and a republic established in 1924. The government of Eleftherios Venizelos, which relied largely on the votes of refugees from Asia Minor, was interrupted by the military dictatorship of Theodoros Pangalos between June 1925 and August 1926, before returning in 1928, until bankruptcy in 1932.

From the late 1920s, local political crises, exacerbated by the global economic crisis, led to the advent of increasingly authoritarian regimes, in a trend that was common to the whole of Europe. In Albania, Ahmet Zogu returned to power at the end of 1924 with the assistance of the Yugoslav government, but moved closer to Italy from 1926, and had himself proclaimed king in 1928, with Mussolini's support. His regime was characterised by the elimination of his main political opponents, a ban on political parties and an impotent parliament. Despite Italy's influence, in the mid-1930s the monarchy developed relatively autonomously around the notion of "enlightened dictatorship" and a personality cult around Zogu, presented as the heir to Skanderbeg, the national hero who had rebelled against the Ottomans in the fifteenth century. In Bulgaria, a coalition government, the Popular Bloc, came to power in 1931 to try to prevent the harmful effects of the economic crisis. However, it fell in 1934, after the signing of the Balkan Pact, which was directed particularly against Bulgaria, and following a putsch carried out by former officers. Nine months later, this authoritarian regime was replaced by the dictatorship of King Boris III. The Greek political scene also became increasingly radical in the second half of the 1930s. A putsch led by Venizelos in 1935 failed. The monarchy was then re-established and Ioannis Metaxas initiated a dictatorship in 1936, which lasted until the country was occupied in 1941. In Romania, where the extremist nationalism of the Iron Guard came to the fore and anti-Semitic measures were taken from 1936 onwards, King Carol II established a dictatorship in 1938, abolishing parliament and the political parties. Finally, in the Kingdom of Serbs, Croats and Slovenes, the tense political situation led King Alexander to suspend the constitution in January 1929. The kingdom, now called the Kingdom of Yugoslavia, was divided into nine provinces (*banovinas*), with the aim of weakening national particularisms. Although a new constitution was promulgated in 1931, the opposition boycotted the elections and the Yugoslav National Party (*Jugoslovenska Nacionalna Stranka*—JNS), which supported the royal dictatorship, emerged as the winner. The dictatorship became slightly less rigid under the regency of Prince Paul, after King Alexander was assassinated in Marseille in October 1934 by a Macedonian nationalist extremist. However, the government of Milan Stojadinović re-aligned the country with the Axis Powers (Italy and Germany). In August 1939, an agreement signed by the new Prime Minister Dragiša Cvetković and the leader of the Croatian Peasant Party Vladimir Maček created a *banovina* of Croatia with a large degree of autonomy within the kingdom.

At this time the Axis Powers already had very significant economic and political influence in Southeast Europe. In April 1939 Italy invaded and annexed Albania. Romania signed an economic agreement with the Third Reich which granted the latter a major role in the Romanian economy. Having sought to remain neutral, the Romanian leaders aligned themselves with the Reich, but were obliged to cede Bessarabia to the USSR in June 1940. Two months later Romania's territory was further reduced, when the country had to abandon Southern Dobruja to Bulgaria, as well as part of Transylvania to Hungary. Bulgaria, which was already close to the Reich, signed the Tripartite Pact (Germany, Italy and Japan) in March 1941. Greece was attacked by the Italian army, from Albania, in October 1940. Despite a counter-offensive, it was forced to surrender in April 1941 when it found itself facing the German troops that had come to reinforce their struggling Italian ally. As for the Kingdom of Yugoslavia, Hitler demanded that it join the Tripartite Pact. Following a coup d'état seeking to go back on Prince Paul's signature of the Pact, the country was attacked by the German army in April 1941. This was the end of the first Yugoslavia.

The victors decided to break up the Yugoslav state in order to create the Independent State of Croatia (*Nezavisna Država Hrvatska*—NDH), which immediately sided with the Axis. This new state, led by Ante Pavelić and the Croatian ultra-nationalists of the Ustasha movement, included Bosnia-Herzegovina, but had to cede a large part of Dalmatia to Italy. Under this arrangement Italy also received part of Slovenia and, through its Albanian satellite, part of Kosovo and Macedonia, giving rise to the creation of a "Greater Albania". Italy also occupied Montenegro and much of Greece. For its part, Germany annexed the north of Slovenia, controlled a rump Serbia placed under the authority of General Nedić, and occupied strategic positions in Kosovo, Macedonia and Greece. Hungary took possession of the Bačka region in Vojvodina. As for Bulgaria, it occupied the eastern parts of Kosovo and Macedonia, as well as a large part of Thrace (see Map 7).

The Second World War was a time of extreme violence in Southeast Europe too. The new regimes deported and exterminated their Jewish and Gypsy populations, along with their political opponents. Several concentration camps were opened in the region, including the Jasenovac camp in the Independent State of Croatia. But many Jews, Gypsies and political opponents were also deported to the Reich's concentration camps, whilst tens of thousands of other people were forced to go and work in Germany. In the Independent State of Croatia the Ustasha committed large-scale massacres against the Serbs, to which the Chetniks (Serbian nationalists) responded by massacring Bosnian Muslims. Tens of thousands of people were killed in these outbreaks of inter-community violence, and hundreds of thousands of others fled. Famine also claimed many victims in Greece.

Resistance movements started to spring up as of 1941, of either communist or nationalist inspiration. The pro-communists were particularly powerful in Yugoslavia, where they were headed by Josip Broz-Tito, as well as in Greece and Albania, though they were only few in number in

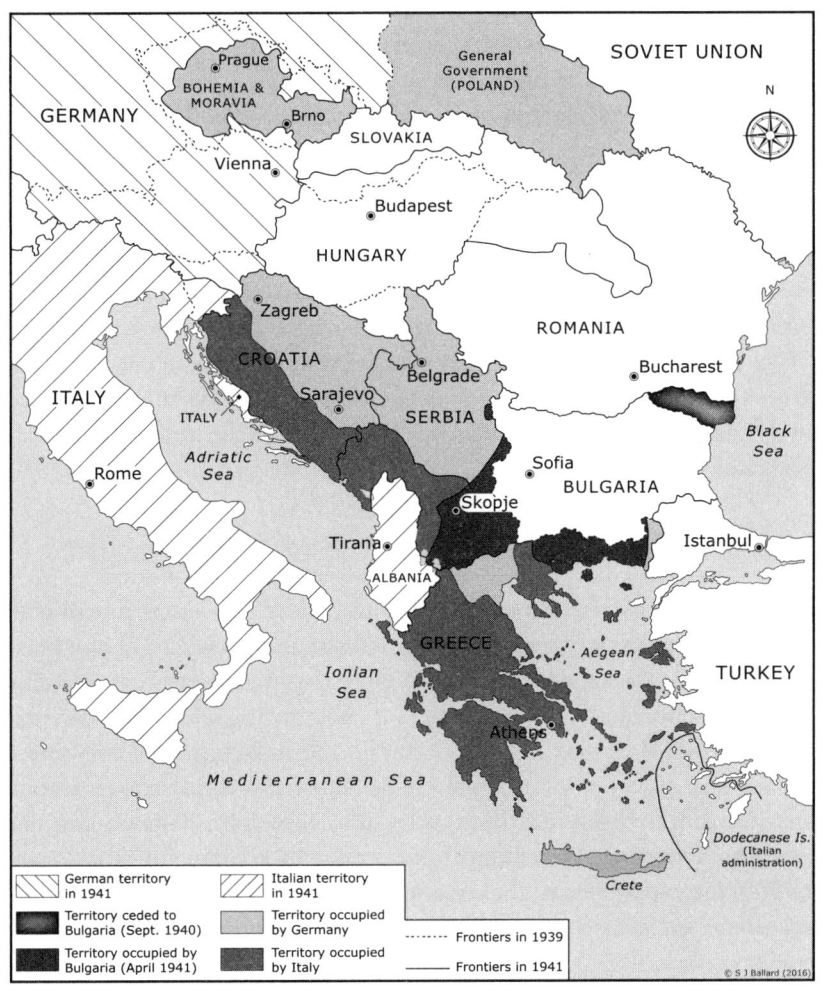

Map 7: Southeast Europe during the Second World War

Bulgaria. They confronted both the occupying troops and the nationalist resistance movements, such as the Chetnik movement in Yugoslavia, the National Front (*Balli kombëtar*) in Albania, and the National Republican Greek League (*Ethnikos Dimokratikos Ellinikos Syndesmos*—EDES) in Greece. As of 1943 the nationalist movements, confronted with the increasing power of the pro-communists, entered into various forms of collaboration with the ruling regimes and occupying troops. But over the same period the situation shifted in the wake of the surrender of Italy, with Germany taking over the areas previously occupied by its ally. The changes in the balance of power at the global level led also to changes in alliances during 1944, as the Soviet troops moved westwards. The regime in place in Romania was overthrown and the country placed itself on the side of the Allies. In Bulgaria, the army allowed the Soviet troops to enter the country, and the new government proclaimed by the Popular Front joined the Allies against Germany. At this time much of Yugoslav, Greek and Albanian territory was controlled by communist partisans, and the Yugoslav communists managed to establish the institutional bases for a new federal Yugoslavia.

Nationalisation of societies and ideological radicalisation

The decade of war between 1912 and 1922 left the countries of Southeast Europe weak and drained. Part of their population had been decimated or displaced, their economies were ravaged and their infrastructures damaged. Serbia, which had been greatly affected, counted a million dead, Romania around 300,000, while in Bulgaria military losses alone accounted for 100,000 men. The shock also came in the form of the waves of refugees that had to be absorbed. John Koliopoulos and Thanos Veremis believe that for Greece, where these flows were the largest, the experience of the refugees played a decisive role in numerous sectors of social and political life.[1] They represented an economic and social challenge, but also brought specific know-how and provided a labour force. They introduced new perspectives into society and their political behaviours were not aligned to the traditional clientelistic networks. Their presence changed the mindset of a part of the elites. The purpose of the land reforms undertaken by practically all the countries of the Peninsula in the early 1920s was to assist the refugees, but also to redistribute agricultural wealth and to satisfy populations that were largely rural and had been impoverished by the war. This did not prevent the reforms also being used for political purposes, to benefit the parties that implemented them, to counter the possible rise of communism, or to serve nationalist ends. The economies of the region's countries, which were suffering the effects of the global crisis but were not as "backward" as communist historiographies seek to portray them, were also transformed by a first, somewhat limited, industrial development, and, above all, by increasingly extensive state intervention in the 1930s.

The political and social landscape of Southeast Europe was also transformed by an external factor linked to the new European order. That new order was based on the principles set out by the US president Woodrow Wilson in 1918. In order to guarantee peace and democracy, he presented fourteen points promoting the principles of national self-determination, freedom and peace. In particular, he demanded that the peoples of Austria-Hungary and the non-Turkish peoples of the Ottoman Empire should be able to develop autonomously. He also recommended the creation of an "association of nations". These principles served as the basis for the 1919 Treaty of Versailles and the treaties that followed, which guaranteed rights for the "minorities", a term which was now officially adopted. The League of Nations, which came into being at the same time, was the result of both the affirmation of the nation-state model and the wish to guarantee the collective rights of minorities.

The states of Southeast Europe remodelled by the treaties were therefore supposed to respect the rights of the "linguistic, racial and religious" minorities, in the words used by the League of Nations.[2] In reality, some minorities were not officially recognised as such: for example the Gypsies in all the countries of the region, the Albanians of Greece or Yugoslavia (recognised as members of the Muslim religious minority, but not as forming an Albanian national minority) and the Vlachs/Aromanians of Albania. Other minorities were recognised, or rather created, but their rights were only imperfectly or temporarily respected. And even when they turned to the League of Nations for assistance, the representatives of the European powers were not always prepared to defend those rights, instead prioritising what they considered to be the interests and stability of the states in the region.

For, in the inter-war period, the Balkan states—which were very heterogeneous in religious and linguistic terms—implemented policies to nationalise their societies and to contribute to both the modernisation and stability of the state. As Irina Livezeanu has shown for Greater Romania, education was one of the principal tools of that nationalisation.[3] Schools were to contribute to the Romanianisation of a population of which only around 70 per cent were of Romanian culture, while non-Romanian educational institutions were to be limited.

Therefore the logic of the nation-state won out over the rights of the minorities. Was the Kingdom of Serbs, Croats and Slovenes different in this regard, since, by its very name, it recognised three groups within its own borders? Did it depart from the nation-state model? This is a complex question. The Yugoslav idea, which made the Serbs, Croats and Slovenes three tribes (*pleme*) of a single nation, did exist. Yet that idea was not shared and understood equally; it evolved in a complex way together with or in opposition to the Serbian, Croatian or Slovenian national ideas, which also varied between individuals and over time. To present the view of Pieter Troch in a simplified version, the dominant position went through three phases.[4] The first was that of "a Yugoslavia with a Serbia-centred compromise", built around the idea of belonging to a single nation divided into three tribes, with the Serbian tribe having the main role to play. The second phase, from 1929, was that of the "integral Yugoslavism" advocated by the dictatorship, which no longer tolerated difference. Finally, in 1935, there was a return to a "realistic Yugoslavism", which took account of the different components. However, the agreement signed in August 1939 by Dragiša Cvetković and Vladimir Maček, which granted Croatia a large degree of autonomy, brought the period of dominance of the Yugoslav idea to a close. Moreover, in the Kingdom of Yugoslavia, economic policies, for example, never really contributed to the integration of the whole territory. Educational policies, which here too were seen as one of the most powerful instruments for nationalising society, were truly unified only at the time of the dictatorship and "integral Yugoslavism", even if the curricula drawn up in the preceding period had already helped to disseminate the Yugoslav idea. In the second half of the 1930s, after Yugoslavism and Yugoslavisation had been closely associated with authoritarianism, the textbooks would gradually move to support the idea of a multinational state.

As Mark Mazower has shown,[5] the nationalisation policies were intended not only to solve the minority problem, but also to exercise social control, eliminate opposition groups and forge citizenship and loyalty to the state. As in the other European countries, youth organisations modelled along the lines of the Czech sokols or the fascist youth organisations appeared more or less everywhere to provide an ideological framework for the young generations. However, not all these organisations supported the national ideology. There were, for example, Catholic youth organisations in Croatia and Albania, while other youth organisations were established by the Iron Guard in Romania. In some cases, the nationalisation of societies also involved changes to the place names (particularly in Albania, Greece, Bulgaria and Turkey) and sometimes surnames (for example, the imposition of—ić endings in Yugoslavia). In the 1930s, the development of eugenics, racial anthropology and technicist approaches reinforced a biopolitical vision of nationalisation and modernisation of societies, as recent studies have shown. Moreover, social changes in some milieus (students, doctors, engineers, etc.) led to a convergence of these trends in the second half of the 1930s with the rise of a fascist movement such as the Iron Guard in Romania and other forms of nationalist and modernising authoritarianism.

In most of the Balkan countries, national ideologies were also redefined with regard to new internal enemies, real or imagined: the communists. In reality, communism found it hard to take root during the 1920s and 1930s. The communist parties that had appeared after the First World War were banned in most of the countries (in 1921 in Yugoslavia, in 1924 in Romania and Bulgaria, in 1936 in Greece). Thus the communists consisted of small groups or individuals who succeeded in publishing journals, and in fomenting strikes and sometimes even uprisings, but who were subject to repression. Some went to study in Moscow, whilst others were in touch with the Komintern, which promised self-determination for peoples. Some were attracted by communism during time spent in Western Europe, such as Enver Hoxha in France. Many, such as Mehmet Shehu, the future number two of communist Albania, even enrolled in the Spanish Civil War. In the late 1930s, the young educated elites, faced with the strengthening of the dictatorships and the rise of fascism, were increasingly attracted by communism. In Zagreb, for example, some young Muslim intellectuals started to publish the journal *Putokaz* ("Road Sign") in 1937.

Like the state authorities, the religious authorities fought to prevent the growth of communism. They also strove to discredit secularising discourses and policies they feared could affect their prerogatives by associating them more widely with communism. Relations between the states and the Churches were, in fact, more complex than they appeared. The Orthodox Church had the status of dominant church in Greece, Romania and Bulgaria. However, the Orthodox Church did not officially have that status in Yugoslavia, or in Albania where, despite—or rather because of—the Muslim majority, the state was declared to have no official or dominant religion. In any case, the political authorities opposed the Church when the state's interests required this. The religious authorities, for their part, sought to respond to their loss of authority and the secularisation of some segments of society, particularly the urban elites. Religious revival and mutual assistance associations flourished. In the 1930s there were interactions between religious nationalist actors and certain radical political movements.

But, more specifically, what was the position of the Muslim populations in the tense circumstances of the inter-war period and during the dramatic period of the Second World War?

Muslims between emigration, the agrarian question and the construction of minorities

In the inter-war period, the Muslim populations in the various Balkan states remained minorities in numerical terms, except in the Albanian state, which had a Muslim majority (69 per cent of the 1 million inhabitants recorded in the 1930 census). The number of Muslims in Romania had increased following the annexation of Southern Dobruja, where they were quite numerous, but even so in the country as a whole there were only between 170,000 and 290,000 according to estimates, which differed widely. In Greece, after the exchange of populations, they numbered around 135,000 (2 per cent of the total population), living mainly in Western Thrace. There were larger groups in Bulgaria and Yugoslavia. Numbering around 800,000, they formed 12–13 per cent of the population of the Kingdom of Bulgaria. In the Kingdom of Serbs, Croats and Slovenes there were almost twice as many Muslims (1.5 million), although they accounted for more or less the same percentage of the total population (around 10 per cent).

From a socio-political point of view, two processes particularly affected the Muslims of the four countries where they formed a minority, with the Muslims of Bosnia-Herzegovina finding themselves in a slightly different situation within Yugoslavia. These processes were emigration—as in earlier periods—and the construction of minorities. The Muslims gradually became minorities, in the sense given to this word by the treaties signed as of 1919 and, later on, by the League of Nations. These two processes were closely linked to the legal status granted to Muslims and the gap between that legal status and everyday reality. They were also closely bound up with the agrarian question, particularly as that question was often considered in national terms.

While some degree of continuity may be seen with the preceding period, the aim of nationalising society that guided political leaders in the Balkans over the inter-war period—including in Turkey—led them to harden their migration policies for Muslims. After 1923, the exchange or displacement of populations—as traumatic as it might be—continued to be seen as a way to resolve what was regarded as a security issue. Moreover, in the late 1930s, Turkey and two Balkan countries signed agreements for "Turks" to emigrate to Turkey: Romania in 1936 and Yugoslavia in 1938.

Nevertheless, recent studies have shown that these policies varied over time and had multiple dimensions, and that not all political leaders had the same attitude to the issue. With regard to "South Serbia", i.e. the regions in southern Yugoslavia (current Sanjak, Kosovo and Macedonia), Edvin Pezo has shown that the Yugoslav authorities first implemented an ambivalent policy of assimilation and encouragement of emigration, against the background of a debate between supporters of integration of Muslims into the new social order and proponents of complete Serbianisation of these regions.[6] To this end, in the early 1920s Muslims were prevented from returning and several laws and decisions came into force concerning land reform, favouring the redistribution of land and the establishment of Serbian and Montenegrin settlers (particularly in the border areas with Albania, for military reasons). In addition, there were repressive measures on the part of the police. Lastly, some legislative measures were taken. According to article 55 of the citizenship law of 1928, former non-Slav Ottoman citizens had the right to renounce Yugoslav citizenship within five years; if they did so, they had to leave the country within one year. This "right" was renewed in 1933. This legislation favoured the departure not only of non-Slav Muslims but also of their Slavic-speaking co-religionists, particularly from Sanjak.

In the 1930s, the failure of integral Yugoslavism and of the policies of assimilation, together with Italian support for Albanian irredentism, led the Yugoslav leaders to opt for a policy of "dissimilation". In 1931 and 1933, new laws concerning the agrarian question introduced an "economic dissimilation" and drove many Muslims to leave for Turkey. In particular, in September 1935, an inter-ministerial conference was organised by the Prime Minister and Minister of Foreign Affairs, Milan Stojadinović, who wanted to introduce measures to "relocate" the Albanians and Turks, either in Turkey, by encouraging their emigration, or within the country but further from the border areas, in order to secure these zones. To do that, the Yugoslav authorities indirectly drove the Muslims to leave, for example by demanding strict compliance with the laws on compulsory schooling and payment of taxes. In 1938, an agreement was also signed with Turkey, which provided for the emigration of 40,000 families, or 200,000 people. However, that policy was not implemented, because of disagreements concerning the financial aspect of the operation.

Nevertheless, Edvin Pezo has emphasised that emigration was also due to other factors. These included the way the local administrative or military authorities acted, at times going much further than the central authorities. There was also Turkey's policy. Turkey, like the other Balkan countries, favoured the immigration of "co-nationals" for demographic and nationalist reasons. However, in 1923 Turkey had to integrate hundreds of thousands of refugees from Greece following the population exchange, and sought to slow the arrival of other migrants. As a result, in 1926 Turkey was constrained to issue a law specifying the people who were and were not wanted (the latter being people who were not of the Turkish race, criminals, anarchists, spies and Gypsies). In 1934, a new law established the criteria for settling migrants according to their degree of adherence to Turkish culture. These criteria of race and culture did not prevent many Albanian-speaking and Slavic-speaking Muslims from emigrating to Turkey. It is true that some spoke Turkish, at least to some degree, but did they all? In any event, each time Turkey adopted a restrictive measure it seems to have slowed these migratory flows. Edvin Pezo estimates that, of the total of 64,000 to 78,000 who left during the inter-war period, the number of departures was insignificant between 1919 and 1922 (the period of the Greco-Turkish War), very high between 1923 and 1926 (40,000 to 50,000), slowed a little between 1927 and 1935 (22,000 to 25,000), and then fell to a relatively low level between 1936 and 1941 (2,000 to 3,000).[7] Thus, the radical measures envisaged in 1935 by the Yugoslavs failed to materialise.

FROM THE END OF THE EMPIRES TO COMMUNISM

In addition to state policies, the global economic crisis also pushed some to seek better living conditions. Emigration was also encouraged by family networks or acquaintanceship networks which made it easier to settle in the host country. In fact, it is often difficult to distinguish between voluntary and non-voluntary migration, as in both cases there is some degree of constraint. People rarely leave their region of origin voluntarily.

In Bulgaria, the agrarian question, the national question and the issue of migration were also interwoven. There was a similar radicalisation in the second half of the 1930s, but with different areas of emphasis. In 1921, under the Stamboliski government, the land redistribution law granted land to each family, both Christians and Muslims. However, from the mid-1920s, while similar laws were voted through, they were often applied according to national criteria in favour of "Bulgarian" refugees from Thrace and Macedonia, at the expense of the Muslims. At times it was the refugee organisations or the fascist organisation *Rodna Zaštita* ("Defence of the Homeland") that drove Muslims to leave. In the 1930s, political radicalisation and the global economic crisis inspired policies to reduce the Turkish presence (but not that of the Pomaks, as we shall see). In fact, while the flow of migrants to Turkey increased (more than 1,000 families left in 1932–4, 1,800 in 1935), the processes at work were more complex. According to Mary Neuburger,[8] while the Bulgarian authorities wanted to redistribute the migrants' lands to Bulgarian peasants, it was speculators who most often succeeded in gaining possession. The Bulgarian state then awarded itself a monopoly over transactions involving migrants' lands; this made it possible to organise in advance colonisation by Bulgarian peasants. However, the Turkish peasants did not remain inactive: they sought to acquire the land of their neighbours who had left, claiming it as Turkish land. During the Second World War, Bulgarian refugees were used as colonists, this time in the lands occupied in Thrace and Macedonia, where Muslims were driven to emigrate.

In Romania, in the newly acquired Southern Dobruja, very similar processes were at work, as the departures of the Turkish and Tatar Muslims were partly linked to the acquisition/seizure of land and redistribution of that land to colonists, partly to Turkey's policy and partly to dynamics coming from the population itself. Here, too, radicalisation—due to the increasing power of the Iron Guard—and the economic crisis caused an increase in migratory flows to Turkey from

1933. The 1936 agreements between the two countries were designed to regulate those flows.

Georgia Kretsi, who has studied the Muslims of Çamëri, the region between Greek Epirus and the Albanian border, shed new light on the relationships between legal status, the agrarian question and the process of constructing minorities.[9] With the creation of the Albanian–Greek border in 1913, the Muslims of Çamëri (in Greek: Thesprotia) became de facto a linguistic–religious minority. Following the Treaty of Lausanne in 1923, they would gradually be ethnicised. Excluded from the population exchange between Greece and Turkey (because of diplomatic pressure from Italy), they were not officially recognised as a minority. However, the Greek authorities recognised their "non-exchangeable" status, while seeking to persuade them to depart as "Turks" and flouting most of their collective rights: access to economic resources, right to open minority schools, right to political representation. The desire to resolve the refugee question and reinforce the loyalty of this border region meant that the land reform of 1922, in particular, favoured the Christian refugees from Anatolia, who were settled in the region's villages. More than half of the 50,000 Çams who lived in the region in the early twentieth century emigrated to Turkey or Albania in the inter-war period. However, Georgia Kretsi also highlights the social dynamics that developed within the minority group, something that is too often overlooked in studies of the Muslims of Southeast Europe. While the religious elites, paid by the Greek state, encouraged emigration and turned a blind eye to the irregularities committed by local administrators, the large landowners behaved as "national agents" of one side or the other, in order to Hellenicise or Albanianise the territory. The strategy adopted by the small landowners was bound up with their desire to acquire land and could fluctuate substantially.

In Greece, another complex process of minority construction and ethnicisation was also at play in Western Thrace. This process was linked to the "non-exchangeable" status granted to the Muslims by the Treaty of Lausanne. It was also related to managing the arrival of the many Christian refugees from Anatolia. It was dependent on the Greek and Turkish land policies and the strategies of the various Muslim actors, for whom emigration was always one of the possible choices. During the Second World War, the occupation of the region by the Bulgarians and their policy of Bulgarianisation, directed at the Pomaks in particular, drove 10,000 Muslims from Western Thrace to take refuge in Turkey.

Conversely, migration became of only marginal significance in Bosnia-Herzegovina, where Muslims were not attracted by the new Turkey. As for Albania, the fact that the majority of the population was Muslim made it a country to which Muslims migrated rather than one they left. The planned land reform was implemented only in a very limited way, precisely because of the settlement of Muslim refugees arriving from the Kingdom of Yugoslavia and Greece. When Muslims did emigrate, their emigration was individual rather than collective and was relatively limited. The main reasons were political exile, education abroad, or economic motives. Emigration for religious reasons was rare, although one could mention the case of the family of Muhammad Nasiruddin al-Albani—the famous neo-Salafist thinker of the Middle East, who died in 1999—who emigrated in the 1920s from Shkodër to Syria to flee the "impious" regime of Ahmet Zogu. However, leaving that particular case aside, the countries to which these Albanian Muslim (in the sociological sense) emigrants went were Italy, Austria, France, or even the United States and Australia, rather than Turkey. This provided early indications of the re-orientation of migratory flows that would occur from the 1960s.

Partial nationalisation, strengthening and control of the Islamic institutions

During the nineteenth century, the Balkan states had already sought to control the Islamic religious hierarchies (and also the Christian religious hierarchies) and to sever their links with Istanbul, but without truly succeeding, as we have seen. In Bosnia-Herzegovina, a relatively autonomous hierarchy had been installed in the 1880s, headed by the *reis-ul-ulema*. This hierarchy was placed under the authority of the *şeyhülislam* again in 1909. In Bulgaria, a similar structure, built around a grand mufti, had been recognised in that same year by a Bulgarian–Ottoman Treaty. The other muftis in Southeastern Europe continued to recognise the higher authority of the *şeyhülislam*.

The abolition of the Ottoman Caliphate and of the office of *şeyhülislam* in 1924 significantly altered a situation which had already undergone changes as a result of a decade of war. The new Turkish Directorate of Religious Affairs (*Diyanet İşleri Reisliği*) now came under the direct authority of the Turkish prime minister and was no longer deemed to have authority over Muslims outside Turkey. Moreover, the treaties signed from 1919 onwards reaffirmed, in the various Balkan countries, the rights of the Muslim minorities concerning education and the exercise and administration of their religion. In most cases, the context of nationalisation and modernisation of local societies also encouraged the nationalisation and strengthening of the Islamic institutions. The efforts on the part of the reformist intellectuals and ulamas to vernacularise Islam—which in some cases had begun as early as the end of the nineteenth century—by translating and producing religious texts in the local languages also contributed to this nationalisation. There were even projects in the inter-war period to produce translations of and commentaries on the Quran in the vernacular languages (Turkish, Albanian and Serbo-Croatian). However, there were also dynamics that ran counter to the nationalisation and strengthening of the Islamic institutions, either for national political and religious reasons or because of local and transnational dynamics.

In Albania, where the Muslims were not in a minority, the institutions set up by the occupying Austro-Hungarian authorities between 1916 and 1918 were subsequently extended to the whole territory, and consolidated around the same group of reformers led by Vehbi Dibra (1867–1937). Several national congresses were arranged in order to design a structure, under tight control of the political authorities. During the first Muslim Congress, which took place early in 1923, Albania's Islamic institutions officially severed their links with the *şeyhülislam* of Istanbul, even before the latter's position was abolished. The purpose was to assert the country's independence, as had been done the previous year at the Congress of Orthodox Christians. In the new state, which had no official religion, the Islamic institutions came under the Ministry of Justice, although the Ministry of the Interior was responsible for overseeing them. They were not allowed to have official links with foreign institutions. The political and religious leaders had both convergent interests (desire for control, nationalisation and reform) and divergent ones. So, for example, the introduction of the civil code in 1929, which brought an end to the sharia courts and the prerogatives in matters of family and inheritance law, was contested by the leaders of the Albanian Muslim Community (*Komuniteti Mysliman Shqiptar*). That same year, new statutes strengthened state control over the Islamic institutions, which were placed under the leadership of the lawyer Behxhet Shapati. With the creation of a Greater Albania under Italian rule in 1941, these institutions were extended to the "liberated lands", that is to say, the western parts of current Kosovo and

Macedonia. However, integration was difficult on several levels. The Muslims of Kosovo initially moved the seat of the religious institutions to which they belonged from Skopje (now under Bulgarian occupation) to Prizren, and some wished to preserve this particular arrangement for reasons that were religious (fear of being subsumed in a less strict form of Islam), economic (control of the income of the local waqfs) and political (ability to exercise political influence through these institutions). The legal regimes in the territories of inter-war Albania, where the civil code had been introduced, continued to differ from that in the "liberated lands", where the sharia courts continued to operate. Support for the reorganisation of the Islamic institutions in 1942, with the creation of a council of ulamas (*Këshilli i Ulemave*) consisting of five members, appointed by the fascist authorities and representing the different regions of Greater Albania, was far from consensual. Moreover, it would be wrong to think that, even in the original Albanian territory, these national institutions controlled the whole religious domain.

Moreover, a particular feature of Albania was that Islamic institutions' prerogatives were restricted due to the recognition of the autonomy of a "Bektashi Community". In fact, the institutionalisation of the Bektashi brotherhood started nationally with the organisation of three successive congresses (in 1921, 1924 and 1929) and the drawing up of statutes or regulations. The link with the mother house of Haji Bektash in Anatolia weakened while, paradoxically, being at the same time strengthened with the installation of Salih Niyazi Dede (the last *dede-baba* in Albania itself) in 1930, five years after the closure of the *tekke*s in Turkey. He became the *kryegjysh* (literally "principal grandfather") and hence the supreme spiritual authority. Contrary to what is frequently affirmed, the Bektashis did not gain full independence. Why was this? From 1920 onwards, the Albanian political and administrative authorities did grant a degree of recognition to Bektashism by appointing a Bektashi lay person as the fourth member of the Regency Council. However, they had difficulties in officially recognising full legitimacy of the Bektashi institutions as those institutions were gradually defined. The main reason seems to have been pressure from some non-Bektashi Muslims, who did not accept the establishment of a second Muslim religious community; for them, all Muslims had to be tied to the official Islamic institutions. Even in Bektashi milieus, institutionalisation generally had little impact, as religious authority continued to be defined locally.

In Bulgaria, from 1919 onwards, a "Regulation of the Organisation and Administration of the Muslim Religious Institutions of Bulgaria" placed the Islamic institutions under the control of the Ministry of Foreign Affairs and Religion. The ministry was able to intervene in the appointment and dismissal of religious officials, as well as in the management of the waqfs, and gained control of charitable activities. From that time, the grand mufti resided in Sofia and directed the Higher Sharia Council, which was the central body of the Islamic institutions. While the sharia courts continued to exist, three appeal courts were set up. However, in 1938, this specific level of jurisdiction was removed. Locally, the Muslim population elected *cemaats* (community councils) that were responsible for managing religious, school and economic (pious foundations) affairs. Nevertheless, the ministry retained a right of oversight, and management of the waqfs was supervised by an official located in the capital. In particular, it should be noted that, from 1938 onwards, the local Islamic institutions in the Smolyan region were taken over by members of *Rodina* ("The Homeland"), a Pomak assimilationist association set up in 1937, to which in 1942, during the Second World War, the ministry even appointed Pomak muftis, as well as in the territories occupied in Thrace and Macedonia. This led to a virtual duplication and an ethnicisation of the Islamic institutions, which were now de facto cut in two—the Turks on one side and the Pomaks on the other.

In Yugoslavia and Romania, centralisation of the religious institutions occurred only in the 1930s, as the regimes in place became more authoritarian. In fact, until 1930, the Yugoslav authorities allowed the pre-existing Islamic institutions to function autonomously in the different regions—in Bosnia-Herzegovina around the *reis-ul-ulema*, and elsewhere around the regional muftis (Belgrade, Niš, Skopje, Podgorica)—contrary to the wishes of the Muslim political and religious elites of Bosnia-Herzegovina, who wanted to see them unified. It was after the establishment of the dictatorship and the creation of the *banovinas* that a law was passed in 1930 proclaiming the unification of the country's Islamic institutions within an Islamic Religious Community (*Islamska Vjerska Zajednica*) under the leadership of the *reis-ul-ulema*, whose seat was now in Belgrade. However, two *ulema-medžlis* and two councils of the waqfs and education were created under the *reis-ul-ulema*, in Sarajevo and Skopje, with authority over the regional structures (muftis, and offices of the waqfs and education) all the way down to the local *džemat*s (community councils) formed around the imams. For political reasons (the entry of the leaders of the main Bosnian Muslim party into the governing coalition), the Yugoslav government agreed to reverse that decision in 1936, re-establishing the seat of the *reis-ul-ulema* in Sarajevo and restoring the autonomy of the religious institutions. In addition to this, the function of mufti was abolished, and the power of the ulamas within the religious institutions was reduced in favour of that of the notables. The fact that the position of *reis-ul-ulema* remained vacant between 1936 and 1938 reflects the struggles between notables and ulamas for control of the Islamic institutions. Those struggles continued during the Second World War within the Independent State of Croatia, with the ulamas organised within the *el-Hidaje* ("The Right Path") association seeking to regain the position they had lost in 1936.

In Romania, the Islamic institutions were organised around four muftiships (*müftülük*)—Constanţa, Silistra, Tulcea and Bazargic (Dobriç)— and the local *cemaat*s. It was only in 1937 that the position of grand mufti (in Turkish: *başmüftülük*) was established in Tulcea, before being transferred to Constanţa in 1940. The way the sharia courts operated had already been changed, and in 1935 they were abolished, although the cadis were retained as experts at the civil courts.

In Greece, on the other hand, no centralised religious hierarchy was set up in the inter-war period. In 1928, there were a dozen muftis in the whole country, three of whom were in Western Thrace. In that region, before the population exchange, the law of 1920 provided that the muftis would also have the prerogatives of cadis, that they were responsible for administration of the mosques, waqfs and personnel, and that they should be elected by the local Muslim population. However, in reality these elections never took place. The muftis were appointed by the state. The same law also provided for the creation of a position of grand mufti, whose seat would be in Athens, although this was never implemented.

These attempts at nationalisation, strengthening and control, which met with varying degrees of success in the different countries, together with the questions of the management of the community schools and integration in political life, were the subject of mobilisations, struggles and debates, both internally and externally. Moreover, the Islamic institutions (and with them the administration of the waqfs and the schools) were places where issues of power, both between Muslims themselves and between Muslims and the state authorities, became concentrated.

EUROPE'S BALKAN MUSLIMS

The specific forms of mobilisation of the Muslim populations

Despite the state policies of assimilation/dissimilation or control, we must be careful not to view the Muslims of Southeast Europe simply as passive objects of state policies. They were also actors who debated, mobilised and acted in different fields (political, religious, economic), despite the constraints to which they were subject. What forms did such mobilisation take? In some cases Muslims formed their own political parties, but due principally to political constraints they also joined parties and especially voluntary associations which were not specific to Muslims. Together with the press these formed the main means of mobilisation drawn upon by Balkan Muslim entrepreneurs. They therefore need to be considered not solely as cultural movements, but also as forms of mobilisation.

As we have seen, partisan mobilisation, in the form of distinct political parties, had existed in Bosnia-Herzegovina since the beginning of the century. The formation of Yugoslavia led to a political reconfiguration and a new party, the Yugoslav Muslim Organisation (*Jugoslovenska Muslimanska Organizacija*—JMO), was formed in 1919. From 1921, it was led by Mehmed Spaho, a middle-class Muslim educated in Vienna. Although initially the leaders of the JMO sought to represent all Yugoslav Muslims, including those of "South Serbia" (current Sanjak, Kosovo and Macedonia), they did not succeed in doing so, as the central authorities opposed this. The JMO succeeded only in putting forward candidates in Sanjak in the 1927 elections. In Bosnia-Herzegovina, in the 1920s, the JMO succeeded in winning the votes of almost all the Muslims, as a dissident party created in 1923 did not survive. However, in 1935 the JMO lost some of its legitimacy as a result of its alignment with Prime Minister Milan Stojadinović and its absorption into the Yugoslav Radical Community (*Jugoslovenska Radikalna Zajednica*—JRZ). Following this, a good proportion of Bosnian Muslims preferred to vote for opposition parties or abstain. The JMO was also weakened by the creation in 1935 of the Muslim Organisation (*Muslimanska Organizacija*), which was close to the Croatian Peasant Party (HSS) and the federalists, while some young students were attracted by communist ideology. An example of the generational divide existing within Muslim elites at that time may be afforded by Nurija Pozderac, a JMO senator in western Bosnia, whose son Hamdija was active in the communist youth. Nevertheless, the integration of the JMO into Yugoslav politics meant that various governments included Muslim ministers during the period.

FROM THE END OF THE EMPIRES TO COMMUNISM

While the JMO did not succeed in mobilising the Muslims of "South Serbia", a political organisation did form there in 1919. The *Džemijet* party was created in 1919, under the leadership of Ferhat Draga, an Albanian notable from Kosovo (*Džemijet* was an abbreviation for *İslam Muhafazayi Hukuk Cemiyeti*, literally: Muslim Committee for the Protection of Rights). However, Bogumil Hrabak's study has shown that this party was plagued by internal divisions, in particular between a "Turkish" faction (which dominated the party between 1919 and 1923) and an "Albanian" faction (which prevailed between 1923 and 1925).[10] After 1925, these internal struggles, as well as the pressure from the central authorities, led to a slow break-up of the party.

Outside Yugoslavia there was no stable specific partisan mobilisation among the Muslims in the inter-war period. In Albania, two parliamentary camps (which were not exclusively Muslim) formed during the period 1920–24, and some parties were founded at the time of the 1924 "revolution", but were quickly banned after the return of Ahmet Zogu at the end of that year. Opposition groups then formed in exile. On the other hand, a degree of political structure did take shape during the Second World War. A fascist party was created after the country was annexed to Italy in 1939, while local guerrillas favouring the return of Ahmet Zogu appeared. Political groups then formed and organised a movement to resist the Italian occupation. The most important of these groups were the Communist Party created towards the end of 1941, the *Balli Kombëtar* (National Front) formed in 1942, and the *Legaliteti* ("Legality") party founded in 1943 and led by monarchist nationalists. Religious affiliation did not play a decisive role in the choice of political affiliation. The fact of belonging to factions with a regional presence was often a determining factor, and these did sometimes include a religious component. A National Liberation Front was also established in 1942 to coordinate the resistance, but disagreements soon appeared between the Communist Party and the other participants. The Italian surrender in September 1943 brought about significant political reconfigurations. The Germans occupied the whole of Albania and proclaimed it "independent" and "neutral", while a regency council was established under the presidency of Mehdi Frashëri and a government was formed under the leadership of Rexhep Mitrovica. Until September 1944, the *Balli Kombëtar* aligned itself with the Germans in its now open struggle against the partisan movement, while trying to maintain contacts with the Allies.

In this new phase, the partisans received official support from the Allies, unlike the *Legaliteti* party, which no longer wished to associate itself with the communists.

Outside inter-war Albania and Greater Albania in the years 1941–4— which were areas where the Muslims were in a majority and where there was no strong link between religion and political affiliation—Balkan Muslim notables also played a part in political life, appearing on the lists of non-Muslim parties. This was the case in Yugoslavia, in particular in "South Serbia" with the Radical Party after 1925 and in Bosnia-Herzegovina after 1935 (the merger with the Yugoslav Radical Community can be seen in this context), as well as in Bulgaria, Greece and Romania. During the Second World War, Muslim notables occupied important positions both nationally and locally in the Independent State of Croatia.

Outside Yugoslavia, because of various types of constraints, mobilisation occurred essentially in the form of clubs and associations of different types, and through the press. In Bulgaria, *Turan*[11] sport and cultural associations were created from 1923 onwards in different places (in 1936, there were 46 with 10,000 members). They formed a union from 1924, and organised national congresses in 1929 and 1936. However, the attempt to form a political movement independent of the Bulgarian parties failed. The dynamics therefore remained largely regional. Also, the clubs and associations diversified. On the one hand they became ethnicised with the emergence of Pomak associations—a Pomak cultural union in 1925, and above all the *Rodina* association in 1937 which, as we shall see, was to play a significant role. On the other hand, several neo-traditionalist Islamic associations appeared. In particular, a Committee of the Defenders of the Islamic Religion (*Dini İslam Müdafileri Cemiyeti*) was founded in 1934, presided over by the grand mufti of Bulgaria.

In the absence of specific political parties, associations also played a preponderant role in Greece. Electoral colleges were set up between 1922 and 1934 for Jews and Muslims. The Muslims had four representatives in parliament elected from the lists of Greek parties, who did not manage to exert any national influence. In these circumstances, associative mobilisation followed the same lines as in Bulgaria, except that there was no Pomak associative movement. A number of associations were created from the 1920s onwards: the Turkish Youth association (*Türk Gençler Birliği*) based on the "Turkish Hearth" model, and charitable or teaching associations. A religious associative movement appeared in the 1930s, with the creation of the Committee for Islamic Union (*İttihad-ı İslam Cemiyeti*) in 1933. Mobilisation of the Muslims of Thrace was limited during the Second World War. The Muslim notables used the Turkish consulate in Komotini to present some claims to the Bulgarian authorities. Generally, however, they adopted a wait-and-see approach towards the Bulgarian authorities and towards the resistance movements. Only some Pomaks became involved in the local nationalist (royalist) guerrilla movement.

In Bosnia-Herzegovina, the existence of a political party representing the Muslims did not prevent the associative movement developing as a form of opposition to that party, as a means of expression during the time the party was banned, and even as a complementary means of action for the party. In his study on Bosnian Muslim women, Fabio Giomi identifies three types of associations active in this area: philanthropic-community associations, cultural-national associations, including the famous *Gajret* ("Zeal") and *Narodna Uzdanica* ("Popular Hope"), and feminist associations (which were not specifically Muslim).[12] There were, however, other types of associations which brought the Bosnian Muslims together, such as sport clubs and professional associations. As in Greece and Bulgaria, a neo-traditionalist associative movement also appeared in the 1930s, with the creation of the Association of Ulamas *el-Hidaje* ("The Right Path") in 1936, under the leadership of Mehmed Handžić.

During the Second World War, when Bosnia-Herzegovina was incorporated into the Independent State of Croatia, the Bosnian Muslims, whom the Ustasha authorities regarded as Islamicised Croats, at first seemed to submit to this policy of authoritarian nationalisation. However, in the autumn of 1941, massacres committed by the Ustashas against the Serbs and by the Chetniks against the Muslims drove certain religious and lay Muslim notables to protest by means of solemn resolutions. As political parties had been banned and the religious institutions weakened, this mobilisation was backed by local notables and religious associations such as *el-Hidaje*. Local Muslim militias were also formed to protect Muslim villages. In 1942, a Committee for National Salvation (*Odbor Narodnog Spasa*) was established, some of whose members demanded autonomy for Bosnia-Herzegovina and sought for the protection of the Third Reich. In response, the German authorities decided to create a Bosnian Muslim SS division: the 13th SS division *Handžar*

("Dagger"). From 1943 onwards, however, the shifts in the global balance of power led some Muslim notables to join the partisan movement. At the same time, an increasing number of Muslims joined the ranks of the partisans. To that end, the Communist Party even created "Muslim brigades", but refused to grant Muslims their own national status within the new federal Yugoslavia.

In "South Serbia", other forms of mobilisation also occurred following the break-up of the *Džemijet* party in the second half of the 1920s. The religious institutions (*ulema-medžlis* of Skopje), with the economic base provided by the waqfs, served as alternative political institutions. However, there were also: a secret society of Albanian students in Belgrade, a secret political committee, and local cultural and sport clubs and associations. The Italian fascist authorities saw their opportunity and, in order to foster irredentism among the Albanians of these Yugoslav regions, sought to finance these various types of organisation. After 1941, many Albanian notables in the "liberated territories" (Kosovo and western Macedonia), such as Xhafer Deva and Rexhep Mitrovica, collaborated with the occupier. The more direct control exerted by the Germans in Kosovo led to the setting up of a "Second League of Prizren" there, which pledged allegiance to the Germans in September 1943, and to the creation in spring 1944 of the 21st SS division *Skanderbeg*, recruited solely in Kosovo. Various resistance groups also emerged in the "liberated territories", including the communist partisans, but only a few Albanians in these regions joined them before 1944.

Whether or not clubs and associations were present, the press played a central role in mobilising people and nurturing polemics. The Tatars of Dobruja gave themselves a showcase with the journal *Emel* ("Hope") founded in 1930. Generally, journals and newspapers published by Muslims were relatively numerous in the whole of the region. In addition to the archives, these publications can help to provide an understanding of some facets of the political and social changes experienced by the Balkan Muslims at this time, as well as some aspects of the power struggles then occurring.

In the cases of Romania, Bulgaria and Greece in particular, the debates and polemics have often been interpreted in terms of an opposition between "Kemalists" and "old Turks", that is to say, between supporters and opponents of the reforms led by Mustafa Kemal in Turkey: adoption of the Latin alphabet, education reform, reform to the manner of dress (with the wearing of hats for men and the abolition of the veil for women), abolition of sharia courts and adoption of the civil code, etc. The Kemalists have also been regarded as having been encouraged or even supported by Turkey and the Old Turks by the Balkan states wishing to cut any link with Turkey. As a result, the importance of local issues and the involvement of Muslims in the local and national arenas have often been played down.

The question of the relationship with the new Turkish Republic did arise. We have seen that the flows of migrants to Turkey did not dry up during the inter-war period, since under certain conditions Turkey needed immigration. We have also seen that Western Thrace was the object of Turkish irredentist ambitions. We know in addition to this, that the Turkish government and diplomats tended to support the adoption, by the Muslims of Romania, Greece and Bulgaria in particular, of reforms similar to the Kemalist reforms. Thus in 1935, following on from a visit to the Muslim seminary at Medgidia by a Turkish government representative, most religious teaching was apparently suppressed there. The only detailed study of the subject based on the Turkish archives—which are difficult to access—concerns Bulgaria.[13] In that study, Ebru Boyar and Kate Fleet show that the Kemalist authorities had an active and multi-faceted policy that was implemented through: diplomatic pressure aimed at altering Bulgarian policy (in 1936 the grand mufti was replaced by a person who was more favourable to them), support for the use of the Latin alphabet in Muslim schools and newspapers, through the provision of financial and material support to the "pro-Kemalist" Turkish press, and through press campaigns. Their study also seems to prove that the actions of the Kemalist authorities were guided above all by the wish to eliminate the development of any opposition to the regime that could reach into Turkey from Bulgaria.

Moreover, opponents of the Kemalist regime (the famous "one hundred and fifty" expelled by Mustafa Kemal, members of the Ottoman dynasty and others) found themselves in some Balkan countries where they were sometimes given important positions in the Islamic institutions or in the press. The former *şeyhülislam*, Mustafa Sabri, passed some of his time in exile in Romania and then, in the second half of the 1920s, in Greece, before leaving for Egypt. In Thrace, with his son who was director of the minority school administration, he was able to publish the influential Islamist newspaper *Yarın* ("Tomorrow"). For the Balkan authorities did indeed make use of Islam to counter the development of Turkish nationalism, or because of their fear of some such development. That was particularly true for Bulgaria and Greece, where the presence of Muslims in the border regions made the authorities highly sensitive to the issue. Thus, the Bulgarian authorities supported Grand Mufti Hüseyin Hüsnü in his policy against the Latin alphabet, just as they supported the publishing of the newspaper *Medeniyet* ("Civilisation"), and the Committee of the Defenders of the Islamic Religion founded in 1934. The Bulgarian authorities also often treated the Bulgarian-speaking Pomak Muslims differently, because of their supposedly natural place in the Bulgarian nation, unlike the Turks and the Gypsies. In that way they indirectly contributed to a process of ethnicisation within the Muslim population. The Greek authorities, for their part, did not do so, and it was only after the Second World War that they started encouraging Pomak identity.

However, insufficient attention has been paid to the transformation of these policies over time, to the differences in how they were drawn up and implemented, and to local dynamics. Mila Mancheva, who has studied the question of schooling in the Bulgarian Muslim minority, emphasises not only the changes due to developments in national and international policies, but also the differences of opinion that existed between different members of parliament, ministers, military leaders and civil servants.[14] Those differences were not without consequences for the policies actually implemented. In particular, the policy as implemented at the local level could differ significantly from the policy designed in the capital. Yannis Bonos has also shown this in his study of the alphabet issue in Western Thrace. Although the central authorities remained neutral, the local authorities, who had already appointed "anti-Kemalists" to a number of positions as muftis, teachers and leaders within the *cemaat*s, took measures against the Latin alphabet.[15]

Moreover, the results were not always those expected by the authorities, whose actions were both constrained and made possible by the dynamics within the Muslim populations. Those dynamics developed around the *cemaat*s—places of power and distribution of resources at the local level—and on their margins, around clubs and associations and press undertakings. They had resources which did not depend solely on the support of the governments involved. Religious reformism, lay reformism, nationalism and conservatism had their own historicity in these regions and were forged through transnational movements of people, which were not necessarily the result of state policies. For example, it is possible to agree with Mary Neuburger when she sees the *Rodina* association as initially a modernist assimilationist movement, formed in 1937 by Pomaks who had received a military education, with the support of a Bulgarian ethnographer; a movement which the Bulgarian authorities would use only later, particularly during the Second World War.[16] Moreover, if we are to understand the dynamics within the Balkan Muslim populations between 1920 and 1944 we must look beyond the opposition between "Kemalists versus anti-Kemalists" or "reformers" versus "conservatives".

Beyond the "reformers"/"conservatives" opposition

Several recent studies have presented a more nuanced view of the opposition between "reformers" and "conservatives" which generally underlies analyses of Balkan Islam in the inter-war period. Xavier Bougarel has shown that it is important to place the debates in their historical context and identify how they have evolved, including during this period.[17] By analysing a polemic that surfaced in 1928 between *Reis-ul-ulema* Čaušević and the *ilmiyye* on the issue of the veil, he identifies three opposing currents at the time: that of the lay reformers established primarily among the intelligentsia, that of the religious reformers supported by some ulamas, and that of the conservatives, also supported by ulamas. However, in the 1930s changes within Yugoslavia and outside favoured the appearance of a new current, namely the neo-traditionalist or revivalist current that formed around Mehmed Handžić (1906–44), an ulama educated in Cairo between 1926 and 1931. Influenced by the Muslim Brotherhood movement founded in Egypt in 1928 by Hasan al-Banna, Handžić was one of the initiators of the new Association of Ulamas *el-Hidaje*, which was established in 1936. Džemaludin Čaušević, who had spent time in Istanbul and Cairo at the beginning of the century, was influenced by Muhammad Abduh—Hasan al-Banna's teacher—and the Ottoman reformers. This partly common genealogy meant they also shared a number of positions (denouncing heterodox practices and materialism, affirming the compatibility of Islam, reason and knowledge, and emphasising the need to use vernacular languages and printing). They did, however, have differing views on other points, although the differences were not always clear: on the issue of the waqfs, the possibility of submitting the sharia to *ijtihad* (reasoned interpretation) and the relationship between the ulamas and the intelligentsia, but also on the definition of the relationship between Islam and the West, and on the place of Muslims in Yugoslavia and their national identification, in the context of the evolution of the south Slavic nationalisms.

Fabio Giomi has studied the issue of Muslim women at that time and distinguishes six types of discourse that had developed on this subject from the end of the nineteenth century in Bosnia-Herzegovina.[18] Following the appearance of an Islamic modernist discourse, which Džemaludin Čaušević continued to support until the 1930s and which argued for the need to enrol girls in school, and an opposing conservative position which also favoured the education of girls but opposed their enrolment at school, a nationalist discourse became established in the years 1920–30. It was now a question of educating the nation's mothers and daughters. Other views emerged among Muslims in the 1930s: the neo-traditionalist position, favouring religious education first and foremost, leading to the opening of a madrasa for girls in Sarajevo, and communist ideology, advocating a new type of emancipation for women. A more specifically feminist discourse, promoted primarily by Serbian and Croatian women, also had some influence in Muslim milieus.

Generally, questions of internal reforms were inextricably linked to issues concerning the political and civic integration of Muslims (or their elites) in the region's states, depending on the specific social and political relationships to be found. In Bosnia-Herzegovina, for example, the leaders of the JMO negotiated the autonomy of the Islamic institutions with the Serbian Radical Party, as well as the maintenance of Bosnia-Herzegovina's autonomy and the protection of the landowners' interests in the face of land reform. They supported the idea of Yugoslavism, which enabled them to protect themselves against Serbian and Croatian nationalisms, affirm their status as a distinct autochthonous group and align themselves with the government. When a group of young intellectuals launched the *Reforma* ("Reform") association in 1928, their desire to modernise religious education and the management of the waqfs, and to abolish the veil for women, was wholly bound up with their desire to see the Muslims integrate fully into a Yugoslav nation. In this, the leaders of the JMO and the *Reforma* activists opposed the leaders of the *Gajret* association, who advocated a Serbian national identification, as well as those of the *Narodna Uzdanica* association, who preferred to opt for a Croatian national identification, while the majority of Muslims did not take a stance on this issue. With the partition of Bosnia-Herzegovina brought about by the creation of the *banovina* of Croatia in 1939, mobilisation for the autonomy of Bosnia-Herzegovina took shape among the Muslims, under the leadership of Džafer Kulenović. In some cases, this mobilisation implied the affirmation of a national identification particular to the Muslims of the province. Support for such a national identification also arose in neo-traditionalist circles, under the guidance of Mehmed Handžić. These neo-traditionalists adopted in particular the Bogomil theory in order to forge a national identity particular to the Bosnian Muslims.

In the south of Yugoslavia, the leaders of the *Džemijet* party were, like their counterparts in the JMO, primarily concerned with the implementation of land reform and with their economic interests. While disagreements emerged within the party between "Turks" and "Albanians", this was mainly a regional (Macedonia/Kosovo) and social (towns/countryside) disagreement, as the Turko-Ottoman identification was a specific feature of those living in urban areas. The resistance movement against the Yugoslav authorities led by the *kaçak*s (literally: "breakaways") until 1924 must be seen as a continuation of a phenomenon that arose towards the end of the Ottoman period and which was partially politicised in 1912 in the context of the opposition to the Young Turks. However, our knowledge of the relationships between political mobilisation, Islam and ethnicisation in "South Serbia" is still lacking, particularly with regard to current Kosovo. It appears that there were similar currents in Macedonia to those in Bosnia-Herzegovina (reformists, conservatives and neo-traditionalists), as we shall discuss with reference to religious education. In the 1930s, communism also spread among young Muslims, particularly those studying at the Great Madrasa in Skopje, as Mustafa Memić has shown.[19] During the inter-war period and the Second World War, politicisation went hand in hand with ethnicisation and the inclusion of a religious component. Albanianist mobilisations appeared, facilitating the establishment of Greater Albania in 1941. These mobilisations had different tendencies according to the balance of power in the different regions. A Turkist mobilisation also appeared. This was the *Yücelciler*[20] movement, founded in Skopje in 1937, which counted many teachers in its ranks. This movement was started by a graduate at the al-Azhar University, from religious milieus in Macedonia, which viewed the Axis powers (not Turkey) as the only possible source of support for the Muslims. In those milieus Greater Albania was also regarded as a state capable of bringing all Balkan Muslims together so that they would no longer be a minority, if it proved impossible to re-establish Ottoman sovereignty. This heterogeneous movement, which subsequently re-orientated itself towards Turkey, would be suppressed by the Yugoslav communist authorities in 1947.

The works of Yannis Bonos and Anna Mirkova also provide a more socio-politically focused reading of the debates of the inter-war period.[21] For Thrace, Yannis Bonos emphasises the fact that each actor could use arguments drawn from different registers: a "reformist" could use a religious justification that would more usually be put forward by the "conservatives". Above all, and with regard to the alphabet issue for example, the notables (whose positions were not always clearly reported by the newspapers) sometimes preferred to remain neutral or adopt an intermediate position, depending on their interaction with other (Muslim or non-Muslim, local or non-local) actors active on the local socio-political scene. Anna Mirkova has shown that the dividing line between "Kemalists" and "old Turks" in Bulgaria cannot be clearly drawn. In her view, the opposition between the two groups resulted above all from different and competing ways of negotiating political affiliation, both among the Muslims themselves and between the Muslims and the Bulgarian state. In all cases, this citizenship was collective rather than individual. This contributed to the ethnicisation of the "minority". Nevertheless, from the end of the 1930s, this ethnicisation acquired another dimension, when Pomak activists proposed a new path linking Bulgarian identity and reform of Islam. The leaders of the *Rodina* association began to take Bulgarian names in 1940–41, asserting that names must relate to nationality and not to religion. During the war, it became compulsory for Pomaks to change name, including in the occupied territories. A law was passed on this issue in July 1942 and then enforced on the ground. According to Mary Neuburger, it was this campaign to change names, and also a change to the dress code and to elements of housing, that have sometimes wrongly been seen as a forced conversion campaign.[22] These highly coercive measures did, however, produce reactions of various kinds on the part of the Pomaks. Some Bulgarian-speaking or Turkish-speaking Muslims holding official positions nevertheless chose to partially Bulgarianise their names (to Ahmedov, for example).

Once again, because of its Muslim majority, Albania was different. Political conflict, nation-building, and the construction of citizenship were not expressed here in terms of opposition between "reformers" on the one hand, and "conservatives" or "reactionaries" on the other. It is true that, once he became king, Zog launched a series of reforms, including reforms of Islam (reformation of the Islamic institutions in 1929, abolition of the sharia courts in 1929, a ban on the veil in 1937). However, the main opposition to his authority was not perceived as religious. Rather, it was denounced as "Bolshevik". Moreover, Muslim reformist circles were close to the authorities. In 1937, the king ordered that religious classes be re-introduced to schools. He did so to avoid future generations being attracted by communism and to reinforce their loyalty to him. Although in 1938 he married a (non-Muslim) Hungarian countess, he strengthened the image of his dynasty by building mosques, the most important of which was the new mosque in Durrës, which bore his name.

A Balkan Islam within new networks

From a more specifically religious perspective, the inter-war period saw significant changes. These changes were linked to local circumstances and also to changes in Islam outside the Balkan Peninsula, and the fact that some Balkan Muslims became members of new transnational networks.

Following the ban on brotherhood activities in Turkey in 1925, the Balkan Sufi networks continued to become regionalised, a process that had first appeared in the nineteenth century in some regions, without becoming generalised. Some level of personal contact still continued between Balkan Sufis and Turkish Sufis, as evidenced by the correspondence of Hafiz Abdullah Zëmblaku, a very active ulama in the Korçë region, with his Naqshbandi teacher in Istanbul. Indeed, some Sufi networks were even strengthened by the arrival of spiritual leaders who had left Turkey, the most notable being the last *dede-baba*, head of the Bektashi brotherhood, who, as we have seen, arrived in Albania in 1930. Other Bektashi *baba*s also settled in southern Yugoslavia (where they had difficulties establishing themselves) and in Albania. One example is Selman Cemali Baba, whom John Kingsley Birge, author of a contemporary monograph on the brotherhood, met in Elbasan in the early 1930s.[23] The Sufi networks also developed in some regions of the Balkan Peninsula as the result of local dynamics. For example, the very orthoprax Tijani brotherhood, which had been introduced in Shkodër in the 1910s by a local ulama returning from the pilgrimage to Mecca, experienced significant success among men of religion and traders in the northern Albanian metropolis, and then in central Albania (Tirana, Durrës) where their spiritual master Qazim Hoxha practised. Halveti networks also experienced some growth in the south of the country thanks to the efforts of certain shaykhs. In the regions of today's Macedonia, on the other hand, some networks were weakened as spiritual leaders and disciples left for Turkey.

The closure of the madrasas in Turkey brought about a re-orientation of the secondary and higher religious educational networks, which now focused inwards or towards Cairo, or even towards "Europe", without severing all links with Turkey.

In Bulgaria, the opening of an establishment for the training of cadis and muftis, which had been provided for in the protocol signed by Bulgaria and the Ottoman Empire in 1913, was again included in the 1919 Regulation. That school, called the School for Cadis (*medrese-i nüvvab*), opened in Šumen in 1922. It would stay open until 1947, when it was converted to a secondary school. Altogether 677 students graduated during its time as a school for cadis and muftis. The curriculum was that of a secondary school, with the addition of religious subjects. Students therefore studied Arabic, Turkish (language and literature), Bulgarian (language and literature), mathematics and physics, Bulgarian history and geography, religious sciences, Bulgarian law, administrative law and civil law. A higher education section was also established in 1930 based on the model of al-Azhar, one of the principal teachers being Shaykh Yusuf Ziyaeddin Ezheri, who graduated from al-Azhar in 1904. A pupil of Muhammad Abduh and son of a Cherkess family in Düzce in Anatolia, he had also been taught by various ulamas and Sufis in Istanbul. He arrived in Bulgaria during the First World War, thanks to the Naqshbandi network of Ahmed Ziyaeddin Gümüşhanevi. During the inter-war period, he contributed significantly to the spreading of the reformist current among Bulgarian Muslims through his teachings, sermons, writings in the press and published works. His approach combined *tafsir* (Quranic exegesis) with the study of the traditions relating to the hadiths (the deeds and sayings of the Prophet). Cairo was not just a model adapted to the Bulgarian situation, however, since in the late 1930s some graduates from the *medrese-i nüvvab* attended the al-Azhar university. They would in turn become teachers at the madrasa from 1940–41.

In July 1935, an article in a Bulgarian Turkish-language newspaper argued that the Šumen *medrese-i nüvvab* had been a model for other establishments of this type in Southeast Europe: in Skopje and Sarajevo in Yugoslavia and in Komotini/Gümülcine in Greece. One could add that the general madrasa in Tirana (which succeeded the Higher Madrasa founded in 1924 and became the only establishment in the country for training religious leaders) was an establishment of the same type, though without the higher education section. Local establishments were opened and curricula introduced in the inter-war period, in order to train religious leaders, who were not only trained in religious sciences but also in general and national culture. However, these schools did not wholly do away with the traditional madrasa approach in which a teacher transmits knowledge of learned works to students. Nor did they prevent young Muslims from attending other, non-religious establishments. In Bosnia-Herzegovina, for example, a Muslim secondary school called the Sharia Academy (*Šerijatska Gimnazija*) was opened in 1918, and the school for cadis (*Šerijatska Sudačka Škola*), founded in the Austro-Hungarian period, was converted in 1937 into a Higher Islamic School of Sharia Law and Theology (*Viša Islamska Šerijatsko-Teološka Škola*). Yet more than fifteen "traditional" madrasas continued to exist, and it was only in 1939 that four reformed madrasas were set up in Sarajevo, Tuzla, Travnik and Bihać.

In the same way as tensions arose around education in the wider sense, others surfaced with regard to the training of religious leaders. In Skopje, the principal city of "South Serbia", for example, the Yugoslav authorities set up the Great Madrasa (*Velika medresa*) in 1924 to train young Muslims in a "modern" and "Western" way. However, the classes—delivered in Serbo-Croatian—dealt only marginally with religion and Islamic sciences. As a result, this establishment was more of a Muslim secondary school and mainly attracted Slavic-speaking Muslims from "South Serbia". In the 1930s, it became not just a centre of modern approaches but also a centre for the dissemination of communism. The pious Muslims of the region largely boycotted the Great Madrasa. From 1923–4, some preferred to send their children to the Meddah madrasa, a private establishment founded by two local ulamas, Ataullah Kurtish and Abdülfettah

Rauf, on the Ottoman model of the Fatih madrasa. From 1932 onwards, religious reformists sought to have a new public establishment opened that would come closer to the model of the reformed madrasas. Eventually such a school, which placed greater emphasis on religious subjects, was opened in 1936 under the name Isa bey madrasa.

In Tirana, the issue of training religious leaders also produced tensions from 1924–5. The reformists who dominated the Islamic institutions wanted to create a higher education madrasa and reform some existing madrasas, such as the one in Shkodër. The neo-traditionalists objected to the curriculum which, in their opinion, left too little space for religious subjects. In 1929, the reformation of the Tirana madrasa was accompanied by the closure of all the local madrasas. However, private teaching continued. Moreover, some representatives of the neo-traditionalist currents, who initially opposed the reforms imposed by the religious and political authorities in Tirana, later became teachers in the new general madrasa, where they could influence the training received by the future religious leaders of the country and other places further afield.

Apart from the Šumen *medrese-i nüvvab*, none of the Balkan establishments mentioned above enabled young Muslims to receive a higher education in Islamic sciences. Those who desired such an education therefore had to continue their studies outside the region. As Istanbul was no longer an option, they headed for one of two centres: Lahore (at that time in British India, now in Pakistan) or Cairo.

Lahore was the centre of a Muslim proselytising movement, the Ahmadiyya, which was born in the late nineteenth century when Muslims were faced with Christian proselytising and Hindu revivalism. Founded by Muhammad Ali, the movement split into two groups: the Lahoris and the Qadianis. The former, who were less numerous, were a group of very active missionaries preaching the compatibility of Islam and modernity and seeking to improve the image that Muslims had of themselves. Lahori Ahmadis were active in Berlin and in London, where they ran mosques (they built the Berlin mosque) and published journals. In 1927, they entered into contact with the publishers of the Albanian Muslim Community's journal. A few years later, they suggested to the Albanian religious authorities that they send young people to complete their Islamic studies in Lahore. In 1934, two young graduates of the Tirana madrasa and one of their comrades left for Lahore. The following year they should have been joined by three others, but those three stopped in Cairo and remained there. At the time, the increasing number of attacks against Ahmadis—in particular the Qadianis who were regarded as heretics because of their belief that Muhammad Ali was a *müceddid* (renewer) and caliph—put sympathisers in a difficult position. It is also possible that the difficulty of adapting and the distance stopped the young Albanian Muslims from leaving for India. The first three students to receive grants to study in Lahore also ended up in Cairo, where they would be forced to renounce the "Ahmadi faith" in the early 1940s.

By disseminating abundant literature in English, German and Arabic, the Lahori-Ahmadiyya did nevertheless have an influence beyond the simple sending of students. In Albania in particular, where the Lahori Ahmadis sought to use the local Islamic institutions as a bridgehead for the whole region, leaders of the Muslim Community adopted the means of action suggested by the Ahmadis, publishing translations of their writings paid for by subscriptions, and distributing them free of charge. In the 1920s, a highly active independent man of religion called Hafiz Abdullah Zëmblaku was also contacted by the Lahori Ahmadis. Like the Ahmadis, with whom he exchanged literature and techniques for transcribing Arabic into the vernacular languages, he regarded himself as a missionary.

However, the actions of the Lahori Ahmadis did not only affect Albania. Muhammad Ali's translation of and commentary on the Quran was used as a basis for commentaries written in Turkey and Bosnia-Herzegovina. In Istanbul Ömer Riza Doğrul, an intellectual, drew very widely on Lahori Ahmadi literature to forge a "modern" Islam. His translation/commentary on the Quran entitled *The Commandments of God*, which appeared in 1934,[24] was then used by *Reis-ul-ulema* Džemaludin Čaušević and Muhamed Pandža to produce a translation and commentary in Serbo-Croatian. That publication caused a scandal on account of its Ahmadi tinge. Other less ambitious works by Ömer Riza Doğrul on Islam and the Quran, inspired by Ahmadi writings, were also translated into Albanian. The Ahmadi network also enabled relationships to be formed between the Muslims of Bosnia-Herzegovina and the small Muslim community in Czechoslovakia, through the Berlin mosque: Islamic literature from Sarajevo was sent to Prague, as were speakers.

Important as they were, in the late 1930s these Ahmadi connections seem to have taken second place to the links formed with Cairo, particularly as regards higher education networks. Increasing numbers of young graduates from the Balkan madrasas followed in the footsteps of their elders, such as Yusuf Ziyaeddin Ezheri or Džemaludin Čaušević, who had already chosen at the beginning of the century to move to Egypt from Istanbul in order to attend the lectures of the famous Muhammad Abduh. As a result, students from Bulgaria, Bosnia-Herzegovina, Greece, "South Serbia" and Albania enrolled at al-Azhar or at the University of Cairo. Their time there also brought them into contact with the Muslim Brotherhood, which was developing at the time under the leadership of Hasan al-Banna. The pan-Islamist Young Muslims organisation (*Mladi Muslimani*) was established in 1941 in Bosnia-Herzegovina along the lines of the Egyptian Young Muslims association (*Jamaat al-shuban al-muslimin*), with the assistance of the Association of Ulamas *el-Hidaje*. The Young Muslims organisation was close to the Muslim Brotherhood, but recruited primarily among non-religious students and secondary school pupils. New forms of activism—including youth or charitable associations—also emerged at that time in Albania, adopting the same model. More impersonal links involving mainly the ulamas also developed as a result of distribution of the Egyptian press, such as Rashid Rida's journal, *al-Manâr* ("The Lighthouse").

In addition to the students who travelled and the Islamic literature that was disseminated, membership of transnational networks also occurred through participation at pan-Islamic conferences organised during the inter-war period. No representative of the Balkan Islamic institutions was present at the Congress of the Caliphate held in Cairo in 1926. However, representatives of the Balkan countries were present at the Congress of Jerusalem in 1931 and at the Congress of Geneva in 1935. Only the representatives of Albanian Muslim institutions were prevented from attending by the political authorities. The Geneva congress, called the "European Muslim Congress", was organised by Shakib Arslan, an activist of Syrian origin, who published the newspaper *La nation arabe* ("The Arab Nation") in Geneva. Between 1932 and 1936, Shakib Arslan's network extended into Southeast Europe; he himself made several journeys in the region, particularly in Yugoslavia and Hungary. In addition, his newspaper reprinted a series of articles on Islam in the countries of East and Southeast Europe previously published by the Bosnian Muslim Smail Aga Ćemalović (Tchémalovitch) in the journal *L'Europe de l'Est et du Sud-Est* ("East and Southeast Europe") in Paris. These articles were included in many periodicals in different languages. Another Arab activist with whom Balkan Muslims were in contact, particularly during the

Second World War, was Amin al-Husayni, the mufti of Jerusalem and main organiser of the Congress of Jerusalem in 1931. In the late 1930s, al-Husayni made common cause with the Third Reich against British, French and Soviet imperialisms, taking refuge in Germany in 1941. There he used his personal contacts with some influential Muslim notables to support Nazi propaganda in Southeast Europe, and played an active part in the creation of the Bosnian Muslim SS division *Handžar*.

In addition to the pan-Islamism and anti-imperialism of these Arab activists whom the representatives of the Balkan Muslims met in search of support for their own minority cause, there was also the attraction of the idea of a "European Islam"—or an "Islam in Europe"—that Shakib Arslan proposed. For the latter, who had been educated in Christian missionary schools, a synthesis needed to be developed in Muslim schools between Islam and modernity, so that Muslims would be at the same level as their Christian co-citizens.

"European Islam", "modern Islam" and local practices

Shakib Arslan's desire to construct a "European Islam"—well before the end of the twentieth century—was in several ways similar to that of some Balkan Muslims. This notion of "European Islam" or rather "Islam in Europe" appeared above all in Albania, the only state where the Muslims were not in a minority. Elsewhere, it could be discerned in the debates on the reform and modernisation of Islam, or on the compatibility of Islam with progress and science. To a certain extent, even though they formed a majority of the population in their country, the Albanian Muslims considered themselves to be in danger, surrounded by "peoples of culture", who were more "educated" and more "civilised"; as a result, they feared for their sovereignty. As in Turkey, some of them had a "civilisational obsession", to use the expression of Hamit Bozarslan.[25] Thus, in 1927, the director general of the waqfs, Salih Vuçitern, enjoined his co-religionists to awaken, because in the civilised world only those who awakened and progressed could survive. For others, who were more radical, such as the lay intellectual and senior official Mehdi Frashëri, it was necessary to reform Islam—to settle the question of Muslim women, to allow intellectuals to access the sources of Islam without intermediaries, to transform the system of religious education, to change the form of prayers—so that Albanians could be included among the "European peoples". Similar arguments were used by young intellectuals in 1935–7 to criticise the veil. In their view, in order to make Albania a European state—which they thought logical because of the country's geographical position—it was necessary to abolish the veil, because it presented foreigners with a poor image of the country and prevented the emancipation of women. When the Albanian government passed a law abolishing the veil in 1937, it was the question of image that carried the day. In fact, the authorities asked local administrators to act prudently when enforcing the law, in order to avoid clashes with the population. The image of Albanian Islam was also forged by emphasising Bektashism, thereby continuing the strain of thought used before 1912 to legitimise the existence of an Albanian nation. Thus, the authorities took important visitors to the Bektashi *tekke* of Fushë-Krujë. In 1928, one of them, the orientalist Franz Babinger, published an account of his visit.[26]

However, presenting a certain image to non-Albanians was not the only motivation for reforming Islam or encouraging certain of its forms. The reformers, both lay and religious, and even the neo-traditionalists, were convinced that in order to reassert the value of Islam it was necessary to change the methods by which it was conveyed, to eliminate *bid'a* ("bad innovation"), superstitions, and to change the place of women in Muslim society. Yusuf Ziyaeddin Ezheri, who played an important role in the *medrese-i nüvvab* in Šumen, was convinced that it was necessary to follow the European example in the Islamic sciences, on which the works of Western orientalists had already had a major influence. At the same time, the secularisation of the Balkan societies also affected Muslims, especially in the towns. Various dynamics were therefore at work, transforming or maintaining day-to-day local Islamic practices. It is difficult to ascertain precisely how those practices evolved, for most available sources are reformist or ethnographic discourse. The reformist discourse denounced the practices they were combating and wished to reform, often drawing on caricature to do so, or else presented the situation as having evolved in accordance with their wishes. The ethnographic discourse presented Islam only in terms of "popular" beliefs and rituals and did not provide any information about the evolution of Islamic thought in intellectual milieus or about religious practices among neo-traditionalists.

It would, for example, be a mistake to look in the statutes of the Albanian Bektashi Community, drawn up following the three congresses, for a description of the life of the Bektashi brotherhood at the time. In reality, there was quite a difference between these regulations and day-to-day practice, including with regard to relations between the local and national religious authorities. In fact, the national authority put in place did not really challenge the relations between the spiritual leader and his disciples at the local level. When two spiritual leaders with different profiles—one having studied in a secondary school and the other not—were in a dispute over the management of the *tekke* in Melçan, near Korçë, the majority of the disciples expressed their support for the *baba* with the traditional profile. They even rejected the authority of the supreme leader of the brotherhood when he arrived from Turkey. In their view, they were entitled to choose their spiritual master, since they themselves had contributed to the building of the *tekke*. This did not prevent Bektashism from taking new forms for some spiritual masters and for some disciples, particularly through the use of books and the press. Their numbers were, however, limited.

Nor do the debates over the issue of Muslim women allow us to measure accurately the changes in women's religiosity and practices. In addition to the measures concerning the ban on wearing the veil taken in Albania and Bulgaria in the late 1930s, we must take account of the social changes experienced by the Balkan urban populations, which also affected Muslims, albeit to a lesser degree. These changes were brought about by the development of non-religious education and new forms of sociability. This led to changes in gender relations and the emancipation of some women. In Bosnia-Herzegovina, for example, associations favoured the education of girls, maintained boarding schools for them, supported vocational education, and provided them with grants. As a result, some young Muslim women from Bosnia-Herzegovina even went to university. In addition, the secularisation of everyday life occurred through public events (theatre performances, festivals, dances) where both sexes had the opportunity to meet. However, as Fabio Giomi has shown, this emancipation remained limited and was always highly paternalist, even when it was driven by feminist associations.[27]

The studies published by orientalists in journals such as *Oriente moderno* ("The Modern East") or *La revue des études islamiques* ("The Journal of Islamic Studies") focus mainly on the normative aspects of Islam. This is the case with the analyses produced by George-Henri Bousquet, professor of law at the University of Algiers, on the subject of the reforms of

Islam in Albania and of Islamic law in Yugoslavia.[28] The articles of Protestant missionaries (Samuel M. Zwemer, Edwin Jacques) or those of Smail Aga Ćemalović, which we have mentioned previously, were more subjective. However, they rarely looked at practices.

Those practices, or rather some of them, were described at the time by local teachers, who published in pedagogical journals. They were concerned, to a certain extent, with denouncing superstitions, as evidenced by the titles of their articles. Professional and amateur ethnographers also took an interest in "popular" practices. In Yugoslavia, in particular, several works provide us with detailed—although often not very analytical—information about the beliefs, practices and rituals that could be observed at the time. From field work carried out in the eastern part of Yugoslavia (Serbia and "South Serbia") in particular, Tihomir Đorđević produced two comprehensive surveys. These works, which dealt not only with Muslims, were *Our Popular Life* in ten volumes[29] and *The Evil Eye in the Beliefs of the Southern Slavs*.[30] Two amateur ethnographers and orientalists with a good knowledge of the field also left important accounts: Gliša Elezović, born in "South Serbia", who based his work extensively on his contacts with the shaykh Saduddin Sirri, at the time head of the Rifai *tekke* in Skopje; and Muhamed Garčević, born in Bosnia-Herzegovina, himself a member of the religious milieus.[31] Muhamed Garčević's career is interesting: born in Bosnia-Herzegovina, he emigrated as a child with his family to Adapazar, in Anatolia, around 1905. There he studied in the local madrasas and with various teachers. However, in 1925, following the closure of the madrasas and *tekke*s, his family undertook the journey back to Bosnia-Herzegovina.

While these studies did not look at the practices and beliefs that existed around the mosques and in some intellectual circles, they do throw light on the presence of the mystical brotherhoods in today's Kosovo and Macedonia (Halveti, Rifai, Kadiri, Shazili, Melami, etc.). In particular, they provide much information on the magical rituals and practices that were extremely common among both the Muslims and their non-Muslim neighbours. For example, Tihomir Đorđević wrote:

> Among the Turks [read: Muslims], there is a deeply-rooted custom when they experience ill-fortune and in particular when they experience illness. This is to visit the *hoca*s and ask them to find a solution in their books. The *hoca*s help in different ways, including, very often, by means of talismans. The talismans are very varied and demand particular attention. I present here what I have

learned [on this subject] to encourage others to study these matters, not only among the Turks [the Muslims], but also among ourselves [the non-Muslims], where they are also very common and very varied. Christians as well as Turks go to the *hoca*s for help. In Niš, in the Belgrade neighbourhood [*u Beograd mahali*], there was a *hoca* to whom people suffering misfortune came seeking a remedy from as far away as Aleksinac and even from more distant regions.[32]

Magical rituals provided very important points of contact between Muslims and Christians and were performed by specialists. These specialists were the *hoca*s, who were imams or other men of religion, sometimes—but not necessarily—with a high level of education. Often, but not always, they were shaykhs and dervishes of various brotherhoods. Women were also sought out to perform some particular rituals. As Đorđević emphasised, the manufacture and use of amulets and talismans was probably the most common practice. Depending on the problem to be treated, the time and the person seeking help from the specialist, the latter would make a talisman designed to provide protection, cure an illness, resolve a problem, or fulfil a wish (such as becoming wealthy). The evil eye—which beliefs generally associated with envy—appears very frequently among the causes identified. Infants, children, cattle, homes and any other property all needed to be protected against the evil eye. Amulets could be made from objects invested with a magical power (horn, wolf's tooth, stone, etc.). However, they were often made from a talisman written in Arabic characters, with different phrases taken from the Quran, names and attributes of Allah, names of angels or magic squares. Quranic text on amulets was used in a literal sense and the numerical value of the letters of the Arabic alphabet was often played with. The talisman's magical power also worked thanks to the precise ways in which it was used (fumigation, dissolving in water which was then drunk, the way it was worn on the body) and the prayers and formulae that accompanied it.

These magical practices were in no way specific to the Balkan Muslims. Divination and the solving of problems by lead (molten lead was poured into water and the specialist analysed the shapes produced) was very common in Turkey, for example. Nor does the less common ritual of *dâ'ira* or summoning of *jinn*s (invisible spirits with supernatural powers), described in detail by Muhamed Garčević, seem to be specific to Southeast Europe. This ritual involved summoning *jinn*s on a reflective surface through a medium (a child), in the middle of a circle (*dâ'ira*).

As for the magical practices associated with Saint George (*Đurđev dan*; in Turkish: *Hidrellez*), celebrated on 6 May and symbolising the start of summer, they too were widely shared with Turkey. The feast was the occasion for spring-cleaning houses, *tekke*s, etc., and moving from winter rooms into summer rooms. It was also the time when people could protect themselves or make wishes for the "new year" (particularly to wish for a child). The associated rituals—for example, going to bathe in running water at dawn—were not very Islamicised, however.

The reformist religious elites fought in vain against these very widespread magical practices. Following the establishment of the communist regimes at the end of the Second World War, efforts to combat them would be increased further.

4

FROM THE ADVENT OF COMMUNISM TO ITS FALL

(1944—1989)

Between Cold War and nationalist fervour

For some countries of Southeast Europe, the human consequences of the Second World War were particularly grave: 1,000,000 dead in Yugoslavia (6 per cent of the total population), 600,000 in Greece (8 per cent), 30,000 in Albania (2.5 per cent). In Romania and Bulgaria, losses represented a lower percentage of the population. There were also contrasting political–military situations at the end of the war: Romania and Bulgaria, which had joined the Allies only in the summer of 1944, were occupied by the Red Army, while Yugoslavia and Albania were in the hands of the triumphant partisans. Drawing inspiration from the Soviet model, the Yugoslav Communist Party created a new Yugoslavia comprising six republics (Slovenia, Croatia, Bosnia-Herzegovina, Serbia, Montenegro and Macedonia), as well as two autonomous entities (Vojvodina and Kosovo) in Serbia (see Map 8). Alongside the "historical" Serbian, Croatian and Slovenian nations, this Yugoslav federation recognised the Macedonian and Montenegrin nations, as well as several national minorities (including the Albanians in Kosovo, Macedonia and Montenegro, and the Hungarians in Vojvodina). Finally, Greece also had a powerful partisan movement. However, that movement came up against the

British troops who landed in October 1944 to support the monarchy. Thus, in 1945 a new geopolitical order stemming from of the upheavals of the war was already taking shape.

Where they had the support of a strong partisan movement or where the Red Army was present as a dissuasive influence, the communist parties succeeded in monopolising power within a few years. While the techniques they used to do this varied from one country to another, there were some constants: taking control of the security apparatus, incorporating part of the non-communist political forces within the popular fronts linked to the Communist Party, ostracising and gradually eliminating the opposition. The abolition of the monarchy was voted through in Yugoslavia (November 1945), Albania (January 1946), Bulgaria (September 1946) and Romania (December 1947), opening the way for people's republics inspired by the Soviet model. In the name of the "dictatorship of the proletariat", the communist parties then became single parties, the population was controlled by various mass organisations and all political opposition was harshly suppressed. The only Balkan country that did not join the Soviet bloc was Greece, where civil war led to 60,000 deaths between August 1946 and August 1949. The Greek Democratic Army (*Dimokratikos Stratos Elladas*—DSE), led by the Communist Party, was eventually defeated by the monarchist forces supported by Great Britain and the United States. Greece was thus left as the only constitutional monarchy in Southeast Europe; there was a degree of political pluralism, but the left suffered from ostracism associated with memories of the civil war. The partition of Southeast Europe between the two blocs that arose out of the Cold War was then exemplified by Greece and Turkey joining the North Atlantic Treaty Organisation (NATO) in 1952, and by Albania, Bulgaria and Romania joining the Warsaw Pact in 1955.

However, unlike in Central Europe, the logic of the Cold War was quickly thwarted in Southeast Europe by political developments specific to some Balkan countries, and by the reactivation of regional conflicts that had not been completely extinguished. In fact, in 1948, a series of political disagreements led to an open breach between Yugoslavia and the Soviet Union. Under the leadership of Josip Broz-Tito, the undisputed leader of the Yugoslav state until his death in 1980, Yugoslavia then set out to build its own model of socialism. The Communist Party— renamed the League of Communists in 1952—allowed Yugoslav intellectuals and artists a degree of creative freedom; however, all political

FROM THE ADVENT OF COMMUNISM TO ITS FALL

Map 8: Southeast Europe during the Cold War

opposition remained banned and the single-party principle was not questioned. Moreover, from the 1960s onwards, Yugoslavia experienced significant decentralisation symbolised by the new constitutions of 1963 and 1974. Most power was transferred to the republics and the autonomous provinces, with Marshal Tito and the army remaining the sole guarantors of the country's unity. In this context, asserting the different national identities that coexisted within the federation became one of the preferred tools used to legitimise the republican and provincial elites, to the detriment of a common Yugoslav project. This phenomenon was best illustrated by the recognition of a Muslim nation by the League of Communists of Bosnia-Herzegovina in 1968, and the points of agreement between the leaders of the League of Communists of Croatia and different nationalist actors at the time of the "Croatian Spring" in 1971. The Albanian demonstrations that broke out in Kosovo in 1968 and then again in 1981, seeking to have the autonomous province made a republic, were an example of how this assertion of national identities threatened the institutional balance of the Yugoslav federation.

While Yugoslavia left the Soviet bloc at a very early stage and participated in the creation of the Non-Aligned Movement in 1961, the other communist states of Southeast Europe evolved in differing ways. In 1948, Albania's communist leaders took advantage of the breach between Tito and Stalin to free the country from the control of neighbouring Yugoslavia. Then, rejecting the de-Stalinisation started by the Soviet Union in 1956, they broke with the Soviet Union and aligned themselves with China. However, this Sino-Albanian relationship ended in 1976 and Albania set itself up as the "besieged fortress" of a pure, hard-line communism. Romania and Bulgaria remained in the Warsaw Pact, but in the 1960s and 1970s Romania displayed stirrings of independence, while Bulgaria was seen as a "model pupil" of the Soviet bloc.

Despite these different political trajectories resulting from the death of Stalin and de-Stalinisation, the communist regimes of Southeast Europe had some common characteristics. Firstly, they were dominated by strong leaders backed by the apparatus of communist dictatorship: this was the case in Albania with Enver Hoxha, in power for four decades (1945–85), in Bulgaria with Todor Živkov (1962–89), in Romania with Gheorghe Gheorghiu-Dej (1952–65) and then Nicolae Ceauşescu (1965–89), and last but not least, in Yugoslavia with Marshal Tito (1945–80). Secondly, as the attraction of the communist project faded, these regimes increasingly used nationalism to legitimise themselves in the eyes of their populations. Unlike multinational Yugoslavia, Albania, Bulgaria and Romania were nation-states within which the dominant national group was in a large majority. However, in each of these three countries, nationalism took a form that reflected certain particular traits of their national construction. In Albania, where the Albanian nation was multi-denominational, exacerbation of nationalist sentiment took the form of an anti-religious campaign, in particular, culminating in a complete ban on religion in 1967. In Bulgaria and Romania, the national minorities were the first victims of the political use of nationalism, as seen in the "revival process" launched by the Bulgarian authorities in 1984 aimed at achieving the complete assimilation of the Turkish minority, and the campaign of "systematisation" of Romanian villages launched in 1988, which sought among other things to facilitate the assimilation of the Hungarian minority. Nationalism was used in a similar way in Serbia in the late 1980s, when the new strong man of the League of Communists of Serbia, Slobodan Milošević, exploited the discontent of the Serbs of Kosovo to reduce the autonomy of that province in 1989. This provoked new Albanian demonstrations, which were brutally suppressed by the police and the army.

While the concept of "Soviet bloc" in Southeast Europe thus conceals diverse and unexpected political trajectories, the concept of "Western bloc" was just as fragile in the region. In fact, the Cold War period also saw a reactivation of the conflict between Greece and Turkey, both members of NATO. Indeed, the rising tensions between Greek and Turkish communities on the island of Cyprus, then a British colony, had repercussions for Greco-Turkish relations in their entirety. Violent anti-Christian riots in 1955 led to the departure of a significant part of the Greek population of Istanbul. The independence of Cyprus on 16 August 1960 did not quell the tensions, and the 1960s saw violent confrontations between the communities. In 1967, a military dictatorship was installed in Greece to prevent the left winning the elections. In order to reinforce their legitimacy, the putschists abolished the monarchy and proclaimed a republic in June 1973. In 1974, they supported an attempted *coup d'état* in Cyprus by supporters of the *enosis* (union) of Greece and Cyprus. Turkey reacted immediately: in July 1974, the Turkish army invaded the north of the island and expelled the Greek inhabitants. This Turkish military intervention resulted in a total of 6,000 deaths. In 1983, the Turkish territory that had been created by force proclaimed itself "Turkish Republic of Northern Cyprus". In Greece itself, the Cyprus crisis led to the return of democracy, with the New Democracy (*Nea Dimokratia*) party and the Socialist Party (*Panellinio Sosialistiko Kinima*—PASOK) dominating Greek political life thereafter. On 1 January 1981, after several years of negotiations, Greece became a member of the European Economic Community. For the first time, the process of European integration begun in the 1950s extended to Southeast Europe.

Authoritarian modernisation and anti-religious policies

The communist regimes' hold over the public sphere and their desire to interfere in the private lives of their citizens have led some analysts to describe them as totalitarian. However, the concept of 'totalitarianism' masks some essential realities of the communist countries. Firstly, it underestimates the population's capacity for adaptation and resistance; people always succeeded in rebuilding spaces of freedom outside the party's control, even though the countries of Southeast Europe did not experience the organised dissidence that occurred in Central Europe. Secondly, it ignores the fact that the communist regimes were also characterised by a desire for accelerated modernisation of society. This modernising enthusiasm manifested itself first of all in economic terms, with the communist period marking the end of the rural societies of Southeast Europe. From the late 1940s onwards, huge land collectivisation programmes were implemented in Albania, Bulgaria and Romania where, by the late 1980s, collectivised land accounted for 99, 90 and 84 per cent of land respectively. Only Yugoslavia, weakened by its breach with the Soviet Union, renounced the collectivisation of land in 1953, and Yugoslav agriculture remained largely one of small landowners. At the same time, the communist authorities nationalised industry, the craft and commerce sectors and encouraged the development of heavy industry. Many state factories and new industrial regions appeared throughout Southeast Europe. Between 1950 and 1990, the urban population as a percentage of total population increased from 26 to 51 per cent in Yugoslavia, from 28 to 65 per cent in Bulgaria, and from 25 to 54 per cent in Romania. Albania was the only partial exception to this rapid urbanisation, as the authorities there wished to retain a large rural population; the percentage accounted for by the urban population was only 36 per cent in 1990.

FROM THE ADVENT OF COMMUNISM TO ITS FALL

Collectivisation, nationalisation and industrialisation contributed to the elimination of the old elites and the emergence of new ones with close links to the communist parties. More generally, these processes were part of the endeavour of the communist authorities to reshape and modernise their societies "from above". For the authoritarian modernisation of Balkan societies at this time was not restricted to the economy. The communist countries developed education in the first place, succeeding in eliminating illiteracy and greatly increasing the number of students completing secondary and higher education. At the same time, elaborate systems of social security and welfare, the first paid holidays, the first mass leisure activities, and even a fledgling socialist consumer society were put in place, despite the chronic shortages and deficits suffered by local economies. Thus, for the inhabitants of the Balkan countries, the communist period was not always a byword for oppression and privation. In the countryside, this period was also one in which roads were tarred, electricity arrived in the villages, and schools and community clinics were built. In the towns it was a period of material security and social progress, access to education and leisure activities, and individualisation of the way of life. Finally, for women, the communist period was one of relative emancipation, with mass access to education and paid work, reform of the civil codes and legalisation of abortion. The realities of communism and post-communism cannot be understood without taking these significant social and cultural transformations into account.

From the development of the road network to the expansion of the education system, from the rural exodus to the circulation of the elites, communist modernisation explains the weakening of parochial and provincial identities and the strengthening of national ones. However, while this nationalisation of the Balkan societies represented a continuation of the changes that had occurred in the first half of the twentieth century, the communist religious policies represented a radical break with those of previous periods. In fact, for the communist parties in power, religion was a sign of backwardness and as such had to be opposed. In the first decade after the war, all the communist regimes of Southeast Europe therefore adopted a similar attitude, confiscating the property of the religious institutions, excluding them from the education system and banning their youth movements and charitable organisations. Religious officials who were guilty of collaboration during the Second World War or suspected of anti-communism were removed from office and, most often, replaced by other, more amenable, officials. At the same time, the communist parties supported atheism and sought to invent a socialist civil religion based on new commemorations and new rituals. It should, however, be noted that certain forms of cooperation were maintained between state and religious institutions: the latter continued to receive salaries and subsidies from the state and, paradoxically, saw their monopoly over religious life strengthened by state repression of non-institutional religious actors.

From the 1960s onwards, differences between the religious policies of the various communist states grew. In Yugoslavia, the pressure exerted on the religious institutions by the government was relaxed, and from then on, those institutions enjoyed a significant increase in activity and visibility. In Albania, on the contrary, the anti-religious campaigns of the Party of Labour (communist party) culminated in February 1967 with the closure of all places of worship, and on 22 November 1967 a ban on all religious activity. Finally, in Bulgaria and Romania, religious institutions struggled to survive despite a shortage of clerics and financial resources; there, religious life was restricted to the private sphere. In all cases, authoritarian modernisation and anti-religious policies combined to bring about the expulsion of religion from the public sphere, a marked reduction in religious practice and a secularisation of society. However, the limits of this secularisation could be glimpsed through the persistence of some individual or informal religious practices. Here Greece was once again an exception: the Orthodox religion occupied a central place in the public sphere and the Greek Orthodox Church was part of the state apparatus, with priests having the status of civil servants. Yet even in Greece the level of religious practice declined from the 1960s onwards, and the Orthodox Church's support for the military dictatorship weakened its legitimacy. After the return of democracy in 1974 and PASOK's arrival in power in 1981, certain reforms challenging the Church's privileges were implemented, such as the introduction of civil marriage in 1982 and the nationalisation of ecclesiastical property in 1987. However, the plan to separate church and state, envisaged by some, was abandoned.

Following Greece's entry into the European Economic Community, in the 1980s it experienced accelerated modernisation. The communist countries of Southeast Europe, on the contrary, suffered a rapid deterioration in their economic situation and a deep crisis of political legitimacy. At the same time, the 1980s were for the whole region—and, beyond that, for the whole of Europe—a period in which religious activity increased and religious actors re-entered the public sphere. This was true in Greece, where the Orthodox Church used its central place in the Greek national identity to protect its privileges. It was even more so in Yugoslavia, where religion served to express the divisions between the south Slavic nations. Thus, the alleged appearance of the Virgin in 1981 in Medugorje, in Bosnia-Herzegovina, led to mass gatherings of the Catholic faithful. In the following years, the Catholic Church increasingly adopted the role of mouthpiece for the Croatian nation. In 1982, the Serbian Orthodox Church aligned itself with the Serbs of Kosovo, protesting against their fate in that Albanian-majority province, and in 1989 it participated in the official celebrations of the 600th anniversary of the Battle of Kosovo. In Bulgaria and Romania, the Orthodox Churches remained subject to the communist regime; however, in Romania, priests and believers of minority denominations (Uniates, Protestants, etc.) joined the ranks of a nascent opposition. Finally, in Albania, some timid alterations were made to the regime's anti-religious policy and, from 1988 onwards, imprisoned religious officials were released and public religious figures such as Mother Teresa, born into an Albanian family in Macedonia, were welcomed by the official authorities. The last decade of the Cold War was thus characterised by religious changes that, without cancelling out the effects of the secularisation of the preceding decades, foretold the future transformations to religious life and to the relationship between religious identity and national identities.

Different ways in which national identities crystallised

The Muslims of Southeast Europe were not immune to the changes that the region experienced during the Cold War. In the communist countries, in particular, their confrontation with the modernising fervour of the new regimes was all the more of a shock given that the previous regimes had often reinforced their social and cultural conservatism. In Yugoslavia, Albania, Bulgaria and Romania, the traditional Muslim elites linked to the land, to trade and to crafts were wiped out by the post-war collectivisation and nationalisation. In the cultural domain too, the process of authoritarian modernisation took particular forms for the Muslims, Islam often being regarded by the communist regimes as the principal cause of the "backwardness" of the Muslim populations. Thus, in Albania, the ban on the veil dating from 1937 was strictly enforced by the new authorities. In Yugoslavia, the desire to emancipate Muslim women led to the abolition of the sharia courts in 1946 and to a ban on the veil in 1950. Likewise in Bulgaria, the communist regime confirmed in 1945 the abolition of the sharia courts decided in 1938, and at the beginning of the 1950s launched an intense campaign against the wearing of the veil and the *şalvar* (baggy trousers). These campaigns were resumed in 1980 with the "revival process". Greece was therefore the only Southeast European country in which the Muslim economic and political elites experienced a degree of continuity, and in which the legal status and dress codes of Muslim women were not overturned by the political authorities.

However, during the following decades, modernisation (including dress) gained ground in Western Thrace as well. In the communist countries, Muslims gradually seized the opportunities offered by communist modernisation and left agriculture to work in industry and the service sector, sent boys and girls to the public schools and adopted socialist lifestyles. This social and cultural modernisation of the Muslim populations explains why, in Bosnia-Herzegovina, Albania and Romanian Dobruja, marriages between Muslims and non-Muslims became markedly more frequent among the urban elites and in some sectors of the working class. Such marriages remained the exception in the rural milieu and, more generally, in Kosovo, Macedonia, Bulgaria and Greece. At the same time, increasing educational attainment was found everywhere, including Greece, with an increase in the number of Muslim men and women working as teachers, doctors, engineers or in other professions linked to the modernisation of Balkan societies.

Against this backdrop the new Muslim elites (in the sociological sense of the term) played an ever more important role within certain communist parties, as shown by the available statistics. In Bosnia-Herzegovina the proportion of Muslims in the League of Communists progressed from 20 per cent in 1946 to 35 per cent in 1984,[1] whilst in Kosovo the proportion of Albanians rose from 30 per cent in 1945 to 65 per cent in 1978.[2] Certain cadres from the Muslim cultural sphere were appointed to the highest positions of state: for example Enver Hoxha, who was president of Albania from 1945 until his death in 1985; Mahmut Bakalli, who was secretary to the League of Communists of Kosovo from 1971 to 1981; and Hamdija Pozderac, who assumed numerous positions of responsibility within the Republic of Bosnia-Herzegovina and the Yugoslav federation between 1965 and 1987.[3] From the 1960s onwards, these elites played an essential role in the secularisation of Muslim populations and in the crystallisation of their respective national identities. However, before considering this political dimension of the modernisation of the Balkan Muslim populations, we must look at the demographic changes in these populations between 1945 and 1990.

As in the previous periods of war, the end of the Second World War was marked in Southeast Europe by the violent expulsion of some national minorities. These included 25,000 Çams from Epirus, who were Muslims and Albanian-speakers, victims of significant massacres and expelled to Albania by the Greek authorities in 1944. While the Çams were the only Muslims of Southeast Europe to be forcibly displaced at the end of the Second World War, in the 1950s other Balkan Muslim populations experienced massive migrations in dramatic circumstances. This was particularly so in 1950–51, when Bulgaria expelled to Turkey some 150,000 Turks who were hostile to collectivisation and nationalisation. Another striking instance occurred between 1953 and 1957 when Yugoslavia, after signing an emigration agreement with Turkey, allowed some 200,000 Muslims, mainly Turkish-speaking and Albanian-speaking Muslims from Macedonia, Kosovo and Sanjak, to leave for Turkey. Subsequent Balkan Muslim migrations were smaller and, above all, less dramatic. Despite the administrative obstacles, several tens of thousands of Greek Muslims emigrated to Turkey. Between 1968 and 1978, Bulgaria allowed some 120,000 Turks to leave under a family reunification policy. In 1963, Yugoslavia reintroduced freedom of movement for its nationals. Eighteen years later, some 900,000 Yugoslav citizens were resident abroad, mainly in Western Europe and North America, including 60,000 Muslims from Bosnia-Herzegovina and Sanjak and 65,000 Albanians from Kosovo and Macedonia. Also, following a bilateral agreement between Greece and Germany in 1960, between 10,000 and 20,000 Muslims from Western Thrace emigrated to Germany. Thus, from the 1960s onwards, Balkan Muslim migrants ceased to converge on Turkey and turned towards the Western world. This major turning point in the history of Balkan Muslim migrations was another sign of their growing integration into European modernity.

The migrations of Balkan Muslims affected their absolute and relative numbers in the different Balkan states. However, to understand the demographic changes between 1945 and 1990, we must also take account of their natural population growth rate. Generally, the Muslims of Southeast Europe had an above average natural population growth rate. This was sometimes the result of a simple time-lag in their demographic transition, as in Albania, and sometimes reflected a more lasting trend, as in Bulgaria and Greece. The case of Yugoslavia is more complex, as the Muslims of Bosnia-Herzegovina gradually aligned their demographic behaviour with that of the Serbs and Croats; while the Albanians of Kosovo and Macedonia maintained a particularly high natural population growth rate throughout the whole of the communist period. These demographic behaviours specific to the Balkan Muslims are explained by the fact that they were often concentrated in rural and under-developed regions such as Kosovo, Western Macedonia and Sanjak in Yugoslavia and the Rhodopes in Bulgaria and Greece. There was another phenomenon at work in these regions: the accelerated emigration of local Christian populations, who had easier access to public-sector jobs in the developed urban centres. Consequently, at the regional level, the percentage of the population accounted for by Muslims continued to grow. It is this conjunction of a higher natural growth rate of the Muslim populations and higher emigration of the Christian populations, that explains, for example, why the percentage of the population of Kosovo accounted for by Albanians increased from 68.5 per cent in 1948 to 82.2 per cent in 1991, while the percentage accounted for by Serbs fell from 23.6 per cent to 10 per cent. This phenomenon was also to be found in Bosnia-Herzegovina, where the percentage of the population accounted for by Muslims rose from 34.5 per cent in 1948 to 43.7 per cent in 1991, and less spectacularly in Macedonia, where Albanians accounted for 17.1 per cent in 1948 and 21 per cent in 1991. In Bulgaria, on a national level, the waves of emigration to Turkey cancelled out the effect of a more rapid natural population growth rate, with Muslims continuing to account for around 12 per cent of the total Bulgarian population during the communist period. However, at the regional level, some regions populated by Muslims, such as the Rhodopes, also became increasingly homogeneous.

Finally, an additional factor influenced the distribution of Balkan Muslims among different national groups: the changes in national affiliation between one population census and the next, where those surveyed could choose between several national categories. Thus, the drop in the

FROM THE ADVENT OF COMMUNISM TO ITS FALL

Turks' share of the population in Macedonia—from 8.3 per cent in 1948 to 4.8 per cent in 1991—was due not only to their emigration to Turkey in the 1950s, but also to the gradual Albanianisation of the Turko-Albanian urban elites. Likewise in Romania, changes in identification took place between Tatars and Turks. In Bulgaria, the tendency of the Muslim Gypsies and the Pomaks to declare themselves to be "Turks" varied according to the region they lived in and over time. A similar phenomenon existed among the Pomaks and the Gypsies of Western Thrace, but cannot be observed in Greek population censuses, since these censuses do not include details about ethnic–national affiliation. In all cases, these changes in national affiliation reflected the nationalisation, and therefore the modernisation, of the Muslim populations of Southeast Europe. Above all, however, they reflected the different ways in which the national question was managed by the region's different states, which we must now examine in more detail.

Since Yugoslavia was a multinational state, it had the most complex attitude towards the national question. Generally, the Yugoslav communists drew to a significant degree on the Soviet model. This can be seen in the federal structure of the country and the recognition of the different constituent nations (*narodi*) and national minorities (*nacionalne manjine* or *narodnosti*). As far as the Muslim populations are concerned, it is necessary to distinguish the case of Bosnia-Herzegovina, where the Bosnian Muslims had to find their place among the south Slavic nations, from that of Kosovo and Macedonia, where the Albanians, more than 90 per cent of whom were Muslims (in the sociological sense of the term), lived alongside other Turkish-speaking, Roma-speaking and Slavic-speaking Muslims.

In Bosnia-Herzegovina, the central issue remained that of the national identification of the Bosnian Muslims. In a continuation of the national liberation struggle, the immediate post-war period was characterised by a partial recognition of their specific identity. Thus, a General Council of Muslims (*Glavni odbor muslimana*) was created in 1945, bringing together the notables supporting the Communist party, and the Muslim cultural society *Preporod* ("Revival") was established one year later to replace the pre-war cultural societies *Gajret* and *Narodna Uzdanica*. However, the General Council of Muslims ceased to exist in 1946, and the cultural society *Preporod* was dissolved in 1949. At the time, the Yugoslav communist leaders were of the opinion that, with the progress of modernisation, the Bosnian Muslims would gradually be led to identify themselves as Croats or Serbs of the Islamic faith. The then national identification of the communist leaders seems to prove them right since, according to David Dyker's calculations, 61.5 per cent of the Bosnian Muslims appearing in the Yugoslav *Who's Who* declared themselves to be of Serbian nationality, and 16.6 per cent of Croatian nationality.[4] However, this was not the case among the general Bosnian population; thus in 1948, 790,000 Bosnian Muslims declared themselves to be of "indeterminate" nationality, against only 70,000 who declared themselves "Serbs" and 25,000 who declared themselves "Croats". Five years later, 890,000 inhabitants of Bosnia-Herzegovina, of whom a huge majority were Bosnian Muslims, declared themselves "indeterminate Yugoslavs". In the 1950s, the nationalisation of the Bosnian Muslims called for by the communist leaders was therefore far from having been realised.

In the 1960s and 1970s, the increasing decentralisation of the Yugoslav political system and the emergence of new Muslim political and intellectual elites led the League of Communists of Bosnia-Herzegovina to reconsider radically the issue of national identification of the Bosnian Muslims. The "Muslim" (*Musliman*) national category, which had been discreetly introduced in the 1961 census, was officially recognised on 17 May 1968 by the League of Communists of Bosnia-Herzegovina. The League therefore decided not to recognise Bosnian Muslims under the national name of "Bosnian" (*Bosanac*) or "Bosniak" (*Bošnjak*), as doing so would have effected too close an identification between Bosnia-Herzegovina and Bosnian Muslims, thereby implicitly reducing Bosnian Serbs and Bosnian Croats to the status of national minorities. The solution adopted was to recognise Bosnian Muslims under the name "Muslim", which had the additional advantage of having being in common use since the end of the nineteenth century. However, this fed into certain ambiguities, in particular with regard to the nature of the link between national identity and religious identity. In order to remedy this, communist intellectuals and leaders emphasised the difference between "*Musliman*" with a capital "M", which designated only Serbo-Croatian-speaking Muslims living mainly in Bosnia-Herzegovina and in Sanjak, and "*musliman*" with a lower case "m", which was the religious name designating all Yugoslav citizens of the Islamic faith. However, this subtle distinction did not prevent many Torbesh from Macedonia, who were Macedonian-speaking Muslims, from declaring themselves to be "Muslims" (national name) in the population censuses.

FROM THE ADVENT OF COMMUNISM TO ITS FALL

Recognition of the Muslim nation did provoke some hostile reactions, in particular within the Leagues of Communists of Serbia and Macedonia. However, the "Muslim" national category had been extended to the whole of the Yugoslav territory by the time of the 1971 census, and the 1974 Constitution recognised Muslims (national name) as the sixth constituent nation of Yugoslavia. In Bosnia-Herzegovina itself, the exact status of the Muslim nation remained a source of uncertainty and tension. In fact, schools and cultural institutions in that republic were common to its three constituent nations: all the pupils in Bosnia-Herzegovina attended the same schools, and the Academy of Sciences of Bosnia-Herzegovina, founded in 1966, had Muslim, Serbian and Croatian members. In this context, some Muslim intellectuals demanded that specific cultural institutions be created for the Muslim nation, while others insisted on the specific features of the Bosnian Muslims' language and literature. These positions were generally condemned by the communist authorities, and from the late 1970s onwards denunciations of "Muslim nationalism" were increasingly frequent in Bosnia-Herzegovina. In the 1980s, they were taken up and amplified by the Belgrade press, which at that time was giving in to the lure of Serbian nationalism. Bosnia-Herzegovina then gradually became the crossroads for antagonistic national ambitions, with a Muslim community that had in the meantime become the largest constituent nation of that republic: in 1948, the Serbian community was the largest in Bosnia-Herzegovina in terms of numbers (41.5 per cent of the total population compared to 34.5 per cent Muslims and 23 per cent Croats); in 1991, the Muslim community was clearly the most numerous (43.7 per cent of the total population, compared to 31.4 per cent Serbs and 17.3 per cent Croats).

In Kosovo and Macedonia, the communist period was dominated by the issue of the Albanian population's political and cultural rights. In 1945, the new Yugoslav communist authorities clashed in Kosovo with the armed resistance of the National Front (*Balli Kombëtar*) and with several local revolts by the Albanian population. In the years that followed, they suppressed the nationalist and anti-communist Albanian National Democratic Movement (*Lëvizja Nacional Demokratike Shqiptare*—LNDSH). However, at the same time, communist Yugoslavia granted its Albanian population the status of national minority, and Kosovo became an autonomous region of Serbia. Albanian then became the second administrative language of Kosovo, an Albanian-language educational system was put in place, and a teacher-training institute was opened in 1958 in Prishtina to train Albanian teachers. Albanian cultural institutions were created and an Albanian-language press developed. However, Kosovo's autonomy remained limited in the first decades of the post-war period and its administration was dominated by Serbs. The Albanian population, suspected of irredentism, suffered unrelenting police repression. In Kosovo too, the Albanian minority had to wait until the 1960s and the emergence of new Albanian intellectual and political elites before it experienced wider changes. The 1963 and 1974 constitutions increased Kosovo's autonomy, elevating it to the status of autonomous province; the presence of Albanians in the provincial administration increased significantly; and the University of Prishtina, founded in 1970, produced a growing body of young Albanian graduates. Finally, at this time, several decisions encouraged closer cultural links between Albania and the Albanians of Yugoslavia: the unified Albanian language used in Albania was adopted in Yugoslavia, the Tirana authorities were involved in the preparation of school curricula, and the use of the Albanian flag was even authorised for certain official or family ceremonial occasions.

However, the improved political status of the Albanian minority did little to conceal the fact that Kosovo remained the least developed region of Yugoslavia. This fed the frustrations of the Albanian youth, who were increasingly educated but often unable to find employment, and many students took part in the Albanian demonstrations of November 1968. Finally, Kosovo's under-development explains the Albanians' high birth rate, Serbian emigration and the resulting imbalances. In the 1980s, these imbalances gradually developed into an open crisis. In March 1981, a few months after Tito's death, there were further demonstrations in Kosovo demanding that the autonomous province become a republic. The demonstrations were harshly suppressed and were followed by a marked deterioration in relations between Serbs and Albanians. During the following years, the Serbs of Kosovo, supported by the Orthodox Church, complained of the discrimination and pressure to which they were subjected. Slobodan Milošević made use of this wave of discontent to take over the leadership of the League of Communists of Serbia in September 1987, to remove the Albanian leaders of the League of Communists of Kosovo in November 1988, and to have constitutional amendments adopted in March 1989 that limited the autonomy of Kosovo. These latter measures provoked a wave of strikes and demonstrations in Kosovo, during which several dozen Albanian demonstrators were killed by the police and army. Thus, on the eve of the collapse of the communist regimes in Southeast Europe, this province was already one of the main crisis zones in the region.

In Macedonia, the Albanian population also enjoyed the status of national minority from 1945 onwards; Albanian was accorded the status of administrative language in the municipalities populated by Albanians, and primary and secondary schools teaching in Albanian were opened. However, compared to the Albanians of Kosovo, the level of education among the Albanians of Macedonia remained low, and their level of representation in the public sector was very low. This did not prevent the Macedonian authorities, frightened by growing Albanian nationalist claims in Kosovo, from closing some Albanian cultural institutions and some Albanian-language secondary schools in the second half of the 1980s. In this republic too, tensions grew between Orthodox Macedonians and Muslim Albanians.

Finally, if we are to understand the changes in the political status of the Muslim populations in Kosovo and Macedonia, we must remember that they were not ethnically homogeneous. In 1947, for example, the authorities in Macedonia harshly repressed the *Yücelciler*, a Turkish nationalist and religious movement. More generally, the Turkish-speaking, Roma-speaking and Slavic-speaking Muslims were squeezed between the assimilationist pressures of the Albanian community and the attempts at manipulation by the Serbian and Macedonian authorities. For example, the reduction in the number of Turks in Kosovo and Macedonia between 1948 and 1991 was partly due to the Albanianisation of the Turko-Albanian urban elites, as we have already shown. Conversely, the increase in the number of Muslims (in the national meaning of the term) reflects the reaction of small groups of Slavic-speaking Muslims, such as the Torbesh of Macedonia and the Goranis of Kosovo, to the recognition of the Muslim nation.[5] Quite soon, the Serbian and Macedonian authorities became concerned by the gradual Albanianisation of the non-Albanian-speaking Muslims and attempted to oppose it. To this end, in the 1970s, the Macedonian authorities supported cultural events arranged by Torbesh activists declaring themselves "Muslim Macedonians". During the following decade, the Serbian authorities sought to obtain the support of the Muslim, Gypsy and Turkish populations of Kosovo in order to create a counterweight to the Albanian demographic predominance and to reinforce the legitimacy of Serbian complaints. Likewise, the Macedonian authorities encouraged teaching in Turkish and in Romany. At the same time, some Gypsy activists started to encourage the assertion of a Roma national identity or, to a lesser extent, an "Egyptian" national identity.[6] In reality the Slavic-speaking, Roma-speaking and Turkish-speaking Muslims of Kosovo and Macedonia were reduced to the status of pawns in a game played by others, in which they had nothing to gain.

The situation in Albania was very different from that in Yugoslavia, as Albania was a relatively homogeneous country in national terms, although the Albanian nation there was multi-denominational. In the 1940s, the new regime fought against different nationalist and royalist guerrilla groups in the north of the country. While those groups did include Muslims, they were not made up of any particular religious community. In the following decades, the communist regime's efforts to strengthen the country's national cohesion resulted in the adoption in 1972 of a unified Albanian language, which was close to the Tosk dialect (Southern Albania), and in the rejection of religious differences, which went as far as an outright ban on religion in 1967. During the 1970s, this anti-religious policy even led the authorities to ban new-born infants being given forenames of a religious origin, and to change forenames and surnames that were not appropriate to the regime's atheist ideology. However, this management of the relations between national identity and religious identity only had specific consequences for the Albanian Muslims when it influenced the definition of the relations between Islam, the Ottoman legacy and Albanian national identity, or when it challenged the Islamic institutions; these two points are dealt with later in this chapter.

Initially, Bulgaria too drew inspiration from the Soviet model in the management of its minority populations. After taking power in September 1944, the Bulgarian communists ended the assimilationist policies of the preceding period and banned the Pomak assimilationist association *Rodina*. In this way they initially attracted the sympathy of the Muslim elites. In December 1944, the Bulgarian Communist Party organised a conference of 200 Turkish delegates supporting the new regime and calling for a cultural modernisation of the Turkish minority, in particular through compulsory school enrolment of children of both sexes and use of the Latin alphabet in all schools teaching in the Turkish language. The same kind of conference was organised one year later for the Pomak minority, and in December 1947 the new constitution officially recognised the existence of a Turkish national minority. However, this recognition went hand in hand with the establishment of the communist party-state: the private Turkish schools were nationalised in 1946, the cultural associations were dissolved one year later, and the traditional elites were wiped out by the economic reforms and the wave of emigration of 1950–51. Nevertheless, the Turkish minority did enjoy significant cultural rights in the 1950s. The Turkish-language press experienced significant growth and new cultural institutions were created. Above all, the number of schools teaching in Turkish grew quickly; three teacher-training institutes were created in Kărdžali, Razgrad and Šumen; and quotas were introduced in the university to encourage the emergence of new Turkish elites linked to the communist regime.

From the mid-1950s, however, the communist authorities became concerned about the "nationalism" of these Turkish elites and the growing identification of the Pomaks with the Turkish national minority. Therefore, in 1956, they reverted to a definition of Bulgaria as a homogeneous nation-state, under which the "Bulgarian socialist nation" was regarded as including the Turkish and Pomak populations. From 1958 onwards, the schools teaching in Turkish were gradually replaced by schools teaching in Bulgarian, with the last vestiges of the Turkish minority's own educational system disappearing in the early 1970s. In 1971, the new Bulgarian constitution made no mention of the existence of national minorities. However, the main targets of the authorities at this time were the Pomaks and Muslim Gypsies. In 1962, and then again in the early 1970s, the authorities launched forced assimilation campaigns that once again saw the imposition of Bulgarian-sounding names and an all-out campaign against the "retrograde" religious and cultural traditions of the Pomak and Gypsy populations. These forced assimilation practices resulted in violent incidents between Pomak villagers and the security forces.

In December 1984, the communist authorities decided to extend these practices to the Turkish population and launched a forced assimilation campaign described as a "revival process" (*văzroditelen proces*). Within the space of a few months, with the support of the police and the army, the forenames and surnames of some 800,000 Turks were changed and their religious and cultural practices were banned, including the circumcision of children, the wearing of the *şalvar* by women and the religious burial of the dead. Use of the Turkish language in public was banned. But this policy too met with strong resistance: the confrontations between the Turkish minority and the security forces left several dozen dead, and hundreds of demonstrators were imprisoned. In the second half of the 1980s, clandestine organisations were set up, such as the Turkish National Liberation Movement in Bulgaria (*Tursko Nacionalno Osvoboditelno Dviženie v Bălgarija*—TNOD), and Turkish intellectuals joined the nascent Bulgarian dissident movement. Thus, paradoxically, the "revival process" increased Turkish national sentiment and led to a politicisation of the Turkish elites produced by the communist modernisation. In May 1989, a new wave of demonstrations and hunger strikes shook the Turkish minority. The communist authorities decided to allow Turks to leave. Between June and August 1989, more than 300,000 sought refuge in Turkey before it closed its border. This emigration of Turks from Bulgaria was the largest exodus in Europe since the end of the Second World War, and Bulgaria became a second crisis zone in Southeast Europe, alongside the autonomous province of Kosovo.

In Romania, management of the Turkish and Tatar minorities was similar to Bulgaria's management of its Turkish minority, though not so dramatic. At the end of the Second World War, the new authorities sought to win the allegiance of Romania's Muslim minorities by creating a Democratic Muslim Bloc (*Blocul Musulman Democrat*) linked to the communist party. Around the same time, they recognised the Turks and the Tatars as national minorities and opened schools teaching in Turkish. In the late 1940s, however, faced with Turkey's pro-Western policy, communist Romania decided to prioritise the assertion of a Dobrujan Tatar identity linked to that of the Tatars of the Soviet Union. Schools teaching in Tatar were therefore opened in 1949, and an alphabet specific to the Tatars of Dobruja was even created in 1955. Shortly afterwards, in 1957, the Romanian authorities changed their policy towards the Turkish and Tatar minorities once again, with the closure of all minority schools. An assimilationist policy then prevailed, which certainly partly explained the emigration of thousands of Turks and Tatars to Turkey, but did not appear to arouse any organised resistance.

It was in Greece that the management of the Muslim minority of Western Thrace presented the greatest degree of continuity with the inter-war period.[7] During the civil war, the majority of the Muslim minority supported the monarchists. After 1949, Muslim members of parliament were again nominated by the Greek political parties, the *cemaat*s continued to manage the minority's local affairs, and the associations that had appeared in the inter-war period, such as the Turkish Union of Xanthi (*İskeçe Türk Birliği*), the Union of Young Turks of Komotini (*Gümülcine Genç Türkler Birliği*) and the Union of Turkish Teachers of Western Thrace (*Batı Trakya Türk Öğretmenler Birliği*), resumed their activities. However, the Cold War led to a military zone being established on the Bulgarian border, increasing the isolation of the Pomaks, whilst relations between the Greek authorities and the Muslim minority remained closely bound up with the evolution of Greco-Turkish relations. In the early 1950s, the time was right for a rapprochement between the two countries. In this context, several bilateral agreements formalised the use of the Turkish language and the Latin alphabet in the minority schools, arranged for teachers to come from Turkey, allowed the opening of a secondary school for the minority in Komotini in 1952[8] and facilitated the enrolment of students from the minority in Turkish universities. For a short period, Greek policy encouraged identification with the Turkish nation amongst the Muslim minority; in 1954 a decree even required the Greek administration to use the word "Turk" instead of "Muslim".

This policy changed radically following the first deterioration in Greco-Turkish relations in 1955 and after the installation of the military dictatorship in 1967. In 1955, article 19 of the new nationality code stipulated that the Greek state could remove Greek nationality from citizens of foreign descent (*allogeneis*) who had left Greece. As a result, some 47,000 Muslims from Western Thrace who settled in Turkey lost their Greek nationality over the following decades. In 1967, the military dictatorship decided that the *cemaat*s would thenceforth be appointed by the Greek authorities and that their role would be limited to managing the waqfs. Two years later, a teacher-training academy was created in Salonica to train minority teachers locally, most of whom were of Pomak origin, and thereby counter the influence of those trained in Turkey. More generally, the Greek authorities opposed the use of the national name "Turk", and the members of the Muslim minority were subject to various forms of discrimination concerning, for example, access to public jobs, the purchase of land, or the obtaining of a trading licence or a building permit.

Neither the restoration of democracy in 1974 nor entry into the European Economic Community in 1981 brought an end to this situation. On the contrary, the 1980s saw a hardening of the Greek authorities' attitude, with a ban on associations using the word "Turk/Turkish" in their names and promotion of a Pomak ethnic identity. However, the restoration of democracy facilitated the politicisation of new generations of young graduates, and then the mobilisation of the whole population. In 1980, the High Council of the Turkish Minority in Western Thrace (*Batı Trakya Türk Azınlığı Yüksek Kurulu*), which brought together political, religious and associative leaders, was established as the main body representing the minority. In 1985, Turkish candidates stood for the first time in legislative elections without being nominated by Greek political parties. In January 1988, a demonstration organised by the High Council of the Turkish Minority to protest against the ban on Turkish associations ended in violent confrontations in Komotini. Finally, a year and a half later, on 18 June 1989, Sadik Ahmet became the first independent Turkish member of parliament elected to the Greek parliament. Thus, a Turkish national identity seems to have crystallised within a large part of the Muslim population of Western Thrace between 1945 and 1989.

If we are to understand the changes that occurred during the communist period and afterwards, we must also take account of the role of the diasporas. In fact, even in this period characterised by the existence of the Iron Curtain, intellectuals and militants who had taken refuge abroad contributed to the construction of the national identities and political claims of their communities of origin. In 1960, Bosnian Muslim emigrants, who until then had been linked to Croatian political émigrés, created a Liberal Alliance of Bosniaks-Muslims (*Liberalni Savez Bošnjaka-Muslimana*), thus rediscovering the national name "Bosniak" (*Bošnjak*) and applying it only to the Muslims of Bosnia-Herzegovina. Also, the National Front (*Balli Kömbetar*) and other Albanian anti-communist organisations rebuilt themselves after 1945 in the diaspora. In 1982, a People's Movement for the Republic of Kosovo (*Lëvizija Popullore për Republikën e Kosovës*—LPRK) was created in Germany by Albanian activists who were natives of Kosovo and admirers of Enver Hoxha's Marxism–Leninism. Finally, in Turkey, the populations of Balkan origin were structured by powerful, semi-official associations, such as the Cultural and Solidarity Association for the Turks of the Rhodopes (*Rodop Türkleri Kültür ve Dayanışma Derneği*), representing Turks from Bulgaria, or the Solidarity Association for the Turks of Western Thrace (*Batı Trakya Türkleri Dayanışma Derneği*). The latter, together with the Federation of Associations of the Turks of Western Thrace (*Bati Trakya Türk Dernekleri*

Federasyonu) created in Germany in 1988, played an important role in internationalising the claims made by Turkish political and associative actors in Western Thrace.

Thus, during the Cold War, the methods used by the Balkan states to manage the national question differed between states and changed over time. In this context, the political status of the Balkan Muslim populations also varied significantly between different places and at different times, as demonstrated by the promotion of a Turkish national identity in Bulgaria and Greece in the 1950s, followed by repression of that identity in the 1970s and 1980s, and by the recognition of the Muslim nation in 1968, after two decades of national indeterminacy of the Muslims of Bosnia-Herzegovina. However, the Muslim populations were not simply passive subjects of state policies; through their elites, and particularly the elites associated with post-war social and cultural modernisation, they participated in the assertion of new national identities, or opposed the policies of assimilation or marginalisation. Crystallisation of the national identities of the different populations could therefore take place either as an extension of state policy or in opposition to it. However, beyond these different specific circumstances, the Cold War period was, for all Balkan Muslims, one in which national identities ceased to be the preserve of small intellectual circles and came to be shared by the ordinary people. From this perspective, the period was also one in which the Muslims of Southeast Europe accessed a certain degree of political modernity.

Scientific socialism and national mythologies

The ways in which the Balkan states chose to manage the national question also explain the types of academic discourse they encouraged concerning their Muslim populations. From that point of view, the Cold War period offers a contrasting picture. On the one hand, it saw significant development of local academic institutions, as evidenced by the creation of new academies of sciences in Bosnia-Herzegovina in 1966, in Albania in 1973 and in Kosovo in 1975. Many archaeological excavations were undertaken, and academic work based on the study of the Ottoman archives greatly increased. In the communist states, however, the academic discourse was more subject than ever to the political authorities and to the yoke of "scientific socialism". Even in Greece, the political regime was characterised by a high level of authoritarianism until 1974, and studies of the Muslim minority of Western Thrace were often motivated by nationalist or security concerns. However, that does not mean that the academic discourses on the different Balkan Muslim populations were monolithic or unchanging. On the one hand, they varied in the same way as state policies; on the other, some dissenting voices succeeded in making themselves heard despite everything. The Muslim intellectual elites took part in the creation of these discourses only when they had a sufficient institutional basis, as was the case in Albania, Bosnia-Herzegovina and Kosovo. They could also adopt the discourses produced in the neighbouring states. Academic publications in the Albanian language circulated, for example, between Albania, Kosovo and Macedonia, and the Turks of Greece used the output of certain official or semi-official academic institutions in Turkey. Throughout Southeast Europe, these academic discourses on the Muslim populations were articulated around three issues, which we shall now examine: the ethnogenesis of the Muslim populations, the causes of their conversion to Islam, and the more general definition of the link between Islam and national identity.

Like the preceding periods, the Cold War period was characterised by intense debates on the ethnogenesis of the Balkan Muslims. In Yugoslavia, the old theories on the Serbian or Croatian origin of the Muslims of Bosnia-Herzegovina were discredited by the tragic experience of the Second World War and banished by the communist regime. That opened the way for the construction of an ethnogenesis peculiar to the Muslims of Bosnia-Herzegovina, reaffirming their Slavic origins but emphasising the existence in the Middle Ages of both a kingdom of Bosnia and a Bosnian Church, described as Bogomil by some historians. In Kosovo, the origin of the local Albanian population was the subject of a lively debate between Albanian historians from Albania and Kosovo on the one hand, and Serbian historians on the other. The former were of the opinion that Kosovo had been populated by Albanians since antiquity, and therefore since before the arrival of the Slavs. According to the latter, the settlement of Albanians in Kosovo dated primarily from the eighteenth century, when the Serbian inhabitants were replaced by Islamicised Albanian settlers, backed by the Ottoman authorities. These debates about the autochthonous nature of the Albanians of Kosovo reflected the Serbian and Albanian territorial claims to the province. Finally, this question of ethnogenesis played an important role in Bulgaria, in particular at the time of the "revival process" in the late

1980s. Bulgarian historians and ethnologists were mobilised to demonstrate that Bulgaria's Pomaks and Turks were descended not from Turkish-speaking populations that arrived from Anatolia, but from Bulgarian populations that were forcibly Islamicised and Turkified in the Ottoman period.

A similar discourse can be found in Greece concerning the Pomaks, who were presented as a forcibly Islamicised population of Thracian-Greek origin. The Greek academic discourse on the Pomaks also tended to identify them en bloc with Bektashism in order to accentuate artificially the difference between Pomaks and Sunni Turks. These Bulgarian and Greek nationalist theories were in opposition to those of the Turkish nationalists, who maintained that the Muslim populations of Bulgaria and Greece were descended from Turkish-speaking peoples (Pechenegs, Cumans) who settled in Southeast Europe in the twelfth and thirteenth centuries, and thus before the Ottoman conquest of the region. This Turkish version of the ethnogenesis of the Muslims of Bulgaria and Greece was promoted in the 1980s in particular. At that time, the Turkish authorities were promoting the so-called "Turko-Islamic synthesis", a current of thought that emphasised the Islamic aspects of Turkish national identity and, within that context, showed an increased interest in the "external Turks" (*dış türkler*).

The question of the ethnogenesis of the Balkan Muslim populations cannot be separated from that of their Islamicisation. This is particularly the case in communist Bulgaria, where historians such as Petar Petrov and Hristo Hristov presented Islamicisation as a violent process imposed upon the Christian Bulgarian population.[9] Only a few historians, such as Antonina Željazkova, disagreed with this simplistic view and emphasised that Islamicisation was a gradual process with multiple causes.[10] In Bosnia-Herzegovina, the theory of a voluntary conversion of the Bosnian Bogomils in the aftermath of the Ottoman conquest was taken up by intellectuals involved in the process of recognition of the Muslim nation, such as Salim Ćerić and Muhamed Hadžijahić.[11] The historian Nedim Filipović, however, questioned the validity of this theory and emphasised the socio-economic factors involved in Islamicisation.[12] Finally, a significant development can be discerned in this period in the Albanian space. Generally, Albanian historians of the communist period adopted the idea, so dear to Albanian nationalist historiography, of a forced and superficial Islamicisation of the Albanians. However, from the 1970s onwards, some Albanian historians from Kosovo and Macedonia, such as Hasan Kaleshi and Muhamet Tërnava, started to present the conversion to Islam as having helped to preserve the Albanian national identity against Greek and Slav assimilationist pressures.[13] Others, such as Muhamet Pirraku and Skënder Rizaj, even extended to the Albanians the Bogomil theory that had arisen in Bosnia-Herzegovina.[14]

In each country, the question of the causes of Islamicisation was related not only to a more general theory concerning the ethnogenesis of the local Muslim populations, but also to a value judgement concerning the Islamic religion and the Ottoman period. In most cases, that judgement was negative in the extreme: Marxist ideology often simply adopted a traditional representation of Islam as a backward religion and the Ottoman Empire as "Asiatic despotism". Albania was no exception to this rule: the country continued to celebrate Skanderbeg, the leader of the Albanian revolts against the central Ottoman authorities in the fifteenth century. In Bosnia-Herzegovina, however, the historians working at the Oriental Institute of Sarajevo sought to offer a more nuanced view of the Ottoman Empire, or even to present it as a progressive economic and political system, in comparison to the medieval kingdoms that had preceded it in the region. At times, some intellectuals even sought to draw out the common aspects of Islam and socialism. Moreover, the Muslim intellectuals of Bosnia-Herzegovina insisted on the existence of Bosnia as a separate political entity within the Ottoman Empire, which justified the elevation of Bosnia-Herzegovina to the rank of republic in 1945 and the recognition of the Muslim nation in 1968.

The question of Islamicisation is also related to the wider question of the relationship between Islam and national identity. In Bulgaria, during the "revival process", Islam was regarded as preventing the Muslims from acceding to Bulgarian national consciousness, hence rituals associated with it were targeted. In Albania, the idea that religion was an obstacle to national consciousness applied to all denominations. Christianisation and Islamicisation were therefore equally portrayed as superficial, and Albanian historians and ethnologists emphasised the vestiges of pagan religions or a supposed "non-religious tradition" among Albanians.[15] On the other hand, as mentioned above, in the 1970s some Albanian historians from Kosovo and Macedonia began to portray Islamicisation as a factor in the preservation of Albanian national identity. Finally, the most complex case was undoubtedly that of the Muslims of Bosnia-

Herzegovina. In order to justify the recognition of the Muslim nation, Bosnian Muslim intellectuals emphasised the fact that Muslim national identity could not be reduced to the religious identity of the same name, and that historically it had been separated from it, just as the Serbian and Croatian national identities had been separated from their Orthodox and Catholic religious substrata. Consequently, they played down Islam as a faith, while emphasising its importance as a cultural heritage, as a set of identity markers positioning the Muslim nation in time and space. This definition of the relations between Islam and Muslim national identity was not without consequences for the Islamic institutions, as we shall see later in this chapter. It was also contested by some lay intellectuals. In the 1960s, for example, the historian Enver Redžić considered the national name "Muslim" to be too closely linked to Islam, and preferred "Bosnian" (*Bosanac*).[16] The sociologist Esad Ćimić, on the contrary, argued that among the Muslims of Bosnia-Herzegovina religious consciousness continued to predominate over national consciousness, and that therefore they did not constitute a nation in the full sense of the term.[17] Declaring himself to be of Croatian nationality, he demonstrated that the definition of the relations between Islam and national identity could impact the very nature of the national identity of some groups of Balkan Muslims.

Finally, the role of the Balkan diasporas must once again be mentioned. Some researchers, such as Speros Vryonis and Stavro Skendi, took part in the debates on Islamicisation.[18] Others, such as Alexandre Popovic, Kemal Karpat and Ali Eminov, researched the Balkan Muslims in the post-Ottoman period.[19] At the same time, political émigrés also adopted certain academic discourses about the Muslim populations, and sometimes anticipated future developments. Thus, in the 1960s, the Albanian emigrants Tajar Zavalani and Abas Ermenji disputed the dogma of a forced Islamicisation of the Albanians.[20] Likewise, Adil Zulfikarpašić and Smail Balić, the two leading figures of the Liberal Alliance of Bosniaks-Muslims, strongly defended the theory of the Bogomil origin of the Bosnian Muslims, and saw in the Islam of Bosnia-Herzegovina the incarnation of an authentic European Islam.[21] Finally, in Turkey, some Turkish intellectuals of Balkan origin worked in the academic institutions that produced the historical discourse of the new "Turko-Islamic synthesis".[22]

EUROPE'S BALKAN MUSLIMS

The contrasting development of the Islamic institutions

Two main factors determined the attitude of each Balkan state to its Islamic institutions: the state's general policy towards religion on the one hand, and its specific policy towards its Muslim population on the other. As we have already seen in this chapter, these policies varied from one state to another and from one decade to another. If we keep these variations in mind, we can understand the changes that the Islamic institutions underwent between 1945 and 1989.

In Yugoslavia, the first post-war years saw a reining in of the Islamic Religious Community (*Islamska Vjerska Zajednica*). In Bosnia-Herzegovina, several of its leaders were sentenced in 1945 and 1947 for having collaborated with the occupying force. In 1947, the Islamic Religious Community adopted a new constitution and appointed Ibrahim Fejić, a cleric who had been a member of the partisan movement, as the new *reis-ul-ulema*. The Islamic Religious Community then sought to present a progressive image by associating itself with campaigns against the wearing of the veil and denouncing magical practices as obscurantist. At the same time, the communist regime set about restricting the activities of the Islamic institutions to the private sphere. In 1946, the sharia courts were abolished, the Higher Islamic School of Sharia Law and Theology was closed, as were all the madrasas (excepting the Gazi Husrev-beg madrasa in Sarajevo), religious education was abolished in public schools and Sufi pilgrimages were banned. The waqfs were nationalised the following year. Finally, in 1952, the *mekteb*s were closed and the Islamic Religious Community banned mystical brotherhoods in Bosnia-Herzegovina and Montenegro, while they continued to be tolerated in Kosovo and Macedonia. The regime's only concession was to allow religious teaching in the mosques again in 1953. By the late 1950s, the Islamic Religious Community had lost most of its resources and a considerable number of its personnel, and its activities were limited to performing the main Islamic rituals. Nevertheless, *ders* (lessons) given to a restricted circle of students by some famous ulamas and shaykhs, *zikr*s (Sufi rituals) held in *tekke*s, mosques or private homes, and *mevlud*s (ceremonies honouring the Prophet) organised informally but at times bringing together thousands of people, did survive on the fringes of the official institutions.

From the 1960s onwards, the Islamic Religious Community experienced a marked renewal in activity, in different ways in the different

FROM THE ADVENT OF COMMUNISM TO ITS FALL

republics. In Bosnia-Herzegovina, this revival was symbolised by the building of several hundred mosques, the development of religious teaching in the mosques and an increase in the number of pupils at the Gazi Husrev-beg madrasa. On the initiative of Husein Đozo, elected president of the Association of Ulamas of Bosnia-Herzegovina in 1964, the Islamic religious press experienced considerable growth; in particular, the newspaper *Preporod* ("Revival") was established, printing several tens of thousands of copies. This renewal of the Islamic institutions is explained by the liberalisation of the Yugoslav communist regime and also, more specifically, by the recognition of the Muslim nation in 1968. In the absence of a national institution specific to the Bosnian Muslims, the Islamic Religious Community played the role of a substitute national institution, as evidenced by its change of name to Islamic Community (*Islamska Zajednica*) in 1969 and its involvement in the 1971 population census. In this context, connections were formed between religious leaders and lay intellectuals, facilitated by the fact that some of the latter—including several historians at the Sarajevo Oriental Institute—had studied before the war at the Gazi Husrev-beg madrasa or at the Higher Islamic School of Sharia Law and Theology. The 1960s were also a period in which exchanges with the Muslim world were resumed; this came about through an increase in the number of Yugoslav pilgrims visiting Mecca, the departure of madrasa graduates to different universities in the Arab world (especially the al-Azhar University in Egypt), the visit of foreign delegations and the presence in Yugoslavia of foreign Muslim students. So it is not surprising that in the 1980s some graduates returning to Yugoslavia from the Arab world began to spread neo-Salafism, a strict interpretation of Islam seeking to imitate the Prophet and his companions, the "pious ancestors" *(al-salaf al sâlih)*,[23] in all things.

This renewal of the Islamic Community continued during the following years, as evidenced by the opening of an Islamic Theology Faculty in Sarajevo in 1977 and the inauguration of an imposing mosque in Zagreb in 1987. However, one of the purposes of the Islamic Theology Faculty was to reduce the number of graduates leaving to study in the Muslim world, and thus to limit outside influences on Yugoslav Islam. More generally, the late 1970s and the early 1980s saw a hardening of the religious policy of the League of Communists of Bosnia-Herzegovina, as will be shown later in this chapter with regard to Husein Đozo and the former members of the pan-Islamist Young Muslims organisation (*Mladi Muslimani*).

In Kosovo and Macedonia too, the renewal of the Islamic Community resulted in the construction of many mosques, a rapid increase in the number of children receiving religious education in the mosques and the development of the religious press. The Alaudin madrasa in Prishtina, which had opened in 1951 as a religious elementary school, became a fully-fledged madrasa in 1962. Twenty-two years later, another madrasa, taking the name Isa-beg, opened in Skopje. However, the Islamic institutions of Kosovo and Macedonia were not at the forefront of the assertion of national identity as was the case in Bosnia-Herzegovina. There were several reasons for this difference. First of all, the Yugoslav authorities promoted the Muslim national identity, while remaining suspicious of the Albanian national identity. Also, the Islamic institutions of Kosovo and Macedonia found it difficult to identify with the atheist Albanian regime or Albanian political movements supporting the Marxism–Leninism of Enver Hoxha. Finally, in Kosovo and Macedonia, the Islamic institutions brought together Albanians, but also Turks, Gypsies and Slavic-speaking Muslims; the president of the Islamic Community of Serbia was, until 1983, a Turk from Kosovo, Ismail Haki. In 1981, the Islamic Community of Serbia—to which Kosovo belonged—condemned the Albanian demonstrations; it was only in the mid-1980s that it moved timidly towards Albanian nationalism. However, this turn created tensions between the *reis-ul-ulema* in Sarajevo and the Albanian leaders of the Islamic Community of Serbia and, within the latter, between those leaders and the mufti of Belgrade Hamdija Jusufspahić, a native of Bosnia-Herzegovina. The Islamic institutions in Kosovo did not fully align themselves with Albanian nationalism until 1990, after the election of Rexhep Boja to the position of president of the Islamic Community of Serbia (renamed at that time the Islamic Community for Kosovo, Serbia and Vojvodina) and the granting of de facto autonomy to the Islamic institutions of Belgrade and Sanjak. The rising tensions had repercussions on the Islamic institutions in Macedonia too; in 1987, the Macedonian authorities banned religious education in the mosques, as they suspected it was being used to Albanianise young Turks and young Torbesh. It was Jakub Selimoski, president of the Islamic Community of Macedonia from 1980 to 1990 and himself a Torbesh, who managed to defuse the crisis.

In order to provide a complete overview of the changes that the Islamic institutions underwent in communist Yugoslavia, it is also necessary to consider the renewal of the mystical brotherhoods from the 1960s onwards. In the 1950s, there was a rapid fall in the number of active *tekke*s in Yugoslavia; in Bosnia-Herzegovina this was due to their banning by the Islamic Religious Community, and in Macedonia and Kosovo to the emigration of numerous Turkish and Albanian shaykhs and dervishes. In the following decades, however, several brotherhoods, mainly Naqshbandi and Halveti, reorganised their activities semi-clandestinely in Bosnia-Herzegovina; and other brotherhoods—Halveti, Rifai, Sadi, Kadiri, etc.—experienced rapid growth in Kosovo and Macedonia. In 1986, Alexandre Popovic estimated that there were between 60 and 100 active *tekke*s in Yugoslavia, some 40 shaykhs and several tens of thousands of dervishes. Xhemali Shehu, a Rifai shaykh from Prizren in Kosovo, succeeded in encouraging the creation of several Rifai *tekke*s among the Gypsies of Macedonia. Shaykh Xhemali was also at the heart of the creation in 1974 of the Community of the Sublime Islamic Dervish Orders (*Zajednica Islamskih Derviškiih Redova Alije*—ZIDRA), which brought together shaykhs from Macedonia, Kosovo and, to a lesser degree, Bosnia-Herzegovina, belonging to various brotherhoods. This initiative was denounced by the Islamic Community, which saw it as challenging its monopoly over the religious life of Yugoslav Muslims. However, during the following years, relations between the Islamic Community and the brotherhoods developed differently in the different republics. In Bosnia-Herzegovina, a compromise quickly emerged, with the Bosnian shaykhs leaving the ZIDRA to join the *Tarikats* Centre (*Tarikatski centar*) created in 1977 by the Islamic Community and led by the Mevlevi shaykh Fejzulah Hadžibajrić. The ban on the activity of the *tarikat*s was therefore implicitly lifted and, in the 1980s, the Islamic religious press in Sarajevo gave more and more room to Muslim mysticism. In Kosovo and Macedonia, on the other hand, a majority of shaykhs—beginning with those who had a personal connection with Shaykh Xhemali—remained members of the ZIDRA and clashed with local leaders of the Islamic Community defending Sunni orthodoxy. Thus, relations between the Islamic Community and the brotherhoods in the communist period were not a simple opposition between "Bosnian ulamas" and "Albanian dervishes".

The history of the Islamic institutions in Albania, Bulgaria and Romania during the communist period is less well known than the history of the Yugoslav Islamic Community, and is dominated by an impression of inexorable decline. From the outset, the new communist authorities in those countries carried out significant purges of the Islamic institutions, installing their agents as religious leaders. Thus, in Bulgaria, Turkish members of parliament meeting in December 1944 called for the replacement of religious dignitaries who had collaborated with the former regime, and the new grand mufti elected in 1947, Akif Osmanov, immediately announced his support for the new regime (although this would not prevent him being removed from office in 1964). Likewise in Albania, Musa Haxhi Ali, a religious dignitary who had joined the partisans, was placed at the head of the Sunni Muslim Community in February 1945 and confirmed in that position by the Third Muslim Congress held three months later. Finally, in Romania, the Tatar Iacub Mehmet Septar was grand mufti of Romania from 1947 until his death in 1990. However, the most striking case of collusion between the Islamic institutions and the communist regimes was Nedim Gendžev who, appointed grand mufti of Bulgaria in 1988, backed the "revival process" launched a few years earlier by the Bulgarian authorities.

The communist authorities were also able to exploit the divisions within the Muslim population in order to control the Islamic institutions. In Albania, the new regime recognised the Bektashi community as a religious community in its own right; this recognition was symbolised by holding the Fourth Bektashi Congress alongside the Third Muslim Congress. However, the regime did not immediately succeed in gaining control of the Bektashi leadership. It had to wait until the suicide of the *kryegjysh* Abaz Hilmi Dede in March 1947, who was replaced by Ahmet Myftar Dede, and then the holding of the Fifth Bektashi Congress in April 1950, in order to bring the Bektashi fully under its influence. In Bulgaria, the new authorities maintained the Islamic institutions that had been created during the war specifically for the Pomaks until the 1980s and even opened an Islamic seminary reserved for Pomak students. On the other hand, the Bulgarian authorities did not appear to have a specific policy for the Alevi-Kizilbash minority, which accounted for around 7 per cent of Bulgaria's Muslims. Finally, in Romania, positions of responsibility within the Islamic institutions were monopolised by the Tatars.

At the same time as they took control of the Islamic institutions, the Albanian, Bulgarian and Romanian authorities drastically restricted their sphere of activity (as they also did for the Christian Churches). This was achieved primarily by nationalising the waqfs, closing the religious schools and abolishing religious education in public schools. In Albania,

FROM THE ADVENT OF COMMUNISM TO ITS FALL

religious education was abolished in public schools in 1946, the Shkodër madrasa was closed in 1947 and the Tirana madrasa in 1964. In Bulgaria, the Šumen *medrese-i nüvvab* was converted into a teacher-training institute in 1947, all the country's madrasas were closed in 1949, and religious education was abolished in public schools in 1952. In Romania, the Medgidia seminary was closed in 1967. In this context, the Islamic institutions experienced a rapid decline: religious personnel were increasingly elderly and fewer in number, religious publications ceased to appear—and even the Quran was no longer reprinted, a number of mosques were destroyed, converted or left to fall into ruin. Consequently, religious knowledge was no longer transmitted to the younger generations, even if the ritual of circumcision or the prohibition on eating pork were widely respected and the main religious feasts were still celebrated in many Muslim families, whether believers or non-believers. It is thus not surprising that from the 1960s onwards, these different religious practices of Islamic origin were targeted by communist propaganda in Albania and Bulgaria. In Albania, this denunciation of practices of Islamic origin formed part of wider anti-religious campaigns that resulted in a ban on all religious activity in November 1967. However, the Albanian authorities' campaign against the Islamic dietary rules (prohibition on eating pork, Ramadan fasting, etc.) had no equivalent in the case of Christians. In Bulgaria too, the authorities combated religion as such: in 1968 an atheism department was opened at the Academy of Science, and in 1978 directives were issued that established a system of socialist holidays and rituals, intended to replace the religious ones. However, the campaign against the religious practices of Islamic origin was also closely linked to the attempts at forcible assimilation of the Pomak and Turkish populations, as demonstrated in the 1980s by the intensification of the attempts to end circumcision, Ramadan fasting and religious burials. In Romania, the policy of the communist authorities seems to have been less proactive, leaving religious institutions and practices to fade away on their own and even authorising the building of a mosque in Bucharest in the 1960s in order to improve their image in the Muslim word. For the communist period was also, for the Islamic institutions of Albania, Bulgaria and Romania, a period in which links with the Muslim world were almost completely severed, despite the participation of a few religious dignitaries in ecumenical peace conferences or in official delegations to foreign countries.

In Greece, the Islamic institutions did not experience an upheaval comparable to that which occurred in the communist countries. In 1945, however, the positions of mufti that still existed in Salonica and Epirus were abolished and, four years later, a decree was issued that redefined the election rules and the competences of the *cemaats* of Western Thrace; thenceforth, the *cemaats* were called "management committees of the communities and foundations" (*Cemaat ve Vakıf İdare Heyetleri*). These local institutions, halfway between politics and religion, saw their legitimacy and spheres of competence decline under the dictatorship. In 1967, the military regime decided that *cemaats* would no longer be elected but would be appointed by the Greek state; ten years later, the authorities ended the *cemaats*' role in the management of minority schools.[24] Renamed "administrative committees for the management of Muslim real estate" (*Müslüman Emlak İdare Memur Heyetleri*), the *cemaats* were now responsible only for managing the waqfs and ceased to play a central role within the Muslim minority. In 1970, the representatives of the minority reacted by creating a committee of sermon and guidance (*Vaaz ve İrşat Heyeti*), which played an important role in organising religious life. Ten years later, the High Council of the Turkish Minority was created as a reaction to a new law that placed the waqfs under strict control by the Greek authorities. It quickly became the principal body representing the Muslim minority.

In the 1980s, tensions between the Greek authorities and representatives of the Muslim minority crystallised around the appointment of the muftis. Traditionally, the muftis of Komotini and Xanthi were appointed by the Greek state, after consulting the local Muslim elites. In 1985, however, those elites refused to recognise the new mufti appointed in Komotini, and in 1990 the committee of sermon and guidance organised the election of an unofficial mufti, Ibrahim Şerif, a former independent candidate in the legislative elections. The same year, a similar crisis broke out in Xanthi, where the unofficial mufti was Mehmet Emin Aga, also a former candidate in the legislative elections. The profile of these two unofficial muftis demonstrates that, in Western Thrace, the boundary between politics and religion was particularly porous, and that the function of mufti became politicised in the late 1980s. In fact, the unofficial muftis participated in the High Council of the Turkish Minority and behaved as true political actors. On the religious level, the situation was more complex as the muftis appointed by the Greek authorities continued to supervise the management of the waqfs and to pass judgements according to sharia law on all personal matters, while the muftis elected by the minority issued simple fatwas (legal opinions) but de facto controlled religious personnel and religious life in Western Thrace.

Finally, the Cold War period was one in which the conflict pitting conservatives against Kemalists since the 1920s gradually lost significance. Until the 1970s, the conservatives continued to be strongly represented in Islamic institutions and maintained their own associations, such as the Committee for Islamic Union (*İttihad-ı İslam Cemiyeti*) founded before the war, the Islamic Awakening Association (*İntibah-ı İslam Cemiyeti*) founded in 1948 and the Association of Madrasa Graduate Muslim Teachers (*Medrese Mezunu Müslüman Muallimler Cemiyeti*) founded in 1960. However, the Kemalist current was clearly dominant within the minority, winning all the elections to the *cemaat*s between 1949 and 1967. Furthermore, the crystallisation of a modern Turkish national identity went hand in hand with the decline in the conservative current, as evidenced by the disappearance of the last Turkish newspapers using Arabic characters in the 1970s. Finally, the 1980s saw Turkey becoming increasingly involved in the religious sphere, having kept a certain distance until then in the face of religious institutions that were Ottoman in appearance. Thus, the Turkish authorities financed the unofficial muftis and the religious personnel connected to those muftis, and the Turkish Presidency of Religious Affairs (*Diyanet İşleri Başkanlığı*) greatly increased exchanges with the Islamic institutions of Western Thrace. While, from that time, the Turkish influence predominated in the religious life of the Muslims of Western Thrace, it was not exclusive, as many pupils from the Komotini and Echinos madrasas travelled to the Arab world to pursue their studies, with the consent of the Greek authorities. The two muftis appointed by those authorities had themselves studied in Saudi Arabia.

So the Cold War period was, for the Islamic institutions of Southeast Europe, one of contrasts. In Greece, the Islamic institutions saw their room for manoeuvre reduced by the Greek authorities but continued to play a central role in the social life of the Muslim minority and became politicised during the 1980s. In Yugoslavia, the liberalisation of the 1960s allowed a renewal of the Islamic institutions and enabled them to make a cautious return to the public sphere. Finally, in Albania, Bulgaria and Romania, the anti-religious policy of the communist authorities led either to an outright ban on the Islamic institutions or to their decline, owing to a lack of clerics and material resources. In this context, the diasporas were sometimes called on to play a significant role in terms of religion too. Admittedly, Balkan Muslims were unable to set up their own religious institutions in Turkey, as the *Diyanet* claimed absolute monopoly over the religious life of Turkey's Muslims. However, in the 1950s, political émigrés opened Albanian or Bosnian Islamic centres in North America and in Australia, while in Germany, Austria and Belgium they participated in the creation of the first local Islamic associations. The Bektashi centre in Detroit, set up in 1954 and led by Baba Rexhepi, even came to be one of the main centres of Bektashi religious life following the banning of all religious activity in Albania in 1967. From the 1970s onwards, economic emigration was added to the post-war political emigration. Among the Yugoslav workers who settled in Western Europe, some Muslims from Bosnia-Herzegovina and Albanians from Kosovo and Macedonia attended Turkish or Arab mosques, and then created their own mosques in collaboration with the Islamic Community and the Yugoslav consular authorities. Likewise in the 1980s, Turks from Western Thrace settling in Germany started to open their own mosques. From this perspective also, the 1980s foreshadowed certain developments that occurred in the following decades.

The Bosnian exception: a pan-Islamist current under communism

In most of the communist states of Southeast Europe, clandestine organisations associated with the Muslim populations continued to exist in the early post-war years, such as the Albanian National Democratic Movement (LNDSH) in Kosovo and the *Yücelciler* movement in Macedonia; or appeared in the 1980s, such as the People's Movement for the Republic of Kosovo (LPRK) in the Albanian diaspora and the Turkish National Liberation Movement (TNOD) in Bulgaria. Bosnia-Herzegovina, however, was the only region of Southeast Europe in which a current, using Islam as a political ideology and carrying on some of its informal activities within the Islamic institutions, existed almost without interruption.

In the months following the end of the Second World War, the members of the pan-Islamist Young Muslims organisation (*Mladi Muslimani*) created in 1941 set about rebuilding their networks. However, as they no longer enjoyed the protection of the Association of Ulamas *el-Hidaje*, which had been banned by the communist regime, they now had to act in a semi-clandestine way. Despite an initial wave of arrests in 1946, they succeeded in recruiting several hundred members throughout Bosnia-Herzegovina, not only in the narrow circles of educated urban youth but also in rural areas. Ideologically, the Young Muslims insisted on some slogans already developed during the war, such as denouncing the decline of the Muslim world, rejecting conservative ulamas and Westernised intellectuals, and calling for a return to the original Islam. Their political utopia remained the creation of a state that would bring together all the Muslim peoples and the introduction of a political order based on the Quran. However, after 1945, the Young Muslims' tone became more militant, and openly challenged the Serbian and Croatian national ideologies on the one hand, and the communist regime and its anti-religious policy on the other. In Herzegovina, this radicalisation even resulted in highly unrealistic preparations for insurrection. It was therefore not long before the Young Muslims organisation attracted the attention of the communist authorities, who carried out several waves of arrests. In August 1949, fourteen of the organisation's leading figures were tried in Sarajevo, and four of them were condemned to death. On that occasion, the leadership of the Islamic Religious Community denounced the organisation as "fascist" and "terrorist". With its leadership removed, the Young Muslims virtually ceased to exist.

In the 1950s, the Young Muslims were not active in Bosnia-Herzegovina, a considerable number of them being in prison or having sought refuge abroad, where they participated in the creation of the Liberal Alliance of Bosniaks-Muslims. From the 1960s onwards, however, some Young Muslims re-established relations among themselves and became involved in the activities of the Islamic Community. In order to understand this choice, it is necessary to take account of the relative political liberalisation that Yugoslavia was experiencing at the time, the recognition of the Muslim nation and the increased room for manoeuvre that this gave the Islamic Community. However, the personal role played by Husein Đozo, elected president of the Association of Ulamas in 1964, must also be emphasised. A former student of the al-Azhar University, Đozo was the leading representative of Islamic reformism in Bosnia-Herzegovina in the communist period. He denounced the sclerosis of the Islamic institutions and called tirelessly for the renewal of Islamic thought through the adoption of *ijtihad* (reasoned interpretation). Faced with a religious life reduced to a few set rituals, he also sought to bring Islam back into touch with contemporary society, even if that meant coming to an accommodation with the communist political order and secularisation of everyday life. Finally, Đozo was without doubt the religious dignitary who best understood that the adoption of the national name "Muslim" was not a threat to the Islamic institutions but that, on the contrary, it provided them with unexpected possibilities for action. In his desire to restore moral and social relevance to the Islamic Community, Đozo sought the support of some former Young Muslims, amongst others, whom he encouraged to write under pseudonyms in the *Takvim* ("Almanac") of the Association of Ulamas and in the newspaper *Preporod*, and to participate in the discussion forums organised in several mosques in Sarajevo and attended by pupils at the Gazi Husrev-beg madrasa, amongst others. Taking the final step, these Young Muslims then became active within the very religious institutions that had publicly disowned them two decades before.

So the 1960s were a period in which the former Young Muslims succeeded in recruiting a new generation of sympathisers, mainly among the students of the Gazi Husrev-beg madrasa and the Islamic Theology Faculty. In this way, they rebuilt an informal network stretching throughout Bosnia-Herzegovina and beyond, as some pupils of those educational institutions were natives of Sanjak, Kosovo and Macedonia. At the same time, these Young Muslims established contacts with Arab students linked to the Muslim Brotherhood and thus accessed the texts of Islamist authors such as Hasan al-Banna, Muhammad Iqbal, Sayyid Qutb and Maulana Mawdudi. At the centre of this network, which was built up over two decades, were some Young Muslims from Sarajevo, and particularly the lawyer Alija Izetbegović, who had been sentenced to three years in prison in 1946. In fact, Izetbegović was not only one of the most active members of the network, but also its principal ideologue. The majority of the texts published by the former Young Muslims in the 1960s and 1970s dealt with religious questions, and those of Izetbegović were no exception to this rule. However, in a series of articles published in *Takvim* in the early 1970s, and later combined into an *Islamic Declaration* that was circulated clandestinely, Izetbegović again sketched the outlines of a pan-Islamist utopia. In this declaration, which included many arguments developed by the Young Muslims organisation and by global Islamist literature, Alija Izetbegović rejected all ideologies other than Islam, beginning with nationalism and secularism, and held up against them pan-Islamism and Islam conceived as a union of faith and politics. He argued that the renewal of Islam must pass through a moral and then a political phase, but struggled to define what the concrete forms of a pan-Islamist state and an Islamic order might be. For lack of anything better, he offered Pakistan as a model of an Islamic republic. At no point does the *Islamic Declaration* mention Bosnia-Herzegovina. However, this reference to Pakistan, a Muslim state born out of the violent partition of a multi-denominational whole, is very significant in the Yugoslav context.

Alija Izetbegović and his companions were soon brought back to the realities of Yugoslav politics. At the end of the 1970s and beginning of the 1980s, the echo of the Iranian revolution, the politicisation of the Catholic and Orthodox Churches and the accusations of "Muslim nationalism" levelled against the Bosnian communist leaders led them to harden their tone against the Islamic Community. In 1979, Husein Đozo, who made no secret of his interest in the Iranian revolution, was fiercely attacked and had to resign the presidency of the Association of Ulamas. Thus, the Young Muslims lost their principal protector. In the following years, the polemics on Muslim nationalism continued in Bosnia-Herzegovina and in the neighbouring republics. Political and intellectual leaders from Bosnia-Herzegovina found convenient scapegoats in the form of the Young Muslims. In March 1983, a wave of searches and arrests took place among the Young Muslims. Five months later, thirteen people, including Alija Izetbegović and four other former Young Muslims, were sentenced for having threatened the fraternity of the Yugoslav peoples, for having circulated the *Islamic Declaration* and, some of them, for having secretly visited Iran. Twelve of them were given long prison sentences. The leaders of the Islamic Community adopted a low profile in the face of these actions, and remained silent. However, this attitude backfired when, as a result of the weakening of the communist regime, a "movement of imams" appeared in Bosnia-Herzegovina in 1988. This movement demanded the resignation of the *Reis-ul-ulema* Husein Mujić and other religious leaders accused of complicity with the communists. The dissident imams finally won out in November 1989, with Husein Mujić being replaced by Jakub Selimoski, who, born in Macedonia, was the first *reis-ul-ulema* since 1882 not to be a native of Bosnia-Herzegovina. Although they were not initiators of the "movement of imams", those sentenced in 1983 (most of whom had been released in the meantime) took advantage of the movement to resume their activities within the Islamic Community and, in particular, to take over the editorship of the newspaper *Preporod*. Without realising it, they were paving the way for their journey to power.

The transformations of Islam through the prism of anthropology

At the end of this chapter, it is certainly worth looking again at the transformations experienced by Balkan Islam between 1945 and 1990. One way of doing this is to use the quantitative studies carried out during this period, measuring the religiosity of the Balkan Muslims. In fact, several of these studies suggest that Balkan Muslims remained more religious than their Christian co-citizens, and were therefore less receptive to the process of secularisation which characterised that half century. Thus, in Bulgaria, a survey carried out by Ali Aliev in 1973 found that 58 per cent of Turkish men and 75 per cent of Turkish women declared themselves to be religious, compared to 32 per cent of Bulgarian men and 42 per cent of Bulgarian women.[25] Likewise in another study carried out by Dragomir Pantić in Yugoslavia in 1990, 64 per cent of people of Catholic tradition, 62 per cent of people of Muslim tradition and 39 per cent of people of Orthodox tradition declared themselves to be religious.[26] However, such data can be misleading; in the case of Yugoslavia, for example, it turns out that 70 per cent of Albanians but only 37 per cent of the Muslims of Bosnia-Herzegovina declared themselves to be religious, so that the latter were very close to the Serbs (34 per cent) and Montenegrins (35 per cent) of Orthodox tradition. The contrast between Muslims of Bosnia-Herzegovina and Albanians of Kosovo and Macedonia suggests that the differences in religiosity are explained not by a hypothetical "impermeability" of Islam to secularization, but by significant differences in the rate of urbanisation, educational attainment and political status of the populations under study. Besides, more subtle questions on religious practice reveal a sharp decline in religiosity among the Balkan Muslims: in Bulgaria, in 1973, only 9.1 per cent of Turks stated that they went to the mosque each Friday, with 18 per cent going there on religious holidays, 11 per cent attending irregularly and 58 per cent never visiting the mosque.[27] In Yugoslavia, according to another study by Dragomir Pantić, carried out in 1989, 69 per cent of young Albanians in Kosovo and 61 per cent of young Muslims in Bosnia-Herzegovina declared that they never went to the mosque, compared to

13 per cent of young Albanians in Kosovo and 14 per cent of young Muslims in Bosnia-Herzegovina who declared that they visited the mosque for religious reasons.[28] Besides the biases inherent in any quantitative survey, these different studies suffer from the major defect that they looked at religion as a homogeneous whole in order to measure its inexorable decline or resistance to change. Consequently, they do not look at how religion involves multiple practices and expectations, and redeploys itself within the very modernity that supposedly destroys it. In order to understand the qualitative, multiple and sometimes paradoxical transformations of Islam in Southeast Europe, it is more prudent to consider the field research carried out by certain anthropologists in the late 1980s.

Cornelia Sorabji's doctoral thesis, submitted in 1989, looks at the Muslim identity and the Islamic faith in Sarajevo at the end of the socialist period.[29] Firstly, she demonstrates how Bosnian Muslims constructed their own identity by distinguishing themselves from the Serbs and Croats on the one hand, and by binding themselves to the *umma* (community of believers) on the other. In this context, the distinction established by the League of Communists between Muslim national identity and Muslim religious identity was not reflected in the population, for whom the two often tended to merge. Sorabji then examines religious practices, and refutes the idea of a clear separation between "orthodox" and "popular" Islam, preferring the more flexible distinctions that the believers themselves established between compulsory, desirable, neutral and banned practices. Finally, she shows that the Islamic Community struggled to maintain its monopoly over religious life, as its compromises with the communist regime damaged its legitimacy and believers often perceived it as merely a service provider:

> Like the secular authorities the Islamska Zajednica is seen as a body to be contributed to, benefited from and otherwise dealt with; it is not taken as the spiritual or social centre of religious life, just as the secular authorities are not taken as embodying the political will of the people.[30]

Sorabji therefore reveals a religious life organised around porous dividing lines and implicit compromises. This is demonstrated by the case of believers who are party members:

> it is clear to everyone that, from the state's point of view, the two are not logically compatible.... However, in daily life the abstract question of the compatibility of the two ideologies does not often arise; Islam and Communism are two facts of life and people's complaints about the system generally focus on

inflation, unemployment and the poor quality of goods rather than on religious matters.[31]

Above all, the Islam described by Cornelia Sorabji is characterised by change. In particular, she notes among the young generations of believers the emergence of new forms of religiosity that were largely outside the control of the Islamic Community. Nor were they expressed within the framework of the traditional mystical brotherhoods which, in Bosnia-Herzegovina, were relatively orthodox and close to the Islamic Community. Sorabji therefore describes as "new mystics" an informal movement organised around charismatic, self-proclaimed "shaykhs" and bringing together young believers of both genders, including some pupils from the madrasa and the Faculty of Islamic Theology. This movement was both mystical, as it practised some Sufi rituals, and scripturalist, as it advocated a return to the letter of the Quran. In the situation in which the Bosnian Muslims found themselves in the late 1980s, that is to say as a minority group facing political repression, this movement did not display any political ambition; instead, it identified strongly with the *umma* and implicitly rejected the official ideology of "fraternity and unity" of the Yugoslav peoples. From this point of view, it was one of the precursors of the politicisation of the 1990s. Above all, however, it signalled the emergence of a more intellectualised and more individualised relationship with the Islamic faith: the "new mystics" experienced the Muslim community as a "community of choice" and, in their eyes, "the nominal Muslims who do not affirm their religious choice are no closer to the Islamic community than the Christians, to whom Islam is potentially open if they choose to embrace it".[32] A new religious current emerging in an urban, educated and modern milieu, the "new mystics" demonstrated how the transformations of Islam during the communist period led both to its politicisation as an identity marker and to its individualisation as a faith.

These processes of politicisation and individualisation were not limited to the urban population, despite a belief that the towns embody change and the villages embody tradition. This is what Yannis Frangopoulos shows in his doctoral thesis based on research carried out between 1988 and 1992 in Western Thrace, in a Pomak village of 2,000 inhabitants.[33] In his thesis, he first describes the historical context of the village of Havari, affected by several competing nation-state projects in Western Thrace, the gradual crystallisation of a Turkish identity within the

Muslim minority and increasing tensions between the Greek state and Turkish nationalists in the 1980s. He then examines the changes that village life experienced in the second half of the twentieth century. On the economic level, traditional activities focused on cattle-farming and maize and tobacco growing had declined and been replaced by new forms of employment, such as salaried jobs for the National Office of Forests or emigration to Athens, Turkey and Germany. This opening up of the village to the outside world was further accentuated by sending children to the teacher-training academy in Salonica or to lower secondary schools in Turkey, and by the arrival of satellite dishes. The ensuing cultural upheavals affected all areas of life, including family life: marriages to people from outside the village multiplied, the extended family gave way to the nuclear family and arranged marriages gradually disappeared as people began to choose their own husbands and wives.

In this context, the ethnic and religious identity of the Havari villagers also underwent significant changes. In fact, Yannis Frangopoulos shows how they managed their "plural identity", at once Pomak, Muslim, Turkish and Greek according to the circumstances and to whom they were speaking. In particular, however, he highlights the division in the village between "old Muslims" and "Kemalists". The "old Muslims", who were culturally on the defensive, as evidenced by the closure of the primary school which was linked to them, nevertheless retained control of the town hall. The "Kemalists" monopolised relations with the minority institutions and in particular with Xanthi's elected mufti. Above all, however, the 1980s saw the emergence of a third group, comprising young people working outside the village, and characterised by a very secular way of life on the one hand and by political engagement in favour of the Greek Socialist Party (PASOK) on the other. These three groups were linked by complex relations. With regard to cultural and religious practices, the first two groups were relatively close to each other and shared the two cafes in the central square, while the young people met in the cafes situated on the outskirts of the village to drink alcohol. However, while the "Kemalists" were led by the principal imam of the village, who officiated in the central mosque, the "old Muslims" and the young people met in the mosque of the upper district, where the imam was a convinced anti-Kemalist. So the source of the main division in the village was not religion but politics: on one side were the "Kemalists", who saw the Greek state as an adversary, and on the other were the "old

Muslims" and the young people, seeking each in their own way to obtain the favour of the Greek state. Thus, in the late 1980s, the Pomak villages in the Rhodopes did not escape the processes of politicisation and individualisation that profoundly affected Islam in Southeastern Europe, producing new divisions and reshaping practices.

5

FROM THE FALL OF COMMUNISM TO EUROPEAN INTEGRATION

(1989–2001)

Between Yugoslav disintegration and Euro-Atlantic integration

In 1989, the communist regimes collapsed one after another. The Berlin Wall, symbol of the Cold War in Europe, fell on 9 November 1989. This collapse of the Soviet bloc was the unexpected result of the *perestroika* that Mikhaïl Gorbachev had encouraged four years earlier, the removal of the conservative leaders by the reformist currents in the communist parties, and the mobilisation of the people—drawn into the street by dissidents or, more discreetly, by the reformers themselves. In Southeast Europe, the end of the communist regimes came relatively late and, from the start, took a dramatic turn: in Bulgaria, the exodus of 300,000 Turks ended up destabilising the regime of Todor Živkov, who was removed on 10 November 1989; in Romania, the December "revolution" led to a thousand deaths and the execution of Nicolae and Elena Ceauşescu on 25 December 1989; in Yugoslavia, the League of Communists divided over the issue of multi-partyism in January 1990, prefiguring the break-up of the Yugoslav federation itself; and in Albania, the authorities yielded to the demonstrations and accepted the introduction of a multi-party system in December 1990.

Over the following decade, the single-party regimes were replaced by multi-party systems based on the organisation of pluralist elections and the restoration of freedom of expression and association. The political life of the Balkan states now came to be dominated by the division between neo-communists and anti-communists, as can be seen in the opposition between the Bulgarian Socialist Party (*Bălgarska Socialističeska Partija*—BSP) and the Union of Democratic Forces (*Sajuz na Demokratičnite Sili*—SDS) in Bulgaria, and between the Socialist Party (*Partia Socialiste*—PS) and the Democratic Party (*Partia Demokratike*—PD) in Albania. To this first division was added a second, between the pro-Europeans and the anti-Europeans. These two divisions did not necessarily coincide. Moreover, the opposition between pro-Europeans and anti-Europeans was also to be found in Greece. The Socialist Party (PASOK) held power in Greece without interruption from 1993 to 2000, but in 1996 its old populist leader George Papandreou was succeeded by the pro-European modernist Kostas Simitis. Only the most pro-European parties avoided the nationalist rhetoric that permeated the political life of the Balkan states in the 1990s. At the same time, the national minorities established their own political parties, such as the Democratic Union of Hungarians in Romania (*Uniunea Democrată Maghiară din România*—UDMR), the Movement for Rights and Freedoms (*Dviženie za Prava i Svobodi*—DPS) for the Turkish minority in Bulgaria, and the Unity for Human Rights Party (*Partia Bashkimi për të Drejtat e Njeriut*—PBDNJ) for the Greek minority in Albania. Compared to Central Europe, the "democratic transition" in Southeast Europe involved considerable turmoil. Authoritarian tendencies and electoral fraud were widespread, on the part of both neo-communists, such as Ion Iliescu in Romania (1990–96), and anti-communists, such as Sali Berisha in Albania (1992–7). A high degree of political instability ensued, characterised by multiple post-election disputes, violent demonstrations and, in the case of Albania, a short civil war resulting in a thousand deaths between January and July 1997. It was not until the late 1990s that the democratic institutions stabilised in Romania, Bulgaria and Albania and political alternation became commonplace.

It was in Yugoslavia that the end of communism took the most dramatic turn. In 1990, following the break-up of the League of Communists of Yugoslavia, separate free elections were organised in each republic. All these elections were won by nationalist parties, such as Slobodan Milošević's Socialist Party of Serbia (*Socijalistička Partija Srbije*—SPS, ex-communist) in Serbia, Franjo Tudjman's Croatian Democratic Union (*Hrvatska Demokratska Zajednica*—HDZ) in Croatia, the Party of

Democratic Action (*Stranka Demokratske Akcije*—SDA, Muslim), the Serbian Democratic Party (*Srpska Demokratska Stranka*—SDS) and the Croatian Democratic Union (HDZ) in Bosnia-Herzegovina. The only partial exception to this rule was Macedonia, where the nationalists of the Internal Macedonian Revolutionary Organisation (*Vnatrešna Makedonska Revolucionerna Organizacija*—VMRO[1]) won a relative majority of the votes, but the Social Democratic Union of Macedonia (*Socijaldemokratski Sojuz na Makedonija*—SDSM, ex-communist) allied itself with the Albanians of the Party for Democratic Prosperity (*Partia për Prosperitet Demokratik*—PPD) to form the government. As for the Albanians of Kosovo, they boycotted the Serbian elections, but created the Democratic League of Kosovo (*Lidhja Demokratike e Kosovës*—LDK), and the provincial parliament dissolved in 1989 clandestinely proclaimed a "Republic of Kosovo" in September 1990.

In the months that followed, four of the six Yugoslav republics proclaimed their independence: Slovenia and Croatia in June 1991, Macedonia in September 1991 and Bosnia-Herzegovina in March 1992. The "Republic of Kosovo" did the same in September 1991, but that proclamation of independence was of no legal value since Kosovo was not one of the constituent republics of the Yugoslav federation. Finally, in April 1992, Serbia and Montenegro established a new Federal Republic of Yugoslavia (FRY) on their own (see Map 9). In Croatia and Bosnia-Herzegovina, independence was followed by a violent armed conflict. The Serbs proclaimed their own secessionist "republics": the "Serbian Republic of Krajina" in Croatia and the "Serbian Republic" (or "Republika Srpska") in Bosnia-Herzegovina. Backed by the Yugoslav army, within a few months they took possession of 30 per cent of the territory of Croatia and 70 per cent of the territory of Bosnia. This military conquest went hand in hand with systematic "ethnic cleansing", i.e. the violent expulsion of the non-Serb populations, accompanied by massacres and various forms of violence. In 1993, it was the turn of the Croats of Bosnia-Herzegovina to proclaim a "Croatian Republic of Herceg-Bosna" and to confront the Bosniak-dominated Bosnian army.[2] In March 1994, however, American diplomacy brought about a halt to the confrontations between Croats and Bosniaks and, with the Washington agreement, supported the creation of a Bosniak-Croatian Federation divided into five Bosniak, three Croatian and two "mixed" cantons. During 1995, changes in the military balance of power on the ground and the growing involvement of the United States led to the disappearance of the "Serbian Republic of Krajina" in Croatia and to the partition of Bosnia-Herzegovina into two entities, the Federation (51 per cent of Bosnia's territory), and the Republika Srpska (49 per cent) (see Map 9). On 14 December 1995, the Dayton agreement was signed, officially ending the war in Croatia and Bosnia-Herzegovina. That war had caused 12,000 deaths and the displacement of 600,000 people in Croatia (out of 4,750,000 inhabitants) and around 100,000 dead and the displacement of 2,100,000 people in Bosnia-Herzegovina (out of 4,400,000 inhabitants).

Sometimes presented as a return to "ancient hatred", the Yugoslav wars were above all the product of post-communist political elites deliberately exacerbating nationalist passions and interethnic conflicts. From this perspective, the extreme nationalism of Slobodan Milošević and the blind militarism of the Yugoslav army were the two main causes of the bloody nature of the break-up of Yugoslavia. At the same time, however, it is necessary to emphasise the similarities between, for example, Slobodan Milošević's policy and that of the Croat Franjo Tudjman, in terms of deliberate use of "ethnic cleansing", exploitation of nationalist feelings, control of the media and the setting up of parallel power structures based on the secret services and organised crime. Such power practices were also to be found in Bosnia-Herzegovina, in both the "Republika Srpska" and Croatian "Herceg-Bosna", and, more ambiguously, in the territories controlled by the legal authorities in Sarajevo. In the Yugoslav space, the war therefore served not only to implement different nationalist projects, but also to perpetuate certain power practices inherited from the communist period and to neutralise the democratic aspirations of the population. Moreover, it is significant that Serbia, Croatia and Bosnia-Herzegovina did not experience political alternation during the 1990s.

With peace having just returned to Croatia and Bosnia-Herzegovina, war threatened again in the south of the Yugoslav space. From 1997 onwards, tensions built up between Serbia and Montenegro, where the Democratic Party of Socialists (*Demokratska Partija Socijalista*—DPS, ex-communist) drew closer to the supporters of independence. Above all, in Kosovo, a Kosovo Liberation Army (*Ushtria Çlirimtare e Kosovës*—UÇK) appeared, which disputed the political hegemony of the LDK and carried out an increasing number of guerrilla actions. In February 1998, Kosovo in turn fell into war, and the Serbian forces once again turned to

FROM COMMUNISM TO EUROPEAN INTEGRATION

Map 9: Southeast Europe at the beginning of the 21st century

"ethnic cleansing". Following an ultimatum concerning acceptance of a peace plan, the NATO air force bombed Serbia from March to June 1999 and, on 9 June, Serbia accepted the deployment of NATO troops in Kosovo, which was then placed under UN administration. The war in Kosovo caused around 11,000 deaths and the displacement of 1,400,000 people (out of 1,950,000 inhabitants).

The late 1990s therefore marked a new stage in the reshaping of the Yugoslav space. They also saw the end of the authoritarian regimes that had dominated the last decade. Croatia's president Franjo Tudjman died in October 1999, and his HDZ party lost the elections three months later. In Serbia, Slobodan Milošević refused to recognise his defeat in the September 2000 elections, but was overthrown in a "revolution" on 5 October. Six months later, he was arrested and handed over to the International Criminal Tribunal for the former Yugoslavia (ICTY). In Bosnia-Herzegovina, in November 2000, an Alliance for Change (*Alijansa za Promjene*) led by the Social Democratic Party (*Socijaldemokratska Partija*—SDP, ex-communist) ended the political hegemony of the SDA and the HDZ in the Federation. In Kosovo, the LDK was now in competition with the Democratic Party of Kosovo (*Partia Demokratike e Kosovës*—PDK) and the Alliance for the Future of Kosovo (*Aleanca për Ardhmërinë e Kosovës*—AAK), both of which emerged from the UÇK. Finally, in Montenegro, the DPS managed to remain in power beyond 2001, but its rallying to independence in 1998 was accompanied by an alliance with the parties representing the Bosniak and Albanian minorities. Thus, a page seemed to have been turned in Southeast Europe. However, in March 2001, a new National Liberation Army (*Ushtria Çlirimtare Kombëtare*—UÇK) appeared in Macedonia, disrupting the precarious balance of Macedonian political life. On 13 August 2001, after five months of fighting that led to around 400 deaths, the main Macedonian and Albanian parties signed an agreement in Ohrid. Although a wider conflict was avoided, the Macedonian crisis is a reminder that several of the states to have emerged from the Yugoslav federation remain particularly fragile.

During the 1990s, the break-up of Yugoslavia was not the only significant geopolitical reconfiguration in Southeast Europe. The Yugoslav wars also provided the opportunity for an in-depth redefinition of NATO's role after the end of the Cold War. In fact, from 1994 onwards, the powerlessness of the UN peacekeepers in Bosnia-Herzegovina led to

NATO becoming increasingly directly involved, and to US diplomacy taking over peace negotiations. In 1995, it was the bombing of Serbian positions by the NATO air force, among other things, that led to the signing of the Dayton agreement and the deployment of 60,000 NATO troops. Four years later, the United States and NATO again played a decisive role in the Kosovo war, and the United Nations Interim Administration Mission in Kosovo (UNMIK), created in 1999, was supported by 50,000 NATO troops. Finally, in 2001, NATO was tasked with supervising the disarmament of the UÇK's fighters in Macedonia. More generally, regional organisations such as NATO, the OSCE and the European Union extended their influence into Southeast Europe through the quasi-protectorates established in 1995 in Bosnia-Herzegovina and in 1999 in Kosovo. OSCE missions were also deployed in the 1990s in Croatia, Serbia, Macedonia and Albania, and the OSCE—with the Council of Europe—played a crucial role in supervising elections, implementing democratisation policies and formulating the rights of national minorities. The European Union participated in the financing of reconstruction in Bosnia-Herzegovina and Kosovo, but its political and military role remained very limited. Even the *Alba* operation in 1997, which was intended to bring back peace to Albania, was entrusted to the UN because of a lack of consensus among the European states. Thus, the process of Euro-Atlantic integration precipitated by the disappearance of the Soviet bloc took indirect and complex forms in Southeast Europe. Only Romania, Bulgaria and Slovenia participated directly in the enlargement of the European Union, as demonstrated by the acceptance of their candidacies in 1995.

Finally, beyond the wars linked to the break-up of Yugoslavia, the 1990s also saw the exacerbation of some regional tensions. It is true that Albania and Greece signed a treaty ending their border conflicts in 1996. However, Greece continued to refuse to recognise Macedonia under that name, and even imposed an economic embargo on Macedonia in 1994 and 1995. At the same time, Greece opposed Turkey over the questions of Cyprus and the Aegean Sea, with serious incidents occurring in 1996 over some islands. Turkey took advantage of the collapse of the communist regimes to sign economic and military cooperation agreements with Macedonia, Albania and Bosnia-Herzegovina, and to normalise relations with Bulgaria. This diplomatic activism reinforced Greece's feeling of isolation and fed into nationalist passions. Here again, it was necessary to wait until the late 1990s for these regional tensions to give way to a normalisation of Greco-Turkish relations, symbolised in 1999 by the mutual assistance the two countries provided to each other after being struck by deadly earthquakes. However, the prospects of enlargement of the European Union seemed to be the real levers for this normalisation, with Cyprus having its candidacy accepted in December 1997 and Turkey two years later. Thus, after twelve years of hesitation, the European Union recognised that Turkey, a country of 75 million inhabitants, was a part of Europe.

"Transition" and the "return of religion"

The complex and dramatic reshaping of Southeast Europe in the 1990s demonstrates the limits of the notion of "transition" to describe the political realities of post-communism. The same is true for economic reforms. Certainly, with varying degrees of enthusiasm, all the post-communist states of Southeast Europe launched programmes to de-collectivise land, privatise trade and industry, and liberalise their economies. However, these programmes took different forms in each country and were accompanied by considerable economic and social difficulties. Industrial output collapsed and the official unemployment rate shot up, reaching 15 per cent in Romania, Bulgaria and Croatia; 20 per cent in Albania and the Federal Republic of Yugoslavia; and as high as 40 per cent in Macedonia and Bosnia-Herzegovina. Moreover, the economic reforms went hand in hand with a rapid increase in inequality, which was further amplified in the Yugoslav space by the consequences of the war. In wartime Bosnia-Herzegovina and Kosovo, a significant proportion of the population lived from international humanitarian aid. Throughout Southeast Europe, many families survived thanks to undeclared work or to money sent by relatives abroad. Ordinary citizens found these difficulties all the more unacceptable as the changes under way often benefited the former members of the communist apparatus, representatives of organised crime and, in the Yugoslav space, "war profiteers". The first decade of the post-communist period was therefore, for the Balkan populations, a time of impoverishment, individual resourcefulness and widespread corruption, rather than a linear transition to a market economy and a gradual catching up with the Western European standard of living.

FROM COMMUNISM TO EUROPEAN INTEGRATION

During the same period, the Balkan countries quickly re-entered the flow of goods, people and ideas generated by globalisation. From the distribution of humanitarian aid to the import of luxury and high technology products, the inflow of foreign goods drastically altered the consumption habits of the Balkan societies. Conversely, the voluntary or forced migrations of the 1990s swelled the ranks of the Balkan diasporas in Western Europe, North America and Oceania. During this decade, some 800,000 Albanians from Albania—a quarter of the country's total population—emigrated to Greece, Italy and other European countries. Likewise, following the Yugoslav wars, hundreds of thousands of refugees from Bosnia-Herzegovina and Kosovo were dispersed among different countries in the West—particularly Germany, Scandinavia, Austria and Switzerland. Subsequently, a number of these refugees found themselves constrained to return to their home countries, but large Bosniak and Albanian communities established themselves in the West, confirming the re-orientation of the migratory flows noted from the 1960s onwards. Only the Turks of Bulgaria continued to migrate mainly to Turkey, with several tens of thousands of them settling there for economic reasons during the 1990s. Greece became a country of immigration. In 2001, it officially received 760,000 foreigners, of which 440,000 were Albanians from Albania, 140,000 were other migrants from Eastern Europe and 70,000 were migrants from Africa and Asia. Finally, the restoration of freedom of opinion, the arrival of various international NGOs and the ground presence of the main international organisations increased the circulation of ideas between Southeast Europe and the rest of the world. Thus, the Balkan societies are not a "black hole" that escaped globalisation, but a place where globalisation takes particularly palpable forms, as also evidenced by the religious changes of the 1990s.

In the whole of Southeast Europe, the restoration of religious freedoms was an essential aspect of the democratisation that was taking place. The ban on religion was lifted in Albania in 1990. Elsewhere religious institutions ceased to be subject to the control of the political authorities, the return of their property was undertaken, despite many legal and practical difficulties, and the opening of private religious schools was authorised again. Romania, Bulgaria, Croatia, Bosnia-Herzegovina and, later, Serbia, Montenegro and Macedonia re-introduced religious education in public schools, most often on an optional basis. Slovenia, Albania and Kosovo were therefore the only countries in the region in which religion and public education remained entirely separate. This restoration of religious freedoms went hand in hand with what some have described as the "return of religion": the building of places of worship increased greatly, religious publications experienced considerable growth and large religious events drew crowds of the faithful and the curious. Moreover, religious dignitaries took part in the main patriotic ceremonies and were sought after by politicians of all sides. This enthusiasm for religion may be detected in opinion surveys, with those surveyed almost all declaring themselves believers and listing religious institutions among the institutions they trusted most. However, these changes attest less to a renewal of faith than to increased visibility of religious symbols and a return of religious institutions to the public sphere, in a context of closer links between national identity and religious identity.

The use of religious symbols and religious institutions in the assertion of national identities was particularly visible in wartime Yugoslavia, where it often led to the systematic destruction of the other side's religious monuments. However, a similar tendency could be found throughout Southeast Europe, including in Greece, where the new Orthodox patriarch, Christodoulos, opposed the pro-European modernism of the Prime Minister, Kostas Simitis. In the former communist countries, the Orthodox Churches or, in Croatia, the Catholic Church established themselves as privileged partners of the state. The "historic religions"[3] thus enjoyed significant privileges compared to the recently established religious movements and Churches, including in the multi-denominational states of Albania and Bosnia-Herzegovina. At the same time, the close links between religious identity and national identity explain many tensions, such as the jurisdictional disputes between the Serbian, Macedonian and Montenegrin Orthodox Churches, the refusal of the Romanian Orthodox Church to return the property confiscated in 1948 to the Uniate Church, and the denunciation by some Albanian nationalists of the links between the Albanian Orthodox Church and the Greek Orthodox Church. To some extent, these disputes are simply a belated manifestation of the nationalisation of the religious institutions begun in the nineteenth century.

However, these same religious institutions did not regain the legal status or moral authority they enjoyed before 1945, and their attempts to do so met strong resistance. The adoption of new laws on religious communities, the introduction of religious education in schools and the attempt to ban abortion gave rise to heated debate. The religious institutions therefore had to learn to position themselves in a pluralist cultural and political environment, at the risk of themselves suffering the effects of that pluralisation. From this perspective, the most significant dispute was without doubt the schism in the Bulgarian Orthodox Church from 1992 onwards, which reflected, among other things, the opposition between the neo-communist BSP and the anti-communist SDS. Other political disputes ranged radical nationalists against moderates within the Serbian Orthodox Church and the Croatian Catholic Church. Moreover, the establishment of political and cultural pluralism was accompanied by new links between the national Orthodox Churches of Southeast Europe, the Russian Orthodox Church and the Ecumenical Patriarchate of Istanbul, the growing involvement of the religious communities set up in the diaspora, and increased proselytising by both the Protestant Churches and the new religious movements arriving from Western Europe and North America. On the religious level too, therefore, liberalisation and globalisation went hand in hand, and challenged the institutional compromises and intellectual certainties of the past. The idea of a simple "return of religion" fails to take account of these complex evolutions. Moreover, despite the closer links between national identity and religious identity, religious life in post-communist Southeast Europe was characterised less by a revival of religious practice than by diversification of such practice and therefore, ultimately, by an individualisation of faith. The proof lies in the fact that the religious institutions found great difficulties in financing their activities and in replacing their religious personnel. They were also unable to have any real influence in public debates, with the faithful often having opinions and attitudes that had little to do with those advocated by their religious hierarchy. As we shall see, the Balkan Muslims were no exception to that rule.

The Balkan Muslims' politicisation

For many Muslims of Southeast Europe, the first post-communist decade was a terrible ordeal. In Bulgaria, when the Živkov regime disappeared in 1989, more than 300,000 Bulgarian Turks had sought refuge in Turkey. In Bosnia-Herzegovina, two thirds of those who died in the war between 1992 and 1995 and 80 per cent of civilian victims were Muslims. The Srebrenica massacre, during which 8,000 Muslim men were killed by the Serbian forces in 1995, was the largest massacre in Europe since the end of the Second World War. Finally, in Kosovo, 90 per cent of the 11,000 victims of the war were Albanians. Yet the violence of the Yugoslav wars should not obscure the fact that the first post-communist decade was also a period of political affirmation and emancipation for the Balkan Muslims. In particular, during the 1990s the different Muslim populations of Southeast Europe set up their own political parties, in widely differing contexts and focusing on very different demands, which are examined below.

In Bosnia-Herzegovina it was the representatives of the pan-Islamist current, reconstituted in the 1960s, who initiated the political mobilisation of the Muslims. In May 1990 they founded the Party of Democratic Action (*Stranka Demokratske Akcije*—SDA), with none other than Alija Izetbegović as president. Over the course of the following months, numerous representatives from the Muslim elites linked to communist modernisation joined the SDA, although its leadership remained under the control of the pan-Islamist current. In November 1990, the SDA won 30 per cent of the votes in the elections, about 70 per cent of the Muslim vote. This means that approximately one third of the Bosnian Muslims supported non-nationalist parties, such as the Social Democratic Party (SDP) or the Union of Reform Forces of Yugoslavia (*Savez Reformskih Snaga Jugoslavije*—SRSJ). After the election, the SDA decided to build a coalition with the Serbian SDS and the Croatian HDZ despite growing disagreements over Bosnia-Herzegovina's future, and Alija Izetbegović became chairman of the Presidency of Bosnia and Herzegovina.

Although controlled by the pan-Islamist current, the SDA, considered as a whole, was no more than an ordinary nationalist party or, at the very most, an Islamic-nationalist party. Its particular aims are difficult to determine, apart from a very general desire to assert the political sovereignty of the Muslim nation. Initially, the SDA supported the continued existence of the Yugoslav federation, but from 1991 onwards, it argued increasingly openly for the independence of Bosnia-Herzegovina. In March 1992, it joined with the HDZ, the ex-communist SDP and several small parties in organising a self-determination referendum (64 per cent participation, 99 per cent voting yes). When war broke out in April 1992, the SDA leaders were faced with a more profound dilemma, between defending the territorial integrity of Bosnia-Herzegovina and asserting the political sovereignty of the Muslim nation, symbolised by the adoption of a new national name "Bosniak" in September 1993. Initially, the SDA set itself up as defender of a multi-ethnic Bosnia-Herzegovina; however, after fighting between Croats and Bosniaks broke out in May 1993, it seemed to be increasingly tempted by the creation of a Bosniak national state covering only part of the Bosnian territory. Thus, in September 1993, a Bosniak Assembly (*Bošnjački sabor*) bringing together the main political, military, religious and intellectual leaders of the Bosniak community made its acceptance of the partition of Bosnia-Herzegovina into three ethnic republics conditional upon additional Serbian territorial concessions. However, the prospect of a Bosniak national mini-state was opposed by the SDP and provoked a significant backlash within the SDA itself. So, for the SDA leaders, the acceptance in March 1994 of the Washington agreement creating the Bosniak-Croatian Federation, and then the Dayton agreement in 1995 dividing Bosnia-Herzegovina into two entities, the Federation and the Republika Srpska, provided a way of avoiding painful choices. More generally, the attitude of the SDA leaders in the face of the break-up of the Yugoslav federation seems to have been one of following rather than leading, as a result of the adverse military balance of power, their desire to win the support of the United States, and their own internal contradictions.

The ambiguities of the SDA leaders were starkly illustrated by how they managed the territories under the control of the Bosnian army. The SDA remained allied to the Croatian nationalists of the HDZ until fighting broke out between Bosniaks and Croats, when it brought the SDP back into the Presidency and government, but then returned to an alliance with the HDZ immediately after the creation of the Federation. Above all, while proclaiming its support for a multi-ethnic Bosnia-Herzegovina, the SDA monopolised power in the territories controlled by the Bosnian army and, in particular, controlled the diplomatic service, the secret services and the army. The foreign policy of the SDA leaders was similarly ambiguous. On the one hand, they counted on intervention by the United States and NATO to overturn the diplomatic and military balance of power in their favour. On the other, they used military and financial support from the Muslim countries to consolidate their hegemony in the territories controlled by the Bosnian army. In particular, they put in place parallel networks to raise funds and arms in the Muslim world and then redistributed them to the different units of the Bosnian army according to the ideological allegiance of their officers. At the heart of this system was the Third World Relief Agency (TWRA), an NGO headed up by Hasan Čengić, sentenced with Izetbegović in the 1983 trial, and Fatih al-Hassanein, a Sudanese member of the Muslim Brotherhood who had been a friend of Izetbegović since the 1970s.

After the war, the SDA continued to adopt conflicting positions. Advocating strengthening the central institutions created by the Dayton agreement, it sought at the same time to perpetuate its domination over the Bosniak part of the Federation. However, the post-war period was, for the SDA, one of relative decline. Firstly, it experienced a serious split in 1996 with the creation of the Party for Bosnia-Herzegovina (*Stranka za Bosnu i Hercegovinu*—SBiH), led by the former Prime Minister Haris Silajdžić. Four years later, in November 2000, the SDP and the SBiH won the legislative elections in the federation and formed the Alliance for Change in order to remove the SDA from power. Moreover, the strong international presence in Bosnia-Herzegovina led to a progressive dismantling of the parallel networks created during the war. The pan-Islamist current was thus weakened and gradually lost its hegemonic position within the SDA. This process was precipitated when Izetbegović withdrew from politics, leaving the Presidency of Bosnia-Herzegovina in 2000 and resigning as president of the party one year later. The "Bosnian exception", which had enabled the representatives of a minority pan-Islamist current to propel themselves to the head of a secularised Muslim/ Bosniak population, had come to an end.

The forms taken by the political mobilisation of Muslim populations (in the sociological sense of the term) in the other Balkan countries were even more complex. In December 1990, the SDA won around 80 per cent of the votes of the Muslims of Sanjak, and had several candidates elected to the parliaments of Serbia and Montenegro. With this support, the SDA claimed the territorial autonomy of Sanjak and the establishment of privileged relations with Bosnia-Herzegovina. It created a Muslim National Council of Sanjak (*Muslimansko Nacionalno Vijeće Sandžaka*—MNVS) in September 1991, and one month later it organised an illegal referendum on the autonomy of the region. During the war in Bosnia-Herzegovina, the Sanjak SDA leaders were the victims of brutal repression, feeding tensions between its president, Sulejman Ugljanin, and its secretary general, Rasim Ljajić. While the former continued to claim autonomy for Sanjak, the latter preferred the idea of regionalisation and aligned himself with the Serbian democratic opposition. In

1994, this led to the existence of two competing SDAs in Serbian Sanjak and then in 2000 to the creation of the Sanjak Democratic Party (*Sandžačka Demokratska Partija*—SDP) by Rasim Ljajić. In Montenegro, the gradual rupture between the Democratic Party of Socialists (DPS) and Slobodan Milošević's regime led the SDA to abandon its demand for the territorial autonomy of the Sanjak and to rejoin the Montenegrin government in 1998; however, this change of direction did not prevent the SDA's electoral decline and its breaking up into a number of small parties. The DPS then succeeded in capturing a majority of the votes of Montenegro's Muslims. Finally, in Serbia, the fall of Slobodan Milošević in October 2000 led the two main Bosniak parties to draw closer to the Serbian political parties that had come to power, the Democratic Party of Serbia (*Demokratska Stranka Srbije*—DSS) for the SDA and the Democratic Party (*Demokratska Stranka*—DS) for the SDP. In Serbia as in Montenegro, allegiance to the state predominated over aspirations for autonomy, with the local Muslim elites distancing themselves from Sarajevo in order to integrate themselves in the political lives of their respective states. A similar process occurred with the two Albanian parties of Montenegro, the Democratic League of Montenegro (*Lidhja Demokratike në Mal të Zi*—LDMZ) and the Democratic Union of Albanians (*Unioni Demokratik i Shqiptarëve*—UDSH), which gave their support to the DPS from 1998 onwards. However, in the valley of Preševo (southern Serbia), the situation remained more tense, with the Party for Democratic Action (*Partia për Veprim Demokratik*—PVD) and the Democratic Party of Albanians (*Partia Demokratike e Shqiptarëve*—PDSH) organising an illegal referendum on the territorial autonomy for the region in March 1992, and an Army for the Liberation of Preševo, Medvedja and Bujanovac (*Ushtria Çlirimtare për Preshevë, Medvegjë dhe Bujanoc*—UÇPMB) appearing in 2000, as a by-product of the Kosovo Liberation Army (UÇK).

In Kosovo, the Democratic League of Kosovo created in 1989 drew its support largely from the secular Albanian elites that had emerged during the communist period; its president, Ibrahim Rugova, was himself the former president of the Union of Writers of Kosovo. Faced with the hardening of Serbian repression, the LDK maintained its claim for the independence for Kosovo and organised an illegal referendum on the question in September 1991. It also opted for a non-violent strategy centred on the creation of a parallel state; the "Republic of Kosovo" proclaimed in September 1991 set up its own government presided over by Bujar Bukoshi, who was charged above all with raising funds in Kosovo and among the diaspora. It then organised clandestine general elections in May 1992. Those elections were won hands down by Ibrahim Rugova (99 per cent of the votes in the presidential elections) and by the LDK (76 per cent of the votes in the legislative elections); the remainder of the votes went to various small parties linked to the LDK. At the same time, various parallel institutions were set up, including an education system using the Albanian language, with 18,000 teachers and 330,000 pupils.

While the claim for independence for Kosovo enjoyed unanimous support in the Albanian community, the non-violent strategy supported by Ibrahim Rugova was soon challenged. Former nationalist activists imprisoned in the communist period criticised this choice as early as 1993 and left the LDK in 1998 to create the Unified Democratic Movement (*Lëvizja e Bashkuar Demokratike*—LBD). More importantly, from 1996 onwards, different armed groups under the name Kosovo Liberation Army (UÇK) led attacks against the police and Serbian civilians. Abroad, the People's Movement for the Republic of Kosovo (LPRK), created in 1982 and renamed the People's Movement of Kosovo (*Lëvizja Popullore e Kosovës*—LPK) in 1993, succeeded in uniting the various components of the UÇK and in making itself the organisation's mouthpiece. The conflict which then arose between the LDK and the LPK mirrored not only a strategic disagreement on the question of armed struggle, but also a more profound division between the leaders of the LDK, most of whom had been socialised in the Yugoslav communist system, and some UÇK leaders who had emerged from clandestine movements inspired by Enver Hoxha's Marxism-Leninism. At the same time as the confrontations between the UÇK and the Serbian security forces were taking on the scale of a veritable war, the conflict between the LDK and the LPK also took a radical and violent turn. In 1998, Bujar Bukoshi sought to promote the Armed Forces of the Republic of Kosovo (*Forcat e Armatosura të Republikës së Kosovës*—FARK), which competed with the UÇK, while the LPK created its own system for raising funds among the diaspora. Several violent incidents ensued, including the assassination of Ahmet Krasniqi, Minister of Defence in Bukoshi's government, in September 1998. Seven months later, with Kosovo in the throes of a full-scale war, the UÇK formed its own provisional government, led by Hashim Thaçi. The LDK refused to participate in that government.

FROM COMMUNISM TO EUROPEAN INTEGRATION

This legitimacy contest between the LDK and the LPK began to be resolved only after the end of the war in June 1999 and the establishment of the United Nations Interim Administration Mission in Kosovo (UNMIK). While the UÇK became the Kosovo Protection Corps (*Trupat e Mbrojtjes së Kosovës*—TMK), and some of its commandants joined the LDK, the LPK launched a new party, the Democratic Party of Kosovo (*Partia Demokratike e Kosovës*—PDK). In July 1999, a Kosovo Transitional Council was put in place, with Bernard Kouchner, UN Special Representative, as president. The LDK, PDK and LBD were represented in the Transitional Council. Two and a half years later, in November 2001, the LDK won the legislative elections with 46 per cent of the votes, compared to 26 per cent for the PDK and 8 per cent for the Alliance for the Future of Kosovo (*Aleanca për Ardhmërinë e Kosovës*—AAK), a party founded by Ramush Haradinaj, a former UÇK regional commander. In March 2002, Ibrahim Rugova was elected president of Kosovo by the new parliament, but the post of prime minister was given to a member of the PDK, Bajram Rexhepi. Thus, the unanimism that had characterised the Albanian community in the early 1990s was replaced by a durable political pluralism, shaped by the strategic disagreements of the past decade and by socio-political divisions going back to the communist period.

In this context, what was happening to Kosovo's small non-Albanian Muslim populations? Caught between the Serbian security apparatus and the Albanian parallel state, they were forced to make difficult choices. A large majority of Kosovo's Gypsies/Romas[4] maintained their clientelistic allegiance to the Socialist Party of Serbia (SPS). The Muslims/Bosniaks and Turks were more divided. Thus, the Kosovo branch of the Party of Democratic Action (SDA) supported the "Republic of Kosovo", while the Democratic Reform Party of Muslims (*Demokratska Reformska Stranka Muslimana*—DRSM), which represented the Muslims of Sredačka Župa (southeast of Prizren), respected the Serbian Constitution. For their part, a majority of the Goranis of the Gora region (south of Prizren) voted for the Socialist Party of Serbia (SPS). Finally, the Democratic Union of Turks (*Türk Demokratik Birliği*—TDB) was close to the Serbian authorities, while the Turkish People's Party (*Türk Halk Partisi*—THP) was linked to the "Republic of Kosovo". After the 1998–9 war, the Roma suffered Albanian reprisals and many of them sought refuge in Serbia or in Western Europe. More generally, the non-Albanian Muslim populations were powerless as a result of their internal divisions, and despite the seats reserved for them in the new Kosovar parliament.[5]

The strategic disagreements and the socio-political divisions that had shaped the Albanian political landscape in Kosovo were also to be found in Macedonia, though in different forms. In April 1990, the Party of Democratic Prosperity (*Partia për Prosperitet Demokratik*—PPD) was created by representatives of the secular elites produced by the communist modernisation. Seven months later, it won 22 per cent of the votes, i.e. 85 per cent of Albanian votes, together with Turkish, Muslim and Roma votes. The PDP then entered a government coalition led by the Social Democratic Union of Macedonia (SDSM, ex-communist). During the following years, however, the PPD gradually lost its dominant position within the Albanian community. Firstly, an internal opposition appeared, led by Arbën Xhaferi and other young party officials. They left the PPD in 1994, and two years later merged with the People's Democratic Party (*Partia Demokratike Popullore*—PDP) to create the Democratic Party of Albanians (*Partia Demokratike e Shqiptarëve*—PDSH). In November 1998, the PPD and the PDSH presented a joint list in the legislative elections (19 per cent of the votes), but in the weeks that followed, the PDSH went its own way and joined a coalition led by the Internal Macedonian Revolutionary Organisation (VMRO). Moreover, in the spring of 2001, a National Liberation Army (*Ushtria Çlirimtare Kombëtare*—UÇK) was created in Macedonia, modelled on the Kosovar UÇK and with the support of former leaders of the LPK, such as Ali Ahmeti. Following the Ohrid agreement that brought the short Macedonian conflict to an end on 13 August 2001, some of the UÇK's commandants created the Democratic Union for Integration (*Bashkimi Demokratik për Integrim*—BDI). In September 2002, the BDI won 12 per cent of the votes in the legislative elections, beating the PDSH (4 per cent) and the PPD (2 per cent). It was then the turn of the BDI to enter into a government coalition led by the SDSM, scarcely a year after the UÇK had ended its military activities.

In Macedonia as in Kosovo, the question of the armed struggle and the opposition between politicians linked to the Yugoslav communist system on the one hand and clandestine or young activists on the other shaped the internal pluralism of the Albanian community. In the case of Macedonia, these divisions were overlaid by the question of the choice of a Macedonian political partner in order to form a governing coalition and thereby access the state's material resources. The PPD took the logical step of allying itself with the ex-communist SDSM, while the PDSH preferred the anti-communist VMRO. In 2002, the BDI, for its part, merely occupied the space left vacant by a declining PPD. It must also be emphasised that the claims put forward by Macedonia's Albanian parties were very similar, concerning the recognition of the Albanians as second constituent nation of the Macedonian state, the use of the Albanian language as an official language, the development of teaching in the Albanian language and the strengthening of the powers of the municipalities. During the 1990s, the mobilisation of the Albanian parties crystallised around the Albanian university in Tetovo, created illegally in 1994. Despite an illegal referendum organised in January 1992 on the issue of territorial autonomy for Western Macedonia, the demand for autonomy was not subsequently taken up by the Albanian parties. On 13 August 2001, the Ohrid agreement satisfied several Albanian demands, giving the members of parliament representing national minorities some right of veto, establishing mechanisms to ensure better representation of the national minorities in the public sector, making Albanian an official language in the municipalities in which Albanians accounted for more than 20 per cent of the population, and extending the powers of the municipalities. Macedonia de facto became a bi-national state. In the months that followed, the UÇK laid down its arms, but the electoral competition between the PDSH and the BDI led to violent incidents. Political violence thus re-appeared within the Albanian community.

In Macedonia too, the non-Albanian Muslim populations struggled to assert themselves in the face of the Albanian community, even though they accounted for a higher proportion of the population than in Kosovo. The Turkish, Roma and Muslim/Bosniak parties succeeded in winning some parliamentary seats by allying themselves with the SDSM or the VMRO. However, these parties were very divided and not really representative. For example, the Party for Complete Emancipation of the Roma (*Partia za Celosna Emancipacija na Romite*—PCER) very soon found itself facing competition from other Roma parties, and the Macedonian branch of the Party of Democratic Action (SDA) split into several rival parties. Only the Turkish Democratic Party (*Türk Demokratik Partisi*—TDP) did not have direct competition and even succeeded in having a member of parliament directly elected in the October 1994 elections by allying itself with the SDA-Islamic Path, a split-off party of the local SDA with an Islamist orientation (seeking to promote a political order founded on Islam).[6] Lastly, throughout this period a proportion of the Turks, Muslims/Bosniaks and Roma from Macedonia voted for the SDSM, which presented candidates from these national minorities.

In Kosovo as in Macedonia, the division between Albanians on the one hand and Serbs or Macedonians on the other coincides with a division between Muslims and Orthodox Christians. This is not the case in Albania, where there is a Greek minority (3 per cent of the population), but where the Albanian majority includes Muslims, Orthodox Christians and Catholics. So in Albania it is not possible to speak of parties representing the Muslim community: in the 1990s, the central division in Albanian political life was between the Socialist Party (PS) and the Democratic Party (DP). This was above all an ideological division between ex-communists and anti-communists, with an underlying regional dimension (the strongholds of the PS were mainly in the south, those of the PD mainly in the north). However, there was no religious dimension to this division: the two parties counted both Muslims and Christians among their members. The adoption in 1991 of a law that banned parties based on ethnicity, faith or regional identity, although only imperfectly enforced, also helps explain why there was no Muslim party in Albania. While a Unity for Human Rights Party (PBDNJ) representing the Greek minority was set up in 1991, and a predominantly Catholic Christian Democrat Party of Albania (*Partia Demokristiane e Shqipërisë*—PDSH) was also created, the Islamic Democratic Union Party (*Partia e Bashkimit Demokratik Islam*—PBDI) was banned in 1993. Contrary to what happened in the rest of Southeast Europe, Albania's Muslim Albanians were not tempted to set up their own political party. This "Albanian exception" is explained by the multi-denominational nature of Albanian national identity in Albania, and by the high degree of secularisation of Albanian society after several decades during which religion had been banned. This does not mean that Albanian political life was devoid of any religious dimension, as will be shown later in this chapter with regard to the PS–PD division.

In Bulgaria, the overthrowing of Todor Živkov in November 1989 was quickly followed by the restoration of some rights that had been abolished in the 1980s, in particular the right for members of the Turkish minority to use their original forenames and surnames and the right to speak Turkish in public. This decision explains why around half of the 300,000 Turks from Bulgaria who had taken refuge in Turkey made the return journey. However, it also created high levels of tension in the Turkish-populated regions, where the ethnic Bulgarians demonstrated against this "betrayal" of national interests. In November 1990, Bulgarian nationalists even proclaimed a "republic of Razgrad" in the north-east of the country. However, relations between the Bulgarian state and the Turkish minority returned to normal quite quickly. The Movement for Rights and Freedoms (DPS) was created in January 1990; its president was Ahmed Doğan, a philosopher who had been imprisoned in 1980 for taking part in the Turkish National Liberation Movement (TNOD). Although Bulgarian law banned parties based on ethnicity or faith, the DPS was allowed to take part in the June 1990 elections, in which it received 7.5 per cent of all votes (around 80 per cent of the Turkish votes). During the following decade, the DPS won between 5.5 and 7.5 per cent of votes in legislative elections, sometimes allying itself with small Bulgarian parties. Its hegemony within the Turkish population was never questioned, even if internal conflicts led to the appearance of small competing parties such as the Turkish Democratic Party (*Turska Demokratičeska Partija*—TDP) created by Adem Kenan in 1993. This hegemonic position of the DPS within the Turkish community enabled it to act as an arbitrator in a parliament long dominated by the opposition between the Bulgarian Socialist Party (BSP) and the Union of Democratic Forces (SDS), and to support various coalition governments led by the SDS (1991–2), by the "independent" Ljuben Berov (1992–5) and by the BSP (1995–7). However, it was not until the elections of June 2001 that the DPS directly participated, with two ministers in the government established by the Simeon II National Movement (*Nacionalno Dviženje Simeon Vtori*).

So, compared to the states that emerged from the Yugoslav federation, Bulgaria seemed to offer a model for pacifying interethnic tensions and integrating national minorities. On the one hand, the main Bulgarian political parties moderated their attacks on a Turkish minority whose elected officials were able to provide essential support in parliament. On the other, the DPS refrained from raising national demands and focused on the economic problems of the Turkish minority, such as the crisis in the tobacco industry. However, this "virtuous circle" must not blind us to the fact that the rights granted to the Turkish minority were rather limited. The new constitution adopted in July 1991 still made no reference to the existence of national minorities. That same year, Turkish language was reintroduced as an optional subject in Bulgarian school curricula; however, ten years later, the number of pupils actually studying Turkish language courses was 35,000, only half of the Turkish pupils. Finally, a National Council on Ethnic and Demographic Issues was created in 1997 and Bulgaria ratified the European Framework Convention for the Protection of National Minorities in 1999; however, this did not bring an end to discrimination, nor to the prejudices suffered by the Turkish population. In the meantime, a new generation of political leaders has emerged within the DPS; they are less marked by the repression of the 1980s and have used the European Convention to demand official recognition for a Turkish national minority. The "Bulgarian model" of interethnic coexistence therefore remains precarious and difficult to export to the wider region.

This is all the more true since the two other Muslim population groups present in Bulgaria, the Pomaks and the Muslim Romas, were not politically integrated in the same way as the Turkish population. After 1990, the Pomaks voted for either the DPS or the BSP, according to their national identification, which will be discussed later in this chapter. In 1992, the attempt to create a Pomak party, the Democratic Party of Labour (*Demokratična Partija na Truda*—DPT), ended in failure. Furthermore, the Roma population—both Muslims and non-Muslims—appeared to be very divided politically, with a coalition of twelve Roma parties receiving only 0.6 per cent of the votes in the 2001 elections and most Roma votes going to the BSP or DPS candidate. The few Romas elected to the Bulgarian parliament were on the lists of the BSP or the SDS. In the "Bulgarian model" created during the 1990s, the Pomaks are still the subject of implicit attempts at assimilation, while the Romas are victims of deep-rooted prejudices and discrimination. Thus, the changes of the 1990s did not affect Bulgaria's different Muslim populations in a uniform way.

In Romania too, the end of communism led to better integration of the Turkish and Tatar minorities, in a context that differed significantly from that in Bulgaria. Concentrated in Dobruja, these two minorities accounted for only a very small minority of the total Romanian population. In December 1989, the Muslim Turkish Democratic Union of Romania (*Uniunea Democrata Turca Musulmana din România*—UDTMR) was created; three months later it split into a Turkish organisation, the Turkish Democratic Union of Romania (*Uniunea Democrata Turca din*

România—UDTR), and a Tatar organisation, the Democratic Union of Turco-Muslim Tatars of Romania (*Uniunea Democrata a Tatarilor Turco-Musulmani din România*—UDTTMR). Each had one member of parliament, as the 1991 constitution reserved seats for the twenty officially recognised national minorities. On the cultural level, teaching in Turkish or Tatar was reintroduced in primary schools in Dobruja, and Turkish or Tatar language newspapers appeared. Thus, the question of the political and cultural rights of the Turkish and Tatar minorities in Romania does not seem to have produced major tensions.

In Greece, the mobilisation of the Muslim minority of Western Thrace, which had begun in the 1980s, reached a peak in 1990. Following the early legislative elections held in November 1989, the independent candidates Sadik Ahmet and İbrahim Şerif saw their candidacies invalidated and were imprisoned for having used the name "Turk" in their electoral propaganda. The High Council of the Turkish Minority then organised a demonstration in Komotini on 29 January 1990. That demonstration was attacked by counter-demonstrators from the extreme right, which carried out violent anti-Turkish exactions. In this tense climate, the two Turkish candidates were released in March 1990. One month later, Sadik Ahmet succeeded in being elected as a member of parliament in fresh early elections. However, this victory was short-lived; as early as November, the Greek parliament passed a new electoral law specifying that, in order to be elected, candidates in the legislative elections had to belong to a political formation that received at least 3 per cent of votes nationally. As a result, in 1993, Sadik Ahmet and Ahmet Faikoğlu received the most votes in the constituencies of Komotini and Xanthi, but failed to win seats in parliament. Sadik Ahmet then created the Friendship, Equality and Peace party (*Dostluk, Eşitlik ve Barış*—DEB), but found himself isolated in this strategy, as most of the Muslim notables preferred to resume the earlier practice of having Muslim candidates included on the lists of the main Greek political parties. Sadik Ahmet's death in a road accident in July 1995 precipitated the marginalisation of the DEB and marked the end of the cycle of mobilisation that had begun in the early 1980s.

The absence of a political party in Western Thrace representing the Muslim minority on a long-term basis was not a return to the status quo ante: in fact, the High Council for the Turkish Minority of Western Thrace—renamed the Consultative Council for the Turkish Minority in

Western Thrace (*Batı Trakya Türk Azınlığı Danış Kurulu*) in 1997—emerged as the minority's principal representative body. Furthermore, the candidates put forward by the Greek Socialist Party (PASOK) did not hesitate to display their Turkish identity, and the use of the Turkish language in election campaigns became widespread. More generally, a certain easing appeared in the 1990s between the Greek state and the Muslim minority of Western Thrace, following the increased tensions of the previous years. Serious disputes persisted around the ban on associations using the word "Turk/Turkish" in their names and the appointment of muftis. However, in 1991, the Greek authorities facilitated the recognition of university degrees obtained in Turkey and, in 1996, set a quota of 0.5 per cent of places reserved for members of the minority in Greek universities. That same year, the military zone established along the Bulgarian border was dismantled and, in 1998, article 19 of the nationality code, which enabled Greek authorities to deprive some Greek citizens of "foreign descent" of their nationality, was abolished. A process of normalisation between the Greek state and the Muslim minority thus began to take shape in the second half of the 1990s, although it continued to be hindered by the very particular legal status granted to the Muslim minority in Western Thrace in 1923.

To sum up, the politicisation of the Balkan Muslims (in the sociological sense of the term) in the 1990s, together with their emergence as an autonomous political factor, was the logical continuation of the process of crystallisation of their national identities during the Cold War period. Almost everywhere, this politicisation was symbolised by the creation of political parties representing the Muslim populations. Albania and Greece are the only exceptions to this rule, for contrasting reasons. In the case of Albania, the absence of a specifically Muslim party may be explained by the widespread reference to a supra-denominational national identity; in the case of Greece, on the contrary, it is accounted for by an attempt to confine the Muslim minority within a strictly religious framework. In the other Balkan states, it has been the secular elites linked to communist modernisation that provided the driving force behind the political parties representing the Muslim populations. The only partial exception in this regard is Bosnia-Herzegovina, where the pan-Islamist current temporarily succeeded in placing itself at the centre of the political reconfiguration of the Muslim community. Finally, the early 1990s were marked by the appearance of political parties that exercised a real hegemony over their respective communities, while the second half of the 1990s saw the development of an intra-community political pluralism. The main exception this time is Bulgaria, where the DPS still do not have any serious competitor. But other than these few traits, shared by a majority of the Balkan Muslim populations, their political trajectories have been very diverse.

Indeed, what does the situation of the Muslims of Bosnia-Herzegovina have in common with that of the Turks of Western Thrace, or the claims of the Albanians in Kosovo with those of the Turks and Tatars in Romania? The differences between the claims advanced are largely explained by the different political contexts. In addition to the differing demographic weights of the various Muslim populations, the stability and legitimacy of the central state play a decisive role in determining their political demands and actions. Yugoslavia was a collapsing multi-national state, while Bulgaria was a stable nation-state. The new Bulgarian authorities opted for a policy of compromise, while Slobodan Milošević's regime chose repression and violence. Against this background, two state entities are special cases: Bosnia-Herzegovina and Kosovo. In these two entities, the break-up of Yugoslavia resulted in the emergence of a state (or quasi-state) in which the Muslims account for a majority of the population. In Bosnia-Herzegovina the majority is relative, with Bosniaks representing around 45 per cent of the total population after the war,[7] while in Kosovo it is absolute, with 90 per cent of the population being Albanians, the great majority of whom are Muslims. The Bosniaks of Bosnia-Herzegovina and the Albanians of Kosovo had been minorities since the end of the Ottoman period, and this change to majority status has been all the more marked because, in both cases, the population displacements caused by the war have resulted in ethnically homogeneous territories, with any areas in which different communities still coexist all but disappearing. Between 1912 and 1990, Albania was the only state in Southeast Europe with a Muslim majority, but in the 1990s two others appeared, providing further impetus for the politicisation of the Balkan Muslims. However, it must be emphasised that none of these three Muslim-majority states grants Islam the status of state religion in the way that, for example, Greece does with the Orthodox Church.

While the Muslims of Southeast Europe were both victims and actors in the building of new nation-states in this region of the world, other processes were also at work. The voluntary or forced emigration of many Balkan Muslims during the 1990s reduced their absolute numbers in some countries, such as Albania and Bosnia-Herzegovina, or their share in the total population, as in Bulgaria. Conversely, the Balkan Muslim diasporas in the Western world experienced rapid growth in the same period. These diasporas sometimes played a significant role in the politicisation of their communities of origin. Thus, during times of war, control of the diaspora's financial resources was a key issue for the leaders of the SDA in Bosnia-Herzegovina and for the LDK and the LPK in Kosovo. The LPK, created in Germany by Marxist–Leninist activists in exile, also succeeded in having a decisive influence on the reshaping of the Albanian political landscape in Kosovo and Macedonia. This political role of the diaspora is to be found in Western Thrace too, in a different context: the Federation of Associations of Turks of Western Thrace in Germany, renamed the Federation of Turks of Western Thrace in Europe (*Avrupa Batı Trakya Türk Federasyonu*—ABBTF) in 1997, influenced the strategies of the local political elites in Western Thrace and was responsible for lobbying the European institutions on behalf of the Turkish minority. In the case of the Muslims of Southeast Europe, politicisation on a nationalist basis, mobilisation of transnational diasporas and participation in the Euro-Atlantic process fed into each other in a complex way, rather than conflicting with each other. Thus, the Muslim minorities of Southeast Europe made use of the European Framework Convention for the Protection of National Minorities, the European Charter for Regional or Minority Languages and the decisions of the European Court of Human Rights in order to renegotiate their relations with the central state. In Bosnia-Herzegovina and Kosovo, NATO, the OSCE and the European Union worked to consolidate the new Muslim-majority state entities. From this perspective, the politicisation experienced by the Balkan Muslims in the 1990s came about not only as the result of the crystallisation of their national identities during the previous half century, but also because of their accelerated integration into the globalised world of the twenty-first century.

Closer links between Islam and national identity

The politicisation of the Balkan Muslims was accompanied by a complex reshaping of their national identity. This was particularly noticeable when it resulted in a change in national name, as in Bosnia-Herzegovina. Shortly after the creation of the SDA, the representatives of the pan-

Islamist current confronted the supporters of the national name "Bosniak" (*Bošnjak*) and succeeded in expelling them from the party in September 1990.[8] However, three years later, on 27 September 1993, they did a U-turn and the SDA-dominated *Bošnjački sabor* decided to abandon the national name "Muslim" in favour of "Bosniak". The purpose of this change of name was to emphasise the accession of Bosnian Muslims to the status of a sovereign political nation, and to strengthen their international legitimacy. The new Bosniak national identity was then taken care of by various national institutions, such as the cultural society *Preporod*, re-established in October 1990, and the Congress of Bosniak Intellectuals, formed in December 1992. The production of a new national identity involved, in particular, the recognition of a Bosnian language as separate from Serbian and Croatian, and the official adoption of certain theories concerning the ethnogenesis of the Bosniak nation, beginning with the Bogomil theory. However, outside Bosnia-Herzegovina, the transition to a Bosniak national identity was not without difficulties: in Sanjak, Kosovo, Macedonia and Croatia, many Muslim Serbo-Croatian speakers continued to declare themselves as Muslims in the population censuses,[9] while the local branches of the SDA became increasingly integrated in the political life of their respective states.

Identity changes of the same order have occurred within the Muslim minority of Western Thrace, where the adoption of the national name "Turk" reflects the politicisation of the local Muslims, including many Pomaks and Romas, but has encountered fierce resistance from the Greek state, which clings to the religious name "Muslim" and encourages the formation of a specific Pomak identity. In Bulgaria, the Turkish national identity is no longer disputed as such, but the question of the national affiliation of the Pomaks remains a major bone of contention between the Bulgarian state and the Turkish minority. More generally, in Southeast Europe, the small groups of Slavic-speaking or Roma Muslims have experienced contrasting identity changes. On the one hand, they tend to identify with the majority Christian population, or with a larger Muslim minority. In Bulgaria, the Pomaks declare themselves to be either Turks or Bulgarians (sometimes keeping the Christian names they have been given during the "revival process"), and in Macedonia the Torbeshis declare themselves to be Albanians, Turks, Muslims or Macedonians. On the other hand, however, there have been attempts to promote new ethnic identities specific to these small groups. In Kosovo, where the institutionalisation of ethnicity has been particularly strong since 1999, some Goranis formed a Gorani Civic Initiative (*Građanska Inicijativa Gorana*—CIG), while the Romas divided between Roma, Egyptian[10] and Ashkali[11] political parties. Several Roma parties also coexisted in Bulgaria and Macedonia. Pomak or Torbesh identity, on the other hand, is expressed in those countries primarily through cultural or religious associations.

The Albanian national identity seems particularly stable in comparison. At first glance, no major identity change occurred within the Albanian nation in the 1990s. However, this is partly a misleading impression. In fact, the opening up of Albania and the politicisation of the Albanians of Kosovo and Macedonia led to more intense exchanges between political and intellectual actors in the Albanian space. Political connections were established between the PD of Albania, the LDK of Kosovo and the PPD of Macedonia, while the PS, the PDK and the PDSH drew closer in response. These trans-Albanian political alliances remain very informal and have gradually given way to dynamics specific to Albanian, Kosovar and Macedonian political life. However, a lasting result of the politicisation of the Albanians of Kosovo and Macedonia has been the shift north of the centre of gravity of Albanian nationalism, previously located in southern Albania. This has also meant that the Sunni Muslim (and Catholic) regions have acquired more weight in the political and intellectual dynamics of the Albanian space, a factor that has influenced the debates on Islam and national identity, as we shall now examine.

It is doubtless in Bosnia-Herzegovina that the identification between Islam and national identity was pushed the furthest. At the initiative of the SDA, the discarding of the national name "Muslim" in favour of "Bosniak" was, paradoxically, followed by an assertion of Islam as the central component of the new Bosniak national identity, opposed to the Orthodox Serbs and the Catholic Croats. In the context of war, the army was used as a vehicle for the re-Islamicisation of the Bosniak national identity; officers responsible for religion and morale were appointed at every level of the military hierarchy; "Muslim brigades" were created, made up of re-Islamicised fighters trained by Iran; and a cult of *šehids*[12] (martyrs of the faith) was established around dead fighters. Moreover, the pan-Islamism of the SDA leaders had very practical implications for the renewal of the Bosniak political elites: direct or indirect affiliation to the

Young Muslims organisation, education at the Sarajevo madrasa or, failing that, a religiosity that was more ostentatious the more recent it was, all ensured a rapid rise within the SDA and the state apparatus. During the war years, Islam ended up occupying within the new party-state set up by the SDA the place that communist ideology had held in communist Yugoslavia. Paradoxically, therefore, the representatives of the pan-Islamist current reproduced some traits of the regime they had fought against for so long. These political practices did not, however, enjoy universal support. The non-nationalist parties such as the SDP continued to defend the idea of a multi-ethnic and secular state, and their representatives in the Bosnian Presidency openly protested against the use of the army as an instrument of re-Islamicisation. Moreover, the end of the war in 1995 brought the gradual ending of the instrumentalisation of religion for ideological purposes, even if Islam continues to occupy a central place in the definition of the new Bosniak national identity.

During this period, there was no equivalent in the Albanian space to the authoritarian re-Islamicisation of identity taking place in Bosnia-Herzegovina. In Kosovo, Ibrahim Rugova's LDK tended rather to promote the role of the Catholic Church in the Albanian national mobilisation, and the cult of fallen soldiers established after 1999 is strictly secular. The Albanian political and intellectual elites, however, are divided over the question of the relationship between Islam and Albanian national identity. One current, which could be described as "Westernist", emphasises the European (and Christian) identity of the Albanians, rejecting everything connecting them to Islam or the Ottoman Empire and regarding Islamicisation as a forced and superficial, even reversible, process. The best known representatives of this dominant current within Albanian nationalism were the writer Ismaïl Kadare and the Kosovo leader Ibrahim Rugova. The second, "multiculturalist" current presents the multi-denominational character of the Albanian nation as the best proof of its tolerant and European nature. It is supported by some intellectuals, such as Fatos Lubonja in Albania and Shkëlzen Maliqi in Kosovo. Finally, an "Islamic-nationalist" current emerged in the early 1990s. Adopting the theories that appeared at the end of the communist period, according to which Islamicisation protected the Albanians from Greek and Slav assimilationist pressures, it emphasises the Muslim and Ottoman aspects of Albanian identity. Politically, this current is supported only by small marginal parties such as Abdi Baleta's Party of

National Recovery (*Partia e Rimëkëmbjes Kombetare*—PRK) in Albania, the SDA-Islamic Path (*Partia për Veprim Demokratik—Rruga Islame*) in Macedonia and the Justice Party (*Partia e Drejtësisë*—PD) in Kosovo. However, it does exercise real influence within the Islamic institutions and in some intellectual circles, as evidenced in Albania by the creation in March 1992 of the Association of Muslim Intellectuals *Kultura Islame* ("Islamic Culture").

In Kosovo and Macedonia, where the Muslim community is multi-ethnic, the Albanian political parties often use Islam to encourage the Albanianisation of the non-Albanian Muslim minorities. Conversely, in Albania, where the Albanian nation is multi-denominational, some politicians are tempted to use religion to deepen political divisions. Sali Berisha's Democratic Party, in particular, has sought to obtain the support of the religious communities against the Socialist Party, heir to the former communist party. Having won the March 1992 elections, Berisha gave his policy a certain Islamic tinge by having Albania join the Organisation of the Islamic Conference (OIC) and appointing Bashkim Gazidede, president of the Association of Muslim Intellectuals, as head of the secret services. When Berisha's authoritarianism plunged Albania into a serious institutional crisis in 1996, and then into a short civil war one year later, the PD accused its political opponents of participating in an "Orthodox plot" against Albania. In fact, the civil war never had a religious dimension, although the insurgents were concentrated in the south of the country, where Orthodox Christians and Bektashis form a majority of the population. When the PS returned to power in the June 1997 elections, it ended Albania's membership of the OIC and, in turn, accused its opponents of being involved in an "Islamic plot" against Albania. In the late 1990s, however, Albanian politics gradually became calmer and such accusations with religious connotations have become increasingly rare.

The links between Islam and national identity have also become closer among the other Balkan Muslim populations. Thus, while the majority of Turkish politicians in Bulgaria and Greece remain close to Kemalist ideology, some are influenced by the "Turko-Islamic synthesis", a current of Islamic-nationalist thought that appeared in Turkey in the early 1980s. In Macedonia, the Turkish Democratic Party (TDP) is dominated by sympathisers with this current, and the Turko-Albanian urban elites are particularly receptive to Islamic-nationalist or pan-Islamist discourses. Moreover, faced with the dominant Albanian or Turkish groups, the representatives of the small groups of Slavic-speaking Muslims are tempted to assert their Muslim identity, or even a hypothetical Arab ethnic origin, in order to strengthen their legitimacy. Finally, only the Romas show little inclination to base their national identity on Islam; admittedly, some use their membership of a Muslim mystical brotherhood as a path to cultural assimilation and social advancement, but others opt to convert to Orthodox Christianity or Protestantism in order to achieve the same ends.

Generally, therefore, during the 1990s the redefinition of the relationship between Islam and national identity was neither consensual nor uniform in Southeast Europe. In particular, it is necessary to distinguish Bosnia-Herzegovina, where there was a real re-Islamicisation of national identity and, during the war, an instrumentalisation of Islam as a substitute political ideology, from the other Balkan states, where the Islamic-nationalist currents are of only marginal significance. Moreover, throughout Southeast Europe, the closer links between Islam and national identity do not prevent national divisions from prevailing over the solidarity of the *umma*. When the SDA was created in 1990, it sought to represent all Yugoslav Muslims (in the religious sense of the term), but the creation of Albanian, Turkish and Roma parties quickly revealed the futility of this pan-Islamic ambition. Between 1992 and 1995, the war in Bosnia-Herzegovina did not provoke any real upsurge of solidarity among Balkan Muslims, even though a few hundred Albanians from Kosovo and the diaspora fought in the Bosnian army. Four years later, in Kosovo, the victory of the Albanian UÇK caused an exodus of Romas and Bosniaks from the province. Finally, these national divisions were also to be found within the Islamic institutions, whose undeniable renewal could not conceal their increased fragility.

The renewal and fragility of Islamic institutions

Following the fall of the communist regimes, the Islamic institutions experienced a marked increase in activity and visibility throughout Southeast Europe. This was particularly evident in Albania where, after a ban on religion lasting twenty-three years, the first collective Muslim prayer was held in Shkodër on 16 November 1990. Three months later, the Sunni Muslim Community (*Komuniteti Mysliman*) was re-established under the leadership of Sabri Koçi, a former mufti of Shkodër who had been imprisoned by the communists for twenty years. During the following decade, hundreds of mosques were rehabilitated or rebuilt in Albania. As for the Bektashi community, it reorganised itself much more slowly under the leadership of the *kryegjysh* Reshat Bardhi. The 6th Bektashi World Congress was held in Tirana in July 1993, but only some ten *tekke*s were reopened in the 1990s. Several other mystical brotherhoods also resumed their activities, such as the Halvetis, the Kadiris, the Rifais, the Sadis and the Tijanis; however, they played only a marginal role in Albanian religious life. In the other Balkan countries too, hundreds of mosques were renovated or built. During the war, 600 mosques had been destroyed in Bosnia-Herzegovina and 200 in Kosovo; rebuilding began in the first years after the war, thanks to donations from the Muslim world and the diaspora. At the same time, some mystical brotherhoods experienced significant growth, such as the Rifais and the Kadiris in Kosovo and Macedonia and the Naqshbandis in Bosnia-Herzegovina. In Bulgaria, the small Alevi-Kizilbash community reopened several *cem evi*s (houses of ritual), closed during the communist period. Throughout Southeast Europe, the visibility of Islam increased considerably. The opening of mosques, the celebration of the main religious festivals and the resumption of some traditional Sufi pilgrimages also provided opportunities for large gatherings. The leaders of the Islamic institutions willingly appeared in the media, and Islamic journals and publishing houses, whether or not linked to the official institutions, multiplied, while ordinary believers also displayed their religious convictions, as evidenced by women wearing the veil and men wearing beards.

On a strictly institutional level, the development of the network of religious schools is the clearest symbol of the renewal of the Islamic institutions. In one decade, the number of active madrasas in Southeast Europe increased from five to twenty-two: six in Bosnia-Herzegovina (Sarajevo, Tuzla, Travnik, Visoko, Cazin, Mostar), one in Croatia (Zagreb), one in Serbian Sanjak (Novi Pazar), one in Kosovo (Prishtina, with one branch in Prizren and one in Gjilan), one in Macedonia (Skopje), seven in Albania (Tirana, Shkodër, Durrës, Berat, Gjirokastër, Kavajë, Cërrik), three in Bulgaria (Šumen, Ruse, Momčilgrad), one in Romania (Medgidia) and two in Greece (Komotini, Echinos). Furthermore, while previously there had been only one Islamic higher education institution (in Sarajevo), by the early 2000s there were seven: in Bosnia-Herzegovina, the Sarajevo Islamic Theology Faculty (founded in 1977 and renamed the Islamic

Sciences Faculty in 1991) and the Islamic Teacher Training Academies in Zenica (founded in 1993) and Bihać (1996); in Serbian Sanjak, the Islamic Teacher Training Institute of Novi Pazar (2001); in Kosovo, the Islamic Sciences Faculty in Prishtina (1992); in Macedonia, the Islamic Sciences Faculty in Skopje (1997); in Bulgaria, the Islamic Higher Education Institute in Sofia (1991). However, while the Islamic institutions succeeded in rebuilding an education system capable of training future imams and teachers of religion, they failed to restore the other traditional religious institutions dismantled by the communist regimes. As already mentioned, religious education was reintroduced to schools in most of the Balkan states, but not in either Albania or Kosovo, two states with a Muslim majority.

Denationalisation of the waqfs came up against multiple legal and practical obstacles, and when restitution of property occurred this was most often on a local, case-by-case and informal basis. Finally, no one seriously raised the possibility of restoring the sharia courts, even though "shariatic marriages" are celebrated in the mosques; these do not replace civil marriage and had only a symbolic value. Therefore, the Islamic institutions did not succeed in nullifying the effects of the authoritarian secularisation of the communist period and, at the dawn of the twenty-first century, Greece was the only Balkan state in which the waqfs played an important role in financing the religious institutions, and where the muftis had legal competence over family matters. Finally, Islamic institutions developed rapidly in the diaspora, with the opening of dozens of Bosniak or Albanian mosques in Western Europe (Germany, Scandinavia, Austria, Switzerland, etc.), North America and Oceania. In order to coordinate and supervise the religious life of their respective diasporas, the Islamic Community of Bosnia-Herzegovina created an Office for the Diaspora in 1996 and the Islamic Communities of Kosovo and Macedonia jointly created a Centre for the Coordination of Albanian Islamic Centres in 1997.

Against a background of closer links between Islam and the national identity of the Balkan Muslims, relations between the Islamic institutions and the Muslim political actors also changed. Numerous Muslim politicians took part in large religious gatherings, displaying their piety and their closeness to the main religious leaders. Some politicians also sat on the governing bodies of local or national religious institutions, or of the charitable associations that were associated with them. At the same time, religious dignitaries returned to the public sphere, taking positions on openly political questions and appearing in the media or before their faithful as champions of the national cause. In Bosnia-Herzegovina, officials of the Islamic Community played an active part in the re-Islamicisation of the Bosniak national identity and some of them made careers in the diplomatic service, the army or the secret services. In Kosovo and Macedonia, the principal religious leaders adopted the Islamic-nationalist discourses that identified Islam with Albanian national identity. However, here too, national divisions prevailed over religious solidarity. In the early 1990s, the Islamic Community of Yugoslavia, led by *Reis-ul-ulema* Jakub Selimoski, announced that it would maintain its unity whatever became of the Yugoslav federation. In April 1993, though, a Restoration Assembly (*Obnoviteljski sabor*)—convened in Sarajevo by ulamas linked to the pan-Islamist current—created an Islamic Community limited to Bosnia-Herzegovina, Sanjak and the Bosniak diaspora,[13] thus bringing an end to the existence of the largest Islamic religious institutions in Europe: the Yugoslav Islamic Community. So, once again, the action of the Bosnian pan-Islamist current ended up following a national rather than religious agenda.

The new *reis-ul-ulema* elected at the head of the Islamic Community of Bosnia-Herzegovina was Mustafa Cerić, formerly the principal imam of the Zagreb mosque.[14] In the following months, separate Islamic Communities were established in Montenegro, Kosovo and Macedonia, led by *Reis-ul-ulema* Idriz Demirović, the mufti Rexhep Boja[15] and *Reis-ul-ulema* Sulejman Rexhepi[16] respectively. The situation was more confused in Serbia, where there was rivalry between the mufti of Novi Pazar, Muamer Zukorlić,[17] who recognised the authority of *Reis-ul-ulema* Mustafa Cerić, and the mufti of Belgrade, Hamdija Jusufspahić, who rejected that authority.[18] In Kosovo and Macedonia, the creation of separate Islamic communities was accompanied by undivided domination by the Albanian ulamas, who displayed their support for the main Albanian parties and discreetly encouraged the Albanianisation of the non-Albanian Muslim populations. In Kosovo, where Albanians accounted for the great majority of the Muslim faithful, this turn was managed without any major difficulty. However, in Macedonia it was followed by serious tensions, with the Torbesh Jakub Selimoski, former *reis-ul-ulema*, even creating a short-lived Religious Community of the Muslims of Macedonia (*Verska Zaednica na Muslimanite vo Makedonija*) in 1996. So it would seem that whilst closer links between Islam and the national identities of the Balkan Muslims benefited the Islamic institutions, they also led to a "nationalisation" of Islam, endangering those institutions in places where the Muslim population is ethnically heterogeneous.

The same is true of the closer relations between Islamic institutions and political parties and, paradoxical as it may seem, of the increase in the financial resources of those institutions. In fact, questions of money were a source of many factional struggles and personal rivalries. In 1996, the Islamic Community of Macedonia experienced a major crisis setting *Reis-ul-ulema* Sulejman Rexhepi against the local religious authorities of Tetovo. The principal cause of this conflict was control of the Islamic Community's financial resources, although it was also partly related to the dispute between the PPD and the PDSH. This increased fragility of the Islamic institutions in the face of partisan divisions and financial disputes is also to be found outside the Yugoslav space. In Bulgaria, the internal conflicts running through the Islamic institutions were exacerbated by the attempts of the BSP, the SDS and the DPS to take control of those institutions; after each change of government coalition a new grand mufti was elected and his legitimacy was disputed by his predecessor. It was not until 1997 that Nedim Gendžev, the last mufti elected in the communist period, was marginalised for good and Ahmed Doğan's DPS imposed its candidate, Mustafa Ališ Hadži, the first Pomak to hold the office of grand mufti of Bulgaria.[19] Finally, in Greece, the rivalry between muftis appointed by the Greek state and muftis elected by the Muslim minority continued throughout the 1990s. A new law on the appointment of muftis was adopted in February 1991 and was followed by legal proceedings against the elected muftis İbrahim Şerif and Mehmet Emin Aga. Thus, throughout Southeast Europe, the 1990s were characterised by a renewal of the Islamic institutions after half a century of authoritarian secularisation, but also by a weakening of those institutions in the face of the ethnic, political and financial disputes they experienced. In the long term, however, the principal challenge they face is loss of their monopoly over religious life and the rapid diversification of Balkan Islam.

Neo-Salafism: what transformations of Balkan Islam does it reveal?

Since the early 1990s, the Balkan and Western media have regularly sounded the alarm at the growing influence in Southeast Europe of

"Wahhabi" ideas, named after Muhammad Ibn Abd-Al Wahhab, father of the official religious doctrine of Saudi Arabia. They see this as a sign of radicalisation of Balkan Islam, or confrontation between a local Islam defined as "European and tolerant" and an imported "Arab and extremist" Islam. However, a caricatural approach of this kind cannot account for recent developments in Balkan Islam. On the one hand, the term "Wahhabism" is too narrow to describe the religious currents that, in Southeast Europe and elsewhere, argue for a strict interpretation of Islam, and the wider term "neo-Salafism" seems more appropriate.[20] On the other hand, the emergence of neo-Salafist currents must be seen in a general context of increased exchanges between Balkan Muslims and the Muslim world, after half a century of isolation caused by the Cold War. Neo-Salafism thus appears as an indicator of deeper religious transformations, which cannot be reduced to a radicalisation of Balkan Islam.

It is undoubtedly true that neo-Salafist ideas have been spread in Southeast Europe by different actors arriving from the Muslim world, and in particular from the Arabian peninsula. In the troubled climate of the 1990s, this took different forms. In Bosnia-Herzegovina, foreign fighters arriving to take part in jihad (holy war) played a significant role in spreading neo-Salafism. Placed together to form the *el-Mudžahid* unit in 1993, they attracted to their ranks several hundred young Bosniak fighters and subjected them to an intense religious re-socialisation. In Kosovo, on the other hand, foreign mujahedeen played only a marginal role, due to the hostility of the UÇK. In Bosnia-Herzegovina, Kosovo and the other Balkan states, the Islamic humanitarian organisations also played an active role in spreading neo-Salafism by organising their own religion classes, offering young people a range of leisure activities and at times requiring people to follow certain religious precepts in order to receive humanitarian aid. In addition to the high committees responsible for coordinating Saudi government aid in Bosnia-Herzegovina and Kosovo, several dozen Islamic NGOs from Muslim or Western countries were active in Southeast Europe. Some, such as the International Islamic Relief Organisation (IIRO) or the *al-Haramain*, *Muwafaq* and *al-Waqf al-islami* foundations, were accused of being a cover for terrorist activities and were subject to police action in Croatia, Macedonia, Albania and Bulgaria. Finally, many students obtained, through the official religious institutions or outside any control, grants to study in different universities in the Muslim world, including at the very highly regarded Islamic

University of Medina. There, they came into contact with neo-Salafist ideas and sometimes adopted them.

The diversity of the ways in which neo-Salafist ideas were spread accounts for the diversity of neo-Salafism itself. In particular, a jihadist-type neo-Salafism must be distinguished from a pietist type. The former emerged from the circles of foreign mujahedeens and the NGOs linked to them; it is characterised by highly political and violently anti-Western discourses, and some of its supporters have been involved in local or international terrorist actions. In the late 1990s, this current was above all represented in Bosnia-Herzegovina by the Active Islamic Youth (*Aktivna Islamska Omladina*—AIO), an organisation created by former fighters of the *el-Mudžahid* unit and openly hostile to the Islamic Community. The pietist-type neo-Salafism, which is more concerned with re-Islamicising everyday life, is primarily the product of students returning from the Muslim world to work within the religious institutions. In the late 1990s, some youth organisations, such as the Union of Islamic Youth (*Bashkimi i Rinisë Islamike*) in Albania and the League of Islamic Youth (*Lidhja e Rinisë Islame*) in Macedonia, joined this pietist current. While the jihadist-type neo-Salafists often deny the *madhhab*s (legal schools) any validity, the pietist-type neo-Salafists are generally content to promote a strict interpretation of the Hanafi *madhhab*s.[21]

The dynamism of the neo-Salafist currents must not obscure the arrival in Southeast Europe of many other religious actors from the Muslim world, bringing with them other interpretations of Islam. Firstly, the end of the Cold War enabled Turkish actors to return to the region in large numbers. The Turkish Presidency of Religious Affairs (*Diyanet*) developed its cooperation with the Islamic institutions of the different Balkan states. In 1998, an agreement with the Bulgarian Directorate of Religious Affairs even placed the three Bulgarian madrasas and the Islamic Higher Education Institute of Sofia under the supervision of the Turkish *Diyanet*. The *Diyanet*'s religious influence also resulted in the establishment in October 1995 of a Eurasian Islamic Assembly in which the Islamic institutions of the states of the Balkans, the Caucasus and Central Asia participated. In addition to this religious activism by the Turkish state, there is that of the Turkish mystical brotherhoods and neo-Sufi movements, such as the *fethullahcı*s of Fethullah Gülen which runs madrasas, lower secondary schools and newspapers in several countries in the region, as well as that of the Turkish Islamists, in particular through the humanitarian organisation Human Rights and Freedom (*İnsan Hak ve Hürriyetleri*—IHH). The Turkish Islamist parties also maintain informal but regular relations with the small Islamist or Islamic-nationalist parties in the region, as well as with some leaders of the main parties representing the Balkan Muslim populations. Finally, a multitude of other actors from outside influence the transformations of Balkan Islam: from Iran, which emphasises the supposed similarities between Shiism and Bektashism in Albania, to Malaysia which offers itself as an example of Islamic modernity, and from the Muslim Brotherhood, whose emblematic figure Yusuf al-Qaradawi is very visible in the Balkan Islamic press, to the Ahmadiyya, a syncretic movement originally from the Indian subcontinent. Finally, the influence that Balkan countries have on each other should not be ignored: for example, the writings of Alija Izetbegović are widely translated and circulated in the Albanian space.

This reintegration of Balkan Islam into global Islam has been instrumental in official Islamic institutions losing their monopoly over the religious life of their respective communities. In fact, part of the renewal of religious activities that characterised the 1990s took place outside those institutions, or even, in the case of some neo-Salafist groups, in opposition to them. This is particularly clear with regard to the translation and publishing of religious works, the issuing of fatwas on various doctrinal issues, the organising of religion classes for adults, the development of leisure activities for young people and women, and the distribution of humanitarian aid. This loss of monopoly by official Islamic institutions cannot be attributed wholly to competition from external religious actors, as certain local actors are also a factor in the de-institutionalisation of religious life. Thus, the mystical brotherhoods often develop in an anarchic way, independent preachers and publishers spread their own conception of Islam, and some mosques have passed under the control of neo-Salafist or Islamist groups. In Albania, several madrasas also operate independently of the control of the religious institutions; and in Bosnia-Herzegovina, the local humanitarian organisation *Merhamet* (Mercy) has even sought to collect the *zakat* (ritual alms-giving) on its own behalf. Finally, while the official religious institutions succeed to varying degrees in preserving their monopoly over the collection of the *zakat*, religious education in schools and management of the madrasas and mosques, in other areas they are compelled to accept the existence of an increasingly diversified religious offering. Furthermore, in those Balkan countries that have experienced significant Muslim immigration, there is a real dichotomy in the religious landscape. In Greece, the dozens of prayer rooms opened in Athens by Muslims of Afro-Asiatic origin have no links with the muftis of Western Thrace, while in Romania, the associations created by Arab students or businessmen ignore the authority of the mufti of Constanța. Thus, in the first post-communist decade, Balkan Islam has been faced with a growing de-institutionalisation of religious life, of which the emergence of neo-Salafist or Islamist currents is only one sign among others.

These transformations of religious life have not taken place without sparking intense debates amongst the various Muslim communities of Southeast Europe. The emergence of neo-Salafist and, to a lesser extent, Islamist currents have provoked sharp reactions; while some ulamas proclaim their support for the Hanafi *madhhab*s, intellectuals and ordinary citizens defend the "tolerant" tradition of Balkan Islam against the "extremist" innovations of imported Islam. The debate about Balkan Islam as a "European Islam" has also taken place within this context. In fact, what the opponents of neo-Salafism and Islamism are seeking to defend is not so much a hypothetical secular tradition of tolerance as certain specific results of the communist modernisation, that is, the secularisation of the law on the one hand and the individualisation of religious practice on the other. In Bosnia-Herzegovina, Enes Karić, an expert in *tafsir* (Quranic exegesis), expresses the view that Islam is the common property of all Muslims and that no political or religious authority can claim monopoly over its interpretation. His colleague Fikret Karčić, an expert in *fikh* (Islamic jurisprudence), is of the opinion that within European secular states sharia has become no more than a set of moral standards that each believer can decide to observe or not. The emergence of neo-Salafist and, to a lesser extent, Islamist currents has thus forced their opponents to specify what they mean by "tolerant European Islam", beyond a simple idealisation of the Ottoman period. In this way neo-Salafists and Islamists have indirectly contributed to the diversification and renewal of Islam in Southeast Europe. More concretely, they seem to carry little weight in the redefinition of the relationship between religion and politics; the neo-Salafists voluntarily refrain from any political involvement and, except for the representatives of the Bosnian pan-Islamist current, the Islamists gather in small and peripheral parties. The increased visibility of Islam in the public sphere is therefore the logical consequence of the restoration of religious freedoms and the closer links between Islam and national identity, rather than some achievement of the neo-Salafist or Islamist currents. These two currents undoubtedly carry greater weight in the area of morals, as their activism compels the Islamic institutions to take more conservative positions on matters concerning the Muslim way of life. However, it is questionable whether these positions are reflected in the behaviour of ordinary believers.

Indeed, the emergence of neo-Salafist currents does not provide sufficient grounds to talk of a re-Islamicisation of the Balkan Muslim populations, and the increased visibility of Islam in the public sphere or the increased activity of the Islamic institutions is not an indication of the level of religious practice on the part of those populations. In fact, it is necessary to distinguish between practices that relate primarily to the return of religion to the public sphere, such as attending the opening of mosques or Sufi pilgrimages, and those relating primarily to the expression of a personal piety, such as not consuming alcohol, praying five times a day or studying the Quran and religious literature.[22] In a context of restoration of religious freedoms and closer links between Islam and national identity, the former have grown spectacularly but at the same time lost much of their sacred character, taking on a national, cultural or even simply a festive character. The latter also spread significantly, if only because the young generations attend religious education at school and are more aware of the precepts of Islam than previous generations. However, regular religious practice remains the preserve of a pious minority, and the Balkan Muslim populations continue, as a whole, to be characterised by a low level of religiosity. The proof of this is that the rare attempts to re-Islamicise everyday life launched during the war in Bosnia-Herzegovina, when the SDA and the Islamic Community castigated mixed marriages, the consumption of alcohol and the celebration of Christmas and the New Year, met strong resistance from the population and had to be abandoned. So it seems that, in this area too, the secularisation that the Balkan Muslims experienced in the communist period is largely irreversible. Besides, believers themselves hold an increasingly individualised faith, knowing how to get around the opinions of the religious authorities and negotiate the enforcement of the different precepts of Islam. It is surely no coincidence that the religious works that enjoy most success among the Balkan Muslims include works on Islam and the family, Islam and sexuality, Islam and health—in short, works revealing as much a concern with the self as a concern with God. The cases, limited in number but nonetheless alarming to the religious authorities, of Muslims converting to Christianity, particularly among the Albanians of Albania and the Roma of Bulgaria, must be seen in this context. Consequently, the neo-Salafist currents must not be seen as a precursor of a general re-Islamicisation of the Balkan Muslims, but as one form of religiosity among others in a diversifying religious landscape.

Once again, taking an anthropological approach enables us to understand more effectively the changes taking place in Southeast Europe. The study of *Muslim Lives in Eastern Europe* by the anthropologist Kristen Ghodsee looks at the small town of Madan in the central Rhodopes in Bulgaria.[23] There, as in the neighbouring towns of Rudozem and Smolyan, new religious practices have developed among the majority Pomak population: a new mosque has opened, which the men attend assiduously each Friday, many women wear the *hijab* (veil), and young lower secondary school pupils claim the right to wear it at school. This increased religiosity has been supported in this region by new religious actors representing an Islam which Kristen Ghodsee describes as "orthodox", and which we would describe as pietist-type neo-Salafism. For Ghodsee this situation cannot be explained without taking into account the Madan Pomaks' identity crisis which, driven by new religious actors, has led them to come up with Arab origins for themselves. Above all, in Madan the economic crisis has resulted in the mines closing and has triggered a profound crisis of masculine identity on the part of adult men reduced to deep poverty and inactivity. For these ex-miners, the new mosque built in the centre of the town represents a new place to socialise, and Islam gives them a way of recreating a positive masculine identity for themselves.

However, there are also strictly religious causes behind the development of "orthodox" Islam. Firstly, the crisis of the official religious institutions, weakened by the never-ending conflict between the former Grand Mufti Nedim Gendžev and the different grand muftis supported by the Turkish DPS party, allowed various Islamic NGOs from the Arab world more room for manoeuvre. At the same time, young Pomaks who have left to study Islam in Saudi Arabia, Jordan and other Muslim countries return with an "orthodox" view of Islam and oppose the older generation of local *hocas*, condemning their heterodox practices. In the central Rhodopes, these "new imams" succeeded in 2003 in taking control of the regional religious institutions, but were sidelined two years later by the grand mufti at the time, Fikri Sali Hasan. They reacted by creating their own religious structure, the Union for Islamic Culture and Development (*Obedinenie za Isljamsko Razvitie i Kultura*), which, with the support of a number of foreign Islamic NGOs, pursues its own religious activities, ranging from publishing Islamic literature, through organising religion classes and leisure activities for young people, to distributing humanitarian aid.

The situation described by Kristen Ghodsee is a good illustration of the process at work in Southeast Europe as a whole, from the increased visibility of Islam in the public space, through the official Islamic institutions' losing of their monopoly and the arrival of new religious actors from the Muslim world, to the diversification of religious practice. However, the revival in religious practice that can be observed in Madan and the surrounding region is linked to specific identity and socio-economic factors, and Kristen Ghodsee herself notes that this phenomenon is not present in Turkish-populated regions or in other Pomak-populated regions. Thus, in Bulgaria as in the rest of Southeast Europe, it is not possible to speak without qualification of a "return of Islam" or a "re-Islamicisation" of the Muslim population.

CONCLUSION

During the nineteenth and twentieth centuries, Southeast Europe experienced profound political, social and cultural changes, often presented as a transition from empires to nation-states, or as a "Europeanisation of the Balkans". These expressions refer to very real processes, but tend to confer on them a linear, inevitable and normative character. However, the contemporary history of Southeast Europe cannot be understood without taking account of the diversity of national and provincial historical trajectories, the complex interactions between local, national and supranational actors, and moments of rupture and uncertainty. This is true for the Balkan societies in general and for the Muslim communities within those societies. It is all the more true for the Ottoman Empire which in the early nineteenth century stretched over three continents: Europe, Asia and Africa.

During the following century, the Ottoman Empire lost most of its European possessions, before being replaced in 1923 by the Republic of Turkey. However, there was nothing linear or inevitable about this process; during the nineteenth century, the Ottoman authorities launched several waves of reforms, reorganising the army and the administration, radically changing the status of the non-Muslim communities, and seeking to promote an Ottomanist sentiment within the population. These reforms often drew inspiration from Western models and resembled those implemented at the same time by the young Balkan states, the creation of which was presented in Western Europe as the result of national liberation movements against the "Ottoman yoke". Yet the first Balkan states that appeared in the early nineteenth century—Montenegro, Serbia, Greece and the Romanian Principalities—took on a truly national character only in the 1860s, and it was not until the late nineteenth century that national irredentisms, alongside the Great Powers, played a decisive role in the dismantling of the Ottoman Empire. In fact, it was the decade of war between 1912 and 1922, and the First World War in particular, that sealed the fate of the Ottoman Empire, along with the fates of two other European empires: the Austro-Hungarian Empire and the Tsarist Empire. Just as it is wrong to see the end of the Ottoman Empire as a foregone conclusion, it does not make sense to contrast "European" Balkan states with an "Asiatic" Ottoman Empire. A fortiori, the trajectories of the Balkan states and modern Turkey after 1923 have many similarities, underlining the latter's European character.

After the decade 1912–22, marked by unprecedented violence and massive population displacements, the national character of the Balkan states seemed to be established. Nationalist ideologies mixed with irredentism and authoritarianism dominated politics in the Balkan Peninsula, and the nationalisation of local societies was accomplished through the army, schools and the press. However, that nationalisation was often only partial and superficial, and went hand in hand with the establishment of national minorities that became bones of contention between neighbouring states. In this context, the young Yugoslav state was a special case, unable to choose between a Yugoslav national project and a federal, plurinational compromise, and torn by the confrontation between Serbian and Croatian nationalisms, to mention only the most significant. Finally, the disappearance of the empires and the formation of the Balkan nation-states did not represent an undivided triumph of the nation-state principle, as evidenced by the continued role of the Great Powers and their involvement in the internal affairs of the region's states. The same contradictions were to be found in the following periods. Certainly, after the Second World War and the renewed violence it brought, the Balkan states had a greater ability to nationalise their societies, including through the authoritarian modernisation implemented by the communist regimes. However, these states escaped the logic of the Cold War only with difficulty, and the new Yugoslavia continued to be a special case, copying the Soviet federal model and recognising several constituent nations within its borders. In the 1990s, the violent break-up of Yugoslavia seemed to put the finishing touch to the bloody triumph of the nation-state in Southeast Europe. However, among the states that emerged from the Yugoslav federation, at least two—Bosnia-Herzegovina

CONCLUSION

and Macedonia—are not nation-states, and the Yugoslav wars were also the subject of a complex process of internationalisation led by the UN, NATO and the Great Powers of the time. Finally, the first post-communist decade saw the Euro-Atlantic integration process, intended to help overcome the logic of the nation-state, extend to Southeast Europe. Thus, at no point during the last two centuries was the nation-state an omnipotent or undisputed actor in Southeast Europe.

A proper understanding of the formation of modern states in this region of the world must consider the context of wider social, political and cultural transformations. During the nineteenth and twentieth centuries, the Balkan societies experienced significant changes, in particular the agricultural reforms of the 1920s and the collectivisations of the 1940s, before the industrialisation and urbanisation of the second half of the twentieth century turned them into mainly urban societies. At the same time, the continued development of educational systems favoured the emergence of new intellectual and administrative elites supporting different nationalist projects, and enabled states to have greater control over their respective populations. Finally, the spreading of modern means of communication and political organisation also contributed to the nationalisation of the Balkan societies, even in the case of authoritarian regimes tolerating only a controlled press and a single party. From this perspective, the establishment of democratic regimes in the 1970s in Greece and twenty years later in the region's other countries marked the completion of a process of transformation of the Balkan societies which did not differ fundamentally from the processes at work in the societies of Western and Central Europe.

Within this context, one of the main features specific to Southeast Europe is its great religious diversity (Orthodox Christianity, Islam, Catholicism, Judaism), with all that means for the relationship between national identity and religious identity. In the nineteenth century, this relationship remained uncertain, as evidenced by the existence of a Yugoslav project competing with Serbian and Croatian nationalisms, which only gradually identified themselves with Orthodox Christianity and Catholicism respectively, and for a long time claimed the Bosnian Muslims as members of their respective nations. However, in the late nineteenth and early twentieth century, the links between national identity and religious identity became closer, as illustrated by the creation of the Bulgarian Exarchate and, more generally, the establishment of national Orthodox Churches by the Balkan states. Albania was the only partial exception to this rule; created in 1912, Albania also sought to create national religious institutions, but the Albanian national identity it promoted was multi-denominational, with each religious community adhering to it in a specific way. In this period, the central role of religious institutions and identities in the formation of national identities contrasted with the beginning of the secularisation of the way of life in urban milieus. This contrast was exacerbated after the Second World War, with the anti-religious policies of the communist regimes contributing, along with the general changes in the way of life, to a rapid secularisation of Balkan societies. From this perspective, the idea of a "return of religion" in the two decades following the fall of the communist regimes must be questioned; admittedly, the closer links between national identity and religious identity led to an increased visibility of religious institutions and symbols, and the restoration of religious freedoms facilitated the appearance of new forms of religiosity. However, those new forms were not always accompanied by increased levels of religious practice, and did not fundamentally challenge the secularisation of Balkan societies.

In this context, what conclusions may we draw about the Balkan Muslims (in the sociological sense of the term)? The multiplicity of their national affiliations partly reflects the diversity of the processes of Islamicisation during the six centuries of Ottoman presence. However, it cannot be understood without taking account of the demographic changes that occurred in Southeast Europe in the nineteenth and twentieth centuries. For Balkan Muslims, in fact, the emergence of the new Balkan states was often accompanied by violence and exile—from the expulsion of the "Turks" by Montenegro, Serbia and Greece in the early nineteenth century to the "ethnic cleansing" of the Bosnian Muslims and Kosovo's Albanians in the 1990s—and it is tempting to see this as the main characteristic of the Balkan Muslims' post-Ottoman history. However, the undeniable feeling of precariousness that this generated for the Muslims of Southeast Europe must not obscure the fact that the causes of their emigration to the Ottoman Empire, Turkey or the Western world differed according to place and time, and that from the late nineteenth century onwards, large Muslim communities have survived the territorial losses of the Ottoman Empire in Europe. In the second half of the twentieth century, the demographic weight of some of them even increased significantly.

CONCLUSION

With the territorial losses of the Ottoman Empire, the Balkan Muslims had to adapt to the new framework of the Balkan states. While the Muslims of Albania accounted for a majority of that state's population, and played a full part in building an Albanian national state, other Muslims did not have access to full citizenship and were reduced to the status of religious minorities whose rights were protected to a greater or lesser extent by international treaties and national constitutions. While Balkan nationalisms were taking shape in the late nineteenth and early twentieth century, the Muslim communities therefore fell back on their religious identity and their religious institutions. The Muslim political elites, dominated by the notables, gave their allegiance to the central state even where they had their own political party, as in Bosnia-Herzegovina with the Yugoslav Muslim Organisation (JMO). The emerging intellectual elites formed associations and promoted Croatian, Serbian or Yugoslav national identities in Bosnia-Herzegovina, Turkish or Bulgarian national identities in Bulgaria, and Turkish or Tatar national identities in Romania; however, they struggled to bridge the gap that separated them from the general Muslim population, which was indifferent to the national question. It was not until the second half of the twentieth century that the Muslims of Southeast Europe could access full citizenship and possessed fully-fledged national identities. The communist modernisation gave birth to new intellectual and political elites, and was accompanied by the promotion of national identities specific to the Muslim populations, as evidenced in 1945 by the recognition of an Albanian national minority in Yugoslavia and a Turkish national minority in Bulgaria, and in 1968 by recognition of a Muslim nation in Bosnia-Herzegovina. Thus, for Balkan Muslims, the communist period was one of nationalisation and, more widely, participation in a certain political, social and cultural modernity.

At the end of the communist period, the promotion of national identities specific to the Balkan Muslims gave way to harsh assimilationist policies, as was the case with the "revival process" in Bulgaria and, to a lesser extent, the suppression of Kosovo's autonomy. However, this hardening only hastened the crystallisation of national identities and the dissidence of the new political elites that had emerged from the communist modernisation. At the same time, the mobilisation of the Muslim minority in Greece around demands for a Turkish national identity, demonstrates that the politicisation of the Balkan Muslims was linked to social and cultural changes encompassing both communist and non-communist countries of the region. Consequently, the 1990s were both one of the most tragic periods in the history of the Muslims of Southeast Europe and one in which they emerged as autonomous political actors. Following trajectories that varied greatly from one state to another, the parties representing Muslim populations put forward national claims ranging from simple cultural rights to full political independence. Sometimes, they turned to armed struggle, as in the case of the Albanian guerrillas in Kosovo and Macedonia. In Bosnia-Herzegovina, a pan-Islamist current that had appeared in the early 1940s and been clandestinely re-formed in the 1960s propelled itself to the head of the Party of Democratic Action (SDA), while in the other Balkan countries, the Islamists were either of marginal significance or non-existent. Towards the end of the decade, the political integration of the local Muslim minorities seemed to be assured in Bulgaria, Romania and Montenegro, but remained more fragile in Macedonia, Serbia and Greece. Above all, two new Muslim-majority states emerged from the ruins of the Yugoslav federation: Kosovo and Bosnia-Herzegovina. Albania, which had had a Muslim majority since 1912, continued to follow a separate trajectory, as the Albanian political parties were not denominational. None of these Muslim-majority Balkan states made Islam a state religion. Indeed, Albania and Kosovo are characterised by a particularly strict secularism. Therefore, the fact that Muslims are now in a majority in Kosovo and Bosnia-Herzegovina will probably not strongly influence the evolution of those states in the coming years and decades. Be that as it may, the diversity of the modes of politicisation of the Balkan Muslims was accentuated by the fact that some of them preferred to support non-nationalist parties and that, in the late 1990s, the weakening of the dominant nationalist parties allowed internal pluralisation to develop within each national group. Hence within a single decade the political situation of the Balkan Muslims (in the sociological sense of the term) has been profoundly transformed, for they have abandoned their status as religious minorities and now view themselves as national minorities or sovereign nations.

While the actual nationalisation of the Balkan Muslims came relatively late, the nationalist myths on which it was based can sometimes be traced to the beginning of the nineteenth century. Many of those myths concern conversion to Islam, presented as voluntary in Bosnia-Herzegovina in accordance with the Bomogil theory, or as forced and superficial in the

CONCLUSION

case of Albania. This emphasis on the question of Islamicisation is not due to a particularly close link between national identity and religious identity. Historically, the first promoters of the national idea among the Balkan Muslims were linked with potentially multi-denominational identity projects such as Ottomanism, Albanianism or Yugoslavism, and to currents of thought that were fascinated by Western modernity, such as Islamic reformism or Kemalism. During the communist period, the promotion of national identities specific to the Muslim populations was designed to facilitate their secularisation, and was supported by new, secular elites. Even in the 1990s, although the links between national identity and religious identity became closer in the Balkan societies, the Muslim communities remained divided between supporters of a "re-Islamicisation" of the Bosniak, Turkish or Albanian national identity, the leading figures of which include the founders of the SDA in Bosnia-Herzegovina, and supporters of a strictly secular definition of the nation. The myths concerning Islamicisation and, more widely, the debates on the relationship between Islam and national identity relate, more specifically, to the constant need for Balkan Muslims to justify their presence in Europe, in the face of Balkan nationalisms that classify them as "Turks" or "renegades". This constraint, which is specific to the Balkan Muslims' nationalist ideologies, also explains their frequent discourses on Balkan Islam as "tolerant" and "autochthonous", contrasted in the 1990s with the "imported" Islam of the neo-Salafists, or in other words their insistence on Balkan Islam as European Islam. However, while these discourses on the supposed essence of Balkan Islam play an important role in structuring the Islamic religious sphere in the Balkans, they are not in any way sufficient to capture its historicity and complexity.

At first sight, the Balkan Muslims are more homogeneous in terms of religion than language: the great majority of them are Hanafi-rite Sunni Muslims, the two main exceptions being the Bektashis in Albania and the small Alevi/Kizilbash communities of Bulgaria and Greece. In the Ottoman period, Balkan Islam did not really differ from Anatolian Islam, and was attached to the same official institutions headed by the *şeyhülislam*, to the same education networks that had Istanbul as their centre of gravity, and to the same mystical brotherhoods. This affiliation to Ottoman Islam survived the territorial losses of the Empire, and until 1923 the Islamic institutions created in the new Balkan states or in Austro-Hungarian Bosnia-Herzegovina maintained close links with the *şeyhülislam* and the religious schools of the Ottoman capital. However, from the late nineteenth century onwards, the religious life of Balkan Muslims increasingly came under the authority of religious institutions whose jurisdiction was limited to the borders of the new Balkan states and which were presided over by a grand mufti or a *reis-ul-ulema*; those institutions were themselves subject to control by the state authorities. The second half of the twentieth century was characterised by a pronounced weakening of those official institutions and, in the communist countries, the definitive abolition of the sharia courts, nationalisation of the waqfs, closure of most of the madrasas and, in Albania, a complete ban on religion in 1967. At the time, only the Islamic institutions of Western Thrace in Greece retained an Ottoman appearance. However, the communist religious policies strengthened the official institutions' monopoly over religious life, and even allowed a degree of institutional renewal in Yugoslavia from the 1960s onwards. The end of the communist regimes and the restoration of religious freedoms in 1989–90 had two contrasting consequences: on the one hand an undeniable renewal of the official institutions, symbolised by the opening of numerous madrasas and Islamic higher education institutions, (although never leading to a return to the status quo ante), and on the other a weakening of their monopoly over religious life, as evidenced by the multiplication of internal conflicts and the emergence of non-institutional religious actors, such as the Islamic NGOs and various youth and women's associations.

For a proper understanding of this evolution of the Islamic institutions, it is necessary to take account of the phenomena of autonomy, competition and circulation that characterised the history of Balkan Islam. Thus, in the Ottoman period, some ulamas exercised their authority more or less independently, on the fringes of the official institutions, which themselves contained different religious currents. Moreover, complex relationships based on rivalry but also complementarity arose between official religious institutions and mystical brotherhoods, between ulamas and shaykhs, with the boundary between them always remaining porous. These complex relationships were also to be found in the interwar period and in the communist period, as evidenced by the unofficial recognition of the Bektashi community in Albania in the 1920s and the autonomy granted to some mystical brotherhoods in Yugoslavia in the 1970s. More generally, the creation of official religious institutions on a national level did not prevent some ulamas and some shaykhs from continuing to exercise a high level of personal authority locally. Finally, Balkan Islam remained part of multiple transnational networks, connected to the Ottoman Empire and to modern Turkey and, increasingly, to other parts of the Muslim world. Thus, in the late nineteenth and early twentieth century, reformist ideas arrived from the Ottoman Empire, but also from Tsarist Russia and British India. In the inter-war period, the anti-Kemalist religious elites exiled in Bulgaria and Greece, the al-Azhar University in Cairo and the Lahore Ahmaddiyya networks in Western Europe helped to shape the internal pluralism of Balkan Islam. From the 1930s onwards, the Kemalist and reformist ideas were countered by new neo-traditionalist currents, including some inspired by the activism of Shakib Arslan or the Islamism of the Muslim Brotherhood. In the early 1940s, the pan-Islamist Young Muslims organisation was launched in Bosnia-Herzegovina, also on the model of an Egyptian association; some of its representatives would create the SDA fifty years later. This participation of the Balkan Muslims in the circulation of people and ideas in the Muslim world came to a halt during the communist period, with the partial exception of Yugoslavia. It resumed with renewed vigour in the 1990s, as evidenced by the development of jihadist or pietist-type neo-Salafist networks in Southeast Europe, the establishment of Turkish neo-Sufi movements, and the departure of Albanian, Bosniak, Turkish or Pomak students for religious universities in the Muslim world. Despite some alarmist interpretations, this reintegration of Balkan Islam within global Islam contributed less to its radicalisation than to its internal diversification—proof that Balkan Islam is no exception to the predominant transformations experienced by all religious communities in Southeast Europe, in a context of restoration of political and religious freedoms.

The debates running through the Muslim communities in Southeast Europe concern not only the abstract link between Islam and Western modernity or the reform of religious institutions such as the madrasas and the waqfs, but also—and perhaps above all—the religious practice of the Muslims themselves. Thus, from the Kadizadelis of the eighteenth century, through the reformists and neo-traditionalists of the inter-war period, to the neo-Salafists of the late twentieth century, hostility to Sufism was a recurrent theme in Southeast Europe. However, it never really threatened the existence of mystical brotherhoods and Sufi teachings, which even survived the bans imposed in communist Yugoslavia in

1952 and in communist Albania in 1967. Similarly, the balance of power between conservatives, reformists and neo-traditionalists, or between modernising states and religious institutions, has often crystallised around the question of the status of women in Islam, their access to education and their dress, as evidenced by the ban on the veil in Albania in 1937 and in Yugoslavia thirteen years later. In the 1990s, this question of the veil again became the subject of heated debate between lay intellectuals, Islamic institutions and neo-Salafist movements, but the emancipation of women brought about by communist modernisation was not seriously challenged. Therefore, the vigour of certain debates and the renewed visibility of some religious symbols must not be allowed to obscure the profound secularisation experienced by the Balkan Muslim communities in the second half of the twentieth century; that secularisation resulted in a perceptible reduction in religious practice, and its effects continued to be felt after 1990. In fact, despite the opening of many mosques and the mass participation in certain pilgrimages and other religious gatherings, regular religious practice and payment of the *zakat* remain for the time being confined to a pious minority. Likewise, political, and therefore collective, manipulation of some religious symbols has not prevented the individualisation of faith. In this context, while the debates among the Muslims of Southeast Europe attest to the diversity of the beliefs and practices of Balkan Muslims, they are not the whole story. Today as yesterday, the internal plurality of Balkan Islam is also the result of a multitude of informal influences, discreet arrangements and intimate beliefs that leave few traces for the historian. However, a subtler and more detailed knowledge of the past and present beliefs of the Balkan Muslims (in the religious sense of the term) is essential to a better understanding of the realities of Balkan Islam.

This book is about the political and religious transformations that Balkan Muslims have undergone over the course of the nineteenth and twentieth centuries. It is however possible to give a certain amount of information here about the situation in the early twenty-first century. In Southeast Europe, the 2000s were also marked by several major political and geopolitical changes. Firstly, they were characterised by a return to peace after the wars of the 1990s, while the independence of Montenegro in 2006 and Kosovo in 2008 marked the final stages in the dissolution of the Yugoslav federation. However, the political stability of Kosovo, Bosnia-Herzegovina and Macedonia continues to be threatened

CONCLUSION

by significant interethnic tensions. At the same time, the attacks on 11 September 2001 and the "war on terrorism" that followed caused the United States to disengage partially from Southeast Europe, while regarding it as an arena for the fight against Islamic terrorism. This American disengagement led the European Union to take the place of the UN and NATO in the peacekeeping missions in Bosnia-Herzegovina and Kosovo, while the enlargement of the EU in Southeast Europe was symbolised by Slovenia joining in 2004 and Romania and Bulgaria in 2007, and by several other of the region's states attaining the status of candidate countries. Thus, the early twenty-first century saw the Euro-Atlantic integration process continue in Southeast Europe. However, in 2012, the three Balkan states that did not have the status of candidate for membership of the European Union were Albania, Kosovo and Bosnia-Herzegovina: the three Muslim-majority states of Southeast Europe. While this situation is explained by political rather than religious factors, it could feed the frustrations of some Balkan Muslims, and reinforce the siege mentality of others. The same holds true for the question of Turkey's membership of the European Union, which will influence how Muslims and Islam are perceived in Europe in general and in Southeast Europe in particular—all the more so as this region is experiencing a significant strengthening of Turkey's influence. A growing economic power, Turkey went through significant political changes with the victory of the Party of Justice and Development (*Adalet ve Kalkınma Partisi*—AKP) in the legislative elections held in 2002, 2007 and 2011. This rise to power of moderate Islamists, accompanied by increased American support for the "Turkish model" after 11 September, has resulted in a strengthening of Turkey's political influence in Southeast Europe, and facilitated the activity of various Turkish religious networks, as will be shown later in this Conclusion.

As regards the Balkan Muslims themselves (in the sociological sense of the term), the 2000s saw the death of Alija Izetbegović in 2003 and that of Ibrahim Rugova in 2006. In Bosnia-Herzegovina, Izetbegović's death and the re-orientation of American policy following the 11 September attacks hastened the marginalisation of the pan-Islamist current within the SDA, with the latter appearing more and more as a moderate nationalist party in the face of the often more entrenched positions of the Party for Bosnia-Herzegovina. In 2010, some of the SDA's founders and dissidents created a new Islamic-nationalist party, the Party for Democratic

Activity (*Stranka Demokratske Aktivnosti*—A-SDA), which received only 1.1 per cent of the votes in the legislative elections. The "Bosnian exception", which had a pan-Islamist current at the centre of the Bosniak nationalist mobilisation, finally ended. The evolution of the SDA also explains the loosening of its links with the Islamic Community, but *Reis-ul-ulema* Mustafa Cerić continued to use his religious mandate for political purposes by strongly influencing the identity-formation process of the Bosniak nation and by supporting candidates opposed to the SDA's candidates in the 2006 and 2010 presidential elections. Religion and politics merged even more obviously in Serbian Sanjak, where the mufti of Novi Pazar, Muamer Zukorlić, opposed the two principal Bosniak parties, the SDA and the Democratic Party of Sanjak (SDP); he created his own party, the Bosniak Cultural Community (*Bošnjačka Kulturna Zajednica*—BKZ) in 2010, and stood with limited success in the Serbian 2012 presidential elections. At the same time, the Bosniaks of Montenegrin Sanjak succeeded in rising above their own political quarrels and in 2006 created the Bosniak Party (*Bošnjačka Stranka*—BS). Interactions of this type between political actors and religious actors did not occur in the case of the Albanian parties, between whom political alternation became commonplace despite the recurrent and sometimes violent tensions between the Democratic Party (PD) and the Socialist Party (PS) in Albania, the Democratic Party of Kosovo (PDK) and the Democratic League of Kosovo (LDK) in Kosovo (the latter being weakened by the death of its leader Ibrahim Rugova), and the Democratic Party of Albanians (PDSH) and the Democratic Union for Integration (BDI) in Macedonia. Finally, in Bulgaria, the Movement for Rights and Freedoms (DPS) retained its dominant position within the Turkish minority, but came under attack from the Bulgarian nationalist extreme right and found itself in opposition after the 2009 legislative elections. At the same time, intense debates continued among the Balkan Muslims concerning the links between Islam and national identity. Thus, in the Albanian case, a lively debate arose in 2006 between Ismail Kadare, Albania's most famous writer, and Rexhep Qosja, an intellectual from Kosovo. The former emphasised the European and Christian identity of the Albanians, while the latter sought to rehabilitate their Ottoman and Islamic past. At the same time, the creation of a Muslim Forum of Albania (*Forumi Musliman i Shqipërisë*) and a Muslim Forum of Kosovo (*Forumi Musliman i Kosovës*) reflected the desire of some religious intellectuals to participate more openly in the debates

CONCLUSION

about Albanian national identity. Similar debates took place throughout Southeast Europe, in the form of controversies concerning the building of cathedrals and statues of Mother Teresa in Albania and Kosovo, the ban on wearing the veil in school in Albania, Kosovo and Bulgaria, and the quasi-compulsory character of religious education in school in Bosnia-Herzegovina.

It is in the religious domain, rather than politics, that Balkan Muslims have experienced serious rifts. Thus, in Albania, the secretary of the Islamic Community was assassinated in 2003, for reasons that remain unclear. In Bulgaria, the struggle to control the Islamic institutions continued and the dissident muftis of Sofia and Smolyan, Selvi Šakirov and Ali Hajraddin, both close to neo-Salafist ideas, each created their own unofficial religious association: the Union for Islamic Development and Culture (*Obedinenie za Isljamsko Razvitie i Kultura*) in 2004 and the Union of Muslims of Bulgaria (*Săjuz na Mjusjulmanite v Bălgarija*) in 2006. The Islamic institutions also experienced serious internal crises in the Preševo valley in South Serbia in 2003 and in Macedonia in 2004–5. Finally, in Serbia, two competing Islamic Communities were formed in 2007: the Islamic Community in Serbia (*Islamska Zajednica u Srbiji*) led by the mufti of Novi Pazar, Muamer Zukorlić, who recognised the authority of the Bosnian *reis-ul-ulema* Mustafa Cerić; and the Islamic Community of Serbia (*Islamska Zajednica Srbije*), which was close to the mufti of Belgrade, Hamdija Jusufspahić, and appointed its own *reis-ul-ulema*, Adem Zilkić. The battle to control the mosques then took a violent turn in Serbian Sanjak, with the police having to intervene on several occasions. In the post-9/11 context, these conflicts have been systematically presented—including by the protagonists themselves—in terms of extremist threat, but in fact very often simply concealed conflicts between generations, personal ambitions or financial interests (the restitution and management of the waqfs, organising the pilgrimage to Mecca, etc.). They bore witness to the fragility of the Islamic institutions in a context of increased cultural and political pluralism. The 2000s were also characterised by a slowing of the development of the Islamic institutions; many mosques continued to be built, but the only madrasa opened during this period was that in Podgorica, Montenegro, in 2009. After 11 September 2001, several madrasas in Albania saw their existence threatened by finance from the Arab world running dry. The Turkish neo-Sufi movement of the *fethullahcı*s came to their aid and took control of them with the blessing of the Albanian religious and political authorities. Finally, the attempts to regain a monopoly over religious life, characterised by the reassertion of the validity of the Hanafi *madhhab*s and the promotion of national religious "traditions", came up against the growing use of the internet by many non-institutional religious actors, amongst other things. This phenomenon was even more pronounced in the diaspora, despite the opening of mosques and the establishment of religious associations linked to the official institutions of the home countries. The authority of the official Islamic institutions therefore remains fragile in the early twenty-first century, in a general context of diversification and individualisation of religious beliefs and practices.

The first decade of the twenty-first century also saw an acceleration of some transformations of the relations between Balkan Islam and global Islam. Following the 11 September attacks, the United States set itself to combat the neo-Salafist networks present in Southeast Europe and pressured the Balkan states to join it in this undertaking; a wave of financial sanctions, arrests and extraditions then swept down upon both the jihadist-type and the pietist-type neo-Salafist milieus. As a result, a considerable number of Islamic NGOs from the Arab world left Southeast Europe, as did most of the mujahedeen who had settled in Bosnia-Herzegovina after 1995. This weakening of the neo-Salafist networks was accompanied by greater internal differentiation; while a minority of jihadists paraded their support for Osama bin Laden, most of them preferred to adopt a legalistic approach in order to continue their missionary work. As for the young ulamas who had frequented the pietist-type neo-Salafists during their studies abroad, they made themselves careers within the official Islamic institutions, where they promoted a strict interpretation of the Hanafi *madhhab*. In the meantime, however, the influence of the Turkish religious networks continued to increase in the 2000s. The Presidency of Religious Affairs (*Diyanet*), together with its *Diyanet Vakfı* foundation, and the Turkish International Cooperation Agency (*Türk İşbirliği ve Kalkınma İdaresi Başkanlığı*—TİKA) formed close links with the official Islamic institutions. A Balkan Islamic Council was created in 2007 at the initiative of the *Diyanet*, and the latter set itself up as mediator between the two rival Islamic Communities in Serbia. Furthermore, beginning with the *fethullahcı*s, the different Turkish neo-Sufi movements continued to set up in Southeast Europe, as evidenced by the opening of several private Turkish universities in Bulgaria,

CONCLUSION

Albania and Bosnia-Herzegovina. The only religious leader to keep some distance from the Turkish "big brothers" was the Bosnian *reis-ul-ulema* Mustafa Cerić. While appearing frequently at the side of the president of the *Diyanet*, he participated in the European Council for Fatwa and Research created in 1997 by ulamas close to the Muslim Brotherhood, with Yusuf al-Qaradawi as its president. Above all, he cast himself as a potential regional leader by publishing, in 2005, a "Declaration of the European Muslims" condemning terrorism and pledging allegiance to the European secular states, but also containing claims put forward by the Muslim Brotherhood in Europe, such as the application of sharia law to family matters or the setting of quotas for Muslim members in the parliaments of the European Union member-states.

The history of Balkan Muslims over the course of the nineteenth, twentieth and early twenty-first centuries shows extensive interaction and circulation with the rest of the Muslim world, as this book has endeavoured to demonstrate. In addition to this, certain historical shifts have affected both Muslims in the Balkans and those elsewhere, such as the formation of modern states and national identities, authoritarian secularisation policies, the emergence of Islamic reformism followed by neo-traditionalism, and the opposition between secularists and Islamists. Nevertheless, fundamental differences remain, and in particular the fact that the Balkan Muslims have never been subjected to colonialism, although their status up until the mid-twentieth century as a religious minority displays some colonial features.

This is not the place to go into these vast and complex issues, but it is important to come back to the question of the definition of Balkan Islam as European Islam. There is no doubt that, living in Southeast Europe, the Balkan Muslims have as much right to call themselves Europeans as their Orthodox Christian or Catholic neighbours. As we have shown in this book, the Balkan Muslims insist on the European and tolerant character of their faith in order to counter the nationalist ideologies that referred to them as "Turks", "Asiatics" or, more recently, "fundamentalists" and "Wahhabis". However, this insistence can lead to a number of biases or misunderstandings. Firstly, it shifts the stigmatisation of Islam rather than abolishing it, as the "European and tolerant" Islam of the Balkan Muslims is implicitly set in opposition to another Islam, that is "not tolerant because it is not European", located beyond the Bosphorus or the Strait of Gibraltar, or even in the suburbs of the large cities of

Western Europe. Secondly, the definition of Balkan Islam as "European and tolerant Islam" often leads to a disregard for its internal diversity, its ceaseless transformations and its multiple links with the Muslim world. The construction of mosques provides a good illustration of this phenomenon; there are many who contrast the "traditional" architecture of the mosques of the Ottoman period with the "Arab" architecture of those built since 1990, and warn against this "degradation" of Balkan Islam. However, the contrast between old and recent mosques is explained above all by the fact that, from the late nineteenth to the late twentieth century, few mosques were built in the Balkan countries and there is therefore no architectural continuum between the two periods. Moreover, whatever one thinks of the aesthetic value of some new buildings, there is no reason that Balkan Muslims should be condemned to build identical copies of Ottoman mosques instead of seeking inspiration in today's Turkey or in the countries of the Persian Gulf, whose architects often draw inspiration from—North American architectural achievements! Of course, reasonings of this type also apply to many other aspects of the practice of Islam in Southeast Europe.

If Balkan Islam can be defined as a European Islam, that is because the Ottoman Empire was a European empire, and because the history of Balkan Muslims is part of the wider history of the European continent. From reduction to the status of religious minorities through nationalisation of the Islamic institutions to communist modernisation, the specific traits of Balkan Islam today are explained by how the Balkan Muslims have been affected by and participated in the major transformations that Europe has experienced over the last two centuries. Thus, the European character of Balkan Islam reflects not a homogeneous and immutable essence, but complex historical trajectories involving a multiplicity of actors. The historical experience of the Balkan Muslims can therefore provide an important source of reflection and inspiration for other European Muslims, although there is no "Balkan model" that can be transposed from one part of the European continent to another. In fact, exchanges between the Balkan Muslims and the Muslims of Western Europe remain limited, even if the formation of significant Albanian and Bosniak diasporas in Western Europe and the enlargement of the European Union in Southeast Europe should favour an intensification of such exchanges. Whatever the case may be, the principal changes in Balkan Islam over the last two centuries, resulting today in growing plu-

CONCLUSION

rality and individualisation of the faith, place it within the general trajectory of religion in Europe as described by the sociologists of religion Danièle Hervieu-Léger[1] and Grace Davie.[2] Therefore, the case of the Balkan Muslims also shows that Islam is not immune to the processes of religious individualisation and pluralisation.

NOTES

INTRODUCTION

1. Around 75 per cent of the Jews of Southeast Europe were exterminated during the Second World War. Many of the survivors migrated to Israel. Thus, from that time the Jewish communities of Southeast Europe are very small.
2. Pronounced: moohajer.
3. On the subject of conversions to Islam in Southeast Europe, see in particular Selim Deringil, *Conversion and Apostasy in the Late Ottoman Empire*, Cambridge, Cambridge University Press, 2012; Gilles Grivaud and Alexandre Popovic (eds), *Les conversions à l'Islam en Asie mineure et dans les Balkans aux époques seldjoukide et ottomane*, Athens, École française d'Athènes, 2011; Marc D. Baer, *Honored by the Glory of Islam: Conversion and Conquest in the Ottoman Empire*, Oxford, Oxford University Press, 2008.
4. See Map 1 showing the locations of Sanjak and Western Thrace.
5. Muslims in the sociological sense of the term account for around 70 per cent of the Albanians in Albania, 95 per cent of the Albanians in Kosovo, 98 per cent of the Albanians in Western Macedonia, 100 per cent of the Albanians in South Serbia and 65 per cent of the Albanians in Montenegro.
6. The Bosniaks present in Kosovo and Macedonia are either descendants of *muhacir*s from Bosnia-Herzegovina and Sanjak who settled in these regions at the end of the nineteenth and beginning of the twentieth century, or members of small Slavic-speaking groups (the Goranis and Torbesh) who have opted for Bosniak nationality.
7. Roy Gutman, *A Witness to Genocide*, New Jersey, Prentice Hall, 1994.
8. Shaul Shay, *Islamic Terror and the Balkans*, London, Translation Publishers, 2007.
9. Christopher Delisso, *The Coming Balkan Caliphate*, Westport, Praeger Security International, 2007.
10. Jørgen Nielsen, *Towards a European Islam*, New York, Palgrave, 1999; Olivier Roy, *Vers un islam européen*, Paris, Esport, 1999.

11. Tariq Ramadan, *Etre musulman européen: étude des sources islamiques à la lumière du contexte européen*, Lyon, Tawhid, 2001.
12. Stephen Schwartz, *The Two Faces of Islam: The House of Sa'ud from Tradition to Terror*, New York, Doubleday, 2002.
13. See for example Felice Dassetto, Brigitte Marechal and Jørgen Nielsen (eds), *Convergences musulmanes. Aspects contemporains de l'islam dans l'Europe élargie*, Paris, L'Harmattan, 2001.
14. Alexandre Popovic, *L'islam balkanique. Les musulmans du sud-est européen dans la période post-ottomane*, Istanbul, Isis, 2009.
15. Nathalie Clayer, *Aux origines du nationalisme albanais: la naissance d'une nation majoritairement musulmane en Europe*, Paris, Karthala, 2007; George Gawrych, *The Crescent and the Eagle: Ottoman Rule, Islam and the Albanians 1874–1913*, London, I. B. Tauris, 2006.
16. Mary Neuburger, *The Orient Within. Muslim Minorities and the Negotiation of Nationhood in Modern Bulgaria*, Ithaca, Cornell University Press, 2004; Ali Eminov, *Turkish and Other Muslim Minorities in Bulgaria*, London, Hurst, 1997.
17. Konstantinos Tsitselikis, *Old and New Islam in Greece. From Historical Minorities to Immigrant Newcomers*, Leiden, Brill, 2012; Samim Akgönül, *Une communauté, deux États: la minorité turco-musulmane en Thrace occidentale*, Istanbul, Isis, 1999.
18. Stefanos Katsikas (ed.), "European modernity and Islamic Reformism among the Late-Ottoman and Post-Ottoman Muslims of the Balkans (1830–1945)", *Journal of Muslim Minority Affairs*, vol. XXIX, no. 4, December 2009, pp. 435–547.
19. Nathalie Clayer and Éric Germain (eds), *Islam in Inter-War Europe*, London, Hurst, 2008.
20. Armina Omerika, *Islam in Bosnien-Herzegowina und die Netzwerke der Jungmuslime 1918–1991*, Wiesbaden, Harrassowitz, 2014.
21. Ali Basha, *Rrugëtimi i fesë islame në Shqipëri (1912–1967)*, Tirana, 2011; Shyqyri Hysi, *Muslimanizmi në Shqipëri në periudhën 1945–1950*, Tirana, Mësonjëtora, 2006.
22. Fikret Karčić, *The Bosniaks and the Challenge of Modernity*, Sarajevo, El-Kalem, 1999; Enes Karić, *Prilozi za povijest islamskog mišljenja u Bosni i Hercegovini XX. stoljeća*, Sarajevo, El-Kalem, 2004.
23. Valeri Stojanov, *Turskoto naselenie v Bălgaria meždu petoljčkata i polumeseca. Bălgarite mjusjulmani i političeskijat režim meždu poljusite na etničeskata politika*, Sofia, Lik, 1997; Mihail Gruev, *Meždu petoljčkata i polumeseca. Bălgarite mjusjulmani i političeskiat režim (1944–1959)*, Sofia, Kota, 2003; Mihail Gruev and Aleksej Kalionski, *Văzroditelnijat proces: Mjusjulmanskite obštnosti i komunističeskijat režim*, Sofia, Siela, 2008.
24. Tone Bringa, *Being Muslim the Bosnian Way. Identity and Community in a Central Bosnian Village*, Princeton, Princeton University Press, 1995.
25. Ger Duijzings, *Religion and the Politics of Identity in Kosovo*, London, Hurst, 2000.

26. Kristen Ghodsee, *Muslim Lives in Eastern Europe: Gender, Ethnicity and the Transformation of Islam in Postsocialist Bulgaria*, Princeton, Princeton University Press, 2010.
27. Burcu Akan Ellis, *Shadow Genealogies: Memory and Identity among Urban Muslims in Macedonia*, Boulder, CO, East European Monographs, 2003.
28. Hugh Poulton and Suha Taji-Farouki (eds), *Muslim Identity and the Balkan State*, London, Hurst, 1997.
29. Xavier Bougarel (ed.), "Balkan Muslims and Islam in Europe", *Südosteuropa*, vol. LV, no. 4, 2007, pp. 339–462; Kerem Öktem, *New Islamic Actors after the Wahhabi Intermezzo: Turkey's Return to the Muslim Balkans*, Oxford, European Studies Centre, December 2010, available at http://www.balkanmuslims.com
30. Xavier Bougarel and Nathalie Clayer (eds), *Le nouvel islam balkanique. Les musulmans, acteurs du post-communisme 1990–2000*, Paris, Maisonneuve & Larose, 2001.

1. FROM THE OTTOMAN PROVINCIAL AUTONOMIES TO THE EASTERN CRISIS, (1800–1876)

1. Gilles Veinstein, "Les provinces balkaniques (1606–1774)", in Robert Mantran (ed.), *Histoire de l'Empire ottoman*, Paris, Fayard, 1989, pp. 287–340.
2. Maria Todorova, *Imagining the Balkans*, Oxford, Oxford University Press, 1997.
3. See for example Antonis Anastasopoulos and Elias Kolovos (eds), *Ottoman Rule in the Balkans, 1760–1850. Conflict, Transformation, Adaptation*, Rethymno, University of Crete, 2007.
4. Pronounced: mejlis.
5. Catherine Durandin, *Histoire des Roumains*, Paris, Fayard, 1995.
6. Kostas Kostis, "The Formation of the State in Greece, 1830–1914", in Marco Dogo and Guido Franzinetti (eds), *Disrupting and Reshaping. Early Stages of Nation-Building in the Balkans*, Ravenna, Longo Editore, 2002, pp. 47–64.
7. Michael R. Palairet, *The Balkan Economies c. 1800–1914: Evolution without Development*, Cambridge, Cambridge University Press, 1997.
8. Maurus Reinkowski, "The State's Security and the Subjects' Prosperity: Notions of Order in Ottoman Bureaucratic Correspondence (19th Century)", in Hakan T. Karateke and Maurus Reinkowski (eds), *Legitimizing the Order: The Ottoman Rhetoric of State Power*, Leiden-Boston, Brill, 2005, pp. 195–212.
9. Pronounced: rushdiye.
10. Pronounced: mesjeed.
11. Pronounced: jemaat.
12. See Tatjana Paić-Vukić, *The World of Mustafa Muhibbi, a Kadı from Sarajevo*, Istanbul, Isis, 2011.

13. David Kushner, "The Place of the Ulema in the Ottoman Empire during the Age of Reform (1839–1918)", *Turcica*, no. 19, 1987, pp. 51–74.
14. Leopold Von Ranke, *Die serbische Revolution, aus serbischen Papieren und Mittheilungen*, Hamburg, F. Perthes, 1829, pp. 523–58.
15. Ami Boué, *La Turquie d'Europe, ou Observations sur la géographie, la géologie, l'histoire naturelle, la statistique, les moeurs, les coutumes, l'archéologie, l'agriculture, l'industrie, le commerce, les gouvernements divers, le clergé, l'histoire et l'état politique de cet Empire*, Paris, Arthus Bertrand, 1840.
16. Felix Kanitz, "Die moslemisch-bulgarischen Pomaci und Zigeuner im nördlichen Balkangebiete", *Mittelungen der Anthropologischen Gesellschaft in Wien*, Band 6, 1876, pp. 76–9.
17. Dora d'Istria, "La nationalité serbe d'après les chants populaires", *Revue des deux mondes*, Second Period, vol. XXXV, 15 January 1865, pp. 315–60, cited in Demetrio Camarda, *Appendice al saggio di grammatologia comparata sulla lingua albanese (Qualque prosa e versi albanesi tradotti e annotati)*, Prato, F. Alberghetti, 1866, vol. II, p. XIV.
18. Panayiotis Aravantinos, *Hronografia tis Epeirou*, Athens, S. K. Vlastou, 1856.
19. See Nathalie Clayer, *Aux origines du nationalisme albanais: la naissance d'une nation majoritairement musulmane en Europe*, Paris, Karthala, 2007, pp. 160–70.
20. Ibid., p. 238.
21. Maria Todorova, "Conversion to Islam as a Trope in Bulgarian Historiography, Fiction and Film", in Maria Todorova (ed.), *Balkan Identities. Nation and Memory*, London, Hurst, 2004, pp. 129–57.
22. Božidar Petranović, *Bogomili. Crkva bosanska i krstjani. Istorička rasprava*, Zadar, Pečatnja Demarki-Ružier, 1867.
23. Franjo Rački, *Bogomili i patareni*, Zagreb, Štamparija D. Albreht, 1870.
24. Konstantin Jireček, *Geschichte der Bulgaren*, Prague, Verlag von F. Tempsky, 1876.
25. The book was subsequently republished in Paris: Moustafa Djelaleddin, *Les Turcs anciens et modernes*, Paris, Lacroix, Verboeken et Cie, 1870.
26. Şemseddin Sami, *Besa yahud ahde vefa*, Istanbul, Tasvir-i Efkar Matbaası, 1292/1875.
27. Sami Frashëri, "Besa ose mbajtja e fjalës së dhënë", *Vepra*, Tirana, Akademia e shkencave e RPS të Shqipërisë, 1988, vol. I, p. 21.

2. FROM THE EASTERN CRISIS TO THE END OF THE EMPIRES, (1876–1923)

1. François Georgeon, *Abdülhamid II. Le sultan calife*, Paris, Fayard, 2003.
2. Kostas Kostis, "The Formation of the State in Greece, 1830–1914", op. cit.
3. Pronounced: chete.

4. İpek Yosmaoğlu, *Blood Ties. Religion, Violence, and the Politics of Nationhood in Ottoman Macedonia, 1878–1908*, Ithaca, Cornell University Press, 2014, p. 41.
5. Erik-Jan Zürcher, "The Young Turks—Children of the Borderlands?", *International Journal of Turkish Studies*, vol. IX, nos. 1–2, 2003, pp. 275–86.
6. Bernard Lory, *Le sort de l'héritage ottoman en Bulgarie. L'exemple des villes bulgares, 1878–1900*, Istanbul, Isis, 1985.
7. Milena Methodieva, *Reform, Politics and Culture among the Muslims in Bulgaria 1878–1908*, unpublished PhD thesis, Princeton University, 2010.
8. Nicole Immig, "The 'New' Muslim Minorities in Greece: Between Emigration and Political Participation 1881–1886", *Journal of Muslim Minority Affairs*, vol. XXIX, no. 4, December 2009, pp. 511–22.
9. Constantin Iordachi, "'The California of the Romanians': The Integration of Northern Dobrogea into Romania, 1878–1913", in Balázs Trencsényi (ed.), *Nation-Building and Contested Identities. Romanian and Hungarian Case Studies*, Budapest/Iaşi, Regio Books/Editura Politom, 2001, pp. 121–52; and *Citizenship, Nation and State-Building: The Integration of Northern Dobrogea into Romania, 1878–1913*, Pittsburgh, Carl Back Papers in Russian and East European Studies, 2002.
10. Alexandre Toumarkine, *Les migrations des populations musulmanes balkaniques en Anatolie (1876–1913)*, Istanbul, Isis, 1995.
11. Alexandre Toumarkine, *Entre Empire ottoman et État-nation turc: les immigrés musulmans du Caucase et des Balkans du milieu du XIXe siècle à nos jours*, unpublished PhD thesis, University of Paris IV, 2000; and Malte Fuhrmann, "Vagrants, Prostitutes, and Bosnians: Making and Unmaking European Supremacy in Ottoman Southeast Europe", in Hannes Grandits, Nathalie Clayer and Robert Pichler (eds), *Conflicting Loyalties: Social (Dis-)integration and National Turn in the Late and Post-Ottoman Balkan Societies (1839–1914)*, London, I. B. Tauris, 2011, pp. 15–46.
12. At that time, censuses and maps were strong power tools in the Balkan Peninsula. İpek Yosmaoğlu, Blood Ties. Religion, *Violence, and the Politics of Nationhood in Ottoman Macedonia, 1878–1908*, Ithaca-London, Cornell University Press, 2014 (see chapters 3 and 4).
13. Erik-Jan Zürcher, *Greek and Turkish Refugees and Deportees 1912–1924*, Leyde, Turkology Update Leiden Project Working Papers Archive, 2003, available at http://www.transanatolie.com/english/turkey/turks/ottomans/ejz18.pdf
14. This and the following quotations are taken from the text of the Treaty of Berlin that can be accessed at http://archive.org/stream/mapofeuropebytre04hert#page/2772/mode/2up
15. Text of the Convention of Constantinople available at http://www.columbia.edu/cu/lweb/digital/collections/cul/texts/ldpd_7229668_000/pages/ldpd_7229668_000_00000713.html?toggle=image&menu=maximize&top=&left

16. François Georgeon, *Abdülhamid II. Le sultan calife*, Paris, Fayard, 2003.
17. Milena Methodieva and Akşin Somel, "Keeping the Bonds: The Ottomans and Muslim Education in Autonomous Bulgaria 1878–1908", *Turcica*, no. 36, 2004, pp. 141–64.
18. Milena Methodieva, *Reform, Politics and Culture among the Muslims in Bulgaria 1878–1908*, op. cit.
19. Xavier Bougarel, *Survivre aux empires. Islam, identité nationale et allégeances politiques en Bosnie-Herzégovine*, Paris, Karthala, 2015, pp. 34–8.
20. Philippe Gelez, *Safvet-beg Bašagić (1870–1934): aux racines intellectuelles de la pensée nationale chez les musulmans de Bosnie-Herzégovine*, Athens, École française d'Athènes, 2009.
21. Fabio Giomi, *Fra genere, classe, confessione e nazione. "Questione femminile musulmana" e associazionismo in Bosnia e Erzegovina (1903–1941)*, unpublished PhD thesis, École des hautes études en sciences sociales in Paris/University of Bologna, 2011.
22. Antun Hangi, *Život i običaji Muslimana u Bosni i Hercegovini*, Sarajevo, A. Kajon, 1907 (2nd edn), pp. 16–17.
23. Jovan Cvijić, *La Péninsule Balkanique. Géographie humaine*, Paris, Armand Colin, 1918.
24. Jovan N. Tomić, *Les Albanais en Vieille-Serbie et dans le Sandjak de Novi-Bazar*, Paris, Hachette, 1913 (also published in Serbian: *O Arnautima u Staroj Srbiji i Sandžaku*, Belgrade, Geca Kon, 1913).
25. Dimitrios Hasiotis, *Diatrivai kai ipomnimata peri Ipeirou*, Athina, 1887.
26. Naim H. Frashëri, *Fletore e Bektashinjet*, Bucharest, s.n., 1896.
27. Frederick W. Hasluck, *Christianity and Islam under the Sultans*, Oxford, Clarendon Press, 1929, 2 vols. (see vol. II in particular).
28. Pronounced: hoja.

3. FROM THE END OF THE EMPIRES TO THE ADVENT OF COMMUNISM, (1920–1944)

1. John S. Koliopoulos and Thanos M. Veremis, *Greece: The Modern Sequel. From 1821 to the Present*, London, Hurst, 2007.
2. Protection of Linguistic, racial or religious minorities by the League of Nations", Geneva, February 1929, http://biblio-archive.unog.ch/Dateien/CouncilMSD/C-24-M-18-1929-I_EN.pdf
3. Irina Livezeanu, *Cultural Politics in Greater Romania: Regionalism, Nation-Building, and Ethnic Struggle, 1918–1930*, Ithaca, Cornell University Press, 1995.
4. Pieter Troch, "Yugoslavism between the World Wars: Indecisive Nation-Building", *Nationalities Papers*, vol. XXXVIII, no. 2, March 2010, pp. 227–44.

5. Mark Mazower, "Minorities and the League of Nations in Interwar Europe", *Daedalus*, vol. CXXVI, no. 2, Spring 1997, pp. 47–63.
6. Edvin Pezo, *Zwangsmigrationen in Friedenszeiten? Jugoslawische Migrationspolitik und die Auswanderung von Muslimen in die Türkei (1918 bis 1966)*, München, Oldenburg, 2013.
7. Pezo, *Zwangsmigrationen in Friedenszeiten?*, pp. 51–77.
8. Mary Neuburger, *The Orient Within. Muslim Minorities and the Negotiation of Nationhood in Modern Bulgaria*, Ithaca, Cornell University Press, 2004.
9. Georgia Kretsi, "From Landholding to Landlessness. The Relationship between the Property and Legal Status of the Cham Muslim Albanians", *Jahrbuch für Geschichte und Kultur Südosteuropas*, vol. V, 2003, pp. 125–38.
10. Bogumil Hrabak, *Džemijet. Organizacija muslimana Makedonije, Kosova, Metohije i Sandžaka 1919–1928*, Belgrade, B. Hrabak, 2003.
11. The literal meaning of *Turan* is "land of the Tur". It refers to central Asia. Towards the end of the Ottoman period, some Turkish and pan-Turkish nationalists adopted this expression to refer to the Turkish peoples' country of origin.
12. Fabio Giomi, *Fra genere, classe, confessione e nazione*, op. cit.
13. Ebru Boyar and Kate Fleet, "A Dangerous Axis: The 'Bulgarian Müftü', the Turkish Opposition and the Ankara Government 1928–1936", *Middle Eastern Studies*, vol. XLIV, no. 5, September 2008, pp. 775–89.
14. Mila Mancheva, *State–Minority Relations and the Education of Turks and Pomaks in Inter-War Bulgaria, 1918–1944*, unpublished PhD thesis, Central European University, Budapest, 2003.
15. Yannis Bonos, "The Turkish Spelling Mistakes Episode in Greek Thrace, June 1929: Beyond Modernists versus Conservatives", in Nathalie clayer and Eric Germain (eds), *Islam in Inter-War Europe*, London, Hurst, 2008, pp. 362–86.
16. Mary Neuburger, *The Orient Within. Muslim Minorities and the Negotiation of Nationhood in Modern Bulgaria*, Ithaca: Cornell University Press, 2004.
17. Xavier Bougarel, *Survivre aux empires*, op. cit.; "Le Reis et le voile: une polémique religieuse dans la Bosnie-Herzégovine de l'entre-deux-guerres", in Nathalie Clayer, Benoît and Alexandre Papas (eds), *L'autorité religieuse et ses limites en terre d'islam*, Leiden, Brill, 2013, pp. 109–57.
18. Fabio Giomi, *Fra genere, classe, confessione e nazione*, op. cit.
19. Mustafa Memić, *Velika medresa i njeni učenici u revolucionarnom pokretu*, Skopje, Fonografika, 1984.
20. Pronounced: Yujeljeeler, lit. "members of the Yücel organization", "yücel" meaning "become accomplished".
21. Yannis Bonos, "The Turkish Spelling Mistakes Episode in Greek Thrace, June 1929: Beyond Modernists versus Conservatives", in Nathalie Clayer

and Eric Germain (eds), *Islam in Inter-War Europe*, London: Hurst, 2008, pp. 362–86; Anna Mirkova, "Citizenship Formation in Bulgaria: Protected Minority or National Citizens?", *Journal of Muslim Minority Affairs*, vol. XXIX, no. 4, December 2009, pp. 469–82.
22. Mary Neuburger, *The Orient Within. Muslim Minorities and the Negotiation of Nationhood in Modern Bulgaria*, Ithaca, Cornell University Press, 2004.
23. John Kingsley Birge, *The Bektashi Order of Dervishes*, London, Luzac & Co., 1937.
24. Ömer Rıza Doğrul, *Tanrı Buyruğu. Kuran'ı Kerim Tercüme ve Tefsiri*, Istanbul, Muallim Ahmet Halit Kitaphanesi, 1934.
25. Hamit Bozarslan, "La Laïcité en Turquie", *Matériaux pour l'histoire de notre temps*, no. 78, April–June 2005, pp. 42–9.
26. Franz Babinger, "Bei den Derwischen von Kruja", *Mitteilungen der Deutsch-Türkischen Vereinigung*, vol. IX, nos. 8–9, 1928, pp. 148–9.
27. Fabio Giomi, *Fra genere, classe, confessione e nazione*, op. cit.
28. See for example George-Henri Bousquet, "Note sur les réformes de l'islam albanais", *Revue des études islamiques*, vol. IV, 1935, pp. 399–410.
29. Tihomir Đorđević, *Naš narodni život*, 10 vol., Belgrade, Srpska Književna Zadruga, 1930–34 (republished in 4 vols. under the direction of Ivan Čolović, Belgrade, Prosveta, 1984).
30. Tihomir Đorđević, *Zle oči u verovanju Južnih Slovena*, Belgrade, Srpska Kraljevska Akademija, 1938 (republished, Belgrade, Prosveta, 1984–5).
31. Gliša Elezović, *Derviški redovi muslimanski. Tekije u Skoplju*, Skopje, Stara Srbija, 1925; Muhamed Garčević, *Zapisi i hamajlije*, Sarajevo, Hrvatska Državna Tiskara and Područnica Sarajevo, 1942.
32. Tihomir Đorđević, "Amajlije", *Naš narodni život*, Belgrade, Srpska Književna Zadruga, 1984, vol. II, p. 199.

4. FROM THE ADVENT OF COMMUNISM TO ITS FALL, (1944—1989)

1. Nedim Šarac, *Istorija Saveza komunista Bosne i Hercegovine*, vol. II, Sarajevo, Institut za istoriju, 1990, pp. 31, 236.
2. Lenard Cohen, *The Socialist Pyramid: Elites and Power in Yugoslavia*, Oakville, Canada, Mosaic Press, 1989, pp. 364–6.
3. Hamdija Pozderac was the son of Nurija Pozderac, a JMO senator who joined the partisans in 1942, and he also fought in their ranks. Taking part in the struggle for national liberation was thus a way for the offspring of certain families of Muslim notables to join the new communist elites.
4. David Dyker, "The Ethnic Muslims of Bosnia—Some Basic Socio-Economic Data", *Slavonic and East European Review*, vol. L, no. 119, April 1972, pp. 238–56.

5. The number of people who declared themselves to be "Muslim" (national name) increased from 8,026 in 1961 to 57,408 in 1991 in Kosovo, and from 3,002 in 1961 to 47,790 in 1991 in Macedonia.
6. In the late 1980s, some Gypsy activists in Macedonia and Kosovo demanded to be recognised as members of an Egyptian national minority. See Ger Duijzings, "The Making of Egyptians in Kosovo and Macedonia", in Cora Govers and Hans Vermeulen (eds), *The Politics of Ethnic Consciousness*, Basingstoke, Macmillan, 1997, pp. 194–222.
7. In 1947, the several thousand Muslims living on the Dodecanese Islands, given to Greece by the Treaty of Paris, became Greek citizens alongside the Muslims of Western Thrace. However, the Muslims of the Dodecanese did not benefit from the provisions of the Treaty of Lausanne, and therefore their mufti did not have legal powers.
8. A second secondary school was opened in Xanthi in 1965.
9. Petăr Petrov (ed.), *Po sledite na nasilieto: dokumenti i materiali za zalaganje na isljama*, Sofia, Nauka i izkustvo, 1987; Hristo Hristov (ed.), *Stranci ot bălgarskata istorija: očerk za isljamiziranite Bălgari i nacionalnovăzroditelnija proces*, Sofia, Nauka i izkustvo, 1989.
10. Antonina Željazkova, *Razprostranenie na isljama v zapadnobalkanskite zemi pod osmanska vlast (XV.-XVIII. vek)*, Sofia, Bălgarskata akademija na naukite, 1990.
11. Salim Ćerić, *Muslimani srpskohrvatskog jezika*, Sarajevo, Svjetlost, 1968; Muhamed Hadžijahić, *Od tradicije do identiteta: geneza nacionalnog pitanja bosanskih Muslimana*, Sarajevo, Svjetlost, 1974.
12. Nedim Filipović, "Specifičnosti islamizacije u Bosni", *Pregled*, vol. LVIII, special issue, 1968, pp. 27–34.
13. Hasan Kalashi, "Das Türkische Vordringen auf dem Balkan und die Islamisierung—Faktoren für die Erhaltung der ethnischen und nationalen Existenz des albanischen Volkes", in Peter Bartl and Horst Glassl (eds), *Südosteuropa unter dem Halbmond*, München, R. Trofenik, 1975, pp. 125–38; Muhamet Tërnava, "Përhapja e Islamizmit në territorin e sotëm të Kosovës deri në fund të shekullit të XVII", *Gjurmime albanologjike*, vol. IX, 1979–80, pp. 45–69.
14. Muhamet Pirraku, *Kultura kombëtare shqiptare deri në lidhjen e Prizrenit*, Prishtina, Instituti albanologjik i Prishtinës, 1989; Skënder Rizaj, "The Islamization of the Albanians during the 15th and 16th Centuries", *Studia Albanica*, vol. II, 1985, pp. 127–31.
15. See for example Elira Cela, *Tradita afetare të populit shqiptar*, Tirana, 8 nëntori, 1991.
16. Enver Redžić, "O posebnosti bosanskih muslimana", *Pregled*, vol. LX, no. 4, April 1970, pp. 457–88.
17. Esad Ćimić, "Osobenosti nacionalnog formiranja Muslimana", *Pregled*, vol. LXIV, no. 4, April 1974, pp. 389–407.

18. Speros Vryonis, *The Decline of Medieval Hellenism in Asia Minor and the Process of Islamization from the Eleventh through the Fifteenth Century*, Berkeley, University of California Press, 1971; Stavro Skendi, *The Albanian National Awakening 1878–1912*, Princeton, Princeton University Press, 1968.
19. Alexandre Popovic, *L'islam balkanique*, op. cit.; Kemal Karpat, *The Turks of Bulgaria: The History, Culture and Political Fate of a Minority*, Istanbul, Isis, 1990; Ali Eminov, *Turkish and Other Minorities in Bulgaria*, op. cit.
20. Tajar Zavalani, *Histori e Shqipnis*, London, Drini Publications, 1966; Abas Ermenji, *Vendi që zë Skënderbeu në historinë e Shqipërisë*, Paris, Komiteti Kombëtar Demokratik "Shqipnia e Li˙rë", 1968.
21. Smail Balić, *Bosna u egzilu 1945–1992: članci, rasprave, razgovori*, Zagreb, Preporod, 1995.
22. Etienne Copeaux, *Espaces et temps de la nation turque. Analyse d'une historiographie nationaliste 1931–1993*, Paris, CNRS Editions, 1997; Binnaz Toprak, "Religion as State Ideology in a Secular Setting: The Turkish–Islamic Synthesis", in Malcolm Wagstaff (ed.), *Aspects of Religion in Secular Turkey*, Occasional Paper Series, no. 4, University of Durham, Centre for Middle East and Islamic Studies, 1990, pp. 10–15.
23. Neo-Salafism is, alongside Islamic reformism, one of the religious currents deriving from the *salafiyya* of the late nineteenth century. However, for the Salafists of the nineteenth century, the return to the Islam of the "pious ancestors" had to allow the removal of outdated traditions, to encourage *ijtihad* (reasoned interpretation) and to legitimise reformist ideas. The neo-Salafists of the late twentieth century, on the other hand, used the example of the "pious ancestors" to promote strict, fixed and anti-Western interpretations of Islam.
24. Religious education in the minority schools and the two madrasas in Komotini and Echinos (Xanthi region) was placed under the control of the Ministry of Education and Religion.
25. Ali Aliev, *Formiraneto na naučno-ateističen mirogled u bălgarskite Turci*, Sofia, Partizdat, 1980, p. 47, quoted in Ali Eminov, *Turkish and Other Muslim Minorities of Bulgaria*, New York, Routledge, 1997, p. 56.
26. Dragomir Pantić, "Religioznost građana Jugoslavije", in Ljiljana Baćević (ed.), *Jugoslavija na kriznoj prekretnici*, Belgrade, IDN, 1991, pp. 241–57.
27. Ali Aliev, *Formiraneto na naučno-ateističen mirogled*, op. cit., p. 55, quoted in Ali Eminov, *Turkish and Other Muslim Minorities of Bulgaria*, op. cit., p. 56.
28. Dragomir Pantić, "Prostorne, vremenske i socijalne coordinate religioznosti mladih u Jugoslaviji", in Srećko Mihailović (ed.), *Deca krize. Omladina Jugoslavije krajem osamdesetih*, Belgrade, IDN, 1990, pp. 203–28.
29. Cornelia Sorabji, *Muslim Identity and Islamic Faith in Sarajevo*, unpublished PhD thesis, University of Cambridge, 1989.
30. Ibid., p. 148.

31. Ibid., pp. 73–4.
32. Ibid., p. 187.
33. Yannis Frangopoulos, *Une minorité musulmane en transition. Approche anthropologique des Pomaques grecs*, unpublished PhD thesis, University of Louvain-la-Neuve, 1996.

5. FROM THE FALL OF COMMUNISM TO EUROPEAN INTEGRATION, (1989–2001)

1. The full name was the Interior Macedonian Revolutionary Organisation—Democratic Party for Macedonian National Unity (*Vnatrešna Makedonska Revolucionerna Organizacija—Demokratska Partija za Makedonsko Nacionalno Edinstvo*—VMRO-DPMNE).
2. On 27 September 1993, a Bosniak Assembly (*Bošnjački sabor*) bringing together the main political, military, religious and intellectual leaders of the Bosnian Muslim community decided to abandon the national name "Muslim" (*Musliman*) and adopt that of "Bosniak" (*Bošnjak*). Whereas the national name "Bosniak" designates only Bosnian Muslims, the name "Bosnian" (*Bosanac*) applies to all inhabitants of Bosnia-Herzegovina regardless of national or religious affiliation.
3. In Southeast Europe, the term "historic religions" includes Orthodox Christianity, Catholicism, Islam, Judaism and some Protestant Churches.
4. From the 1990s onwards, a majority of the Gypsy population of Southeast Europe claimed a Roma identity, and the term "Gypsy" was more and more regarded as pejorative.
5. In the Kosovo parliament (120 seats), 10 seats are reserved for the Serbian minority, 4 for the Roma, Ashkali and Egyptian minority, 3 for the Bosniak minority, 2 for the Turkish minority and 1 for the Gorani minority.
6. The SDA-Islamic Path (in Albanian: PVD-*Rruga Islam*; in Turkish: DHP-*İslam Yolu*), led by Kenan Mazllami, became the SDA-True Path (*Rruga e Vërtetë*; *Hak Yolu*) in 1995.
7. In the Federation, one of the two entities of Bosnia-Herzegovina, Bosniaks account for around 75 per cent of the total population.
8. The supporters of the national name "Bosniak", led by Adil Zulfikarpašić, then created the Bosniak Muslim Organisation (*Muslimanska bošnjačka organizacija*—MBO), which won only 1 per cent of the votes in the November 1990 elections.
9. According to the population censuses conducted in the early 2000s, there were 136,087 Bosniaks and 19,053 Muslims in Serbia, 48,184 Bosniaks and 24,625 Muslims in Montenegro, 17,018 Bosniaks and 2,553 Muslims in Macedonia, 20,755 Bosniaks and 19,677 Muslims in Croatia.
10. See chapter 4, note 119.

11. After 1999, certain Albanian-speaking Roma activists from Kosovo claimed a separate Ashkali identity, in order to move closer to the majority Albanian community.
12. Pronounced: shehid
13. The Islamic institutions of Croatia and Slovenia are attached to the Islamic Community of Bosnia-Herzegovina, but in practice enjoy a wide degree of autonomy.
14. Mustafa Cerić, born in 1952, studied at the Sarajevo madrasa and then at the al-Azhar University in Egypt. He was principal imam at the Bosnian Islamic Centre of Chicago from 1981 to 1987, and then at the Zagreb mosque from 1987 to 1993.
15. Rexhep Boja, born in 1946, attended primary school in Kosovo and then received his secondary and higher education in Saudi Arabia. He taught at the Prishtina madrasa from 1985 to 1990.
16. Sulejman Rexhepi, born in 1947, studied at the Prishtina madrasa and then in Kuwait. He was in charge of educational matters at the Islamic institutions of Macedonia.
17. Muamer Zukorlić, born in 1970, studied at the Sarajevo madrasa, then in Algeria. He was elected mufti of Novi Pazar in 1993.
18. To complicate matters even further, the local Islamic institutions in Preševo, Medvedja and Bujanovac, in the south of Serbia, recognise only the authority of the Islamic Community of Kosovo.
19. Mustafa Ališ Hadži, born in 1962, studied theology in Jordan between 1993 and 1997.
20. For discussion of neo-Salafism, see Chapter 4, note 136.
21. Sunni Islam is divided into four *madhhab*s (in Turkish: *mezheb*s; legal schools) which appeared in the eighth and ninth centuries: the Maliki, Shafi'i, Hanbali and Hanafi *madhhab*s, the latter being the official *madhhab* of the Ottoman Empire and the one to which Balkan Muslims belong historically.
22. Some religious practices are related to both the public sphere and personal piety, such as observing the Ramadan fast or wearing a veil or beard.
23. Kristen Ghodsee, *Muslim Lives in Eastern Europe: Gender, Ethnicity, and the Transformation of Islam in Postsocialist Bulgaria*, Princeton, Princeton University Press, 2009.

CONCLUSION

1. Danièle Hervieu-Leger, *Le pèlerin et le converti: la religion en mouvement*, Paris, Flammarion, 2001.
2. Grace Davie, *Europe, the Exceptional Case: The Parameters of Faith in the Modern World*, London, Darton, Longman & Todd, 2002.

BIBLIOGRAPHY

This bibliography contains the main recent publications concerning the Muslims of Southeast Europe or the regional context for the period discussed in this book. It does not include all the references, particularly those in local languages, which can be found in the bibliographies of the studies presented here.

Adanir, Fikret and Faroqhi Suraiya (eds), *The Ottomans and the Balkans. A Discussion of Historiography*, Leiden: Brill, 2002.

Adanir Fikret, "The Formation of a 'Muslim' Nation in Bosnia-Herzegovina: A Historiographic Discussion", in Fikret Adanir and Suraiya Faroqhi (eds), *The Ottomans and the Balkans. A Discussion of Historiography*, Leiden: Brill, 2002, pp. 267–304.

Adiyeke Ayşe Nükhet, *Islamic Community Brotherhood Administrations in Greece: Cemaat-i Islamiye 1913–1998*, Ankara: Ncsrs, 2002.

Agai Bekim, *Zwischen Netzwerk und Diskurs: Das Bildungsnetzwerk um Fethullah Gülen (geb. 1938). Die flexible Umsetzung modernen islamischen Gedankenguts*, Hamburg: Eb-Verlag, 2004.

Akagül Deniz and Vaner Semih, "La Turquie dans les Balkans", in Edith Lhomel and Thomas Schreiber (eds), *L'Europe centrale et orientale*, Paris: La Documentation française, 1993, pp. 53–64.

Akan Ellis Burcu, *Shadow Genealogies: Memory and Identity among Urban Muslims in Macedonia*, Boulder, CO: East European Monographs, 2003.

Akgönül Samim, *Une communauté, deux états: la minorité turco-musulmane de Thrace occidentale*, Istanbul: Isis, 1999.

Akgönül Samim, "L'émigration des musulmans de Thrace occidentale", *Mésogeios*, no. 3, 1999, pp. 31–49.

Aleksov Bojan, "Perceptions of Islamization in the Serbian National Discourse", *Southeast European and Black Sea Studies*, vol. V, no. 1, January 2005, pp. 113–27.

BIBLIOGRAPHY

Alibašić Ahmet, *Traditional and Reformist Islam in Bosnia and Herzegovina*, Cambridge: Center of International Studies, 2003.

Anagnostou Dia, *Regional Political Economy, Turkish Muslim Mobilization and Identity Transformation in Southeastern Europe*, unpublished PhD thesis, Cornell University, 1999.

———, "Breaking the Cycle of Nationalism: The EU, Regional Policy and the Minority of Western Thrace, Greece", *South European Society and Politics*, vol. VI, no. 1, Summer 2001, pp. 99–124.

———, "Nationalist Legacies and European Trajectories: Post-Communist Liberalization and Turkish Minority Politics in Bulgaria", *Southeast European and Black Sea Studies*, vol. V, no. 1, January 2005, pp. 89–111.

———, "National Interpretations in Bulgarian Writings on the Pomaks from the Communist Period through the Present", *Journal of Southern Europe and the Balkans*, vol. VII, no. 1, April 2005, pp. 57–74.

Anastassiadis Tassos and Clayer Nathalie (eds), *Society, Politics and State-Formation in South-Eastern Europe during the 19th Century*, Athens: Alpha Bank Historical Archives, 2011.

Anastasopoulos Antonis and Kolovos Elias (eds), *Ottoman Rule in the Balkans 1760–1850. Conflict, Transformation, Adaptation*, Rethymno: University of Crete, 2007.

Antoniou Dimitris, "Western Thracian Muslims in Athens, from Economic Migration to Religious Organization", *Balkanologie*, vol. IX, nos. 1–2, December 2005, pp. 79–101, available at http://balkanologie.revues.org/index579.html

Apostolov Mario, "The Pomaks: A Religious Minority in the Balkans", *Nationalities Papers*, vol. XXIV, no. 4, 1996, pp. 727–45.

Aruçi Muhammed, "The Muslim Minority in Macedonia and its Educational Institutions during the Inter-War Period", in Nathalie Clayer and Eric Germain (eds), *Islam in Inter-War Europe*, London: Hurst, 2008, pp. 344–61.

Atanovski Gligor, "Les Roms en Macédoine", *Migrations et société*, vol. XI, no. 63, May–June 1999, pp. 71–8.

Babuna Aydın, *Die nationale Entwicklung der bosnischen Muslime. Mit besonderer Berücksichtigung der österreichisch-ungarischen Periode*, Bern: Peter Lang, 1996.

———, "National Identity, Islam and Politics in Post-Communist Bosnia-Herzegovina", *East European Quarterly*, vol. XXXIX, no. 4, Winter 2006, pp. 405–64.

Baer Marc David, *Honored by the Glory of Islam. Conversion and Conquest in Ottoman Europe*, Oxford: Oxford University Press, 2008.

———, *The Dönme. Jewish Converts, Muslim Revolutionaries, and Secular Turks*, Stanford: Stanford University Press, 2009.

Bagaric Oliver, "Museum und nationale Identitäten: Eine Geschichte des Landesmuseums Sarajevo", *Südost-Forschungen*, vol. LVIII, 2008, pp. 144–67.

BIBLIOGRAPHY

Bagherzadeh Alireza, "L'ingérence iranienne en Bosnie-Herzégovine", in Xavier Bougarel and Nathalie Clayer (eds), *Le nouvel islam balkanique. Les musulmans, acteurs du post-communisme (1990–2000)*, Paris: Maisonneuve & Larose, 2001, pp. 397–428.

Balić Smail, *Das unbekannte Bosnien: Europas Brücke zur islamischen Welt*, Wien: Böhlau, 1992.

——— (ed.), "Islam in the Balkans", *Islamic Studies*, vol. XXXVI, nos. 2–3, Summer-Fall 1997, pp. 137–581.

Banac Ivo, *The National Question in Yugoslavia: Origins, History, Politics*, Ithaca: Cornell University Press, 1984.

Barany Zoltan, "The Roma in Macedonia", *Ethnic and Racial Studies*, vol. XVIII, no. 3, July 1995, pp. 515–31.

Bartl Peter, *Die albanischen Muslime zur Zeit der nationalen Unabhängigkeitsbewegung (1878–1912)*, Wiesbaden: Otto Harrassowitz, 1968.

Basha Ali, *Rrugëtimi i fesë islame në Shqipëri (1912–1967)*, Tirana: s.n., 2011.

Begić Esnaf, *Die bosnisch-herzegowinischen Muslime in Deutschland und ihre religiöse Organisation*, unpublished Master's thesis, University of Bochum, 2002.

Bein Amit, *Ottoman Ulema, Turkish Republic. Agents of Change and Guardians of Tradition*, Stanford: Stanford University Press, 2011.

Bellion-Jourdan Jérôme, "Les réseaux transnationaux islamiques en Bosnie-Herzégovine", in Xavier Bougarel and Nathalie Clayer (eds), *Le nouvel islam balkanique. Les musulmans, acteurs du post-communisme (1990–2000)*, Paris: Maisonneuve & Larose, 2001, pp. 429–72.

Benthall Jonathan and Bellion-Jourdan Jérôme, *The Charitable Crescent: Politics of Aid in the Muslim World*, London: I. B. Tauris, 2003.

Bieber Florian, "Muslim Identity in the Balkans before the Establishment of Nation States", *Nationalities Papers*, vol. XXVIII, no. 1, March 2000, pp. 13–28.

Bielenin-Lenczowska Karolina, "The Construction of Identity in a Multiethnic Community: A Case Study on the Torbeši of Centar Župa Commune, Western Macedonia (FYROM)", *Ethnologia Balkanica*, no. 12, 2008, pp. 167–81.

Bilici Faruk, "Le parti islamiste turc (Refah Partisi) et sa dimension internationale", *Les annales de l'autre islam*, no. 4, 1997, pp. 35–60.

Billion Didier and Da Lage Olivier, "La guerre du Kosovo et le monde musulman", *Revue internationale et stratégique*, no. 36, hiver 1999/2000, pp. 139–45.

Blumi Isa, "The Islamist Challenge in Kosovo", *Current History*, vol. CII, no. 662, March 2003, pp. 124–8.

———, *Political Islam among the Albanians: Are the Talibans Coming to the Balkans?*, Prishtina: Kipred, 2003.

———, "Defining Social Spaces by Way of Deletion: The Untold Story of Albanian Migration in the Post-War Period", *Journal of Ethnic and Migration Studies*, vol. XXIX, no. 6, November 2003, pp. 649–65.

BIBLIOGRAPHY

———, *Reinstating the Ottomans: Alternative Balkan Modernities 1800–1912*, New York: Palgrave Macmillan, 2011.

Bonos Yannis, "The Turkish Spelling Mistakes Episode in Greek Thrace, June 1929: Beyond Modernists versus Conservatives", in Nathalie Clayer and Eric Germain (eds), *Islam in Inter-War Europe*, London: Hurst, 2008, pp. 362–86.

Bora Tanıl, "Turkish National Identity, Turkish Nationalism and the Balkan Problem", in Günay Göksü Özdoğan and Kemâli Saybaşili (eds), *Balkans. A Mirror of the New International Order*, Istanbul: Eren, 1995, pp. 101–20.

Bougarel Xavier, "Ramadan during a Civil War (as Reflected in a Series of Speeches)", *Islam and Christian–Muslim Relations*, vol. VI, no. 1, 1995, pp. 79–103.

———, *Bosnie, anatomie d'un conflit*, Paris: La Découverte, 1996.

———, "From Young Muslims to the Party of Democratic Action: The Emergence of a Pan-Islamist Trend in Bosnia-Herzegovina", *Islamic Studies*, vol. XXXVI, nos. 2–3, Summer-Fall 1997, pp. 533–49.

———, "Le ramadan, révélateur des évolutions de l'islam en Bosnie-Herzégovine", in Fariba Adelkhah and François Georgeon (eds), *Ramadan et politique*, Paris: CNRS Editions, 2000, pp. 83–96.

———, "Trois définitions de l'islam en Bosnie-Herzégovine", *Archives de sciences sociales des religions*, vol. XLVI, no. 115, July–September 2001, pp. 183–201, available at http://assr.revues.org/18673

———, "L'islam bosniaque, entre identité culturelle et idéologie politique", in Xavier Bougarel and Nathalie Clayer (eds), *Le nouvel islam balkanique. Les musulmans, acteurs du post-communisme (1990–2000)*, Paris: Maisonneuve & Larose, 2001, pp. 79–132.

———, "Bosnie-Herzégovine: comment peut-on être bochniaque?", in Alain Dieckhoff and Riva Kastoryano (eds), *Nationalismes en mutation en Méditerranée orientale*, Paris: CNRS Editions, 2002, pp. 173–93.

———, "Islam and Politics in the Post-Communist Balkans", in Dimitris Keridis and Charles Perry (eds), *New Approaches to Balkan Studies*, Dulles, VA: Brassey's, 2003, pp. 345–60.

———, *The Role of Balkan Muslims in Building a European Islam*, Brussels: European Policy Center, 23 novembre 2005, available at http://www.epc.eu/pub_details.php?pub_id=62&cat_id=2

———, "Balkan Muslim Diasporas and the Idea of a 'European Islam'", in Tomislav Dulić (ed.), *Balkan Currents. Essays in Honour of Kjell Magnusson*, Uppsala: Uppsala Multiethnic Papers, 2005, pp. 147–65.

———, "Islam balkanique et intégration européenne", in Rémy Leveau and Khadija Mohsen-Finan (eds), *Musulmans de France et d'Europe*, Paris: Cnrs Editions, 2005, pp. 21–48.

———, "Bosnian Islam as European Islam: Limits and Shifts of a Concept", in

BIBLIOGRAPHY

Aziz Al-Azmeh and Effie Fokas (eds), *Islam in Europe. Diversity, Identity and Influence*, Cambridge: Cambridge University Press, 2007, pp. 96–124.

——— (ed.), "Balkan Muslims and Islam in Europe", *Südosteuropa*, vol. LV, no. 4, 2007, pp. 339–462.

———, "Farewell to the Ottoman Legacy? Islamic Reformism and Revivalism in Inter-War Bosnia-Herzegovina", in Nathalie Clayer and Eric Germain (eds), *Islam in Inter-War Europe*, London: Hurst, 2008, pp. 313–43.

———, "Balkan Islam as 'European Islam': Historical Background and Present Challenges", in Christian Voss and Jordanka Telbizova-Sack (eds), *Islam und Muslime in (Südost)Europa im Kontext von Transformation und EU-Erweiterung*, München: Otto Sagner, 2010, pp. 15–31.

———, "Nuovi orizzonti, nuove sfide: i musulmani nello spazio jugoslavo dopo il communismo", in Antonio D'alessandri and Armando Pitassio (eds), *Dopo la pioggia. Gli stati della ex Jugoslavia e l'Albania (1991–2011)*, Lecce: Argo, 2011, pp. 451–67.

———, "Le Reis et le voile: une polémique religieuse dans la Bosnie-Herzégovine de l'entre-deux-guerres", in Nathalie Clayer, Benoît Fliche and Alexandre Papas (eds), *L'autorité religieuse et ses limites en terre d'islam*, Leiden: Brill, 2013, pp. 109–57.

———, *Survivre aux empires. Islam, identité nationale et allégeances politiques en Bosnie-Herzégovine*, Paris: Karthala, 2015.

Bougarel Xavier and Clayer Nathalie (eds), *Le nouvel islam balkanique. Les musulmans, acteurs du post-communisme (1990–2000)*, Paris: Maisonneuve & Larose, 2001.

Bougarel Xavier and Iseni Bashkim, "Islam et politique dans les Balkans occidentaux", *Politorbis*, no. 43, 2007, pp. 3–71, available at http://www.eda.admin.ch/etc/medialib/downloads/edazen/doc/publi.Par.0227.File.tmp/Politorbis%2043.pdf

Bougarel Xavier and Mihaylova Dimitrina (eds), "Diasporas musulmanes balkaniques dans l'Union européenne", *Balkanologie*, vol. IX, nos. 1–2, décembre 2005, pp. 57–211, available at http://balkanologie.revues.org/index547.html

Boussiakou Iris Kalliopi, *The Educational Rights of the Muslim Minority under Greek Law*, Flensburg: Ecmi, 2007, available at http://www.ecmi.de/fileadmin/downloads/publications/Jemie/2007/Issue1/1-2007_Boussiakou.pdf

Bowers Stephen, "The Islamic Factor in Albanian Policy", *Journal of Muslim Minority Affairs*, vol. V, no. 1, January 1984, pp. 123–35.

Boyar Ebru and Fleet Kate, "A Dangerous Axis: The 'Bulgarian Müftü', the Turkish Opposition and the Ankara Government 1928–1936", *Middle Eastern Studies*, vol. XLIV, no. 5, September 2008, pp. 775–89.

Bozarslan Hamit, "La Laïcité en Turquie", *Matériaux pour l'histoire de notre temps*, no. 78, April–June 2005, pp. 42–9.

BIBLIOGRAPHY

———, *Histoire de la Turquie contemporaine*, Paris: La Découverte, 2007.
Bringa Tone, *Being Muslim the Bosnian Way. Identity and Community in a Central Bosnian Village*, Princeton: Princeton University Press, 1995.
———, "Islam and the Quest for Identity in Post-Communist Bosnia-Herzegovina", in Maya Schatzmiller (ed.), *Islam and Bosnia: Conflict Resolution and Foreign Policy in Multi-Ethnic States*, Montreal: Mc Gill-Queen's University Press, 2002, pp. 24–34.
Broun Janice, "Rehabilitation and Recovery: Bulgaria's Muslim Communities", *Religion, State & Society*, vol. XXXV, no. 2, June 2007, pp. 105–38.
Brubaker Rogers, *Nationalism Reframed: Nationhood and the National Question in the New Europe*, Cambridge: Cambridge University Press, 1996.
Brunnbauer Ulf, "The Perception of Muslims in Bulgaria and Greece: Between the 'Self' and the 'Other'", *Journal of Muslim Minority Affairs*, vol. XXI, no. 1, 2001, pp. 39–61.
———, "An den Grenzen von Staat und Nation. Identitätsprobleme der Pomaken Bulgariens", in Ulf Brunnbauer (ed.), *Umstrittene Identitäten. Etnizität und Nationalität in Südosteuropa*, Bern: Peter Lang, 2002, pp. 97–121.
———, "Fertility, Families and Ethnic Conflict: Macedonians and Albanians in the Republic of Macedonia 1944–2002", *Nationalities Papers*, vol. XXXII, no. 3, September 2004, pp. 565–98.
Brunner Georg, "The Status of Muslims in the Federative Systems of Soviet Union and Yugoslavia", in Georg Brunner, Andreas Kappeler and Gerhard SIMON (eds), *Muslim Communities Re-emerge: Historical Perspectives on Nationality, Politics and Opposition in the Former Soviet Union and Yugoslavia*, Durham, NC: Duke University Press, 1994, pp. 183–213.
Bulut Esra, "'Friends, Balkans, Statesmen, Lend Us Your Ears': The Trans-State and State in Links between Turkey and the Balkans", *Ethnopolitics*, vol. V, no. 3, September 2006, pp. 309–26.
Burg Steven, *The Political Integration of Yugoslavia's Muslims: Determinants of Success and Failure*, Pittsburgh: Carl Beck Papers in Russian and East European Studies, 1983.
Buturovic Amila and Schick Irvin Cemil (eds), *Women in the Ottoman Balkans*, London: I. B. Tauris, 2007.
Canapa Marie-Paul, "L'islam et la question des nationalités en Yougoslavie", in Olivier Carre and Paul Dumont (eds), *Radicalismes islamiques*, Paris: L'Harmattan, 1986, pp. 100–150.
Capelle-Pogacean Antonela and Ragaru Nadège, "En quoi les 'partis ethniques' sont-ils 'ethniques'? Les trajectoires du MDL en Bulgarie et de L'UDMR en Roumanie", *Questions de recherche*, no. 25, June 2008, pp. 1–93, available at http://www.sciencespo.fr/ceri/sites/sciencespo.fr.ceri/files/qdr25.pdf
Ćehajić Džemal, *Derviški redovi u jugoslovenskim zemljama sa posebnim osvrtom na Bosnu i Hercegovinu*, Sarajevo: Orijentalni institut, 1986.

BIBLIOGRAPHY

Clayer Nathalie, *L'Albanie, pays des derviches. Les ordres mystiques musulmans en Albanie à l'époque postottomane (1912 1967)*, Berlin Wiesbaden: Otto Harrassowitz, 1990.

———, *Mystiques, état et société. Les Halvetis dans l'aire balkanique de la fin du XVe siècle à nos jours*, Leiden: Brill, 1994.

———, "Le renouveau de l'islam et l'enseignement religieux en Albanie depuis 1990", in Nicole Grandin and Marc Gaborieau (eds), *Madrasa. La transmission du savoir dans le monde musulman*, Paris: Arguments, 1997, pp. 289–94.

———, "National and Religious Identity among Albanian Muslims after the Political Upheaval of 1990", *Islamic Studies*, vol. XXXVI, nos. 2–3, Summer-Fall 1997, pp. 403–12.

———, "Islam, State and Society in Post-Communist Albania", in Hugh Poulton and Suha Taji-Farouki (eds), *Muslim Identity and the Balkan State*, London: Hurst, 1997, pp. 115–38.

———, "Quelques réflexions sur le phénomène de conversion à l'islam à travers le cas des catholiques albanais observé par une mission jésuite à la fin de l'époque ottomane", *Mésogeios*, no. 2, 1998, pp. 16–39.

———, "Islam et identité nationale dans l'espace albanais (Albanie, Macédoine, Kosovo) 1989–1998", *Archives de sciences sociales des religions*, vol. XLVI, no. 115, July–September 2001, pp. 161–81, available at http://assr.revues.org/18443

———, "L'islam, facteur des recompositions internes en Macédoine et au Kosovo", in Xavier Bougarel and Nathalie Clayer (eds), *Le nouvel islam balkanique. Les musulmans, acteurs du post-communisme (1990–2000)*, Paris: Maisonneuve & Larose, 2001, pp. 177–240.

———, *Religion et nation chez les Albanais XIXe—XXe siècles*, Istanbul: Isis, 2003.

———, "Der Balkan, Europa und der Islam", in Karl Kaser and Dagmar Gramshammer-Hohl and Robert Pichler (eds), *Europa und die Grenzen im Kopf*, Klagenfurt: Wieser, 2003, pp. 303–28.

———, "La Ahmadiyya lahori et la réforme de l'islam albanais dans l'entre-deux-guerres", in Véronique Bouiller and Catherine Servan-Schreiber (eds), *De l'Arabie à l'Himalaya. Chemins croisés en hommage à Marc Gaborieau*, Paris: Maisonneuve & Larose, 2004, pp. 211–28.

———, *Aux origines du nationalisme albanais: la naissance d'une nation majoritairement musulmane en Europe*, Paris: Karthala, 2007.

———, "Behind the Veil. The Reform of Islam in Inter-War Albania on the Search for a 'Modern' and 'European' Islam", in Nathalie Clayer and Eric Germain (eds), *Islam in Inter-War Europe*, London: Hurst, 2008, pp. 128–55.

———, "Islam und Zivilgesellschaft auf dem Westbalkan", in Ulf Brunnbauer and Christian Voss (eds), *Inklusion und Exklusion auf dem Westbalkan*, München: Otto Sagner, 2008, pp. 53–64.

———, "The Tijaniyya: Reformism and Islamic Revival in Interwar Albania", *Journal of Muslim Minority Affairs*, vol. XXIX, no. 4, December 2009, pp. 483–94.

BIBLIOGRAPHY

———, "Construction de mosquées en Albanie 1920–1939", *Archives de sciences sociales des religions*, no. 151, July–September 2010, pp. 91–105, available at http://assr.revues.org/22350

———, *Muslim Brotherhood Networks in South-Eastern Europe*, Mainz: Institute of European History, European History Online (EGO), 2011, available at http://www.ieg-ego.eu/en/threads/european-networks/islamic-networks/nathalie-clayer-muslim-brotherhood-networks-in-south-eastern-europe

———, "The Bektashi Institutions in Southeastern Europe: Alternative Muslim Official Structures and their Limits", *Die Welt des Islams*, no. 52, 2012, pp. 183–203.

Clayer Nathalie and Germain Eric (eds), *Islam in Inter-War Europe*, London: Hurst, 2008.

Clayer Nathalie and Popovic Alexandre, "Les Balkans", in Henri Chambert-Loir and Glaude Guillot (eds), *Le culte des saints dans le monde musulman*, Paris: Ecole française d'Extrême-orient, 1995, pp. 335–52.

———, "Le culte d'Ajvatovica et son pèlerinage annuel", in Henri Chambert-Loir and Glaude Guillot (eds), *Le culte des saints dans le monde musulman*, Paris: Ecole française d'Extrême-Orient, 1995, pp. 353–65.

———, "Les courants anti-confrériques dans le Sud-Est européen à l'époque post-ottomane (1918–1990). Les cas de la Yougoslavie et de l'Albanie", in Frederick De Jong and Bernd Radtke (eds), *Islamic Mysticism Contested. Thirteen Centuries of Controversies and Polemics*, Leiden: Brill, 1999, pp. 639–64.

Cohen Lenard, *Serpent in the Bosom: The Rise and Fall of Slobodan Milošević*, Boulder, CO: Westview, 2002.

Copeaux Etienne and Yerasimos Stéphane, "La Bosnie vue du Bosphore", *Hérodote*, no. 67, Winter 1992, pp. 151–9.

Cossuto Giuseppe, "I musulmani di Romania e il nuovo corso politico", *Oriente moderno*, vol. XIII, nos. 7–12, July–Decembre 1994, pp. 203–18.

———, "Il senso d'identita dei turco-tatari di Romania dal 1878 ad oggi", *Oriente moderno*, vol. XV, no. 3, September 1996, pp. 113–66.

———, *Breve storia dei Turchi di Dobrugia*, Istanbul: Isis, 2001.

Courbage Youssef, "Les transitions démographiques des musulmans en Europe orientale", *Population*, vol. XLVI, no. 3, May–June 1991, pp. 651–78.

Crowe David, "Muslim Roma in the Balkans", *Nationalities Papers*, vol. XXVIII, no. 1, March 2000, pp. 93–128.

Dalegre Joëlle, *La Thrace grecque. Populations et territoire*, Paris: L'Harmattan, 1997.

———, "Grèce: comment peut-on être musulman?", in Xavier Bougarel and Nathalie Clayer (eds), *Le nouvel islam balkanique. Les musulmans, acteurs du post-communisme (1990–2000)*, Paris: Maisonneuve & Larose, 2001, pp. 289–314.

Daniel Odile, "The Historical Role of the Muslim Community in Albania", *Central Asian Survey*, vol. IX, no. 3, Summer 1990, pp. 1–28.

Dassetto Felice, Marechal Brigitte and Nielsen Jorgen (eds), *Convergences musul-*

BIBLIOGRAPHY

manes. Aspects contemporains de l'islam dans l'Europe élargie, Paris: L'Harmattan, 2001.

Davie Grace, *Europe, the Exceptional Case: The Parameters of Faith in the Modern World*, London: Darton, Longman & Todd, 2002.

Davie Grace and Hervieu-Leger Danièle (eds), *Identités religieuses en Europe*, Paris: La Découverte, 1996.

De Jong Frederick, "The Turks and Tatars in Romania", *Turcica*, no. 18, 1986, pp. 165–89.

———, "The Muslim Minorities in the Balkans on the Eve of the Collapse of Communism", *Islamic Studies*, vol. XXXVI, nos. 2–3, Summer-Fall 1997, pp. 413–27.

De Rapper Gilles, "*Vakëf*: lieux partagés du religieux en Albanie", in Dionigi Albera and Maria Couroucli (eds), *Religions traversées. Lieux saints partagés entre chrétiens, musulmans et juifs en Méditerranée*, Arles: Actes Sud, 2009, pp. 53–83.

———, "Religion on the Border: Sanctuaries and Festivals in Post-Communist Albania", in Galia Valtchinova (ed.), *Religion and Boundaries. Studies from the Balkans, Eastern Europe and Turkey*, Istanbul: Isis, 2010, pp. 247–65.

———, *Les Albanais à Istanbul*, Istanbul: IFEA, 2000.

Deringil Selim, *The Well-Protected Domain. Ideology and the Legitimation of Power in the Ottoman Empire 1876–1909*, London: I. B. Tauris, 1998.

———, *Conversion and Apostasy in the Late Ottoman Empire*, Cambridge: Cambridge University Press, 2012.

Dick Christiane, "Aus Muslimen werden Bosniaken. Der Beitrag Adil Zulfikarpašićs zur Konstruktion und Anerkennung des 'Bosniakentums'", *Jahrbuch für Geschichte und Kultur Südosteuropas*, vol. IV, 2002, pp. 109–29.

Dikici Ali, "The Torbeshes of Macedonia: Religious and National Identity Questions of Macedonian-Speaking Muslims", *Journal of Muslim Minority Affairs*, vol. XXVIII, no. 1, April 2008, pp. 27–43.

Dimitrov Rumen, "Türken, Tabak, Politik: Zur Ökonomisierung ethnischer Konflikte in Bulgarien", in Margaditsch Hatschikjan and Peter Weilemann (eds), *Nationalismen in Umbruch. Etnizität, Staat und Politik im neuen Europa*, Köln: Wissenschaft und Politik, 1996, pp. 75–88.

Dimitrovova Bohdana, "Bosniak or Muslim? Dilemma of One Nation with Two Names", *Southeast European Politics*, vol. II, no. 2, October 2001, pp. 94–108.

Djokić Dejan (ed.), *Yugoslavism: Histories of a Failed Idea, 1918–1992*, London: Hurst, 2003.

———, *Elusive Compromise. A History of Interwar Yugoslavia*, New York: Columbia University Press, 2007.

Dogo Marco, "Religion und Ethnizität in Albanien", in Georg Brunner and Hans Lemberg (eds), *Volksgruppen in Ostmittel- und Südosteuropa*, Baden-Baden: Nomos, 1994, pp. 195–201.

———, "The Balkan Nation-States and the Muslim Question", in Stefano

Bianchini and Marco Dogo (eds), *The Balkans. National Identities in a Historical Perspective*, Ravenna: Longo Editore, 1998, pp. 61–74.

Dogo Marco and Franzinetti Guido (eds), *Disrupting and Reshaping. Early Stages of Nation-Building in the Balkans*, Ravenna: Longo Editore, 2002.

Dogo Marco (eds), *Schegge d'impero, pezzi d'Europa. Balcani e Turchia fra continuità e mutamento 1804–1923*, Gorizia: Leg, 2006.

Donia Robert, *Islam under the Double Eagle. The Muslims of Bosnia-Hercegovina 1878–1914*, New York: Columbia University Press, 1981.

———, *Sarajevo. A Biography*, Ann Arbor: University of Michigan Press, 2006.

Duijzings Ger, *Religion and the Politics of Identity in Kosovo*, London: Hurst, 2000.

Dulić Tomislav, *Utopias of Nation. Local Mass Killing in Bosnia-Herzegovina 1941–42*, Uppsala: Uppsala University Press, 2005.

Durandin Catherine, *Histoire des Roumains*, Paris: Fayard, 1995.

Dyker David, "The Ethnic Muslims of Bosnia—Some Basic Socio-Economic Data", *Slavonic and East European Review*, vol. L, no. 119, April 1972, pp. 238–56.

Džaja Srećko, *Bosnien-Herzegowina in der österreichisch-ungarischen Epoche (1878–1918): die Intelligentsia zwischen Tradition und Ideologie*, München: Oldenbourg, 1994.

Eminov Ali, *Turkish and Other Muslim Minorities in Bulgaria*, London: Hurst, 1997.

———, "Islam and Muslims in Bulgaria: A Brief History", *Islamic Studies*, vol. XXXVI, nos. 2–3, Summer-Fall 1997, pp. 209–41.

———, "Turks and Tatars in Bulgaria and the Balkans", *Nationalities Papers*, vol. XXVIII, no. 1, March 2000, pp. 129–64.

Featherstone Kevin, Papadimitriou Dimitris and Mamarelis Argyris and Niarchos Georgios, *The Last Ottomans. The Muslim Minority of Greece 1940–1949*, Basingstoke: Macmillan, 2011.

Filandra Šaćir, *Bošnjačka politika u XX. stoljeću*, Sarajevo: Sejtarija, 1998.

———, *Bošnjaci nakon socijalizma. O bošnjačkom identitetu u postjugoslavenskom dobu*, Sarajevo: BZK Preporod, 2012.

Fischer Bernd, *Albania at War 1939–1945*, London: Hurst, 1999.

Fleet Kate, Suraiya Faroqhi and Resat Kasaba (eds), *The Cambridge History of Turkey* (4 vols.), Cambridge: Cambridge University Press, 2013.

Fleming Katherine E., *The Muslim Bonaparte: Diplomacy and Orientalism in Ali Pasha's Greece*, Princeton: Princeton University Press, 1999.

Fortna Benjamin C., *Imperial Classroom. Islam, the State, and Education in the Late Ottoman Empire*, Oxford: Oxford University Press, 2002.

Fraenkel Eran, "Urban Muslim Identity in Macedonia: The Interplay of Ottomanism and Multilingual Nationalism", in Eran Fraenkel and Christina Kramer (eds), *Language Contact–Language Conflict*, Bern: Peter Lang, 1993, pp. 27–41.

BIBLIOGRAPHY

———, "Turning a Donkey into a Horse: Paradox and Conflict in the Identity of Makedonci muslimani", *Balkan Forum*, vol. III, no. 4, 1995, pp. 153–63.

Frangopoulos Yanis, "La minorité musulmane et les Pomaques de la Thrace: entre islam et ethnisme", *CEMOTI*, no. 17, January–June 1994, pp. 152–66.

———, *Une minorité musulmane en transition. Approche anthropologique des Pomaques grecs*, unpublished PhD thesis, University of Louvain-la-Neuve, 1996.

———, "Religion, Identity and Political Conflict in a Pomak Village in Northern Greece", in Steven Vertovec and Ceri Peach (eds), *Islam in Europe: The Politics of Religion and Community*, Basingstoke: Macmillan, 1997, pp. 73–90.

Fuhrmann Malte, "Vagrants, Prostitutes, and Bosnians: Making and Unmaking European Supremacy in Ottoman Southeast Europe", in Hannes Grandits, Nathalie Clayer and Robert Pichler (eds), *Conflicting Loyalties: Social (Dis-)integration and National Turn in the Late and Post-Ottoman Balkan Societies (1839–1914)*, London: I. B. Tauris, 2011, pp. 15–46.

Gaber Natasha, "The Muslim Populations in FYROM (Macedonia): Public Perceptions", in Hugh Poulton and Suha Taji-Farouki (eds), *Muslim Identity and the Balkan State*, London: Hurst, 1997, pp. 103–14.

Gaber Natasha, Najcevska Mirjana and Simoska Emilja, "Muslims, State and Society in the Republic of Macedonia: The View from Within", in Tim Niblock, Gerd Nonnenman and Bogdan Szajkowski (eds), *Muslim Communities in the New Europe*, Reading, Berks: Ithaca Press, 1996, pp. 75–97.

Gaborieau Marc and Popovic Alexandre (eds), "Islam et politique sans le monde (ex-) communiste", *Archives de sciences sociales des religions*, vol. XLVI, no. 115, July–September 2001, pp. 5–201, available at http://assr.revues.org/17583

Gangloff Sylvie, "La Turquie dans le réseau balkanique", *Relations internationales et stratégiques*, no. 15, automne 1994, pp. 63–76.

———, "La politique balkanique de la Turquie et le poids du passé ottoman", in Xavier Bougarel and Nathalie Clayer (eds), *Le nouvel islam balkanique. Les musulmans, acteurs du post-communisme (1990–2000)*, Paris: Maisonneuve & Larose, 2001, pp. 317–56.

——— (ed.), *La perception de l'héritage ottoman dans les Balkans*, Paris: L'Harmattan, 2005.

Gawrych George, *The Crescent and the Eagle: Ottoman Rule, Islam and the Albanians 1874–1913*, London: I. B. Tauris, 2006.

Gelez Philippe, *Petit guide pour servir à l'étude de l'islamisation en Bosnie et en Herzégovine*, Istanbul: Isis, 2005.

———, *Safvet-beg Bašagić (1870–1934): aux racines intellectuelles de la pensée nationale chez les musulmans de Bosnie-Herzégovine*, Athènes: Ecole française d'Athènes, 2009.

———, "La spécificité musulmane dans l'évolution démographique de la Bosnie-Herzégovine durant la seconde moitié du XIXe siècle (1850–1914)",

BIBLIOGRAPHY

European Journal of Turkish Studies, no. 12, 2011, available at http://www.ejts.revues.org/index4382.html

Georgeon François, *Abdülhamid II. Le sultan calife*, Paris: Fayard, 2003.

Germain Eric, "The First Muslim Missions on a European Scale: Ahmadi-Lahori Networks in the Inter-War Period", in Nathalie Clayer and Eric Germain (eds), *Islam in Inter-War Europe*, London: Hurst, 2008, pp. 89–127.

Ghodsee Kristen, "Minarets after Marx. Islam, Communist Nostalgia, and the Common Good in Postsocialist Bulgaria", *East European Politics and Societies*, vol. XXIV, no. 4, Fall 2010, pp. 520–42.

———, *Muslim Lives in Eastern Europe: Gender, Ethnicity and the Transformation of Islam in Postsocialist Bulgaria*, Princeton: Princeton University Press, 2010.

Gingeras Ryan, *Sorrowful Shores: Violence, Ethnicity and the End of the Ottoman Empire 1912–1923*, Oxford: Oxford University Press, 2011.

Giomi Fabio, "Fuori dal dar al-islam. Intellettuali musulmani di Bosnia e Bulgaria nel periodo post-ottomano 1878–1941", *Contemporanea*, vol. XII, no. 2, April 2009, pp. 253–73.

———, "Reforma—The Organization of Progressive Muslims and its Role in Interwar Bosnia", *Journal of Muslim Minority Affairs*, vol. XXIX, no. 4, December 2009, pp. 495–510.

———, *Fra genere, classe, confessione e nazione. 'Questione femminile muslimana' e associazionismo in Bosnia e Erzegovina (1903–1941)*, unpublished PhD thesis, Ecole des hautes études en sciences sociales, Paris/University of Bologna, 2011.

Gradeva Rositsa and Ivanova Svetlana, "Researching the Past and Present of Muslim Culture in Bulgaria: the 'Popular' and 'High' Layers", *Islam and Christian–Muslim Relations*, vol. XII, no. 3, 2001, pp. 317–37.

Grandits Hannes, *Herrschaft und Loyalität in der spätosmanischen Gesellschaft. Das Beispiel der multikonfessionellen Herzegowina*, Wien: Böhlau, 2008.

Grandits Hannes, Clayer Nathalie and Pichler, Robert (eds), *Conflicting Loyalties in the Balkans. The Great Powers, the Ottoman Empire, and Nation-Building*, London: I. B. Tauris, 2011.

Greble Emily, *Sarajevo 1941–1945. Muslims, Christians and Jews in Hitler's Europe*, Ithaca: Cornell University Press, 2011.

Grivaud Gilles and Popovic Alexandre (eds), *Les conversions à l'islam en Asie mineure et dans les Balkans aux époques seldjoukide et ottomane*, Athènes: Ecole française d'Athènes, 2011.

Grünenberg Kristina, "Constructing 'Sameness' and 'Difference': Bosnian Diasporic Experiences in a Danish Context", *Balkanologie*, vol. IX, nos. 1–2, December 2005, pp. 173–93, available at http://balkanologie.revues.org/index587.html

Gruev Mihail, *Meždu petolăčkata i polumeseca. Bălgarite mjusjulmani i političeskijat režim (1944–1959)*, Sofia: Kota, 2003.

BIBLIOGRAPHY

Gruev Mihail and Kalionski Aleksej, *Văzroditelnijat proces: Mjusjulmanskite obštnosti i komunističeskijat režim*, Sofia: Siela, 2008.

Haenni Patrick, *L'islam de marché: l'autre révolution conservatrice*, Paris: Seuil, 2005.

Hajdarpašić Edin, "Out of the Ruins of the Ottoman Empire: Reflections on the Ottoman Legacy in South-Eastern Europe", *Middle Eastern Studies*, vol. XLIV, no. 5, September 2008, pp. 715–34.

———, *Whose Bosnia? National Movements, Imperial Reforms, and the Political Re-ordering of the Late Ottoman Balkans, 1840–1875*, unpublished PhD thesis, University of Michigan, 2008.

Hanioğlu Şükrü, *The Young Turks in Opposition*, Oxford: Oxford University Press, 1995.

———, *Preparation for a Revolution. The Young Turks, 1902–1908*, Oxford: Oxford University Press, 2001.

———, *A Brief History of the Late Ottoman Empire*, Princeton: Princeton University Press, 2008.

Hann Chris, *The Post-Socialist Religious Question: Faith and Power in Central Asia and East-Central Europe*, Münster: LIT, 2006.

Hasanbegović Zlatko, *Jugoslavenska Muslimanska Organizacija 1929–1941*, Zagreb: Bosana, 2012.

Hasanović Sabina, "Fes oder Hut? Der Islam in Bosnien zwischen den Weltkriegen", *Wiener Zeitschrift zur Geschichte der Neuzeit*, vol. V, no. 2, 2005, pp. 69–85.

Hatiboğlu Ibrahim, "*Inshai* Interpretation of Islamic Sciences in Transition to a Multicultural Environment in Bulgaria during the First Half of the 20th Century: The Case of Yusuf Ziyaeddin Ezheri", in *Proceedings of the Second International Symposium on Islamic Civilization in the Balkans*, Istanbul: Ircica, 2006, pp. 135–48.

Hećimović Esad, *Kako su prodali Srebrenicu i sačuvali vlast*, Sarajevo: Dani, 1998.

———, *Garibi. Mudžahedini u BiH 1992–1999*, Zenica: Fondacija Sina, 2006.

———, "Politischer Islam mit bosnischem Migrationshintergrund", in Thomas Schmidinger and Dunja Larise (eds), *Zwischen Gottesstaat und Demokratie. Handbuch des politischen Islams*, Wien: Denticke, 2008, pp. 183–206.

Hersant Jeanne, "Minorité/communauté. La *cemaat* comme principe d'organisation sociale", *Labyrinthe*, no. 21, 2005, pp. 85–93.

———, "Transmission de l'identité et culte du héros. Les associations de Turcs de Thrace occidentale en Allemagne", *Balkanologie*, vol. IX, nos. 1–2, December 2005, pp. 103–30, available at http://balkanologie.revues.org/index581.html

———, *Mobilisations politiques, co-gouvernementalité et construction ethnique. Sociologie du nationalisme turc à travers le cas des Turcs de Thrace occidentale*, unpublished PhD thesis, Ecole des hautes études en sciences sociales, Paris, 2007.

———, "Surveillances croisées et rivalité gréco-turque en Thrace occidentale:

entre coercition et contrôle social", *European Journal of Turkish Studies*, no. 8, 2008, available at http://ejts.revues.org/index2693.html

———, "Souveraineté et gouvernementalité: la rivalité gréco-turque en Thrace occidentale", *Critique internationale*, no. 45, 2009, pp. 141–62.

Hersant Jeanne and Yatropoulos Nepheli, "Mobilisation identitaire et représentation politique des 'Turcs' en Thrace occidentale: les élections législatives grecques de mars 2004", *European Journal of Turkish Studies*, stand-alone article, 2008, available at http://ejts.revues.org/index1342.html

Hervieu-Leger Danièle, *La religion pour mémoire*, Paris: Cerf, 1993.

———, *Le pèlerin et le converti: la religion en mouvement*, Paris: Flammarion, 2001.

Hoare Marko, *How Bosnia Armed*, London: Saqi Books, 2004.

———, *The Bosnian Muslims in the Second World War*, London: Hurst, 2013.

Höpken Wolfgang, "Modernisierung und Nationalismus: sozialgeschichtliche Aspekte der bulgarischen Minderheitspolitik gegenüber den Türken", in Roland Schönfeld (ed.), *Nationalitätenprobleme in Südosteuropa*, München: Oldenbourg, 1987, pp. 255–80.

———, "Emigration und Integration von Bulgarien-Türken seit dem Zweiten Weltkrieg", in Gerhard Seewann (ed.), *Minderheitfragen in Südosteuropa*, München: Oldenburg, 1992, pp. 359–75.

———, "Türken und Pomaken in Bulgarien", *Südosteuropa-Mitteilungen*, vol. XXXII, no. 2, 1992, pp. 141–51.

———, "Yugoslavia's Communists and the Bosnian Muslims", in Georg Brunner, Andreas Kappeler and Gerhard Simon (eds), *Muslim Communities Re-emerge: Historical Perspectives on Nationality, Politics and Opposition in the Former Soviet Union and Yugoslavia*, Durham, NC: Duke University Press, 1994, pp. 214–47.

———, "Konfession, territoriale Identität und nationales Bewusstsein: die Muslime in Bosnien zwischen österreichisch-ungarischer Herrschaft und zweitem Weltkrieg", in Eva Schmidt-Hartmann (ed.), *Formen des nationalen Bewusstseins im Lichte zeitgenössischer Nationalismustheorien*, München: Oldenburg, 1994, pp. 233–53.

———, "Flucht vor dem Kreuz? Muslimische Emigration aus Südosteuropa nach dem Ende der osmanischen Herrschaft (19./20. Jahrhundert)", *Comparativ*, vol. VI, no. 1, 1996, pp. 1–24.

———, "From Religious Identity to Ethnic Mobilization: The Turks of Bulgaria before, under and since Communism", in Hugh Poulton and Suha Taji-Farouki (eds), *Muslim Identity and the Balkan State*, London: Hurst, 1997, pp. 64–71.

Hrabak Bogumil, *Džemijet. Organizacija muslimana Makedonije, Kosova, Metohije i Sandžaka 1919–1928*, Belgrade: B. Hrabak, 2003.

Hüseyinoğlu Ali, *Islam in Western Thrace—Greece after 1923. The Role of Internal and*

BIBLIOGRAPHY

External Actors, Oxford: European Studies Centre, 2010, available at http://www.balkanmuslims.com/pdf/Chouseiinoglu-Gr.pdf

Hysi Shyqyri, *Muslimanizmi në Shqipëri në periudhën 1945–1950*, Tirana: Mësonjëtorja, 2006.

Ilchev Ivan and Perry Duncan, "The Muslims of Bulgaria", in Tim Niblock and Gerd Nonnenman and Bogdan Szajkowski (eds), *Muslim Communities in the New Europe*, Reading, Berks: Ithaca Press, 1996, pp. 115–37.

Immig Nicole, "The 'New' Muslim Minorities in Greece: Between Emigration and Political Participation 1881–1886", *Journal of Muslim Minority Affairs*, vol. XXIX, no. 4, December 2009, pp. 511–22.

Iordachi Constantin, "'The California of the Romanians': The Integration of Northern Dobrogea into Romania, 1878–1913", in Balázs Trencséniy (ed.), *Nation-Building and Contested Identities. Romanian and Hungarian Case Studies*, Budapest/Iaşi: Regio Books/Editura Politom, 2001, pp. 121–52.

———, *Citizenship, Nation and State-Building: The Integration of Northern Dobrogea into Romania, 1878–1913*, Pittsburgh: Carl Back Papers in Russian and East European Studies, 2002.

Irwin Zachary, "The Islamic Revival and the Muslims of Bosnia-Hercegovina", *East European Quarterly*, vol. XVII, no. 4, January 1984, pp. 437–58.

———, "The Fate of Islam in the Balkans: A Comparison of Four State Policies", in Pedro Ramet (ed.), *Religion and Nationalism in Soviet and East European Politics*, Durham, NC: Duke University Press, 1989, pp. 207–25.

Iseni Bashkim, *La question nationale en Europe du Sud-Est: genèse, émergence et développement de l'identité nationale albanaise au Kosovo et en Macédoine*, Bern: Peter Lang, 2008.

Jahić Adnan, *Islamska zajednica u Bosni i Hercegovini za vrijeme monarhističke Jugoslavije 1918–1941*, Zagreb: Bošnjačka nacionalna zajednica/Islamska zajednica, 2010.

Jaljmov Ibrahim, *Istorija na turskata obštnost v Bălgarija*, Sofia: IMIR, 2002.

Janjetović Zoran, *Deca careva, pastorčad kraljeva. Nacionalne manjine u Jugoslaviji 1918–1941*, Belgrade: INIS, 2005.

Kadler Hermann, "Ahmed Sadik (1947–1995): politischer 'Spaltpilz' Griechisch-Thrakiens", *Orient*, vol. XXXIX, no. 2, June 1998, pp. 285–307.

Kalčić Špela, "Changing Contexts and Redefinitions of Identity among Bosniaks in Slovenia", *Balkanologie*, vol. IX, nos. 1–2, December 2005, pp. 149–71, available at http://balkanologie.revues.org/index585.html

Kamberović Husnija, *Hod po trnju. Iz bosanskohercegovačke historije 20. stoljeća*, Sarajevo: Institut za istoriju, 2011.

Kaneff Deema, "When 'Land' Becomes 'Territory': Land Privatisation and Ethnicity in Rural Bulgaria", in Sue Bridger and Frances Pine (eds), *Surviving Post-Socialism: Local Strategies and Regional Responses in Eastern Europe and the Former Soviet Union*, London: Routledge, 1998, pp. 16–32.

BIBLIOGRAPHY

Karagiannis Evangelos, *Zur Ethnizität der Pomaken Bulgariens*, Münster: LIT, 1997.

Karateke Hakan T. and Reinkowski Maurus (eds), *Legitimizing the Order: The Ottoman Rhetoric of State Power*, Leiden: Brill, 2005.

Karčić Fikret, *Šerijatski sudovi u Jugoslaviji 1918–1941*, Sarajevo: Vrhovno starešinstvo Islamske zajednice u SFRJ, 1986.

———, "Islamic Revival in the Balkans 1970–1992", *Islamic Studies*, vol. XXXVI, nos. 2–3, Summer-Fall 1997, pp. 565–81.

———, *The Bosniaks and the Challenge of Modernity*, Sarajevo: El-Kalem, 1999.

———, "The Reform of Shari'a Courts and Islamic Law in Bosnia and Herzegovina, 1918–1941", in Nathalie Clayer and Eric Germain (eds), *Islam in Inter-War Europe*, London: Hurst, 2008, pp. 253–70.

———, *Islamske teme i perspektive*, Sarajevo: el-Kalem, 2009.

Karčić Harun, "Islamic Revival in Post-Socialist Bosnia and Herzegovina: International Actors and Activities", *Journal of Muslim Minority Affairs*, vol. XXX, no. 4, 2010, pp. 519–34.

Karić Amir, *Panislamizam u Bosni*, Sarajevo: Connectum, 2006.

Karić Enes, "Islamic Thought in Bosnia-Herzegovina in the 20th Century: Debates on Revival and Reform", *Islamic Studies*, vol. XLI, no. 3, 2002, pp. 391–444.

———, "Is 'Euro-Islam' a Myth, a Challenge or a Real Opportunity for Muslims and Europe?", *Journal of Muslim Minority Affairs*, vol. XXII, no. 2, 2002, pp. 435–42.

———, *Prilozi za povijest islamskog mišljenja u Bosni i Hercegovini XX. stoljeća*, Sarajevo: El-Kalem, 2004.

Karpat Kemal, *The Turks of Bulgaria: The History, Culture and Political Fate of a Minority*, Istanbul: Isis, 1990.

———, "The Turks of Bulgaria: The Struggle for National-Religious Survival of a Muslim Minority", *Nationalities Papers*, vol. XXIII, no. 4, 1995, pp. 725–49.

———, *The Politicization of Islam. Reconstructing Identity, State, Faith, and Community in the Late Ottoman State*, Oxford: Oxford University Press, 2001.

Katsikas Stefanos (ed.), "European Modernity and Islamic Reformism among the Muslims of the Balkans in the Late-Ottoman and Post-Ottoman Period (1830s-1945)", *Journal of Muslim Minority Affairs*, vol. XXIX, no. 4, December 2009, pp. 435–547.

Katsikas Stefanos, "Millets in Nation-States: The Case of Greek and Bulgarian Muslims 1912–1923", *Nationalities Papers*, vol. XXXVII, no. 2, March 2009, pp. 177–201.

Kentel Ferhat, "Les Balkans et la crise de l'identité nationale turque", in Xavier Bougarel and Nathalie Clayer (eds), *Le nouvel islam balkanique. Les musulmans, acteurs du post-communisme (1990–2000)*, Paris: Maisonneuve & Larose, 2001, pp. 357–95.

BIBLIOGRAPHY

Kentrotis Kyriakos, "Der Verlauf der griechisch-albanischen Beziehungen nach dem Zweiten Weltkrieg und die Frage der muslimischen Tschamen", *Balkan Studies*, vol. XXXIV, no. 2, 1993, pp. 271–99.

Kepel Gilles, *Jihad: The Trail of Political Islam*, London: I. B. Tauris, 2002.

———, *The War for Muslim Minds: Islam and the West*, Cambridge, MA: Harvard University Press, 2004.

Kiel Machiel, "La diffusion de l'islam dans les campagnes bulgares à l'époque ottomane (XVe-XIXe siècles): colonisation et conversion", *Revue du monde musulman et de la Méditerranée*, no. 66, 1992, pp. 39–53.

Kirişci Kemal, "Post Second World War Immigration from Balkan Countries to Turkey", *New Perspectives on Turkey*, no. 12, Spring 1995, pp. 61–77.

Kisić-Kolanović Nada, *Muslimani i hrvatski nacionalizam 1941–1945*, Zagreb: Školska knjiga, 2009.

Köksal Yonca, "Transnational Networks and Kin States: The Turkish Minority in Bulgaria 1878–1940", *Nationalities Papers*, vol. XXXVIII, no. 2, March 2010, pp. 191–211.

Koliopoulos John S. and Veremis Thanos M., *Greece, the Modern Sequel. From 1821 to the Present*, London: Hurst, 2007.

Koller Markus, *Bosnien an der Schwelle zur Neuzeit. Eine Kulturgeschichte der Gewalt (1747–1798)*, München: Oldenburg, 2004.

Konstantinov Yulian, "An Account of Pomak Conversions in Bulgaria (1912–1990)", in Gerhard Seewann (ed.), *Minderheitfragen in Südosteuropa*, München: Oldenburg, 1992, pp. 343–57.

———, "Nation-State and Minority Types of Discourse—Problems of Communication between the Majority and the Islamic Minorities in Contemporary Bulgaria", *Innovation*, vol. V, no. 3, 1992, pp. 75–89.

———, "Strategies for Sustaining a Vulnerable Identity: The Case of the Bulgarian Pomaks", in Hugh Poulton and Suha Taji-Farouki (eds), *Muslim Identity and the Balkan State*, London: Hurst, 1997, pp. 33–53.

Kostis Kostas, "The Formation of the State in Greece, 1830–1914", in Marco Dogo and Guido Franzinetti (eds), *Disrupting and Reshaping. Early Stages of Nation-Building in the Balkans*, Ravenna: Longo Editore, 2002, pp. 47–64.

Kraljačić Tomislav, *Kalajev režim u Bosni i Hercegovini (1883–1903)*, Sarajevo: Veselin Masleša, 1987.

Kramer Martin, *Islam Assembled. The Advent of Muslim Congresses*, New York: Columbia University Press, 1986.

Krasniqi Gëzim, *The 'Forbidden Fruit': Islam and the Politics of Identity in Kosovo and Macedonia*, Oxford: European Studies Centre, 2010, available at http://www.balkanmuslims.com/pdf/krasniqikosmac.pdf

Krasteva Anna (ed.), *Communities and Identities in Bulgaria*, Ravenna: Longo Editore, 1998.

Kretsi Georgia, "Austauschbar—nicht austauschbar. Albanophone Muslime und

BIBLIOGRAPHY

andere Grenzbevölkerungen des Epirus der Zwischenkriegszeit im Kräftefeld zwischen ethnischer Identitätskonstruktion und Entmischungspolitik", *Jahrbuch für Geschichte und Kultur Südosteuropas*, vol. IV, 2002, pp. 205–31.

———, "The 'Secret' Past of the Greek–Albanian Borderlands. Cham Muslim Albanians: Perspectives on a Conflict over Historical Accountability and Current Rights", *Ethnologia Balkanica*, no. 6, 2002, pp. 171–95.

———, "From Landholding to Landlessness. The Relationship between the Property and Legal Status of the Cham Muslim Albanians", *Jahrbuch für Geschichte und Kultur Südosteuropas*, vol. V, 2003, pp. 125–38.

———, "Shkëlzen ou Giannis? Changement de prénom et stratégies identitaires, entre culture d'origine et migration", *Balkanologie*, vol. IX, nos. 1–2, December 2005, pp. 131–48, available at http://balkanologie.revues.org/index583.html

Krstić Tijana, *Contested Conversions to Islam*, Stanford: Stanford University Press, 2011.

Kurz Marlene (ed.), "Islam am Balkan", *Wiener Zeitschrift zur Geschichte der Neuzeit*, vol. V, no. 2, 2005, pp. 3–130.

Kuşat Ali, "The Influence of Minority Feelings on the Formation of Religious Concept and Individual Identity: The Case of Bulgarian Muslims", *Journal of Muslim Minority Affairs*, vol. XXI, no. 2, 2001, pp. 363–72.

Kushner David, "The Place of the Ulema in the Ottoman Empire during the Age of Reform (1839–1918)", *Turcica*, no. 19, 1987, pp. 51–74.

Kut Şule, "Turkish Diplomatic Initiatives for Bosnia-Herzegovina", in Günay Göksü Özdoğan and Kemâli Saybaşili (eds), *Balkans. A Mirror of the New International Order*, Istanbul: Eren, 1995, pp. 295–315.

———, "Turkey in the Post-Communist Balkan: Between Activism and Self-Restraint", *Turkish Review of Balkan Studies*, no. 3, 1996/1997, pp. 39–45.

Lacroix Stéphane, *Les islamistes saoudiens: une insurrection manquée*, Paris: PUF, 2010.

Lakshman-Lepain Rajwantee, "Albanie: les enjeux de la réislamisation", in Xavier Bougarel and Nathalie Clayer (eds), *Le nouvel islam balkanique. Les musulmans, acteurs du post-communisme (1990–2000)*, Paris: Maisonneuve & Larose, 2001, pp. 133–76.

Lampe John R. and Mazower Mark (eds), *Ideologies and National Identities: The Case of Twentieth-Century Southeastern Europe*, Budapest: Central European University Press, 2004.

Lausevic Mirjana, "The *Ilahiya* as a Symbol of Bosnian Muslim Identity", in Mark Slobin (ed.), *Retuning Culture: Musical Changes in Central and Eastern Europe*, Durham, NC: Duke University Press, 1996, pp. 117–35.

Lederer György, "Modern Islam in Eastern Europe", *Journal of Muslim Minority Affairs*, vol. XV, nos. 1–2, January–July 1994, pp. 74–83.

BIBLIOGRAPHY

———, "Islam in Albania", *Central Asian Survey*, vol. XIII, no. 3, Summer 1994, pp. 331–59.

———, "Islam in Romania", *Central Asian Survey*, vol. XV, nos. 3–4, Summer-Fall 1996, pp. 349–68.

———, "Islam in East Europe", *Central Asian Survey*, vol. XX, no. 1, Winter 2001, pp. 5–32.

Lipsius Stephan, "Politik und Islam in Albanien—Instrumentalisierung und Abhängigkeiten", *Südosteuropa*, vol. XLVII, nos. 3–4, March–April 1998, pp. 128–34.

Livezeanu Irina, *Cultural Politics in Greater Romania: Regionalism, Nation-Building, and Ethnic Struggle, 1918–1930*, Ithaca: Cornell University Press, 1995.

Lockwood William, *European Moslems: Economy and Ethnicity in Western Bosnia*, New York: Academic Press, 1975.

Lopasic Alexander, "Bosnian Muslims: A Search for Identity", *Bulletin of the British Society for Middle Eastern Studies*, vol. VIII, no. 2, 1981, pp. 115–25.

———, "The Muslims of Bosnia", in Tim Niblock, Gerd Nonnenman and Bogdan Szajkowski (eds), *Muslim Communities in the New Europe*, Reading, Berks: Ithaca Press, 1996, pp. 99–114.

Lory Bernard, *Le sort de l'héritage ottoman en Bulgarie. L'exemple de villes bulgares, 1878–1900*, Istanbul: Isis, 1985.

———, "Strates historiques des relations bulgaro-turques", *CEMOTI*, no. 15, 1993, pp. 149–67.

——— (ed.), "Contentieux micro-territoriaux dans les Balkans, XIXe-XXe siècles", *Balkanologie*, vol. VI, nos. 1–2, December 2002, available at http://balkanologie.revues.org/index426.html

———, *Les Balkans: de la transition post-ottomane à la transition post-communiste*, Istanbul: Isis, 2005.

Lučić Iva, "In the Service of the Nation: Intellectual's Articulation of the Muslim National Identity", *Nationalities Papers*, vol. XL, no. 1, January 2012, pp. 23–44.

Machacek Štepan, "'European Islam' and Islamic Education in Bosnia-Herzegovina", *Südosteuropa*, vol. LV, no. 4, 2007, pp. 395–428.

Makrides Vasilios (ed.), *Religion, Staat und Konfliktkonstellationen im orthodoxen Ost- und Südosteuropa: vergleichende Perspektiven*, Bern: Peter Lang, 2005.

Malcolm Noel, *Bosnia. A Short History*, London: Macmillan, 1994.

———, *Kosovo. A Short History*, London: Macmillan, 1998.

Mancheva Mila, "Image and Policy: The Case of Turks and Pomaks in Inter-War Bulgaria 1918–1944 (with Special Reference to Education)", *Islam and Christian–Muslim Relations*, vol. XII, no. 3, July 2001, pp. 355–74.

———, *State–Minority Relations and the Education of Turks and Pomaks in Inter-War Bulgaria, 1918–1944*, unpublished PhD thesis, Central European University, Budapest, 2003.

BIBLIOGRAPHY

Mandaci Nazif, "Turks of Macedonia: The Travails of the 'Smaller' Minority", *Journal of Muslim Minority Affairs*, vol. XXVII, no. 1, April 2007, pp. 5–23.

Marechal Brigitte, *Les Frères musulmans en Europe*, Paris: PUF, 2009.

Markou Katerina, "Les Pomaques de Grèce", *Cahiers balkaniques*, no. 25, 1998, pp. 51–9.

Marushiakova Elena and Popov Vesselin, "New Ethnic Identities in the Balkans: The Case of the Egyptians", *Facta Universitatis—Philosophy and Sociology*, vol. II, no. 8, 2001, pp. 465–77.

Mavrogordatos George, *Stillborn Republic: Social Coalitions and Party Strategies in Greece 1922–1936*, Berkeley: University of California Press, 1983.

Mazower Mark, *The Balkans. From the End of Byzantium to the Present Day*, London: Phoenix, 2000.

———, "Minorities and the League of Nations in Interwar Europe", *Daedalus*, vol. CXXVI, no. 2, Spring 1997, pp. 47–63.

McCarthy Justin, *Death and Exile. The Ethnic Cleansing of Ottoman Muslims 1821–1922*, Princeton: Princeton University Press, 1996.

Memić Mustafa, *Velika medresa i njeni učenici u revolucionarnom pokretu*, Skopje: Fonografika, 1984.

Mentzel Peter (ed.), "Muslim Minorities in the Balkans", *Nationalities Papers*, vol. XXVIII, no. 1, March 2000, pp. 7–204.

Methodieva Milena, *Reform, Politics and Culture among the Muslims in Bulgaria 1878–1908*, unpublished PhD thesis, Princeton University, 2010.

Methodieva Milena and Somel Akşin, "Keeping the Bonds: The Ottomans and Muslim Education in Autonomous Bulgaria 1878–1908", *Turcica*, no. 36, 2004, pp. 141–64.

Michel Patrick, *La société retrouvée: politique et religion dans l'Europe soviétisée*, Paris: Fayard, 1988.

Michel Patrick, Antonela Capelle-Pogacean and Pace Enzo (eds), *Religion(s) et identité(s) en Europe. L'épreuve du pluriel*, Paris: Presses de Sciences Po, 2008.

Micheletta Luca, *La resa dei conti: Il Kosovo, l'Italia e la dissoluzione della Jugoslavia (1939–1941)*, Roma: Edizione Nuova Cultura, 2008.

Miloslavlevski Slavko and Tomovski Mirche, *Albanians in the Republic of Macedonia. 1945–1995*, Skopje: NIP Studenski Zbor, 1997.

Mirkova Anna, "Citizenship Formation in Bulgaria: Protected Minority or National Citizens?", *Journal of Muslim Minority Affairs*, vol. XXIX, no. 4, December 2009, pp. 469–82.

Mitri Tarek, "La Bosnie-Herzégovine et la solidarité du monde arabe et islamique", *Maghreb-Machrek*, no. 139, January 1993, pp. 123–36.

Moe Christian, "A Sultan in Brussels? European Hopes and Fears of Bosnian Muslims", *Südosteuropa*, vol. LV, no. 4, 2007, pp. 374–94.

Morozzo Della Rocca Roberto, *Nazione e religione in Albania (1920–1944)*, Bologna: Il Mulino, 1990.

BIBLIOGRAPHY

Morrison Kenneth and Roberts Elizabeth, *The Sandžak. A History*, London: Hurst, 2013.

Mufaku Al-Arnaut Muhamed, "Islam and Muslims in Bosnia 1878–1918: Two Hijras and Two Fatwas", *Journal of Islamic Studies*, vol. V, no. 2, July 1994, pp. 242–53.

Müller Dietmar, *Staatsbürger auf Widerruf. Juden und Muslime als Alteritätspartner im rumänischen und serbischen Nationscode 1878–1941*, Wiesbaden: Harrassowitz, 2005.

Müller Stefan, "Zur Situation der Roma in Kosovo", *Südosteuropa*, vol. XLVIII, nos. 9–10, September–October 1999, pp. 506–19.

Neuburger Mary, "Pomak Borderlands: Muslims on the Edge of Nations", *Nationalities Papers*, vol. XXVIII, no. 1, March 2000, pp. 181–98.

———, *The Orient Within. Muslim Minorities and the Negotiation of Nationhood in Modern Bulgaria*, Ithaca: Cornell University Press, 2004.

Niblock Tim, Nonnenman Gerd and Szajkowski Bogdan (eds), *Muslim Communities in the New Europe*, Reading, Berks: Ithaca Press, 1996.

Nielsen Jorgen, *Towards a European Islam*, New York: Palgrave, 1999.

Nitzova Petya, "Bulgaria: Minorities, Democratization and National Sentiments", *Nationalities Papers*, vol. XXV, no. 4, December 1997, pp. 729–39.

Nizami Farhan A. (ed.), "Islam in the Balkans", *Journal of Islamic Studies*, vol. V, no. 2, July 1994, pp. 163–273.

Okey Robin, *Taming Balkan Nationalism. The Habsburg 'Civilizing Mission' in Bosnia, 1878–1914*, Oxford: Oxford University Press, 2007.

Öktem Kerem (ed.), *After the Wahhabi Mirage: Islam, Politics and International Networks in the Balkans*, Oxford: European Studies Centre, December 2010, available at http://www.balkanmuslims.com

———, *New Islamic Actors after the Wahhabi Intermezzo: Turkey's Return to the Muslim Balkans*, Oxford: European Studies Centre, December 2010, available at http://www.balkanmuslims.com/pdf/Oktem-Balkan-Muslims.pdf

———, *Muslim Identities in New Contexts: Rijaset, Diyanet and Interaction with Regional Actors in Bosnia-Herzegovina and Southeast Europe*, Hohenheim: Akademie der Diözese Rottenburg-Stuttgart, 18 November 2011, available at http://www.akademie-rs.de/fileadmin/user_upload/download_archive/interreligioeser-dialog/111118_oektem_muslim-identities.pdf

Omerika Armina, "The Role of Islam in the Academic Discourses on the National Identity of Muslims in Bosnia and Herzegovina 1950–1980", *Islam and Muslim Societies*, vol. II, no. 2, 2006, pp. 351–76.

———, *Islam in Bosnien-Herzegowina und die Netzwerke der Jungmuslime 1918–1991*, Wiesbaden: Harrassowitz, 2012.

Oran Baskın, "Religious and National Identity among the Balkan Muslims: A Comparative Study on Greece, Bulgaria, Macedonia and Kosovo", *CEMOTI*, no. 18, July–December 1994, pp. 307–23.

BIBLIOGRAPHY

Özervarli Sait, "Alternative Approaches to Modernization in the Late Ottoman Period: Izmirli Ismail Hakkı's Religious Thought Against Materialist Scientism", *International Journal of Middle East Studies*, vol. XXXIX, no. 1, February 2007, pp. 77–102.

Özgür Nurcan, *Etnik Sorunların Çözümünde Hak ve Özgürlükler Hareketi*, İstanbul: Der Yayınları, 1999.

Özgür Baklacioğlu Nurcan, *Dış Politika ve Göç: Balkanlar'dan Türkiye'ye Arnavut Göçleri*, İstanbul: Derin Yayınları, 2010.

Palairet Michael R., *The Balkan Economies c.1800–1914: Evolution without Development*, Cambridge: Cambridge University Press, 1997.

Panzac Daniel (ed.), "Les Balkans à l'époque ottomane", *Revue du monde musulman et de la Méditerranée*, no. 66, Winter 1992, pp. 5–158.

Paulwitz Michael, "Nation und Religion in '*Preporod*'", in Thomas Bremer (ed.), *Religion und Nation im Krieg auf dem Balkan*, Bonn: Justitia et Pax, 1996, pp. 151–61.

Pechoux Pierre-Yves and Sivignon Michel, "L'éviction des Tchamidès d'Épire occidentale en 1944", *L'ethnographie*, vol. LXXXV, no. 2, 1989, pp. 113–19.

Perica Vjekoslav, *Balkan Idols: Religion and Nationalism in the Yugoslav States*, Oxford: Oxford University Press, 2002.

Pezo Edvin, *Zwangsmigrationen in Friedenszeiten? Jugoslawische Migrationspolitik und die Auswanderung von Muslimen in die Türkei (1918 bis 1966)*, München: Oldenburg, 2013.

Pickles John, '*There Are No Turks in Bulgaria*': *Violence, Ethnicity, and Economic Practices in the Border Regions and Muslim Communities of Post-Socialist Bulgaria*, Halle: Max Planck Institut, 2001, available at http://www.eth.mpg.de/pubs/wps/pdf/mpi-eth-working-paper-0025.pdf

Pollack Detlef, Borowik Irena and Jagodzinski Wolfgang (eds), *Religiöser Wandel in den postkommunistischen Ländern Ost- und Mitteleuropas*, Würzburg: Ergon, 1998.

Popovic Alexandre, "Sur les récits de pèlerinage à la Mecque des musulmans yougoslaves (1949–1972)", *Studia islamica*, vol. XXXIX, 1974, pp. 129–44.

———, "Le pèlerinage à La Mecque de musulmans des régions yougoslaves", *Correspondance d'Orient*, no. 13, 1975, pp. 335–63.

———, "The Contemporary Situation of the Muslim Mystic Orders in Yugoslavia", in Ernest Gellner (ed.), *Islamic Dilemmas: Reformers, Nationalists and Industrialization*, Berlin: Mouton, 1985, pp. 240–54.

———, "Les ordres mystiques musulmans du Sud-Est européen dans la période post-ottomane", in Alexandre Popovic and Gilles Veinstein (eds), *Les ordres mystiques dans l'islam. Cheminements et situation actuelle*, Paris: Editions de L'ehess, 1985, pp. 63–99.

———, *L'islam balkanique. Les musulmans du sud-est européen dans la période post-ottomane*, Berlin-Wiesbaden: Otto Harrassowitz, 1986.

BIBLIOGRAPHY

———, "Le 'radicalisme islamique' en Yougoslavie", in Olivier Carre and Paul Dumont (eds), *Radicalismes islamiques*, Paris: L'Harmattan, 1986, pp. 151–61.

———, "Le waqf dans les pays du Sud-Est européen à l'époque post-ottomane", in Faruk Bilici (ed.), *Le waqf dans le monde musulman contemporain (XIXe–XXe siècles)*, Istanbul: IFEA, 1994, pp. 199–213.

———, *Les derviches balkaniques hier et aujourd'hui*, Istanbul: Isis, 1994.

———, *Cultures musulmanes balkaniques*, Istanbul: Isis, 1994.

———, *Les musulmans des Balkans à l'époque post-ottomane. Histoire et politique*, Istanbul: Isis, 1994.

———, "Les *medrese* dans les Balkans. Des premières innovations du milieu du XIXe siècle à nos jours", in Nicole Grandin and Marc Gaborieau (eds), *Madrasa. La transmission du savoir dans le monde musulman*, Paris: Arguments, 1997, pp. 279–88.

———, "Muslim Intellectuals in Bosnia-Herzegovina in the Twentieth Century", in Stéphane Dudoignon (ed.), *Intellectuals in the Modern Islamic World: Transmission, Transformation and Communication*, London: Taylor & Francis, 2006, pp. 211–25.

———, "La magie chez les musulmans des Balkans (III): l'apport de Tihomir R. Djordjević (1868–1944)", *Balkanologie*, vol. IX, nos. 1–2, December 2005, pp. 291–308, available at http://balkanologie.revues.org/index601.htm

———, "Les autorités religieuses musulmanes de Yougoslavie face à la magie (1933–1992)", *Südost-Forschungen*, vol. LXVIII, 2008, pp. 349–67.

Popovic Alexandre and Veinstein Gilles (eds), *Les voies d'Allah. Les ordres mystiques dans le monde musulman des origines à aujourd'hui*, Paris: Fayard, 1996.

Poulton Hugh, *The Balkans. Minorities and States in Conflict*, London: Minority Rights Publications, 1993.

———, "Changing Notions of National Identity among Muslims in Thrace and Macedonia: Turks, Pomaks and Roma", in Hugh Poulton and Suha Taji-Farouki (eds), *Muslim Identity and the Balkan State*, London: Hurst, 1997, pp. 82–102.

———, "Turkey as Kin-State: Turkish Foreign Policy towards Turkish and Muslim Communities in the Balkans", in Hugh Poulton and Suha Taji-Farouki (eds), *Muslim Identity and the Balkan State*, London: Hurst, 1997, pp. 194–213.

———, "The Muslim Experience in the Balkan States 1919–1991", *Nationalities Papers*, vol. XXVIII, no. 1, March 2000, pp. 45–66.

Poulton Hugh and Taji-Farouki Suha (eds), *Muslim Identity and the Balkan State*, London: Hurst, 1997.

Proceedings of the Second International Symposium on Islamic Civilisation in the Balkans, Tirana, Albania, 4–7 December 2003, Istanbul: IRCICA, 2006.

Proceedings of the Third International Symposium on Islamic Civilisation in the Balkans, Istanbul: IRCICA, 2010.

BIBLIOGRAPHY

Promitzer Christian, Trubeta Sevasti and Turda Marius (eds), *Health, Hygiene and Eugenics in Southeastern Europe to 1945*, Budapest: CEU Press, 2011.

Ragaru Nadège, "Recompositions identitaires chez les musulmans de Bulgarie: entre marqueurs ethniques et religieux", *Balkanologie*, vol. III, no. 1, September 1999, pp. 121–45, available at http://balkanologie.revues.org/index290.html

———, "Islam in Post-Communist Bulgaria: An Aborted Clash of Civilization?", *Nationalities Papers*, vol. XXIX, no. 2, 2001, pp. 293–324.

———, "Islam et coexistence intercommunautaire en Bulgarie post-communiste", in Xavier Bougarel and Nathalie Clayer (eds), *Le nouvel islam balkanique. Les musulmans, acteurs du post-communisme (1990–2000)*, Paris: Maisonneuve & Larose, 2001, pp. 241–88.

———, "Quel islam en Bulgarie post-communiste?", *Archives de sciences sociales des religions*, vol. XLVI, no. 115, July–September 2001, pp. 125–59, available at http://assr.revues.org/18393

——— (ed.), "Les politisations de l'identité dans les Balkans contemporains", *Revue d'études comparatives Est-Ouest*, vol. XXXVIII, no. 4, December 2007, pp. 5–224.

———, "Faire taire l'altérité. Politique de la langue et mobilisations linguistiques au temps de l'assimilation forcée des Turcs de Bulgarie (1984–1989)", *Cultures & Conflits*, nos. 79–80, Fall-Winter 2010, pp. 73–96, available at http://www.cairn.info/revue-cultures-et-conflits-2010-3-page-73.htm

Ramet Pedro, "Primordial Ethnicity or Modern Nationalism: The Case of Yugoslavia's Muslims", *Nationalities Papers*, vol. XIII, no. 2, Fall 1985, pp. 165–87.

———, *Cross and Commissar: The Politics of Religion in Eastern Europe and the USSR*, Bloomington: Indiana University Press, 1987.

Ramet Sabrina, "Primordial Ethnicity or Modern Nationalism: The Case of Yugoslavia's Muslims Reconsidered", Georg Brunner, Andreas Kappeler and Gerhard Simon (eds), *Muslim Communities Re-emerge: Historical Perspectives on Nationality, Politics and Opposition in the Former Soviet Union and Yugoslavia*, Durham, NC: Duke University Press, 1994, pp. 111–38.

Rechel Bernd, "The 'Bulgarian Ethnic Model'—Reality or Ideology?", *Europe-Asia Studies*, vol. LIX, no. 7, November 2007, pp. 1201–15.

———, "Ethnic Diversity in Bulgaria: Institutional Arrangements and Domestic Discourse", *Nationalities Papers*, vol. XXXXVI, no. 2, May 2008, pp. 331–50.

Redžić Enver, *Bosnia and Herzegovina in the Second World War*, London: Routledge, 2005.

Reinkowski Maurus, *Die Dinge der Ordnung. Eine vergleichende Untersuchung über die osmanische Reformpolitik im 19. Jahrhundert*, München: Oldenburg, 2005.

———, "Hidden Believers, Hidden Apostates: The Phenomenon of Crypto-Jews and Crypto-Christians in the Middle East", in Dennis Washburn and

BIBLIOGRAPHY

Kevin A. Reinhart (eds), *Converting Cultures: Religion, Ideology, and Transformations of Modernity*, Leiden: Brill, 2007, pp. 409–33.

Reuter Jens, *Die Albaner in Jugoslawien*, München: Oldenburg, 1982.

———, "Islam in Jugoslawien in der Offensive?", *Südosteuropa*, vol. XXXIII, no. 9, September 1984, pp. 482–90.

Riedel Sabine, "Die Politisierung islamischer Geschichte und Kultur am Beispiel Südosteuropas", *Südosteuropa*, vol. XLVI, no. 11, November 1997, pp. 539–61.

Roux Michel, *Les Albanais en Yougoslavie. Minorité nationale, territoire et développement*, Paris: Editions de la MSH, 1992.

Roy Olivier, *The Failure of Political Islam*, London: I. B. Tauris, 1994.

———, *Vers un islam européen*, Paris: Esprit, 1999.

———, *Globalized Islam: The Search for the New Ummah*, London: Hurst, 2004.

Sahara Tetsuya, "The Islamic World and the Bosnian Crisis", *Current History*, no. 92, November 1994, pp. 386–9.

Sarajlić Eldar, *The Return of the Consuls: Islamic Networks and Foreign Policy Perspectives in Bosnia and Herzegovina*, Oxford: European Studies Centre, 2010, available at http://www.balkanmuslims.com/pdf/Sarajlic-Bosnia.pdf

Scarcia Amoretti Biancamaria (a cura di), "Problematiche islamiche in area balcanica: Albania, Bulgaria, Romania", *Oriente moderno*, vol. XV, no. 3, September 1996, pp. 1–166.

Scheer Tamara, *"Minimale Kosten. Absolut kein Blut". Österreich-Ungarns Präsenz im Sandžak von Novipazar (1879–1908)*, Frankfurt: Peter Lang, 2013.

Schmidt-Neke Michael, "Makedoniens Albaner: Konfliktpotential oder Stabilitätsfaktor?", *Südosteuropa*, vol. XLVIII, nos. 3–4, March–April 1999, pp. 191–212.

Schmitt Oliver Jens, "Skanderbeg reitet wieder. Wiederfindung und Erfindung eines Nationalhelden", in Ulf Brunnbauer, Andreas Helmedach and Stefan TROEBST (eds), *Schnittstellen. Festschrift für Holm Sundhaussen zum 65. Geburtstag*. München: Oldenburg, 2007, pp. 401–19.

———, *Kosovo. Kurze Geschichte einer zentralbalkanischen Landschaft*, Wien: Böhlau, 2008.

——— (ed.), *Religion und Kultur im albanischsprachigen Südosteuropa*, Bern: Peter Lang, 2010.

———, *Die Albaner: Eine Geschichte zwischen Orient und Okzident*, München: Beck, 2012.

Schrameyer Klaus, "Ahmed Dogan—hat der Königsmacher überreizt?", *Südosteuropa*, vol. LIII, no. 3, 2005, pp. 356–75.

Sciarra Lino, "L'islam in Albania", *Oriente moderno*, vol. XV, no. 3, 1996, pp. 1–77.

Šehić Nusret, *Autonomni pokret Muslimana za vrijeme austrougarske uprave u Bosni i Hercegovini*, Sarajevo: Svjetlost, 1980.

Seyppel Tatjana, "Das Interesse an der muslimischen Minderheit in Westthrakien

BIBLIOGRAPHY

(Griechenland) 1945–1990", in Gerhard Seewann (ed.), *Minderheitfragen in Südosteuropa*, München: Oldenburg, 1992, pp. 377–92.

———, "Pomaks in Northeastern Greece: An Endangered Population", *Journal of Muslim Minority Affairs*, vol. X, no. 1, January 1989, pp. 41–9.

Shoup Paul, *Communism and the Yugoslav National Question*, New York: Columbia University Press, 1968.

Sigalas Nikos and Toumarkine Alexandre (eds), "Demographic Engineering, Part I", *European Journal of Turkish Studies*, no. 7, 2008, available at http://ejts.revues.org/index2073.html

——— (eds), "Demographic Engineering, Part II", *European Journal of Turkish Studies*, no. 12, 2011, available at http://ejts.revues.org/index4381.html

Silverman Carol, "Roma of Shuto Orizari, Macedonia: Class, Politics, and Community", in David Kideckel (ed.), *East European Communities: The Struggle for Balance in Turbulent Times*, Boulder, CO: Westview, 1995, pp. 197–215.

Skendi Stavro, *The Albanian National Awakening*, Princeton: Princeton University Press, 1967.

Solberg Anne Ross, "The Role of Turkish Islamic Networks in the Western Balkans", *Südosteuropa*, vol. LV, no. 4, 2007, pp. 429–61.

Somel Selçuk Akşin, *The Modernization of Public Education in the Ottoman Empire 1839–1908. Islamization, Autocracy and Discipline*, Leiden: Brill, 2001.

Sorabji Cornelia, "Islamic Revival and Marriage in Bosnia", *Journal of Muslim Minority Affairs*, vol. IX, no. 2, July 1988, pp. 331–8.

———, *Muslim Identity and Islamic Faith in Sarajevo*, unpublished PhD thesis, University of Cambridge, 1989.

———, "Mixed Motives: Islam, Nationalism and Mevluds in an Unstable Yugoslavia", in Camillia Fawzi El-Solh and Judy Mabro (eds), *Muslim Women's Choices*, Oxford: Berg, 1994, pp. 108–27.

Speziale Fabrizio, "Adapting Mystic Identity to Italian Mainstream Islam: The Case of a Muslim Rom Community in Florence", *Balkanologie*, vol. IX, nos. 1–2, December 2005, pp. 195–211, available at http://balkanologie.revues.org/index589.html

Steindorff Ludwig, "Von der Konfession zur Nation: die Muslime in Bosnien-Herzegowina", *Südosteuropa-Mitteilungen*, vol. XXXVII, no. 4, 1997, pp. 277–90.

Stojanov Valeri, "Die türkische Minderheit Bulgariens bis zum Ende des Zweiten Weltkrieges", *Österreichische Osthefte*, vol. XXXVI, no. 2, 1994, pp. 279–94.

———, *Turskoto naselenie v Bălgarija meždu poljusite na etničeskata politika*, Sofia: Lik, 1997.

———, "Ausgrenzung und Integration: die bulgarischen Türken nach dem Zweiten Weltkrieg", *Österreichische Osthefte*, vol. XXXIX, no. 2, 1997, pp. 193–221.

BIBLIOGRAPHY

Stoppel Wolfgang, "Bewegung in Albaniens Religionspolitik?", *Südosteuropa*, vol. XXXVIII, nos. 11–12, November–December 1989, pp. 729–38.

Szajkowski Bogdan, "Muslim People in Eastern Europe: Ethnicity and Religion", *Journal of Muslim Minority Affairs*, vol. IX, no. 1, January 1988, pp. 103–18.

Telbizova-Sack Jordanka, *Identitätsmuster der Pomaken Bulgariens*, Marburg: Biblion, 1999.

———, "Identitäten islamischer Gemeinschaften", *Ost–West Gegeninformationen*, vol. XV, no. 4, February 2004, pp. 37–41.

Todorova Maria, "Die Osmanenzeit in der bulgarischen Geschichtsforschung seit der Unabhängigkeit", in Hans-Georg MAJER (ed.), *Die Staaten Südosteuropas und die Osmanen*, München: Südosteuropa Gesellschaft, 1989, pp. 127–61.

———, "The Ottoman Legacy in the Balkans", in Carl L. Brown (ed.), *Imperial Legacy: the Ottoman Imprint on the Balkans and the Middle East*, New York: Columbia University Press, 1996, pp. 45–77.

———, *Imagining the Balkans*, New York: Oxford University Press, 1997.

———, "Identity (Trans)Formation Among Pomaks in Bulgaria", in Laszlo Körti and Juliet Langman (eds), *Beyond Borders. Remaking Cultural Identities in the New East and Central Europe*, Boulder, CO: Westview, 1997, pp. 63–82.

——— (ed.), *Balkan Identities. Nation and Memory*, London: Hurst, 2004.

———, "Conversion to Islam as a Trope in Bulgarian Historiography, Fiction and Film", in Maria Todorova (ed.), *Balkan Identities. Nation and Memory*, London: Hurst, 2004, pp. 129–57.

Tomic Yves, *La Serbie du prince Miloš à Milošević*, Bern: Peter Lang, 2003.

Toumarkine Alexandre, *Les migrations des populations musulmanes balkaniques en Anatolie (1876–1913)*, Istanbul: Isis, 1995.

———, *Entre Empire ottoman et Etat-nation turc: les immigrés musulmans du Caucase et des Balkans du milieu du XIXe siècle à nos jours*, unpublished PhD thesis, University of Paris IV, Paris, 2000.

Trix Frances, "The Resurfacing of Islam in Albania", *East European Quarterly*, vol. XXVIII, no. 4, January 1995, pp. 533–49.

Troch Pieter, "Yugoslavism between the World Wars: Indecisive Nation-Building", *Nationalities Papers*, vol. XXXVIII, no. 2, March 2010, pp. 227–44.

Troebst Stefan, "Zum Verhältnis von Partei, Staat und türkischer Minderheit in Bulgarien 1956–1986", in Roland Schönfeld (ed.), *Nationalitätenprobleme in Südosteuropa*, München: Oldenburg, 1987, pp. 231–51.

Trubeta Sevasti, "Die Minderheitenpolitik Athens am Beispiel der Pomaken und derer sozialer Integration", *Südosteuropa*, vol. XLVI, no. 12, December 1998, pp. 632–58.

———, *Die Konstitution von Minderheiten und die Ethnisierung sozialer und politischer Konflikte. Eine Untersuchung am Beispiel der im griechischen Thrakien ansässigen 'Moslemischen Minderheit'*, Bern: Peter Lang, 1999.

BIBLIOGRAPHY

———, "Balkan Egyptians and Gypsy/Roma Discourse", *Nationalities Papers*, vol. XXXIII, no. 1, March 2005, pp. 71–95.

Tsitselikis Konstantinos, "Personal Status of Greece's Muslims: A Legal Anachronism or an Example of Applied Multiculturalism?", in Roberta Aluffi Beck Peccoz and Giovanna Zincone (eds), *The Legal Treatment of Islamic Minorities in Europe*, Leuven: Peeters, 2004, pp. 109–31.

———, "The Pending Modernisation of Islam in Greece: From Millet to Minority Status", *Südosteuropa*, vol. LV, no. 4, 2007, pp. 354–73.

———, *Old and New Islam in Greece. From Historical Minorities to Immigrant Newcomers*, Leiden: Brill, 2012.

Turan Ömer, *The Turkish Minority in Bulgaria (1878–1908)*, Ankara: Türk Tarih Kurumu, 1998.

Ülker Erol, "Assimilation of the Muslim Communities in the First Decade of the Turkish Republic (1923–1934)", *European Journal of Turkish Studies*, stand-alone article, 2007, available at http://ejts.revues.org/index822.html

———, "Assimilation, Security and Geographical Nationalization in Interwar Turkey: The Settlement Law of 1934", *European Journal of Turkish Studies*, no. 7, 2008, available at http://ejts.revues.org/index2123.html

Valtchinova Galia, "La 'crise turque' de 1984–1989 et l'identité bulgare", *Cahiers d'histoire immédiate*, no. 5, Spring 1994, pp. 93–102.

Vassileva Darina, "Bulgarian Turkish Emigration and Return", *International Migration Review*, vol. XXVI, no. 2, Summer 1992, pp. 342–52.

Veinstein Gilles, "Les provinces balkaniques (1606–1774)", in Robert Mantran (ed.), *Histoire de l'Empire ottoman*, Paris: Fayard, 1989, pp. 265–340.

Verdery Katherine, *National Ideology under Socialism: Identity and Cultural Politics in Ceaucescu's Romania*, Berkeley: University of California Press, 1991.

Vezenkov Alexander, "Reconciliation of the Spirits and Fusion of the Interests: 'Ottomanism' as an Identity Politics", in Diana Mishkova (ed.), *We, the People. Politics of National Peculiarity in Southeastern Europe*, Budapest: Central European University Press, 2009, pp. 47–78.

Voss Christian and Telbizova-Sack Jordanka (eds), *Islam und Muslime in (Südost) Europa im Kontext von Transformation und EU-Erweiterung*, München: Otto Sagner, 2010.

Woodward Susan, *Balkan Tragedy: Chaos and Dissolution after the Cold War*, Washington, DC: Brookings Institution, 1995.

Yavuz Hakan, "Towards an Islamic Liberalism? The Nurcu Movement and Fethullah Gülen", *Middle East Journal*, vol. LIII, no. 4, Fall 1999, pp. 584–605.

———, *Islamic Political Identity in Turkey*, Oxford: Oxford University Press, 2003.

———, *Secularism and Muslim Democracy in Turkey*, Cambridge: Cambridge University Press, 2009.

BIBLIOGRAPHY

Yosmaoglu-Turner İpek, *The Priest's Robe and the Rebel's Rifle: Communal Conflict and the Construction of National Identity in Ottoman Macedonia 1878–1908*, unpublished PhD thesis, Princeton University, 2005.

Zhelyazkova Antonina (ed.), *Relations of Compatibility and Incompatibility between Christians and Muslims in Bulgaria*, Sofia: International Center for Minority Studies and Intercultural Relations, 1995.

———, "Islamization in the Balkans as an Historiographical Problem: The Southeast-European Perspective", in Fikret Adanir and Suraiya Faroqhi (eds), *The Ottomans and the Balkans. A Discussion of Historiography*, Leiden: Brill, 2002, pp. 223–66.

Zürcher Erik Jan, "The Young Turks—Children of the Borderlands?", *International Journal of Turkish studies*, vol. IX, nos. 1–2, Summer 2003, pp. 275–86.

———, *Greek and Turkish Refugees and Deportees 1912–1924*, Leiden: Turkology Update Leiden Project Working Papers Archive, 2003, available at http://www.transanatolie.com/english/turkey/turks/ottomans/ejz18.pdf

———, *Turkey: A Modern History*, London: I. B. Tauris, 2004.

INDEX

Abaz Hilmi Dede 154
Abduh, Muhammad 70, 73, 107, 112, 116
Abdülhamid, Sultan 34, 46, 63–5, 68, 70, 77
Abdülmecid, Sultan 22, 28
Active Islamic Youth (*Aktivna Islamska Omladina*, AIO) (Bosnia) 203
Adapazar 120
Adrianople, Treaty of 16
Aegean Sea and islands 54, 57, 60, 173
Afghani, Jamal ad-Din al- 70, 73
Aga, Mehmet Emin 156, 210
Ahmadiyya 114–15, 204
Ahmet, Sadiq 144, 189
Ahmet, Myftar Dede 154
Ahmeti, Ali 184
Ajvaz, Dede 33
Akçura, Yusuf 67
Alaeddin 77
Alaudin madrasa 152
al-Azhar (university) (Cairo) 110, 112, 116, 152, 159
Alba operation 173
Albani, Muhammad Nasiruddin al- 95
Albania, Albanians 11, 19, 22, 29, 33, 35, 36, 37–8, 42, 45, 46, 51, 55, 65–7, 75–8, 78, 79, 80, 82, 83–6, 87, 89, 90, 92, 94, 95, 96–7, 101–2, 104, 109, 111–12, 114–16, 117–20, 213; Communist era 123, 124, 126–7, 128, 130, 131, 132, 133, 134, 135, 137–40, 144, 145–6, 147–9, 152–5, 162, 217–18; post-Communist era 167–8, 169, 172, 173, 175–6, 181, 182, 185, 186, 190, 191, 194, 195–6, 197–8, 202–3, 204, 206, 212, 215, 219, 220–21, 224
Albanian Muslim Community (*Komuniteti Mysliman Shqiptar*) 96
Albanian National Democratic Movement (*Lëvizja Nacional Demokratike Shqiptare*, LNDSH) 137, 158
Albanianism 41, 42, 65–6, 76, 109, 215
Alevi, 33, 38, 76–8, 154, 198, 215
Alexander I, King of Yugoslavia 83
al-Haramain (Islamic NGO) 202
al-Manâr (newspaper) 70, 116
al-Waqf al-islami (Islamic NGO) 202
Ali Pasha 16, 22, 29, 35, 77
Ali Suavi 55

INDEX

Alliance for Change (*Alijansa za Promjene*, Bosnia) 172
Alliance for the Future of Kosovo (*Aleanca për Ardhmërinë e Kosovës*, AAK) 172, 183
alphabet questions 42, 66, 73–4, 105, 106, 110, 140, 143
Anatolia 28, 34, 36, 50, 54, 57, 77, 82, 94, 97, 120, 147, 215
Arabs, Arab states 46, 52, 160, 205, 207, 221, 224
Aravantinos, Panayiotis 37
Arbëresh 41
*armatole*s 16
Armenians 25, 50, 52, 57, 68
Army for the Liberation of Preševo, Medvedja and Bujanovac (*Ushtria Çlirimtare për Preshevë, Medvegjë dhe Buhanoc*, UPÇMB) (Serbia) 181
Arnautaši 75–6
Arslan, Shakib 116, 117, 217
Arta 46
Ashkali 194
Association of Madrasa Graduate Muslim Teachers (*Medrese Mezunu Müslüman Muallimler Cemiyeti*) (Greece) 157
Association of Ulamas of Bosnia-Herzegovina 151, 159, 161
Athens 17, 99, 165, 205
Athos, Mount 58
Australia 56, 95, 158
Austria 95, 158, 175, 199
Austria/Austria-Hungary (Habsburg Empire) 11, 12, 13, 17, 18, 19, 25, 27, 40, 46, 51, 52, 55, 56–7, 58, 62, 63, 65, 66, 79, 87, 96, 210, 215
Azapagić, Mehmed Tevfik 62
Azeris 67

Babadag 60

Bačka 84
Bakalli, Mahmut 132
Baleta, Abdi 195
Balkan Islamic Council 222
Balkan Pact 80, 83
Balkan Wars 51–2, 56–7, 66, 67
Balkan, Mount 37
Balli Kombetar (National Front, Albania) 86, 101
Balta-Liman, Convention of 16
Banna, Hasan al- 107, 116, 160
Bar 46, 60
Bardhi, Reshat 198
Bašagić, Ibrahim-beg 41
Bašagić, Safvet-beg 69, 75
Bazargic 99
Bedreddin Simavi 34
Bektashi 32, 34, 35–6, 38, 76–7, 78, 97, 111, 118–19, 147, 154, 158, 198, 204, 215, 216
Belgium 158
Belgrade 27, 28, 29, 34, 98, 104, 152, 200, 221
Berisha, Sali 168, 196
Berlin 114, 115; Berlin Wall 167
Berlin, Treaty of 45–6, 51, 54, 57
Berov, Ljuben 187
Bessarabia 13, 18, 83
Beyanülhak 71
Bihać 113, 199
bin Laden, Osama 222
Bitola/Manastir 30, 51, 55
Bogomils 39, 40, 69, 74–5, 109, 146, 147, 148, 193
Boja, Rexhep 152, 200
Boris II, King of Bulgaria 83
Bosnia/Bosnia-Herzegovina 11, 19, 20, 22, 29, 33, 34, 36, 39, 40, 41, 46, 51, 52, 53, 55–6, 58, 59, 62, 63, 64, 65, 69–70, 71, 73–5, 78, 84, 90, 95, 98–9, 100, 102, 103–4,

INDEX

108–9, 113–15, 116, 119; Communist era 123, 126, 131, 132, 133, 134, 135–7, 144, 145, 146, 149, 150–53, 158–62, 164, 213; post-Communist era, independence and war 169–70, 173, 174, 175, 176, 177–80, 190, 191, 192–3, 194–5, 197, 198–200, 202–3, 204, 205, 206, 214, 217, 218–20
Bosniak (adoption and use of the name) 144, 183–6, 191, 193, 194–5, 200, 215, 220
Bosniak Assembly (*Bošnjacki sabor*) 179, 193
Bosniak Cultural Community (*Bošnjačka Kulturna Zajednica*, BKZ) 220
Bosniak Party (*Bošnjačka Stranka*, BS) (Montenegro) 220
Bosniak-Croatian Federation 179
Bosnianism 69
Boué, Ami 37
Britain 17, 26, 51, 124, 127
British and Foreign Bible Society 42
Bucharest 155
Bukoshi, Bujar 182
Bulgaria 12, 19, 23, 25, 29, 30, 33, 36, 39, 45, 49, 50–52, 53–4, 57, 58, 59, 61–2, 63, 64, 67–9, 71–3, 75, 79, 80, 82, 83, 86, 89, 90, 93, 94, 102, 105, 106, 110–11, 112–13, 116, 119, 213; Communist era 123, 126–7, 128, 130, 131, 133, 134, 140–45, 146–8, 153–4, 158, 162; Post-Communist era 167–8, 173, 174, 175, 177, 186–8, 190, 193, 196, 198–9, 202, 203, 207–8, 211, 213, 215, 219, 220–21
Bulgarian Socialist Party (*Bălgarska Socialističeska Partija*, BSP) 168, 176, 187, 188, 201

Bushatli, Mustafa Pasha 22

cadis 31, 32, 35, 60, 61, 63, 112
Cairo 70, 73, 107, 112, 114, 115–16
Caliphate 63, 116
Camarda, Demetrio 38
Çamëri 94
Çams 95, 133
Carol I, King of Romania 18
Carol II, King of Romania 83
Catharism 39
Catholics, Catholic Church 25, 30, 40, 66, 67, 131, 149, 161, 162, 176, 194, 195, 211, 223
Caucasus 28, 55, 70, 203
Čaušević, Džemaludin 73, 107, 108, 115, 116
Cazin 198
Ceauşescu, Nicolae 126, 167
cem evi 198
*cemaat*s 98, 99, 106, 143, 156, 157
Ćemalović, Smail Aga 116
Čengić, Hasan 180
Central Asia 203
Centre for the Coordination of Albanian Islamic Centres 199
Čepino 39
Cerić, Mustafa 200, 220, 221, 223
Cërrik 198
Chalcis 34
Cherkess 28, 112
Chetniks 84, 103
China 126
Christian Democratic Party of Albania (*Partia Demokristiane e Shqipërisë*, PDSH) 186, 194, 220
Christians, see also Catholics; Orthodox; Protestants 26–31, 35, 36, 37–42, 54, 56, 62, 63, 65–9, 75, 77, 93, 94, 134, 147, 154–5, 162, 164, 186, 193, 195, 207, 220

INDEX

Christodoulos, Patriarch 176
Ćimić, Esad 149
collectivisation 128–9, 131, 133, 174, 211
Committee for Islamic Union (*İttihad-ı İslam Cemiyeti*, Greece) 103
Committee for National Salvation (*Odbor Narodnog Spasa*) (Bosnia) 103
Committee of Defenders of the Islamic Religion (*Dini İslam Müdafileri Cemiyeti*) (Bulgaria) 102
Committee of Union and Progress 51, 56, 57, 67
Communism, Communists, Communist parties (Leagues of Communists in Yugoslavia) 80, 84–6, 89, 101, 104, 109, 167–72, 182, 192, 199, 206, 210, 212, 216, 217–18
Community of the Sublime Islamic Dervish Orders (*Zajednica Islamskih Derviškik Redova Alije*, ZIDRA) (Yugoslavia) 153
Congress of Bosniak Intellectuals 193
Constanţa 60, 99, 205
Constantinople, Convention of (1881) 58
Constantinople, *see* Istanbul
Consultative Council for the Turkish Minority in Western Thrace (*Batı Trakya Türk Azınlığı Daniş Kurulu*) 189–90
conversion to Islam 26, 29, 37–41, 68, 69, 75–7, 147–9, 195, 212, 214–15
conversion to Christianity 19, 26, 37, 68
Corfu 13
Council of Europe 173
Crete 17, 19, 30, 49, 51, 53, 54, 59–60, 66

Crimea 28, 71; Crimean War 17, 19, 22
Croatia, Croats 13, 52, 70, 74, 80, 82, 83, 88, 89, 99, 102, 108, 109, 123, 159, 163, 168–72, 173, 174, 175, 176, 177, 179, 193, 194, 198, 210, 211, 213
Croatian Democratic Union (*Hrvatska Demokratska Zajednica*, HDZ) 168, 169, 172, 178, 179
Croatian Peasant Party (*Hrvatska Seljačka Stranka*, HSS) 82, 83, 100
Croatian Republic of Herceg-Bosna 169, 170
Crypto-Christians 30, 38, 77
Cultural and Solidarity Association for the Turks of the Rhodopes (*Rodop Türkleri Kültür ve Dayanışma Derneği*) 144
Cumans 147
Cuza, Alexandru Ioan 18
Cvetković, Dragiša 83
Cvijić, Jovan 75
Cyprus 127–8, 173–4
Cyrenaica 54
Czechoslovakia 80, 89, 115

Dalmatia 13, 84
Danilo, Crown Prince of Montenegro 18
Danube vilayet 22, 24
Danube 11, 18
darülharb 28
darülislam 28
Dayton agreement 170, 179
Declaration of the European Muslims 223
Dede-baba 97, 111
Deli Orman 33
Demir Baba 33
Demirović, Idriz 200
Democratic Entente (Bulgaria) 80

INDEX

Democratic League of Kosovo (*Lidhja Demokratike e Kosovës*, LDK) 169, 181, 182, 183, 192, 194, 195, 220
Democratic League of Montenegro (*Lidhja Demokratike në Mal të Zi*, LDMZ) 181
Democratic Muslim Bloc (*Blocul Musulman Democrat*) (Romania) 142
Democratic Party (*Partia Demokratike*, PD) (Albania) 168, 194, 196, 220
Democratic Party (*Demokratska Stranka*) (Serbia) 181
Democratic Party of Albanians (*Partia Demokratike e Shqiptarëve*, PDSH) (Macedonia) 181, 184, 185
Democratic Party of Kosovo (*Partia Demokratike e Kosovës*, PDK) 172, 183, 220
Democratic Party of Serbia (*Demokratska Stranka Srbije*, DSS) 181
Democratic Party of Socialists (*Demokratska Partija Socijalista*, DPS) (Montenegro) 170
Democratic Reform Party of Muslims (*Demokratska Reformska Stranka Muslimana*, DRSM) (Kosovo) 183
Democratic Union for Integration (*Bashkimi Demokratik për Integrim*, BDI) (Macedonia) 184, 185, 220
Democratic Union of Albanians (*Unioni Demokratik i Shqiptarëve*, UDSH) (Montenegro) 181
Democratic Union of Hungarians in Romania (*Uniunea Democrată Maghiară din România*, UDMR) 168
Democratic Union of Turco-Muslim Tatars of Romania (*Uniunea Democrată a Tatarilor Turco-Musulmani din România*, UDTTMR) 189
Democratic Union of Turks (*Türk Demokratik Birliği*, TDB) (Kosovo) 183

dervishes, *see also* Sufism; *tekke*s 32–5
Detroit 158
Deva, Xhafer 104
devşirme 13, 22, 39
diaspora 144, 149, 158, 175, 182, 192, 198, 199
Dibra, Vehbi 96
Diyanet (*Diyanet İşleri Başkanlığı*) (Turkey) 157, 203, 222
Diyanet Vakfı foundation 222
Dobruja 12, 28, 33, 49, 52, 54, 60, 80, 83, 90, 93, 104, 132, 142, 188–9
Dodecanese 54
Doğan, Ahmed 187, 201
Doğrul, Ömer Riza 115
*dönme*s 78
Đorđević, Tihomir 120–21
Đozo, Husein 151, 159–60, 161
Draga, Ferhat 101
Draginov, Pope Metodi 39
Drina 27
Durrës 77, 111, 112
Düzce 112
Džabić, Ali Fahmi 63
Džemijet, see Muslim Committee for the Protection of Rights

Echinos 157, 198
Ecumenical Patriarchate 177
education, *see also* madrasas 23, 24, 30, 35, 72, 74, 88, 106, 108, 112–16, 129, 137–9, 140, 141, 142, 143, 145–6, 150, 154–5, 175, 182, 185, 189, 190, 195, 198–9, 204, 207, 217, 221, 222–3
Egypt 17, 56, 64, 70, 105, 107, 116
Egyptian 116, 140, 194, 217
Elbasan 37, 111
Elezović, Gliša 120
el-Hidaje (ulama association) (Bosnia) 99, 103, 107, 116, 158

INDEX

el-Mudžahid (military unit) (Bosnia) 202, 203
Emel 104
Epidaurus 16
Epirus 29, 35, 42, 45, 46, 56, 60, 80, 94, 133
Ethniki Hetairia (National Society) (Greece) 50
Euboea 27, 34
Eurasian Islamic Assembly 203
European Charter for Regional or Minority Languages 192
European Council for Fatwa and Research 223
European Court of Human Rights 192
European Economic Community (EEC) 128, 130, 143
European Framework Convention for the Protection of National Minorities 188, 192
"European Islam" 117, 205–8, 215, 223–5
European Union 173, 219, 223, 224
Exarchate (Bulgarian) 25, 50, 61, 211
exchange of populations (Greece and Turkey) 27, 57, 86, 90, 92, 93
Ezheri, Shaykh Yusuf Ziyaeddin 112, 116, 118

Faikoğlu, Ahmet 189
Fatih madrasa 31, 114
fatwa, 32, 55, 62, 157, 204
Federation of Associations of Turks of Western Thrace in Germany 192
Federation of Turks of Western Thrace in Europe (*Avrupa Batı Trakya Türk Federasyonu*, ABBTF) 192

Fejić, Ibrahim 151
*fethullahcı*s 203, 221, 222
fikh, 71, 205
France 13, 17, 21, 23, 25, 26, 52, 80, 89, 95
Franz Ferdinand, Archduke 49
Frashëri, Mehdi 101, 117
Frashëri, Naim 76
Frashëri, Shemseddin Sami 42
Friendship, Equality and Peace Party (*Dostluk, Eşitlik ve Barış*, DEB) (Greece) 189
Füshe-Krujë 118

Gagauz 29
Gajret (cultural society) (Bosnia) 70, 103, 108, 135
Garašanin, Ilija 18
Garčević, Muhamed 120, 121
Gasprinski, Ismail 68, 71, 73
Gazi Ali Pasha waqf 60
Gazidede, Bashkim 196
Gendžev, Nedim 154, 201, 207
General Council of Muslims (*Glavni odbor muslimana*) (Bosnia) 135
Geneva, Congress of 116
George I, King of Greece 27
Germany 80, 83, 101, 103, 104, 117, 133, 144, 145, 158, 165, 167, 175, 192, 199
Gheorghiu-Dej, Gheorghe 126
Ghika, Elena 37
Gjilan 198
Gjirokastër 198
Gorani Civic Initiative (*Građanska Inicijativa Gorana*, CIG) (Kosovo) 194
Gorani 139, 183, 194
Gorbachev, Mikhail 167
Great Madrasa (*Velika madrasa*) (Skopje) 109, 113

INDEX

Greece, Greeks 11, 13, 15–16, 19, 20, 25, 26–30, 34, 40, 42, 46, 49, 51, 52, 53, 54, 57, 58–60, 68, 76, 79, 80, 82, 83–4, 89, 90, 92, 94, 95, 99, 102, 105, 106, 209; post-World War II 123, 124, 127, 130, 132, 133, 134, 142–4, 145, 146, 156, 164–6, 168, 173–4, 175, 176, 189–90, 191, 199, 201, 205, 211, 212, 213, 214, 215, 216
Greek Democratic Army (*Dimokratikos Stratos Elladas*, DSE) 124
Gülen, Fethullah 203
Gulf states 224
Gülşen-i Saray (newspaper) 24
Gümüşhanevi, Ahmed Ziyaeddin 112
Gypsy, see Roma

Hadži, Mustafa Ališ 201
Hadžibajrić, Fejzulah 153
Hahn, Johann Georg 38
Haji, Bektash 34, 97
Hajraddin, Ali 221
Haki, Ismail 152
Halveti 32, 34, 36, 78, 120, 153, 198
Hamidiye 50
Hanafi rite 33, 203, 205, 215, 222
Handžar division 103–4, 117
Handžić, Mehmed 103, 107, 109, 113
Hangi, Antun 74
Haradinaj, Ramush 183
Hasan, Fikri Sali 208
Hasluck, Frederick W. 76–7
Hassanein, Fatih al- 180
Havari 164–5
Hellenism 25, 41, 42
High Council of the Turkish Minority in Western Thrace (*Batı Trakya Türk Azınlığı Yüksek Kurulu*) 144, 156, 189

Higher Islamic School of Sharia Law and Theology (*Viša Islamska Šeriatsko-Teološka Škola*) (Sarajevo) 113, 150, 151
Higher Sharia Council (Albania) 63
Higher Sharia Council (Bulgaria) 98
Hirsch, Baron 23
hocas 77, 78, 120–121, 207
Hoxha, Enver 89, 126, 132, 144, 152, 182
Human Rights and Freedom (*İnsan Hak ve Hürriyetleri*, IHH) 204
Hungary, Hungarians 11, 12, 41, 83, 84, 116, 123, 127, 168
hurufism 34
Husayni, Amin al- 117
Hüseyin Hüsnü 106
Husrev-beg madrasa 31, 150, 151, 160

Ibrahim Pasha 17
ijitihad, 73, 108, 159
Iliescu, Ion 168
Ilinden revolt 50
Illyrism 40, 41, 67
Imams 33, 121, 161, 199
Independent State of Croatia (*Nezavisna Država Hrvatska*, NDH) 84, 99, 102, 103
India 114, 115, 217
Internal Macedonian Revolutionary Organisation (*Vătrešna Makedonska Revoljucionna Organizacija*, VMRO) 50, 169, 184, 185
International Criminal Tribunal for the Former Yugoslavia (ICTY) 172
International Islamic Relief Organisation (IIRO) (Islamic NGO) 202
Ioannina 16, 17, 22, 29, 35, 42, 65, 77
Ionian Islands 13

INDEX

Iqbal, Muhammad 160
Iran 161, 194, 204
Iron Guard 83, 89, 93
Isa bey madrasa 114, 152
Islamic Awakening Association (*İntibah-ı İslam Cemiyeti*) (Greece) 157
Islamic Community (*Islamska Zajednica*) (Bosnia-Herzegovina and Sanjak) 199, 200
Islamic Community (*Islamska Zajednica*) (communist Bosnia-Herzegovina) 151, 153, 163, 164
Islamic Community for Kosovo, Serbia and Vojvodina 152
Islamic Community in Serbia (*Islamska Zajednica u Srbiji*) 221
Islamic Community of Macedonia 201
Islamic Community of Serbia (*Islamska Zajednica Srbije*) 152, 221
Islamic Community of Yugoslavia 200
Islamic Community, Albania 221
Islamic Declaration 160, 161
Islamic Democratic Union Party (*Partia e Bashkimit Demokratik Islam*, PBDI) (Albania) 186
Islamic higher education institutions 198–9
Islamic humanitarian organisations 202–3
Islamic NGOs 202–3, 208, 216, 222
Islamic Religious Community (*Islamska Vjerska Zajednica*) (interwar Yugoslavia) 98, 150–51, 159
islamism, islamist 65, 67, 71, 105, 160, 185, 193, 203, 204, 205, 206, 214, 219, 223
Istanbul/Constantinople 16, 20, 21, 23, 25, 30, 31, 35, 41, 45, 50, 56, 57, 60, 65, 70, 73, 78, 94, 107, 111, 112, 114, 115, 127, 177, 215
Istria 13
Italy 17, 19, 41, 51, 66, 67, 80, 82, 83, 84, 91, 95, 96, 101, 104
Izetbegović, Alija 160–61, 178, 180, 204, 219

Jadidism 68
janissaries 13, 22, 39
Jasenovac 84
Jerusalem 17, 117; Congress of Jerusalem 116
Jews 30, 78, 84, 102
jihad, jihadist 7, 202, 203, 217, 222
Jinns 121
Jireček, Konstantin 40
Jordan 207
Junimists 24
Justice Party (*Partia e Drejtësisë*, PD) (Kosovo) 196
Jusufspahić, Hamdija 152, 200, 221

*kaçak*s 109
Kadare, Ismail 195, 220
Kadiri 32, 36, 78, 120, 153, 198
Kadizadeli 34, 217
Kállay, Benjamin 69–70
Kanitz, Felix 37
Karađorđe Petrović, ruler of Serbia 13, 15
Karadžić, Vuk 40
Karčić, Fikret 205
Karić, Enes 205
Kavajë 198
Kemal, Mustafa; Kemalism 51, 104–5, 107, 110, 157, 165, 196, 215, 217
Kenan, Adem 187
Këshilli i Ulemave (council of ulama, Albania) 97

276

INDEX

Kingdom of Serbs, Croats and Slovenes, *see also* Yugoslavia 52, 79–83, 88, 90
Kıraathane 71
Kizilbash, *see* Alevi
Kladovo 28
klefts 16
Koçi, Sabri 197
Kolašin 46
Kolettis, Ioannis 19
Komotini/Gümülcine 113, 144, 156, 157, 189, 198
Korçë 111, 119
Kosovo Liberation Army (*Ushtria Çlirimtare e Kosovës*, UÇK) 170–72, 181–5, 197, 202
Kosovo Protection Corps (*Trupat e Mbrojtjes së Kosovës*, TMK) 183
Kosovo Transitional Council 183
Kosovo 29, 35, 46, 49, 52, 55, 60, 75, 76, 77, 78, 80, 84, 91, 96, 100, 101, 104, 109; post-Communist era 126, 127, 131, 132, 133, 137–40, 142, 144, 145, 146, 150, 152–3, 158, 160, 162, 163, 169; war and independence 170–74, 175, 178, 181–6, 191–2, 194–7, 198–9, 200, 202, 212, 214, 218–21
Kosovo, Battle of 40, 49, 131
Kouchner, Bernard 183
Krajina (Croatia) 169–70
Krasniqi, Ahmet 182
Kruja 33
Kryegjysh 97
Küçük Kaynarca, Treaty of 17
Kulenović, Džafer 109
Kurtćehajić, Mehmed Šakir 41
Kurtish, Ataullah 113

La nation arabe 116

Lahore 114
Lahori Ahmadis 114–15, 217
land issues 21, 29–30, 39, 54, 74, 86–7, 91, 92, 93, 94, 95, 108, 128–9
Lausanne, Treaty of 57, 80, 94
League of Islamic Youth (*Lidhja i Rinisë Islame*) (Macedonia) 203
League of Nations 57, 87, 91
League of Prizren 65–6
Legaliteti 100–1
Liberal Alliance of Bosniaks-Muslims 144, 149, 159
Little Entente 80
Ljajić, Rasim 180
Loveč 37, 39
Lubonja, Fatos 195

Macedonia 12, 46, 49, 50–52, 55, 56, 60, 66, 75, 78, 80, 84, 91, 93, 97, 98, 100, 104, 109, 110, 112; Communist era 123, 131, 132, 133–7, 139–40, 146, 148, 150, 152–3, 158, 160, 161, 162; post-Communist era 169, 172, 173, 184, 193, 196, 198–201, 202–3, 214, 218, 220, 221
Maček, Vladimir 83
Madan 207–8
madhhabs 203, 205, 222
madrasas 23, 31, 60, 71, 113–14, 150, 151, 152, 155, 198, 203, 204, 216, 221
magic 34, 74, 78, 120, 121–122, 150
Mahmud II, Sultan 22, 34
Malaysia 204
Mali Zvornik 27
Maliqi, Shkëlzen 195
Manastir, see Bitola
Marriages 38, 132, 165, 206
Marseille 83

277

INDEX

Mawdudi, Maulana 160
Mecra-i Efkâr 24
Meddah madrasa 113
Medeniyet 105
Medgidia/Mecidiye 28, 60, 105, 155, 198
Medina University 203
Međugorje 131
Megali Idea 19, 49, 82
Mehmed II, Sultan 39
*mekteb*s 72, 150
Melami 32, 78, 120
Melamiyye-Nuriyye 78
Melçan 119
Memić, Mustafa 109
Merhamet 204
Metaxas, Ioannis 83
Mevlevi 32, 77, 153
mevlud 150
Midhat Pasha 22, 23
migrations, refugees, displacement 28–9, 35, 52–7, 86, 91–5, 105, 133–5, 141, 142, 158, 170, 175, 186–7, 212
Mihailo, Prince of Serbia 17
Milan, King of Serbia 17, 19
millet 25, 68
Miloš Obrenović, Prince of Serbia 13, 17
Milošević, Slobodan 127, 138, 168, 170, 172, 181, 191
mission, missionary 77, 114, 115, 173, 222
Mitrovica, Rexhep 103
Moldavia 11, 16, 18
Momčilgrad 198
Montenegro 11, 15, 17, 18, 19, 26, 29, 45–6, 51, 58, 60–61, 64, 79, 91, 123, 150, 152, 170, 172, 181, 209, 212, 214, 218, 220, 221
Morava 27

Morea, see Peloponnese
mosque 31–35, 60, 74, 99, 111, 114, 115, 120, 150, 151, 152, 155, 158, 160, 162, 163, 165, 198, 199, 200, 204, 206, 207, 218, 221, 222, 224
Mostar 30, 198
Movement for Rights and Freedoms (*Dviženie za Prava i Svobodi*, DPS) (Bulgaria) 168, 187, 191, 201, 207, 220
müderris 31, 32, 35
mufti general (*Myftiu i Përgjithshëm*) 63
muftis 32, 60–63, 95, 98, 99, 152, 154, 156–7, 200, 201, 207, 221
*muhacir*s, see also refugees, migrations, displacement 55–6
Prophet Muhammad 31
Muhammad Ali (founder of Ahmadiyya) 114–15
Muhammad Ali (ruler of Egypt) 17, 22
Muhammad Nur al-Arabi 78
Muhibbi 34
mujahedeen 202, 222
Mujić, Husein 161
Musa Haxhi Ali 154
Muslim Brotherhood 107, 116, 160, 180, 204, 217, 223
Muslim Committee for the Protection of Rights (*Islam Muhafazayi Hukuk Cemiyeti*) (Yugoslavia) 101, 104, 109
Muslim Forum of Albania (*Forumi Musliman i Shqipërisë*) 220
Muslim Forum of Kosovo (*Forumi Musliman i Kosovës*) 220
Muslim nation in Yugoslavia 136–7, 139, 148, 159, 213
Muslim National Council of Sanjak (*Muslimansko Nacionalno Vijeće Sandžaka*, MNVS) 180

INDEX

Muslim Organisation (*Muslimanska Organizacija*) (Yugoslavia) 100
Muslim People's Organisation (*Muslimanska Narodna Organizacija*, MNO) (Yugoslavia) 70
Muslim Turkish Democratic Union of Romania (*Uniunea Democrata Turca Musulmana din România*, UDTMR) 188
Mussolini, Benito 82
Mustafa Celaleddin Pasha 41
Mustafa Sabri 105
Muwafaq 202

Namik Kemal 24, 68, 70
Nansen, Fridtjof 57
Napoleon 13
Naqshbandi 32, 34, 36, 78, 111, 112, 153, 198
Narodna Uzdanica 103, 109, 135
National Council on Ethnic and Demographic Issues, Bulgaria 188
National Front (*Balli Kombetar*) (Albania) 86, 101, 137, 144
National Liberation Front, Albania 100
National Republican Greek League (*Ethnikos Dimokratikos Ellenikos Syndesmos*, EDES) 86
NATO 124, 172, 179, 192, 211, 219
Navarino, Battle of 17
Nedić, General Milan 84
neo-Salafism 95, 151, 201–7, 215, 217, 218, 221, 222
neo-traditionalist 103, 107, 109, 114, 118, 217
Neuilly, Treaty of 57
New Democracy (*Nea Dimokratia*) (Greece) 128
Nikola, King of Montenegro 18
Nikšić 46

Niš 22, 23, 46, 60, 98
Non-Aligned Movement 126
Novi Pazar, city of 46, 60, 75, 91, 100, 133, 134, 136, 152, 160, 180, 193, 198, 199, 200, 220, 221
Numanagić, Hadži Hafiz Husni Efendi 78

Odessa 15, 16
Ohrid 36, 172, 184, 185
Omerović, Mustafa Hilmi 62
Organisation of the Islamic Conference (OIC) 196
Orthodox Christians and Churches 17, 21, 39, 40, 41, 42, 50, 57, 61, 66, 67, 68, 90, 130–31, 139, 149, 161, 162, 176–7, 186, 191, 196, 197, 211–12, 223
OSCE 173, 192
Osmanov, Akif 154
Otman Baba 34
Otto, King of Greece 17, 19, 20, 27, 49
Ottoman Empire, 45–71, 78, 79–80, 87, 109, 110, 112, 145, 146–8, 195, 209–10, 212, 215–16, 217, 220, 224
Ottomanism 23, 42, 67, 68, 69, 70, 71, 209, 215

Pakistan 161
Pandža, Muhamed 115
Pangalos, Theodoros 82
pan-Islamism, pan-Islamist 63, 116, 160, 161, 178, 180, 190, 196, 197, 200, 205, 214, 219
pan-Turkism, pan-Turkist 41, 65, 67, 68
Papandreou, George 168
partisans (Greece) 123
partisans (Yugoslavia) 104

INDEX

Party for Bosnia-Herzegovina (*Stranka za Bosnu i Hercegovinu*, SBiH) 180
Party for Complete Emancipation of the Roma (*Partia za Celosna Emancipacija na Romite*, PCER) (Macedonia) 185
Party for Democratic Action (*Partia për Veprim Demokratik*, PVD) (Albanians in Serbia) 181
Party for Democratic Activity (*Stranka Demokratske Aktivnosti*, ASDA) (Bosnia) 219–20
Party for Democratic Prosperity (*Partia për Prosperitet Demokratik*, PPD) (Macedonia) 169, 184, 194, 201
Party of Democratic Action (*Stranka Demokratske Akcije*, SDA) (Bosnia) 169, 172, 178–81, 183, 192, 193, 194–5, 197, 206, 214, 215, 219–20
Party of Justice and Development (*Adalet ve Kalkınma Partisi*, AKP) (Turkey) 219
Party of National Recovery (*Partia e Rimëkëmbjes Kombëtare*, PRK) (Albania) 195–6
PASOK (*Panellinio Socialistiko Kinima*; Socialist Party) (Greece) 128, 130, 165, 168
Patarenism 39, 40
Paul, Prince of Yugoslavia 83
Pavelić, Ante 84
Pazvanoğlu, Osman 22
Pechenegs 147
Pelasgians 66, 67
Peloponnese 12, 16, 17
People's Movement for the Republic of Kosovo (*Lëvizija Popullore për Republikën e Kosovës*, LPRK) 144, 158, 182

People's Movement of Kosovo (*Lëvizja Popullore e Kosovës*, LPK) 182, 183, 184, 191
Petar I Njegoš, Bishop of Montenegro 15
Petar II Njegoš, Prince-Bishop of Montenegro 15, 18, 19
Petranović, Božidar 40
Phanariots 16
Philhellenes 16
Philiki Hetairia 15–16
Piedmont-Sardinia 17
Pilgrimage 33, 112, 150, 198, 206, 218
Pirot 46
Plovdiv 53
Podgorica 46, 60, 98, 221
Poland 41
Pomaks 39, 40, 62, 68–9, 93, 94, 98, 102, 103, 106, 107, 110, 135, 140, 143, 147, 154, 155, 164, 165, 166, 188, 193, 201, 207, 208, 217
Popular Bloc (Bulgaria) 82–3
population 9, 10, 134–5
poturica 26
Pozderac, Hamdija 132
Pozderac, Nurija 100
Preporod 135, 151, 160, 162, 193
Preševo 181, 221
Presidency of Religious Affairs (*Diyanet İşleri Başkanlığı*) (Turkey) 157, 158, 203, 222
press 24, 41, 71–2, 73–4, 104, 105, 137, 157, 211
Pressburg, Treaty of 13
Princip, Gavrilo 49
Prishtina 138, 152, 198, 199
Prizren 22, 25, 36, 97, 153, 183, 198
Protestants 25, 30, 42, 177, 197
Provincial Museum (Bosnia-Herzegovina) 74

INDEX

Prusac 33
Prussia 17
Putokaz 89

Qadiani 114, 115
Qaradawi, Yusuf al- 204, 223
Qazim Hoxha 112
Qosja, Rexhep 220
Quran 31, 75, 96, 115, 121, 155, 164
Qutb, Sayyid 160

racial theories and origin myths 36–42, 65–9, 75–6, 146–9, 192, 207
Rački, Franjo 40
Radić, Stjepan 82
Radical Party (Yugoslavia) 102
railways 23
ramadan 155
Ramadan, Tariq 7
Ranke, Leopold von 37
Rauf, Abdülfettah 113–14
Red Army 123–4
Redžić, Enver 149
Reforma 108
reformism, reformist 60, 67, 70–74, 96, 111, 119–20, 159–60, 167, 215, 217, 223
refugees, migrations, displacement 28–9, 35, 52–7, 86, 91–5, 105, 133–5, 141, 142, 158, 170, 175, 186–7, 212
reis-ul-ulema 62, 74, 98–9, 107, 150, 152, 161, 200–1, 220, 221
Religious Community of the Muslims of Macedonia (*Verska Zaednica na Muslimanite vo Makedonija*) 200
religious persecution 129–31, 140, 155, 157, 217–18
religious revival post-Communism 175–7, 216

Renan, Ernest 70
Republika Srpska 169–70, 179
Restoration Assembly (*Obnovitelski sabor*) 200
Rexhepi, Baba 158
Rexhepi, Bajram 183
Rexhepi, Sulejman 200, 201
Rhodope mountains 39, 69, 134, 166, 207
Rida, Rashid 55, 70, 116
Rifai 32, 36, 120, 153, 198
Rodina 98, 102, 107, 110, 140
Rodna Zaštita 93
Roma 28, 84, 92, 106, 135, 139–40, 141, 152, 153, 183–6, 188, 193, 197, 207
Romania 15–18, 20, 21, 24, 40, 45–50, 52, 53, 54–5, 58, 59, 60, 64, 67–8, 79, 80, 83, 86, 88, 90, 91, 93–4, 98–9, 102, 104, 105; Communist era 123–4, 126–7, 128, 130, 131, 132, 135, 142, 154–5; post-Communist era 167, 173, 175, 176, 188–9, 191, 198, 205, 213, 214, 219
Rudozem 207–8
Rugova, Ibrahim 181–3, 195, 219, 220
Rumelia 22, 33, 34, 35, 41, 45, 46, 51, 53, 55, 69, 71
*rüşdiye*s 71, 72
Ruse 23, 24, 53, 198
Russia 12, 13, 15–18, 26, 28, 35, 45, 50, 51, 52, 53, 68, 79, 210, 217

Šabac 28
Sadi 34, 36, 153, 198
Saduddin Sirri 120
Safavid Islam 33
Saint George 122
Saint Nicholas 77

281

INDEX

Sakar 27
Šakirov, Selvi 221
salafiyya, see also neo-Salafism 70–71
Salih Niyazi Dede 97
Salonica 24, 78, 67, 143, 156, 165
şalvar 132, 141
San Stefano, Treaty of 45, 49, 50
Sanjak Democratic Party (*Sandžačka Demokratska Partija*, SDP) 181, 195, 220
Sanjak of Novi Pazar 46, 60, 75, 91, 100, 133, 134, 136, 152, 160, 180, 193, 198, 199, 200, 220, 221
Sarajevo 24, 36, 49, 62, 73, 98, 99, 113, 148, 150, 151, 152, 159, 160, 163, 198, 220
Sari Saltik 33
Saudi Arabia 157, 202, 207
Scandinavia 175, 199
School for Cadis (*medrese-i nüvvab*) (Bulgaria) 112, 113, 118, 155
School for Cadis (*muallim-hane-i nüvvab*) (Istanbul) 35, 73
School for Cadis (*Šerijatska Sudačka Škola*) (Bosnia-Herzegovina) 73, 113
SDA-Islamic Path (*Partia për Veprim Demokratik–Rruga Islame*) (Macedonia), *see also* Party of Democratic Action (*Stranka Demokratske Akcije*, SDA) 185, 196
šehid 194
Selim III, Sultan 21
Selimoski, Jakub 152, 161, 200
Seljuks 77
Selman Cemali Baba 111
Septar, Iacub Mehmet 154
September 11 2001 attacks 219, 221, 222
Serbia, Serbs 11, 13–15, 17–19, 20, 21, 24, 25, 27–30, 40, 41, 45–52, 58, 60, 64, 69, 70, 74, 75, 79–80, 84, 86, 88, 91, 100, 102, 103, 104, 108, 109, 113, 120, 209, 210, 212; Communist era 123, 127, 134, 136, 137, 138, 139, 146, 149, 152, 159, 163; post-Communist era and wars 168–73, 175, 176, 181, 182, 191, 193, 194, 198–9, 211, 213, 214, 220
Serbian Democratic Party (*Srpska Demokratska Stranka*, SDS) (Bosnia) 169, 176, 201
Serbian Radical Party 108
Serbian Scholarly Society 40
Serbs, Croats and Slovenes, Kingdom of, *see also* Yugoslavia 52, 79–83, 88, 90
Şerif, İbrahim 189, 201
Sèvres, Treaty of 80
şeyhulislam 31, 61–2, 63, 64, 95–6, 105, 216
Shapati, Behxhet 96
Sharia Academy (*Šerijatska Gimnazija*) (Bosnia) 113
Sharia courts 32, 34, 35, 60, 62, 99, 105, 111, 132, 150, 199, 216
Shaykh 121, 153, 164, 216
Shazili 36, 120
Shehu, Mehmet 89
Shehu, Xhemali 152
Shiite Muslims 33–4, 38, 204
Shköder 15, 22, 55, 95, 112, 114, 155, 197
Shpatiotes 37
Silajdžić, Haris 180
Silistra 99
Simeon II National Movement (*Nacionalno Dviženje Simeon Vtori*) (Bulgaria) 187
Simitis, Kostas 168, 176
Sırat-i müstakim/Sebilürreşad 71
Skanderbeg division 104
Skanderbeg 82, 148

INDEX

Skopje 30, 97, 98, 109, 113, 120, 198, 199
Skopska Crna Gora 30
Slovenia, Slovenes 13, 52, 84, 88, 123, 173, 219
Smederevo 28
Smolyan 98, 207–8, 221
Social Democratic Party (*Socijaldemokratska Partija*, SDP) (Bosnia) 172, 178
Social Democratic Union of Macedonia (*Socijaldemokratski Sojuz na Makedonija*, SDSM) 169
Socialist Party (*Partia Socialiste*, PS) (Albania) 168, 196, 220
Socialist Party of Serbia (*Socijalistička Partija Srbije*, SPS) 168, 183
Sofia 61, 63, 98, 199, 221
Solidarity Association for the Turks of Western Thrace (*Batı Trakya Türkleri Dayanışma Derneği*) 144
Soviet Union 83, 86, 123, 124–6, 128, 167, 210
Spaho, Mehmed 100
Spain 89
Special Organisation (*Teşkilat-ı mahsusa*) 57
Srebrenica 177–8
Sredačka Župa 183
St Germain, Treaty of 79
Stalin, Josif 126
Stamboliski, Aleksandar 80, 93
Stambolov, Stefan 71
Stojadinović, Milan 83, 92, 100
Strossmayer, Bishop Josip 40
Sufism, *see also names of brotherhoods* 78, 111–12, 150, 153, 164, 198, 206, 215–16, 217–18, 221, 222
Süleymaniyye 31
Šumen 53, 112, 113, 114, 118, 155, 198

Sunni Muslim Community (*Komuniteti Mysliman*) (Albania) 197
Sunni Muslims 33, 38, 76, 77, 147, 154, 194, 197
Supreme Organisation (*Vărhovna Organizacija*) 50
Switzerland 175, 199
Syria 95

Takvim 160
Tanzimat 20, 22, 26, 29, 37, 40
*Tarikat*s Centre 153
Tatars 28, 67, 68, 71, 93, 104, 135, 142, 154, 191
teacher training 71, 199
*tekke*s 32–3, 34, 35, 77, 78, 97, 118, 119, 120, 150, 152–3
Temo, Ibrahim 64
Teresa, Mother 131, 220
terrorism 219, 222, 223
Tetovo 185, 201
Thaçi, Hashim 182
Thessaly 12, 28, 39, 46, 53, 54, 59
Third Muslim Congress (Albania) 154
Third World Relief Agency (TWRA) 180
Thrace 12, 33, 46, 51, 52, 55, 57, 80, 90, 93, 94, 96, 98, 99, 103, 105, 106, 110, 132, 135, 142–5, 147, 156–8, 164–6, 189–90, 191, 193, 205, 216
Tijani 112, 198
Tirana 36, 112, 113, 114, 155, 198
Tito, Josip Broz 84, 124–6, 138
Tomić, Jovan 75
Torbesh 136, 139, 152, 193, 194, 200
Transylvania 11, 52, 83
Travnik 39, 78, 113, 198
Tripartite Pact 83–4
Tripolitania 51

INDEX

Tudjman, Franjo 168, 170, 172
Tulcea 62, 99
Turan associations 102
*türbe*s 33, 74
Türk Ocakları 67
Turkey (post-Ottoman), *see also* Ottoman Empire 52, 79–80, 89, 91–5, 97, 104–5, 112, 117, 121, 122, 124, 127–8, 133, 134, 135, 142, 143, 147, 149, 157, 165, 173–4, 177, 190, 196, 203–4, 209, 210, 217, 219, 221, 222–3, 224
Turkish Democratic Party (Bulgaria) 187
Turkish Democratic Party (*Türk Demokratik Partisi*, TDP) (Macedonia) 185, 196
Turkish Democratic Union of Romania (*Uniunea Democrata Turca din România*, UDTR) 188–9
Turkish International Cooperation Agency (*Türk İşbirliği ve Kalkınma İdaresi Başkanlığı*, TİKA) 222
Turkish National Liberation Movement in Bulgaria (*Tursko Nacionalno Osvoboditelno Dviženie v Bălgarija*, TNOD) 142, 158, 187
Turkish People's Party (*Türk Halk Partisi*, THP) (Kosovo) 183
Turkish Union of Xanthi (*İskeçe Türk Birliği*) 143
Turkish Youth association (*Türk Gençler Birliği*) (Greece) 102
Turkism 41, 66, 67, 68
Turkology 41
Turks in Balkan countries 36–7, 91–4, 98, 101, 106, 109, 110–11, 127–8, 133, 135, 139–45, 147, 149, 153, 155, 156, 158, 162, 164–5, 167, 175, 177, 183–8, 191, 196, 197, 207–8, 213, 215, 217, 220, 222

Tuzla 113, 198

UÇK (*Ushtria Çlirimtare e Kosovës*, Kosovo Liberation Army) 170–72, 181–5, 197, 202
Ugljanin, Sulejman 180
ulama 24, 31, 34, 35, 54, 62, 63, 73–4, 107, 116, 159, 216, 223
ulema-medžlis 62, 74, 98, 104
Ulcinj 46, 60
umma 72, 163, 164, 197
Unified Democratic Movement (*Lëvizja e Bashkuar Demokratike*, LBD) (Kosovo) 182, 183
Unified Serbian Youth 24
Union for Islamic Development and Culture (*Obedinenie za Isljamsko Razvitie i Kultura*) (Bulgaria) 208, 221
Union of Democratic Forces (*Sajuz na Demokratičnite Sili*, SDS) (Bulgaria) 168, 176, 187
Union of Islamic Youth (*Bashkimi i Rinisë Islamike*) (Albania) 203
Union of Muslims of Bulgaria (*Săjuz na Mjusjulmanite v Bălgarija*) 221
Union of Reform Forces of Yugoslavia (*Savez Reformskih Snaga Jugoslavije*, SRSJ) 178
Union of Turkish Teachers of Western Thrace (*Batı Trakya Türk Öğretmenler Birliği*) 143
Union of Young Turks of Komotini (*Gümülcine Genç Türkler Birliği*) 143
United Nations Interim Administration Mission in Kosovo (UNMIK) 173, 183
United Nations 172–5, 183, 211, 219
Unity for Human Rights Party (*Partia Bashkimi për të Drejtat e Njeriut*, PBDNJ) (Albania) 168, 186

INDEX

USA 56, 87, 95, 124, 158, 169–70, 173, 179, 219
Ustasha 84, 103, 103

Varna 23, 53
Vasojević 26
veil issue 107, 118, 132, 207, 218, 221
Venice 11, 13
Venizelos, Eleftherios 82, 83
Versailles, treaty of 87
Vidin 53
Vienna 12, 23
Vienna, Congress of 13
Visoko 78, 198
Vlachs/Aromanians 87
Vladimirescu, Tudor 16
Vlora, Ismail Kemal bey 66
Vlorë 77
Vojvodina 84, 123, 152
Vranje 46
Vučić-Perišić, Toma 15
Vuçitern, Salih 117
Vuçitrn/Vushtrri 55

Wahhabism 202, 223
Wallachia 11, 16, 18, 20
waqfs 33, 34–5, 59, 60, 61, 62, 72, 154, 156, 198, 199
Warsaw Pact 124, 126
Washington Agreement 1994 194
Wilson, Woodrow 87
women's situation and issues 72, 73, 103, 108, 119, 129, 132, 218, 219
World War, First 51–2, 57, 63, 75, 79
World War, Second 93, 94, 98, 99, 101–2, 103–4, 107, 117, 133, 146, 210

Xanthi 156, 165, 189
Xhaferi, Arbën 184

Yarın 105
Young Muslims (*Mladi Musulmani*) 116, 151, 158–9, 161
Young Muslims association (*Jamaat al-shuban al-muslimin*) (Egypt) 116
Young Ottomans 40, 41, 70
Young Turks 50–51, 66, 67, 71, 76, 78, 109
Ypsilantis 15
Yüceleiler 109–10, 139, 158
Yugoslav Muslim Organisation (*Jugoslovenska Muslimanska Organizacija*, JMO) 100–1, 108, 209, 213
Yugoslav National Party (*Jugoslovenska Nacionalna Stranka*, JNS) 83
Yugoslav Radical Community (*Jugoslovenska Radikalna Zajednica*, JRZ) 100, 102
Yugoslavia, *see also* Bosnia-Herzegovina, Croatia, Kosovo, Macedonia, Montenegro, Serbia, Slovenia 80, 82–6, 88, 90, 91, 95, 98–9, 100–4, 107–9, 111, 113–14, 115–17, 119–21; Communist era 123–7, 128, 130–40, 144–6, 148–53, 157–64, 167; break-up 168–73, 210–11, 213–14
Yugoslavism 40, 88, 91, 215

Zagreb 151, 198
zakat 204, 218
Zakhariev, Stefan 39
Zëmblaku, Hafiz Abdullah 111, 115
Zenica 199
zikr 150
Zilkić, Adem 221
Živkov, Todor 126, 167, 177, 186
Zogu, Ahmet (King Zog) 82, 95, 101, 111
Zukorlić, Muamer 200, 220, 221
Zvornik 27

285